ANDRÉ and FRANÇOIS ANDRÉ MICHAUX

ANDRÉ and

MIC

HENRY SAVAGE, JR. *and*

FRANÇOIS ANDRÉ
HAUX

ELIZABETH J. SAVAGE

University Press of Virginia   *Charlottesville*

Publication of this book was assisted by a generous grant from
the Michaux Committee of the American Philosophical Society.

THE UNIVERSITY PRESS OF VIRGINIA

First published 1986

Design by Janet Anderson

Library of Congress Cataloging-in-Publication Data
Savage, Henry, 1903–
   André and François André Michaux.
   Bibliography: p.
   Includes index.
   1. Michaux, André, 1746–1802. 2. Michaux, François
André, 1770–1855. 3. Botanists—United States—
Biography. 4. Botanists—France—Biography. 5. Botany—United
States—History. I. Savage, Elizabeth J., 1908–   . II. Title.
QK31.M45S28 1987   580′.92′2 [B]   86-5612
ISBN 0-8139-1107-9

Whereas Andrew Michaux, a native of France, and inhabitant of the United States has undertaken to explore the interior country of North America from the Missisipi along the Missouri and Westwardly to the Pacific ocean, or in such other direction as shall be advised by the American Philosophical society, & on his return to communicate to the said society the information he shall have acquired of the geography of the said country, it's inhabitants, soil, climate, animals, vegetables, minerals & other circumstances of note: We the Subscribers, desirous of obtaining for ourselves relative to the land we live on, and of communicating to the world, information so interesting to curiosity, to science, and to the future prospects of mankind, promise for ourselves, our heirs executors & administrators, that we will pay the said Andrew Michaux or his assigns, the sums herein affixed to our names respectively, one fourth part thereof on demand, the remaining three fourths whenever, after his return, the said Philosophical society, shall declare themselves satisfied that he has performed the sd journey & that he has communicated to them freely, all the information which he shall have acquired & they demanded of him: or if the sd Andrew Michaux shall not proceed to the Pacific ocean and shall reach the sources of the waters running into it, then we will pay him such part only of the remaining three fourths as the said Philosophical society, shall deem duly proportioned to the extent of unknown country explored by him, in the direction prescribed as compared with that omitted to be so explored. And we consent that the bills of exchange of the sd Andrew Michaux, for monies said to be due to him in France, shall be recieved to the amount of two hundred Louis, & shall be negociated by the sd Philosophical society, and the proceeds thereof retained in their hands, to be delivered to the sd Andrew Michaux, on his return, after having performed the journey to their satisfaction, or, if not to their satisfaction, then to be applied towards reimbursing the subscribers the fourth of their subscription advanced to the said Andrew Michaux. We consent also that the said Andrew Michaux shall take to himself all benefit arising from the publication of the discoveries he shall make in the three departments of Natural history, Animal, Vegetable and mineral, he concerting with the said Philosophical society, such measures for securing to himself the said benefit, as shall be consistent with the due publication of the said discoveries. In witness whereof we have hereto subscribed our names and affixed the sums we engage respectively to contribute.

G: Washington one hundred Dollars

John Adams Twenty Dollars

Benjamin Hawkins Twenty Dollars.

Ra: Izard — Twenty Dollars

Sam Johnston Twenty Dollars

Rob: Morris Eighty Dollars

Ja. Henry — ten dollars

G Cabot — Ten Dollars

John Rutherford Twenty dollars

H Knox fifty dollars

Th: Jefferson fifty dollars

Alexander Hamilton fifty Dollars

Rufus King — Twenty Dollars

John Langdon Twenty Dollars

Peter Edwards Sixteen Dollars

John Brown Twenty Dollars

Tho Mifflin Twenty Dollars

Jon.a Trumbull Twenty Doll.rs

Jam.s Madison Jr. Twenty dollars

J Parker — Twenty Dollars

Alex White Twenty Dollars

John Page twenty Dollars

John Beckle 100 D.rs

Wm Smith Twenty Dol.rs

Jere Wadsworth Thirty

Richard Bland Lee ten dollars

Tho.s Fitzsimons ten dollars

Saml Griffin Ten dollars

Wm B. Giles Ten Dollars

Jn Witherow Ten Dollars.

Subscription list for proposed western journey of André Michaux. January 1793. Subscribers included George Washington, John Adams, Thomas Jefferson, James Madison, Alexander Hamilton, Henry Knox, Ralph Izard, Robert Morris, John Rutherford, Rufus King, Thomas Mifflin, John Trumbull, Benjamin Franklin Bache, John Vaughan, and David Rittenhouse. (Courtesy of the American Philosophical Society)

ᕁ Contents

PART TWO
⋞ FRANÇOIS ANDRÉ MICHAUX

◁§ Acknowledgments

Until now neither André Michaux nor his son, François André, has been the subject of a full-length biography. In preparing this volume we have had the benefit of memoirs by their contemporaries and of various scholarly articles, but the foundation of this book has been the Michauxs' own work and their unpublished correspondence. During the six years we have spent in research and writing, since first undertaking this project for the University Press of Virginia, our task has been greatly facilitated by the cooperation, support, and encouragement of many persons and institutions, and it is with grateful memories that we express our appreciation.

The American Philosophical Society is the principal repository in this country of Michaux source material, and we are deeply indebted to the Society and its staff, not only for giving us access to their extensive collection, but also for making available to us their microfilm collection of Michaux letters and documents from the following institutions of France, whose directors graciously granted permission for their use: Archives de France, Bibliothèque Nationale, Muséum National d'Histoire Naturelle. We wish to express our thanks to these French Institutions as well as to the American Philosophical Society for this material, which proved essential to our study.

Our thanks are also due to the Bibliothèque de Versailles for a copy of the manuscript in their collection of André Michaux's journal of his Persian travels, and to Jacques Rousseau of the Montreal Botanical Garden for a copy of his article on André Michaux's journey to Lake Mistassini.

We would like to express our appreciation to the many libraries and other institutions that have made their research facilities available to us: The Libraries of Harvard University, particularly Widener, Houghton, the Arnold Arboretum, and the Gray Herbarium Libraries; the Massachusetts Historical Society; the Massachusetts Horticultural Society; the Boston Public Library, Rare Book Room; the Library of the New York Botanical Garden, to which we are indebted for both French and English versions of the J. P. F. Deleuze memoir of the life of André Michaux; the Charleston Library Society; the South Carolina Historical Society; the Thomas Cooper Library, especially the Rare Book Room, of the University of South Carolina, and the South Caroliniana Library; the South Carolina Department of Archives and History, with particular thanks to Dr. Charles Lee, Director; also, the Library of Congress, which supplied us with a copy of the rare manuscript of André Michaux's memoir of his journeys, addressed to Citizen Genet.

We wish to express our thanks to the many individuals who have helped us in one way or another. Especially we acknowledge most gratefully our indebtedness to Stephen Catlett, Manuscript Librarian of the American Philosophical Society, who responded with never-failing patience to our many requests and queries, supplying us with many significant documents, including extensive copies from the French microfilms and photographs from the Society's collections. Our thanks are also due to Dr. F. K. Jouffroy, of the Muséum National d'Histoire Naturelle, for her research in France on our behalf and for a copy from the Muséum collection of E. T. Hamy's account of André Michaux's Persian journey; to Dr. George C. Rogers, of the History Department of the University of South Carolina; to Margaret Seaborn, for her Oconee research on our behalf.

We wish especially to thank Anne de Brunhoff for her skill and enterprise in obtaining for us photographs of the Harcourt Château and arboretum and the Michaux home in Vauréal, and we gratefully acknowledge the permission granted by Madame Claude Brasseur for the Vauréal photographs.

We wish also to thank our typists, Sandra Hendley and Everose Alexander for their excellent work on our manuscript.

Finally, we are most grateful to Walker Cowen, Director of the University Press of Virginia, for his support and guidance throughout this undertaking, and to our editor, Gerald Trett, for his careful attention to every aspect of our work, his discerning criticism, and generous encouragement, from all of which both we and our manuscript have profited.

Part One
~§ ANDRÉ MICHAUX

I HAVE ALWAYS FELT THAT ANDRÉ MICHAUX
MORE THAN ANY OTHER TRAVELER WAS
POSSESSED BY THE ANIMUS OF OUR NA-
TURE . . . . HE LOVED FLOWERS AS AUDUBON
LOVED THE BIRDS; HE TOO CAME FROM THE
STRICT GRACES OF FRANCE TO WOO THE
AMERICAN WILDERNESS, AND HIS HIGH AND
SELFLESS ADVENTURING LED HIM AT LAST
TO A GRAVE IN FAR-OFF MADAGASCAR I
LOVE HIM FOR THE GENTLEMAN EXPLORER
THAT HE WAS, THE CHEVALIER UNDER THE
LIVE-OAKS AND THE SPANISH MOSS, THE
PLANTSMAN WHO WOULD LIFT A PLANT
FROM THE GROUND AS IF IT HAD BEEN A
CHILD. NO MERE COLLECTOR OF SPECI-
MENS, HE LOVED THE LIVING PLANT; HE
SOUGHT THE USEFUL OR THE BEAUTIFUL
AND DREAMED ONLY HOW HE COULD MAKE
IT COSMOPOLITAN.

DONALD CULROSS PEATTIE

CHAPTER 1

ᘓ Youth and Apprenticeship, 1746–1782

THIS IS THE STORY of the life and times of two remarkable Frenchmen, father and son, richly endowed naturalists, whose lives spanned the latter half of the eighteenth century and the first half of the nineteenth. Both have been strangely neglected, although separately and together they made significant contributions to the advancement of botany, horticulture, and forestry in the United States, a nation to which each gave a selfless devotion with results yet visible in our day. They left no other posterity. Their names, André Michaux and François André Michaux, are seen daily in hundreds of places in works of botany, horticulture, and forestry, but rarely beyond these circles. The intent of this book is to make amends to some degree for their undeserved neglect. The times in which they flourished were dramatic chapters in history, during which significant progress was made not only in the fields of their special interests but in the whole realm of science.

The winter of 1785–86 was a severe one in New York City. The ground was already frozen in the nearby countryside as early as November, when the French vessel *Le Courrier de New York* hove in sight on Sunday, the thirteenth, and dropped anchor in the harbor. Among the passengers who stepped ashore next day in the crisp, chill air was a French naturalist, André Michaux, recently appointed botanist to Louis XVI of France. He had been sent by His Majesty to the new republic across the sea on a scientific mission designed to enrich both countries with botanical exchanges and thereby cement in peace the ties forged in war in the struggle for American independence. Essentially, the purpose of his mission was to collect and ship to his native land American seeds and plants to enrich the gardens, farms, and forests of France, particularly the forests, sadly depleted by the long naval war with England.

This was a formidable assignment for any botanist, but to Michaux it seemed a magnificent prospect. Waiting in the port of Lorient to embark for America, he had written exultantly to a friend: "Our ship is under sail and the wind is favorable. I imagine myself setting out to the conquest of the New World."[1] The conquest he dreamed of was the botanical exploration of the vast and virgin wonderland of the American wilderness. Qualified for his task by intelligence and training, he was already, at thirty-nine years of age, seasoned by scientific expeditions in France, Spain, England, and, most recently, Persia. Fortunately, he brought to his mission other less tangible but significant assets: a passionate dedication to the gentle science of botany, an indomitable and adventurous spirit, and the courage and vitality to meet the challenges of the American wilderness, to which he would devote the next eleven years of his life.

During that relatively brief span of time in what became the United States, he would travel, sometimes alone and sometimes companioned by his young son, François André, who had accompanied him, thousands of miles over eastern North America, from southern Florida to the region of Hudson Bay, and westward to the Mississippi, recording in his journal and letters the botanical wealth of the American wilderness—which he called "Les Wilderness," multiple and many faceted—enduring hardships and dangers but tirelessly observing, discovering, collecting, and describing the thousands of trees and plants he found on his journeys.

As the first trained botanical explorer to travel extensively in North America, his contributions to botany are recognized in the annals of science in the species of plants named for him; for example, a beautiful lily of eastern United States, the Turk's-cap, or Carolina, lily, *Lilium michauxii*. Also he is the established authority for many genera, species, and varieties of plants.

Moreover, Michaux's name is immortalized and his memory kept green in the continuing enrichment of our lives through his introduction into American horticulture of European and Asian trees and plants he brought to this country as gifts and helped to establish here.[2] All are of oriental origin. Among the best known and most treasured are two evergreen shrubs, *Camellia japonica,* the glory of southern gardens in late winter and early spring, when its exquisite flowers, ranging from white to red, blossom among the glossy, dark green foliage, and *Osmanthus fragrans,* or sweet olive, whose tiny white or yellow blooms perfume the gardens of the South. He brought in also at least one and probably several species of "Chinese azalea."

Michaux gave us too the graceful mimosa, or silk tree, *Albizzia julibrissin,* whose delicate, fragrant flowers seem made of slender, silken threads tipped with crimson, a tree described by William Bartram in a letter to Thomas Jefferson, to whom he sent some seeds of mimosa, as "a native of Persia and Armenia, lately brought to us by the celebrated Michaux the elder"; and the popular crape myrtle tree, as well, *Lager-*

stroemia indica, whose long-lasting, striking, and abundant blossoms of intricate design range from white to deep crimson.

We owe to this celebrated naturalist some of our most interesting and ornamental exotic trees. These include the maidenhair tree, *Ginkgo biloba,* a living fossil, the most ancient surviving species of broad-leafed tree, once found growing wild on the forested mountains of western China and cultivated for centuries on the grounds of eastern temples. Now successfully naturalized in this country, it often graces the streets and public parks as well as gardens of our cities, where it has proved particularly resistant to air pollution. The *Ginkgo* is especially glorious in autumn when the alternate, fan-shaped leaves turn a brilliant gold and fall in a sudden golden shower as the season ends. Other interesting and beautiful trees introduced by Michaux are the varnish tree, or Chinese parasol tree, *Firmiana platanifolia,* a native of both China and Japan, a relative of the chocolate tree, now sparingly escaped in some of our southern states—a curious tree with very large, heart-shaped leaves and bark that remains green on trunk and branches even in maturity, and with seeds borne in open pods from their beginning so that they are clearly visible from outside; and the Chinese tallow tree, *Sapium sebiferum,* now rather freely naturalized in the low country of the Southeast and sometimes called the popcorn tree because of the round white seeds that cling in clusters to its branches. Another popular Michaux import is the pride of India, or chinaberry tree, *Melia azedarach,* of the mahogany family, a sacred tree of Persia, though generally considered a native of India. This striking tree, often called the Persian lilac for the similarity of its lilac or lavender flowers to those of the lilac, has escaped in the southern states, where it is welcomed for the shade of its leafy branches, for its flowers, and for its insect-repellent yellow drupes. Exotic fruit trees brought from Persia to France by André Michaux and hence to this country include the pomegranate, *Punica granatum,* the Persian peach, plum, and almond.

One should mention a plant of the same family as the Camellia, the tea plant, *Thea sinensis,* which André Michaux is believed to have introduced into South Carolina with the intention of establishing tea production. He is said to have planted the first tea plants at Middleton Place near Charleston. Moreover, legend or tradition attributes to Michaux the introduction of the true laurel, *Laurus nobilis,* and a fragrant spicebush, the Asian *Lindera,* as well as a sweet-scented flowering vine with sausage-shaped, edible fruits, *Akebia quinata,* a native of Japan, which Michaux is said to have brought to America from the gardens of Versailles.

Whatever the provenance of the purple-flowering *Akebia,* it may well have been those fabulous gardens of Versailles that first awakened in André Michaux his profound and lifelong love of flowers. For he was born on March 7, 1746, in the royal domain of Satory in the great park of Versailles, the son of a farmer in the service of the king, Louis XV, then in the thirty-first year of his long reign. Michaux's father, another André, was entrusted with the management of the Satory domain, 500 fertile acres of good French soil, which had been in the care of his forebears for generations and would, God willing, be handed down to his sons. Or so it seemed. Thus, in preparation for his anticipated stewardship of the farm, the lad André labored beside his father, absorbing from childhood a love of the soil and developing a taste for a simple, wholesome way of living and a habit of steady, persevering toil that would persist throughout his career.

Yet his life from its beginning was lived in the midst of dramatic contrast. Beyond the woods, edging their green fields on the north, lay one of the largest and most magnificent gardens in the world, surrounding palaces of imperial splendor. The imagined glories of fairy-tales castles pale beside the factual descriptions of the opulence of Versailles as created by Louis XIV, at a cost that beggared the kingdom but with results which dazzled Europe and which still, muted and dimmed by time, resist the erosions of the centuries.

The Château, or great palace, with accommodations for 6,000 persons, was built in 1672 in a park of 4,000 acres, converted into wonderful gardens designed by André le Nôtre, with terraces, tree-shaded avenues ornamented by statuary, lagoons, a great canal, and always and everywhere flowers in astonishing variety and quantity, cared for and rotated according to the season by hundreds of skilled gardeners, to furnish blossoms year around. Whole forests are said to have been moved in and planted, and rivers diverted to furnish water for the hundreds of fountains. To supplement the great Château, the palaces of the Grand and Petit Trianon were erected, but the finest piece of architecture at Versailles was the Orangery, designed by Mansard and built in 1685. Within its glass-protected interior, with a central gallery 508 feet long, grew 1,200 orange trees, some 500 years old, as well as 300 other varieties of trees. On the south of the great Château two splendid staircases led past the Orangery to the Swiss lake, beyond which rose the forests of Satory, the oldest part of Versailles, bordering the bountiful fields of the Michaux farm and the little village, dominated by the ancient Cathedral of St. Louis, with which the Michaux family were affiliated.

Thus, within the environs of these 4,000 acres André Michaux spent his childhood, except for four years at boarding school, where he proved a ready pupil, especially in the classics. At fourteen, his formal education at an end, he was summoned home to work beside his father and assume in earnest the duties of his apprenticeship as his father's heir on the Satory domain.

From the first he revealed a marked aptitude for the work and an eager interest in the science of agriculture, which inspired him to experiment with new methods of cultivation and to explore the neighboring gardens. Not least, one surmises, the magnificent gardens of Versailles. Yet he found time not only to study the theories and principles of agriculture but also to carry on his study of Latin and even to embark on a study of the Greek language.

The death of both parents by the time he was twenty left André and his younger brother to share the management of the large farm as well as the guardianship of their sisters' welfare and fortunes, a partnership that lasted until 1769, when the two brothers separated their shared concerns.

In October of the same year André married Cécile Claye, daughter of a prosperous farmer of Beauce. In the spring of 1770 the young couple may have watched beyond the dark woods, separating Satory from the royal park, the glittering display of fireworks and illuminations lighting up the night skies in celebration of the marriage of the dauphin to his Austrian princess, Marie Antoinette.

The future of both young couples looked bright. André Michaux seemed destined to follow his father in the rooted and useful life of his forebears, in the service of the king. A few months later, however, the pattern of his life was shattered by the death, after less than a year of marriage, of his young wife, following the birth of their son François André. Her death was not only a tragic loss to Michaux but the end of his old way of life.

In his grief and loneliness he sought solace in a passionate dedication to work, plunging with renewed intensity into the study and practice of his art. It was in these circumstances that his sad situation came to the attention of the king's personal physician, Dr. Lemonnier, a distinguished naturalist, who invited the young widower to visit him at his estate at Montreuil, near Versailles.[3] Touched by Michaux's melancholy and impressed by his evident ability as a cultivator, Lemonnier set out to encourage his already eager interest in botany and especially to engage him in the principles and practice of naturalizing exotic plants, an interest close to Lemonnier's heart. The friendship, thus initiated, rapidly deepened, and persisted until Lemonnier's death. Fortune could hardly have provided Michaux with a wiser mentor or a kinder friend.

When this friendship began, Louis Guillaume Lemonnier was already a celebrated scientist, high in the favor of Louis XV. As professor of botany at the Jardin du Roi in Paris, the exploration for plants in all corners of the world and the naturalization of the exotic discoveries in French soil had long been matters of intense interest to him, and he had welcomed to the garden the botanical treasures sent back by naturalists in the field, such as Pierre Poivre and Pierre Sonnerat with their shipments of fragrant spices, scented acacias, irises, lilacs, camellias, and other exotics.[4]

Ever alert to detect and encourage gifted young scientists, Lemonnier was quick to direct the interests of his protégé in the direction of plant exploration. Michaux needed no urging. Stimulated by his need to escape the still painful associations of his home, his latent hunger for travel and far horizons began to stir. Even as a boy of fourteen, construing the life of Alexander the Great by Quintus Curtius, he had been so enthralled by the descriptions of the fabled countries of the Greek hero's conquests that he had dreamed of one day seeing for himself the marvelous lands of the East.

He now resolved to prepare himself, with Lemonnier's aid and advice, through study and practical experience, for a career as a naturalist explorer and collector, to serve his country and the cause of science, and at the same time satisfy his longing to visit all the green kingdoms of the world.

Lemonnier suggested that he devote a part of the land at his disposal to experimenting with the cultivation of madder and rice. When these first trials succeeded admirably, Lemonnier took the significant step of presenting the young farmer to the comte D'Angiviller, who was destined to become one of the most influential men in the court of Louis XVI.[5]

As the count was also to play a significant role in Michaux's life for many years, it is appropriate to introduce him more fully. Charles-Claude De La Billarderie, comte D'Angiviller (1730–1809), had begun his association with the French court at an early age as a royal page to Louis XV. Handsome, capable, generous, and magnetic, he advanced steadily in his court career to reach eminence under Louis XVI, who loved and trusted him, and, upon his accession to the throne in 1774, appointed him to the office of counselor to the king, and director of the buildings of the king, including gardens, academies, the arts, manufacturing, and the like, as well as administrator for His Majesty of his château and private domain of Rambouillet, and overseer of the Jardin du Roi.

Louis XVI had chosen well. Behind the facade of the elegant courtier dwelt a genuine friend of artists and scientists, and a singularly capable administrator who enormously enriched the academies and museums, imposing his often costly reforms and innovations through a mixture of benevolence and tenacity.[6]

At the time of his meeting with Michaux, the count was at the height of his power. Interested in Lemonnier's report of Michaux's success with madder and rice, he requested the young man to try his hand in the cultivation of a particularly desirable pasture grass called teff, with seeds brought back from Abyssinia by Bruce.[7] The successful results were further confirmation of Michaux's ability in the naturalization of exotic plants.

Now wholly committed to the science of botany and plant research, and realizing his need for more profound knowledge in the field, Michaux surrendered his share of farm duties to his brother in order to devote himself to study with the single-minded fervor characteristic of all his efforts.

On the advice of Lemonnier, he began his formal studies in botany at the Trianon in 1777 under Bernard de Jussieu, celebrated brother of Antoine de Jussieu and demonstrator in botany at the Jardin du Roi (now Jardin des Plantes) for many years.[8] In 1779 Michaux moved to Paris, taking lodgings near the garden, then as now a mecca for dedicated students in all facets of natural history.

The capital of France at this time was the largest city in Europe, with approximately 650,000 inhabitants, and the intellectual center for savants from all over Europe, attracted by its academic institutions, museums, and the intoxicating intellectual atmosphere, produced by the ferment of ideas known as the Enlightenment, particularly potent in Paris.

Change was in the air, though few, if any, could have foreseen the cataclysmic nature of coming events. Many of the great figures, the movers and shakers in the world of ideas, were gone from the scene by the time Michaux settled in Paris, but their influence remained. The year 1778 saw the deaths of Voltaire, Rousseau, and Linnaeus.[9] Diderot lingered on for a few more years, his monumental *Encyclopédie* attacked and banned, but his luminous mind undimmed.

Still dominant in the field of science was Buffon, the arbiter of natural history in France for more than a quarter of a century, now old and tired but still able to bring out in the eventful year of 1778 his highly praised *Epogues de la Nature* and still gallantly struggling to complete his monumental *Histoire Naturelle,* eventually to come to forty-four volumes, embracing all nature as its province.[10]

One of the more inspired acts of Louis XV had been the appointment in 1739 of this scientific scion of the petite noblesse of Burgundy as overseer of the Jardin du Roi. During the years of his administration, the area devoted to the garden had been tripled, the greenhouses and cultivated areas enriched with hundreds of exotic plants from all over the world, and a school of botany established. It was here then that André Michaux came to study. The Jardin du Roi was then, in essential ways, much like the establishment as we see it today.[11]

Even in 1778 the student of botany would have found at the Jardin du Roi an establishment second to none dedicated to scientific research. Michaux was privileged to work also under that green-thumbed genius of the soil André Thouin, reputed to know more about the naturalization of foreign plants than anyone of his day.[12] The gentle and beloved Bernard de Jussieu had died in 1777, but his nephew, Antoine de Laurent de Jussieu, had taken his place as professor of botany. So closely had he lived and worked with his Uncle Bernard and so profoundly had he absorbed his teachings that he developed, extended, and established the new system of the natural classification of plants first conceived by Bernard.

As his knowledge of the science of botany deepened and his skill in cultivation and naturalization increased, Michaux's desire to begin his own green pilgrimage to distant countries intensified. While he waited for an opportunity to travel to eastern lands, it seemed advisable to try his wings nearer home and, probably late in 1779 or early 1780, he set out for England.

England was a logical choice. In the eighteenth century France's ancient friend and foe across the Channel led the nations of Europe in botanical exploration and the naturalization of exotic plants. There was enough and more to enchant a young scholar in the London of Samuel Johnson, Edmund Burke, and the great naturalist Sir Joseph Banks, who had sailed with James Cook to the Pacific, and of James Smith, who, on the death of Linnaeus, had brought that great naturalist's incomparable collection to London to be carefully preserved for study.[13] We can picture Michaux's absorption in the renowned gardens of eighteenth-century London, such as the Apothecaries' Garden at Chelsea, on the banks of the sweetly flowing, unpolluted waters of the Thames, where at the gate stood magnificent Cedars of Lebanon planted there in 1683. Here were the first greenhouses and "stoves" in England, established to nurture the tender exotics such as the 800 Jamaican specimens collected by Sir Hans Sloane, patron of the garden, whose statue can be seen from Swans Walk.[14] Philip Miller, author of the famous *Dictionary of Gardening*, who had served as director of the Apothecaries' Garden for nearly fifty years, had died, but the garden still welcomed foreign naturalists to study its rich resources.

Michaux must surely have visited also the newly established British Museum to observe the remaining collections of Sloane's long and brilliant career, which included 16,000 natural history specimens.

We also fancy him spending delightful hours at Kew Gardens, already a paradise for botanists, which, under the inspired direction of Sir Joseph Banks, was beginning its development into the botanical world center we know today;[15] and at Mile End near the City, strolling absorbed through the establishment of James Gordon, a skilled cultivator who successfully naturalized plants from all over the world and whose botanical skill has been commemorated in the name of the genus *Gordonia,* which later would become one of Michaux's favorites among native plants of North America.

On his return to France, Michaux shared with his friends the botanical treasures he had brought back from England, setting out some of his plants in the gardens of Lemonnier and of the duc de Noailles. He had developed his own methods of grafting, which he used successfully, taking scions from the trees of his friends' gardens to graft on the trees of the Versailles forest.

In a few months he was off again, this time in the company of fellow naturalists, on an expedition into the French province of Auvergne, a region of dramatic scenery, volcanic mountains, and beautiful valleys. Among his companions were André Thouin and Jean-Baptiste Lamarck, men very close to his own age but already well established in their scientific careers.

André Thouin, chief gardener of the Jardin du Roi, Michaux's teacher and his lifelong friend, seems as intimately associated with the garden as the trees that grow on its soil. Born in 1742 at the garden, where his father was chief gardener before him, and trained as a botanist under Bernard de Jussieu, he succeeded to his father's position at the age of seventeen. Under his care the garden expanded and flourished. The plantation of the school of botany, over which he presided, is said to have had, at the time of his death, 6,000 living plants.[16]

Jean Baptiste de Monet, chevalier de Lamarck, whose family, like

View of the Jardin des Plantes, Paris, c. 1800. (Courtesy of the Bibliothèque Nationale, Paris; photograph by Lauros-Giraudon)

that of Buffon, belonged to the petite noblesse, was born in Picardy, educated by the Jesuits, but commissioned as a soldier, a career from which he is said to have been converted to the study of botany by a chance encounter with Rousseau, botanizing along the Seine.[17] Be that as it may, he became a pupil of that best of masters, Bernard de Jussieu, while he himself served as tutor to Buffon's son. At the time of his journey with Michaux, he had already published his *Flora Française,* designed to facilitate the determination of plant species, and had become a member of the Academy of Sciences.

As the company journeyed over the rugged terrain of Auvergne, Michaux's enthusiasm, as recorded by his companions, seemed boundless. Each day, equipped with gun, knapsack, notebook, and collection boxes, he ran far ahead of the rest, only pausing now and then to fire off his gun, or to speak to a shepherd, or to sow in some favorable spot the Cedar of Lebanon seeds he carried in his pocket—perhaps brought back from the famous old trees at the entrance to the London Apothecaries' Garden—already practicing his lifelong custom of enriching the earth wherever he found himself. Laden with the trophies of the day's collection of plants, birds, insects, and minerals, he rejoined his friends each evening.[18]

No sooner had he returned from Auvergne than he set off again, this time to journey through the Pyrenees into Spain, collecting seeds and plants for the royal gardens and nurseries, a successful expedition that brought him an official appointment as correspondent of the Royal Gardens.

Eager to undertake plant research in distant lands, Michaux appealed to Lemonnier for help in obtaining a commission, preferably for the East, which continued to hold a strong attraction for him.

It so happened that there had arrived in Paris, from Persia, Jean François Rousseau, a native of Esfahan but of European parentage, who had served the French government effectively as provisional consul to Baghdad and Bassorah (now Basra, Iraq) during the critical years of the seventies and been rewarded on his return to France with an appointment as consul to Persia.[19] Rousseau and his wife had made a sensational appearance at Versailles, both gorgeously attired in oriental costume and glowing with tales of eastern adventure, charming Marie Antoinette and the court. Persia became the fashion.

Here was a rare opportunity and Michaux seized upon it, presenting, with the help of Lemonnier, whose influence at court was great, the following petition to Marie Antoinette:

Madam,

André Michaux, correspondent of the garden of the mu-
seum of the king, being fervently dedicated to botany, desires to
extend his knowledge and augment the progress of this science
through botanizing in regions of the world which have not yet
been visited for this purpose. On the advice of several botanists,
members of the Academy of Sciences, he had decided upon Persia,
knowing that the country produces the most beautiful trees, the
best fruits, and the most beautiful flowers, and that they can
thrive in France. He begs your Majesty to order Sieur Rousseau,
consul, to obtain for him the necessary recommendations and as-
sistance. He will consider himself too fortunate if the harvest of
trees and plants which he intends to collect can give pleasure to
Your Majesty and enrich the beautiful garden of the Trianon.[20]

In consequence, Michaux was appointed to accompany Rousseau
on his return to Baghdad to take up his duties as consul. For the
expenses of the journey, necessary supplies, and equipment, including
scientific instruments for studies in physics and astronomy, the resourceful Lemonnier solicited Monsieur, brother of the king, who
graciously assigned to Michaux a pension of 1,200 francs.[21] Michaux
himself quietly supplemented this sum at his own expense, an expedient he was to find repeatedly necessary when serving royalty. He was
inspired on this occasion, however, only with profound gratitude to
Monsieur for his patronage. The journal in which he was to record his
three years in Asia reveals in its opening paragraphs the intensity of his
ardor: "The passionate love of Botany has led me to traverse the
mountains of Auvergne, and to visit the Pyrenees and the mountains of
Spain. I burned with the longing to undertake a journey into the most
distant countries. . . . The desire to extend my knowledge and to contribute to the progress of natural history moved me to search for several
years for the opportunity to travel into parts of the world which had not
yet been visited for that purpose." Thus it was joyfully and with the
most exalted expectations that the botanist prepared to set out for
Persia.[22]

CHAPTER 2

∾§ Persian Expedition,
1782–1783

AFTER FOND FAREWELLS to Lemonnier, Thouin, Jussieu, and others, the young naturalist departed Paris on February 2, 1782, for the legendary East, beginning a green odyssey that would take him, in a span of twenty years, from the Persian Gulf to the Caspian Sea, from Florida to Hudson Bay, from the eastern shores of the Atlantic Ocean westward to the Mississippi River and, at long last, to a fevered death on the island of Madagascar.

Traveling by Cholins, Lyons, and Avignon, the Rousseau party reached Marseilles three weeks later, where the Syrian convoy awaited them.[1] Embarking on March 4 on the frigate *L'Aurore,* they sailed in a little over a week into the magnificent harbor of Malta. On this rocky island, still ruled by the Knights of Malta, last of the crusading orders, Michaux visited Caumont, French chargé d'affaires and an amateur botanist as well.[2]

Near Cyprus a violent storm struck the convoy. For three days the tempest raged. Though water poured into the ship from all sides and the cannons, in spite of their strong moorings, crushed against the sleeping berths stationed between them, the ships withstood the battering and, on March 29, dropped anchor in the Gulf of Alexandretta.

Eager as the passengers were to land after twenty-six days at sea, they had no sooner set foot on the earth on the thirty-first than they were forced to retreat quickly to the ship for two more days to escape the fierce fighting then in progress between the inhabitants of the town of Canton and the neighboring and warlike Payas.[3]

Alexandretta (now İskenderun) was at that time, as Michaux described it, "only a wretched village composed of some twenty houses," located on the Mediterranean coast of what is now southern Turkey.[4] Only two of the houses were tolerable, those of the consular agents of France and England. Situated in a low area on the edge of the sea, the village was subject to flooding in times of high tides when the waves broke against the houses and even inundated the shops where the imported goods destined for Aleppo were stored. Between the town and the neighboring mountain, half a league away, lay reed-covered marshes of foul-smelling stagnant water.

Michaux soon recognized that the deplorable health conditions and high mortality rate among the people who lingered long in the town could be attributed to the "mauvaise qualité de l'eau" drawn from a muddy stream that had circulated through these putrid marshes. As pure water from the nearby mountain was obviously easily obtainable by digging a canal, he was inspired to comment that "the health and life of men are counted for so little no one will soon remedy this deplorable condition."[5]

However strongly Michaux deplored the lack of enterprise among the inhabitants, who bothered neither to drain their marshes nor to cultivate the land but lived solely on fish, he responded joyfully to the experience of botanizing in this strange and fertile countryside, "where all was new." During the eight days he spent in İskenderun he went botanizing every day along the edges of the sea, in the lowlands and prairies, and in the neighboring mountains, finding among many other plants several kinds of irises, the *Nerium oleander,* and *Laurus nobilis,* species which it seems probable he later introduced into America. Some of his rapture is reflected in a letter to Thouin:

> *I cannot express to you the delight with which I run about the country here. In examining the multitude of plants with which the fields abound, I was often transported beyond myself, and compelled to pause and tranquillize my mind for some moments. At night I could not sleep but awaited the dawn of day with impatience. What happiness! to find myself in Asia, and at my pleasure to traverse the mountains and valleys covered with liliaceous plants, orchideae, daphnes, laurus, vitices, myrtles, andrachnes, styrax, palms, and other vegetable productions, different from those of Europe. The seashore abounded with shell-fish, varied in form and colour; land and sea birds came every morning to feed upon them. The flamingos came in flocks of three and four hundred each. The marshes abounded with reptiles.*[6]

In addition to the flamingos, Michaux noted the herons, ducks, hooded crows, swallows, sparrows, red-legged partridges, francolins, and pigeons, though the carrier pigeon had been eliminated by Kurdish guns forty years earlier.[7] Among the reptiles were dozens of sea and land turtles and several different snakes.

By April 10 their caravan was organized and they set out for the journey to Antioch, fifteen in number, all well armed: six travelers, four janissaries, and five baggage conductors. It seemed a propitious beginning for Michaux's first mission into distant lands. None could have foreseen that the journey across the Turkish provinces to the Persian Gulf would require nearly a year of arduous and dangerous travel, interspersed with periods of frustrating delays.

Whenever possible along the route, Michaux eagerly botanized, guarded by a janissary assigned by Rousseau to protect him—a wise precaution, for during the eight-hour journey from Beylan to Antioch, their first stop, the caravan was repeatedly harassed by ragged bands of Turks and Turkomen who could be driven off only by payment of bribes.[8]

Thus it was a weary band of travelers who crossed the swift-flowing Orontes River on April 11 and entered the town of Antioch. Little remained of the once flourishing trade center of the ancient world, "Golden Antioch," queen of the East, the pride of vanished empires, the guardian of many faiths. It was here that Paul and Barnabas brought the new gospel, here that the name "Christian" was used for the first time, here that a Christian principality, established by crusaders, endured for two centuries.

The remorseless erosion of centuries and the ravages of earthquakes and wars had left of the old city only a few ruins. "Antioch," observed Michaux, "is now a little village agreeably situated at the foot of high mountains, on which one sees still the thick high walls that once formed the encircling ramparts. They are fallen in ruins."[9]

Leaving Antioch, the travelers journeyed across pleasant and fertile fields to Salghim, where Michaux noted especially the hedgerows of almond trees surrounding the plantations. Their way was now along difficult mountain paths for two more days before arriving on April 14 at the ruined and abandoned fields surrounding Aleppo. Once a favored rendezvous for caravans from Arabia, India, and Persia, this city, whose population Michaux estimated to be 100,000 people, had declined into decadence.

"The town is situated on the side of a valley," wrote Michaux, *in which are gardens abounding with trees, none of which are grafted: the rest of the country is dry, stony, and uncultivated. For six leagues around not a single tree or shrub is to be seen. Beyond are vast plains, whose fertility if cultivated would be prodigious. On these were formerly villages which have been successively destroyed. The predecessor of the present pacha destroyed more than eighty on the pretext that the inhabitants had formerly revolted. His soldiers committed unheard of cruelties among them. They ransacked the houses and cut off the heads of women and children to make themselves masters of the pieces of gold or-*

*namenting their headdresses. It is by such vexations that the
pachas indemnify themselves for the tributes they must pay to the
grand Seignior. These ruined villages are now the haunts of robbers.*[10]

During the six months the Rousseau party was forced to remain in
Aleppo until arrangements could be made to continue their journey
toward Baghdad, Michaux devoted himself to his mission, recording
detailed observations on the flora and fauna and on the modes of
agriculture, listing all the plant species he had identified. Despite the
ever-present dangers, he made three excursions into the surrounding
mountains. "One would never go out," he commented, "if one wished
always to be safe."[11]

As he explained to Thouin,
*Excursions are equally painful and dangerous throughout the
whole of this part of Asia, which extends from Syria to the frontiers of India. The traveller carries his provisions and sleeps on
the ground, avoiding the caravanseries on account of their filthi-
ness and the insects with which they abound. He must, however,
follow the caravans; otherwise, he would be plundered by the
Arabs on the plains, and the Kurds who infest the mountains.
The caravans are often attacked: in March last the robbers took
from that of Alexandretta 380 camels; and the one which is now
ready to depart has been compelled to wait ten days beyond their
time, expecting troops which the pacha of Aleppo and Antioch
has detached for their escort. Every traveller must take with him
an Armenian with whom he must stand guard alternately; for the
conductors of the caravans are for the most part knaves who
watch for an opportunity to rob the travellers.*[12]

The most extensive of his excursions from Aleppo was one to
Laodicea (now Latakia) and Selucia in the company of Beauchamp,
who was the nephew and vice-general of the bishop of Baghdad, and
amateur archeologist as well, interested especially in medallions. The
two Frenchmen journeyed first to Latakia, where they found, among
other ruins of the ancient world, six well-preserved granite columns
from a temple to Bacchus, and, in a garden, an octagonal pillar with still
legible Greek inscriptions on its eight faces, one of which Michaux
transcribed.

Embarking on a Greek boat, they visited Selucia, ancient seaport
of Antioch. A multitude of sepulchers, hollowed out of the rocks, some
in the form of underground caverns large enough for several coffins,

gave evidence of the considerable size of the vanished city. After their stopover in Antioch, en route back to Aleppo, Michaux once more explored the countryside, discovering several new species of plants and listing the birds, animals, and reptiles. Among the latter he noted land and water turtles, scorpions, chameleons, a large gray and black spotted lizard, "hideous to see," and a few snakes which, he observed with relief, were "pas méchant," for Michaux, fearless in the face of the most awesome dangers, had a genuine dread of "serpents," especially the venomous species he would encounter in years to come in the American wilderness. In that wilderness also, in the southern regions of America, he would meet again an insect that now delighted him in the Aleppo countryside, the firefly, which he called *mouche luisante*, "glittering fly," saying that "it flies from all sides at night and sheds a bright light, very cheerful and pleasant to see."

Before setting out on this expedition to Selucia, he had assured André Thouin: "On my return I shall send you and Monsieur Malesherbes[13] some specimens of seeds. The consul and the merchants can tell you that no one labors with more ardor to make his fortune than I do for the interests of botany."[14] Back in Aleppo, he devoted himself "with zeal and untiring work" to preparing his first collection for shipment to France, "a good collection of rare and new plants, some birds, some old medallions, some Greek inscriptions, some minerals."

Lemonnier, who received the shipment, wrote appreciatively, "I have greatly entertained Monsieur at Fontainebleau . . . by showing him your dried plants, the medallions, the inscriptions, and in presenting to him the engraved stone of which he is going to have a ring made. I cannot praise you enough for the care which you have put into this shipment, your plants are perfectly preserved, and it seems to me you have many new things."[15]

Lemonnier promptly classified the seeds and sowed them in his orangerie for protection against the winter cold. He advised Michaux to prepare a report of all the fruit trees, culinary plants, and beautiful flowers he should discover in Persia, as this would interest Monsieur far more than botanical research. This letter, sent care of Consul Rousseau, was long delayed in reaching Michaux, as the ship on which it was carried was damaged by storms and held in Cyprus for repair.

Meanwhile the Rousseau caravan, delayed from travel by extreme heat, was at last preparing to depart for Baghdad. They were awaiting, Michaux explained in his journal, the outcome of negotiations with an Arab chieftain, through whose lands they must pass, who demanded as a price for the passage of the Europeans "les presens d'usage"—the customary gifts.[16] The French had offered him 200 sequins (nine francs) and were awaiting his response. This chieftain was camped three leagues from Aleppo, with 2,000 soldiers who roamed over the countryside and only the day before had pillaged a company of Turkish travelers.

"This country," commented Michaux, "which would be the best country in the world for its fertility and purity of air, is a country of desolation and continual civil war caused by the abuses of the powerful against the people whom they force into rebellion. There had been a great massacre only eight days before my last journey to Antioch."[17] On this occasion, Michaux reported, 700 or 800 persons, huddled in a mosque for sanctuary, were strangled to death by order of the governor, and eight rebellious princes, or chiefs, tied in bundles and thrown living into the Orontes River.

"It is not the same in Persia and in India," he wrote hopefully. "One can travel as safely in those countries as in Europe; one lacks, in truth, many conveniences, as in all of Asia; one finds no inn, one even avoids sleeping in the caravanseries because of the vermin and infections found in them; one must carry a rug for sleeping at night, some rice, a cooking pot, and some water; wine is extremely rare as the Turks do not use it. The most effeminate carry a tent but one can do without, for it never rains in summer, rarely in winter."[18] Thus, even in his journeys in far countries, Michaux's dedication led him to accept with grace the terms of his service and to find a night beneath the brilliant stars of the eastern deserts or below the shadowing trees of the western forests only a fitting prelude to the constantly renewed wonder of each day's revelations in the green kingdoms of the world.

Rousseau and his companions, who had been waiting for six months in Aleppo, set out finally on October 10 on the long journey across the desert to Baghdad. The caravan consisted of 180 camels and 120 to 130 persons, of whom only a dozen were Europeans: M. and Mme Rousseau, their two-year-old child and French governess, Martin, a doctor who had accompanied Rousseau from Paris, Senez, Rousseau's secretary, and an interpreter from Constantinople; Beauchamp, vicar-general of Baghdad, another Frenchman met at Aleppo, who was en route to India, a baron, German or French, from Alsace, and his wife, also en route to India.[19] The rest of the number consisted of 10 traveling Jews who had joined the caravan and over 100 Arab guides, including 3 very honest and very courageous chieftains, for, said Michaux, one must justly admit that the Arabs are the most humane of all those who make a business of pillaging the caravans, as they do not kill, but after taking everything away, often furnish the victim with some poor garments and provisions sufficient for him to reach the nearest town.

This journey of less than 200 leagues from Aleppo to Baghdad consumed forty-two days, being prolonged by detours to find grass or water for the camels or avoid encounters with brigands. Perhaps the travelers, like Chaucer's pilgrims, beguiled the hours with tales, but one of their company at least kept his eye on the landscape: "I have had the satisfaction of collecting something each day, either during the march or the remainder of the day after our arrival at the place where we were to camp," Michaux wrote to his patron. "We set out every day before seven o'clock in the morning, and stopped ordinarily about two o'clock in the afternoon."[20]

Heavy rains halted the caravan for a day, during which Michaux botanized without interruption, discovering near their halt a new species of almond tree he called *Amygdalus juncea.* However, most of the journey took place under a burning desert sun that scorched everything and forced the botanist to dig deep into the hot, hard soil in search of the bulbs of rare and new species of lileaceaus plants sometimes found there.

On All Saints' Eve, October 31, the arrival of the hot and weary caravan at the Euphrates River was a day of rejoicing—"*un jour de fête.*" Fresh water to drink and a cool bath in the river for all, including the camels, who gratefully submerged themselves in the cool waters for more than three hours. "At this spot," Michaux reported, "the river is a little larger than the Seine at Les Invalides." Beyond the wide plain of dry mud, "thickets of mimosa and tamarin" gave an idea of the extent of the surrounding land submerged at high water—one to two leagues. It was like a valley of flood lands contained within its boundaries by terraces, thirty or forty feet above the water level at that season. Along those dry banks Michaux was pleased to come upon a new species of "vanneau," an oriental lapwing, or peewit, to add to his ornithological collection.

As the caravan continued its journey along the Euphrates, a turn in the river revealed a grazing herd of 400 to 500 gazelles, which, startled at their approach, quickly fled from sight. Farther on they crossed the Euphrates, spending four days ferrying across it on miserable barges—men, camels, and baggage. Pushing in a wide northward detour across a desolate plateau of sterile soils composed mostly of gypsum and clay in a steadily increasing cold, more than once freezing the water in their flasks, the caravan, tired and dusty, arrived at the mud flats bordering the Tigris River, which, at high water, Michaux reported, sometimes flooded twenty leagues of countryside.

In November they turned southward, following down the Tigris aiming for Baghdad. Along the way they camped at the edge of the river in the holy Muhammadan city of Iman-Moussa, a holy place of the Shiite Muslims, sacred to the memory of the prophet's great-grandson, Moussa, whose glittering tomb and mosque could be seen shining in the sun north of their encampment. Early in December they reached Baghdad. The arrival of the French consul was anticipated, and Rousseau and his party were welcomed by the Carmelite Fathers of the city and hospitably lodged in their monastery, where Michaux was to spend nearly three months. His Persian journal gives an evocative description of the fabled city:

> *This city is situated on the Tigris which flows through its midst. There is a bridge of boats across the river which is six hundred feet wide at this spot. There are several mosques. The houses are built of bricks baked in the fire, though a few houses inhabited by Arab tribes are made of sun dried bricks. The interior of the houses is roughly plastered. The mosques as well as the towers that accompany them are of fire-baked bricks. These towers are called minarets and their surface is covered with a glaze similar to that of the pottery used in France. The bricks which are to be placed on the exterior of these edifices are prepared with this glaze at the time of construction so that one can conveniently form then the symmetry of design which they create on the glaze.*
>
> *The city at both extremities is bordered by gardens which are very fertile, planted in palm trees, oranges and lemons. They cultivate vegetables there too because of the frequent irrigation necessary to carry off the saltiness with which the soil is impregnated. Outside of these gardens, in places where there is no irrigation, the soil, although of clay, is so sterile that no plants grow there. There are no forests in the environs, and the inhabitants use for their stoves the wood of old palm trees that die in the gardens or more generally the wood of tamarisk which grows abundantly in the desert in all the places innundated by the flooding of the Euphrates and the Tigris. In the proximity of these two rivers the city is surrounded by a ditch and walls of sun-dried brick. These walls are in good condition and are well maintained, but they would offer no resistance to European artillery.*
>
> *I have seen no vestige of antiquity save only a granite column which serves as a threshold to one of the principal portals of*

*the city. Three hours distant from the city toward the Southwest
one sees a considerable tower called Tower of Nimrod. There is
another tower nearby called Tower of Babel. I have not seen it
but its construction was so considerable that most of the houses of
Hella are constructed of bricks taken from the tower and people
have taken these bricks by river even as far as Baghdad.*[21]

Though he does not refer to the city's historical and intellectual associations, one may assume that his pulse beat faster when he trod for the first time the streets of this legend-haunted, four-thousand-year-old city, once the glory of Mesopotamia, the center of art and learning under Harun ar-Rashid in the time of Charlemagne, and the fabled scene of many a tale from the *Arabian Nights.*

Legend and romance may well have enhanced Michaux's stay in Baghdad but in no way distracted him from his scientific mission. Throughout December of 1782 and the following January he kept precise records of the temperature variations in Baghdad weather. "The coldest day," he wrote, "was the 7th of January, 1783; the thermometer Réaumur was, at 6 o'clock in the morning at 2 degrees below zero, at noon at 7° above, and in the evening at 2° below."

By the end of January he was able to send a new collection of seeds by caravan to Aleppo on the first stage of their long journey to Paris. "The seeds that I have the honor to send to you," he wrote to his patron, Monsieur,

*have been collected during the crossing of the desert from Aleppo
to Baghdad. I would have liked to add a large herbarium but
most of the plants were withered and the shrubby trees denuded of
leaves. There are several very interesting ones whose seeds I have
been able to gather only by searching for a considerable time at
the foot of the plant and in places where I surmised the wind
would have brought them together. I beg you to believe that I
have made every possible effort; I was often obliged to turn aside
from the caravan which always followed its route, and to avoid
being surprised by Arabs or ferocious beasts, especially beside the
Euphrates, I took the precaution of being well armed.*

*I have gathered more than a hundred kinds of seeds, and I
have put together in the same package the most interesting ones. I
have put separately those of which I have been able to procure
samples to make a herbarium. I presume all these plants can survive in the Orangery and a few will succeed out of doors, for in
the month of November we experienced in the desert two degrees*

*below zero, by the Réaumur thermometer. The water which flowed
from our leather bottles one uses for travel was frozen in the
morning on three occasions. I am giving you more complete details in the letter which I have the honour to write to you by way
of Constantinople. There is now a caravan ready to set out for
Aleppo, it is very numerous and I hope this shipment will reach
you safely. As shipments addressed to consuls are exempt from
customs examinations, I address this one to M. Arne, consul of
Aleppo, who is entrusted to send it on to the Chamber of Commerce of Marseilles, whence it will be sent immediately to you.*

*I will take advantage of the first courier we have for Con-
stantinople in order to give you notice of this shipment and of my
departure for Persia, by passing through Basra, Bushire, Shiraz,
and Esfahan. I have not yet received, Monsieur, any words from
you since my departure from Paris; they will however be very precious to me and your consideration would give me a great deal of
confidence in my journeys.[22]*

Over a year had elapsed since Michaux departed Paris when at
last, on March 1, 1783, he bade farewell to Consul Rousseau and set out
from Baghdad on the final stage of his journey into Persia. On that
expedition he had for companions Father Ferdinand, a monk from the
Baghdad mission, whose frivolities had made his superiors eager to be
rid of him, and Cotinant, a Frenchman en route to India to make his
fortune, who was a diplomatic courier as well, entrusted with important
political messages. As planned, the little band set out on March 1, across
the canal connecting the Tigris and Euphrates, and two days later
reached Hella.[23] Here they took a boat to visit the pasha of Baghdad,
who received them well and provided them with not only the necessary
letters of safe conduct to officials in towns on their route but also the
company of a sheikh and four of his men as escorts.

It was soon apparent that the pasha's precautions were justified.
"It was after having traveled for seven hours," wrote Michaux, "that we
saw at a great distance some Arabs who, having also seen us, came upon
us at full speed. They were armed with lances; most were naked,
wearing only a belt, and many bare-headed. Three or four of the
chieftains had shields of rhinoceros hide; one had a coat of mail. Their
number was about sixty. They were uttering shrieks and the alarming
howls customary among these people. Fortunately, their sheikh was a
friend of the pasha of Baghdad; so only pointed out to us the route we
should take to avoid their enemies."[24] After another encounter with a

friendly tribe who even offered to share with them their meager meal and another meeting with a band of hostile Arabs, too wretched and too few in numbers to challenge them, Michaux and his companions arrived at the appointed village on the shore of the Euphrates where the promised boat and four new guards awaited them for their descent of the river.

Downstream, beyond the junction of the Euphrates and Tigris, which unite to form the Shatt-al-Arab, one bank was bordered with palm trees and dotted with reed houses; but on the opposite side lay an immense expanse of marshlands harboring water birds in great numbers, ducks, geese, and pelicans, some of which Michaux secured for his collection.[25]

Though the travelers reached Basra on March 12, another six months were to pass before Michaux would be able to enter Persia. Hostilities between the Arab tribes and the Turkish authorities and wars among the various tribes themselves continually frustrated the efforts of the European travelers to leave Basra for the East, an enforced interval of delay that Michaux used profitably in learning Persian and even compiling a dictionary of the Persian language. "But," he lamented, "there was nothing for me to do in Basra in Botany. The soil is covered with a crust of salt on the surface and no plant grows there."

Among his surviving letters written from Basra is one to his son, directed to Paris to the home of Murat, possibly the tutor of the twelve-year-old lad. "I have received, my dear friend," wrote the father, "several letters from you, enclosed with those from your aunts." Though the approach was that of any conscientious eighteenth-century parent, replete with admonitory dictums and moral precepts, the letter clearly revealed the concerns and hopes of the absent father, nearly a third of the way around the world away from his only child whom he had not seen in more than a year. He was pleased with the good reports of his son's progress given by uncles and aunts, and urged him to strive continually to become an honorable, honest man and a gentleman "without reproach from God, from men, and from oneself." With messages of respect to his tutors, and of affection to the aunts and uncles in Paris and Satory, the letter concluded fondly. "I embrace you and am your affectionate father."[26]

Late in the month of May 1783 Michaux, in the company of a Dominican father, bound for Esfahan to take up his duties as vicar-general, embarked on a boat for Bandar Abu Shehr (now Bushire), a port on the Persian Gulf, only to have their little flotilla overwhelmed by thirty ships of the warring Arabs—a desperate experience from which they escaped with great difficulty and then only through the intercession of the British consul, De la Touche.

This gentleman showed the botanist every consideration throughout his prolonged stay in Basra, often inviting him to stay at his country place on the river where the two men formed a congenial friendship. In spite of the hostilities between their two nations, the consul assured him, Michaux reported, that, as he worked for the good of mankind and, "as natural history discoveries benefit all nations, I should not refuse any assistance he could give me."[27]

It was not until late summer that the English consul considered the situation safe enough to arrange for the departure of Michaux and his companion, who embarked hopefully on September 9 in a boat provided him. Yet after only one day of sailing they were set upon at a turn in the river by eight vessels manned by hostile Arabs, pillaged of all their possessions, and carried off to separate camps in the interior, where Michaux was eight days in captivity before the consul's efforts succeeded in obtaining his freedom. His books, his medicines, his two guns, his money, and a few articles of clothing rejected by the Arabs were returned to him, but his Wilson microscope, his magnifying glass, meridian telescope, carpentry tools, cooking gear, and most of his clothing remained in the hands of his captors. Nevertheless, although now meagerly equipped with the tools of his profession, Michaux again bade farewell to his benefactor and set out once more for the voyage down the gulf, on the consul's ship, destined once more for the Persian port of Bushire on the eastern shore of the gulf.

The long and perilous journey from İskenderun to the Persian Gulf had been a formidable initiation in the trials, tribulations, and triumphs of botanical research in foreign lands, demanding extraordinary resources of character, as revealed in Michaux's Persian journal. Naturally courageous, he seldom expressed fear. Yet one marvels at the astonishing intrepidity with which he faced the most fearful dangers, from the head-on charge of the wild and shouting desert horsemen armed with spears, and the repeated attacks on land and sea by hostile Arab tribes, to capture and captivity alone among enemies, not forgetting the relatively mild threat during his almost daily botanizing of encounters with savage beasts—lions, lynx, and wild boars—lurking even in the impenetrable thickets of tamarisk and mimosa and poplar along the mud flats of the Euphrates. Perhaps his restless and adventurous nature found these hazards less difficult to bear than the prolonged delays, frustrations, and petty obstacles that threatened to interfere with his mission, as when, on one occasion, in describing a voyage

he had made on the Tigris, he regretted not being able to botanize on
the shores of the river, because, he lamented, the Arabs had taken away
his shoes and the sun was so burning hot that it was not possible to put
one's feet down except in places covered with water. It was not the loss
of his shoes that distressed him so much as the loss of the possible plants
he might have found. One is impressed too by his ready adaptability to
circumstance and stubborn persistence in the face of obstacles, and by
the wide scope of his interests, from every aspect of natural history to
the ways of life of the natives, and the monuments of antiquity, but
perhaps, most of all, by his deep satisfaction and transcendent joy in his
work. Now from the deck of his ship, borne south-by-east with the wind,
he watched the blue waters of the gulf flowing by, with no misgiving but
only an elated anticipation of botanizing at last in Persia, where who
knew what myriads of unknown plants awaited his coming.

CHAPTER 3

⤦ Persia, 1783–1785

ON SEPTEMBER 21, 1783, the consul's ship dropped anchor in the
ancient port of Bushire. As the botanist stepped ashore in "the land of
the Lion and the Sun," his heart must have thrilled with pride and joy.
His Persian adventure had begun. The boundaries of this ancient and
romantic kingdom were very much the same in 1783 as they are today.
Then as now Persia extended from the Caspian Sea on the north to the
Persian Gulf and the Gulf of Oman on the south. Fortunately for
Michaux the kingdom, long racked by internal struggles, was enjoying
a rare interlude of calm under the benign rule of Karim Khan, who had
restored a measure of prosperity to the country. Europeans could travel
with relative safety as Michaux later reported to Lemonnier: "When
one has arrived at Bushire, one has no longer anything to fear if one
accompanies the caravans. This is what I have proved for myself since I
advanced as far as Rasht and Enzeli on the Caspian Sea."[1]

At Bushire, Michaux had observed with interest that great numbers of fossil shells were to be found in the limestones on the edge of the
sea, and pieces of reddish or milky white transparent agates as well. The
mountains along the coast were covered with gray, calcereous rocks

with, here and there, clay nodules like grinding stones. From the port a steep climb led, stage by stage, up to the high Persian plateau country. Here Michaux noted gypsum and salt mines and, thirty or forty fathoms down in the pits, he discovered pudding stones of ancient formation. Although the winter was severe, with snows of more than a month's duration, Michaux was able to send Lemonnier a precious harvest of seeds, of celandines, milkworts, mignonettes, carnations. Among the useful or attractive species the botanist was able to collect were some excellent melons, a certain little wood rose, *Rosa simpliciflora*, a favorite of his, and a very fragrant mountain mint.

Persians were then noted in Europe for their knowledge of medicinal drugs and, at Shiraz, Michaux visited the drug establishments, procuring resins and gums, especially the Persian gum used to heal wounds, called *Sarcocolla*, and a kind of Persian manna used to sweeten pastries. To his mineral collection he was now able to add samples of quartz "le plus beau quartz possible" from which Persian artisans fashioned their exquisite crystal creations.

It was at Shiraz, inland a hundred miles east of Bushire, that the second of the surviving letters from Asia to François André was written, at the beginning of the spring of 1784. In it Michaux père, so recently rescued from fearful dangers, urged his son to strive to develop good habits and self-discipline, the better to be able to endure the suffering inevitable in the course of any life, and, above all, to have faith in God: "If you had accompanied me, you would have seen that all men together would not have been able to save me from the dangers in which I found myself. But I hope that the One who preserved me then will take care of me in other circumstances." With expressions of gratitude to relatives and friends for their kindness to his son, the letter concluded, "A Dieu, mon cher fils." On the cover of the packet addressed to François André at the home of his uncle, Desaint, the printer, rue St. Jacques, Paris, Michaux noted that he had included some curios he thought might interest his son, but they were first to be examined by the Desaints. Included in the bulky package were also objects for Lemonnier.[2]

From Shiraz to Esfahan, by Yazd-e Khvast, the road wound its tortuous way through sterile and rocky valleys, among high mountain ranges, whose precipitous slopes were devoid of vegetation, a landscape with an awesome beauty of its own, but nothing to delight a botanist's eyes. Though snow still covered the highest summits, the rivers were swollen with spring floods by the time Michaux arrived at the ancient city of Esfahan. It was April 1784.

We have no record of the botanist's impressions of the once glorious cities in his path, no word pictures of the magnificent mosques of Esfahan or of the lonely ruins of Persepolis, evocative of Darius and of Cyrus, which he passed on his mountain journey from Shiraz to Esfahan. Perhaps he felt no need to add to the eloquent descriptions of earlier travelers, such as Sir John Chardin, whose Persian travels he carried with him on his journey;[3] or perhaps he preferred to restrict himself to his observations of natural history and the works of nature, always paramount in his interest over the works of man.

As he approached the city of Hamadan, the harsh landscape mellowed. With the advancing season the countryside grew steadily more verdant and more botanically appealing day by day as far as Azerbaijan. As the mountains became lower and less rugged, one could ride on horseback from one summit to another in search of plants. Hamadan, which Darius is said to have rebuilt from the classical city of Ecbatana as a refuge for his family from Alexander, is situated at the foot of Mount Alwand. The botanist made the ascent of this 11,900-foot mountain and passed the night on the summit in a little cabin dedicated to Ali, son-in-law of Muhammad. As his precision instruments had been confiscated by the Arabs, he could take no measurements, but he was able to make a herbarium of mountain plants, and a mineral collection, noting that "all the rocks of the mountain, as of neighboring mountains, are of granite, in which one distinguishes traces of quartz, mica, and school."[4]

From Hamadan he traveled to Rasht on the Caspian Sea by way of Qazvin. When still two days away from this city, as the road emerged from a very narrow valley shut in by mountains, one could see the snow-covered peak of Mount Damavand, soaring skyward. Michaux reached Qazvin at the beginning of summer to find himself in a veritable Garden of Eden that, day after day, yielded a rich harvest of new and interesting species. Of this region he reported to his protector, the brother of the king:

> In Persia, only the northern provinces are profitable for researches in natural history. As those of the Gilan and of the Mazandaran are fertile and covered with forests, one finds there a great many plants. The shores of the Caspian Sea (seen at Rasht and at Enzeli) abound with a great variety of birds. And as for mineralogy, the province of Khorasan surpasses all others. I have brought back some samples from this province which I obtained at Qazvin.
>
> The shipment of seeds sent herewith is scarcely half of the

*seeds gathered this year (1784) and I will arrange for the other
half to arrive before the end of the springtime. For greater order
and facility, I have put together the different species (a little package of each) of the same family in a general package, that is to
say the* Gramineae *with* Gramineae, *the* Cruciferae *with the*
Cruciferae, *etc. The seeds with the mark • on the package which
encloses them are for the most part new or very interesting, some
marked with an X are those which seemed to me the most precious
and the greatest number are indicated by their specific name. . . .*

*In my last letter from Hamadan I have informed you, Mon-
sieur, that the province of Gilan differs totally from all the other
more southern ones by its productions; that I have found there
many North American trees,* Diospyrus[5] *and* Gleditsia,[6] *the
one called Siberian elm, a new very interesting tree even from the
few observations that circumstances have not allowed me the leisure to increase.*

*Although I have not been as fortunate as I would have de-
sired in the search for trees and shrubs, as this part of botany is
the most popular with amateurs, I have nevertheless the satisfaction of having discovered new ones. . . . I can, with modesty and
without conceit, congratulate myself upon having used my time
well this year and particularly upon not allowing to escape at the
moment of maturity many plants previously identified. I regret
only two or three plants, seen in flower, whose seeds it was not
possible for me to recover.*[7]

In addition to his botanical discoveries and collections, Michaux
contributed to the science of botany by verifying that the regions of
Persia lying between the thirty-fifth and forty-fifth degrees of latitude
are the natural habitat of some of our best-known plants: cereals and
legumes—such as wheat and alfalfa, chick peas and onions—and of
useful trees such as walnut and cherry, as well as of lilies, tulips, and
many other flowers.[8]

A letter from his sister urged Michaux to return without continuing his journey further. We do not know the exact content of this letter,
but, having seen and collected in the rich region south of the Caspian,
he set out to return and by August was back in Hamadan. One wonders
whether his sister's message reflected concern for the traveler's safety or
a need for his presence in Paris, where the young François André, in
her charge, had entered upon the difficult period of adolescence.
Whatever the urgency, in response to his sister's appeal Michaux left

Hamadan by caravan on August 23, aiming directly for Baghdad, which was reached without difficulty. There, in the city of Aladdin and of Ali Baba, he lingered day after day, loath to depart for Europe without seeing again his friend and traveling companion Consul Rousseau, detained en route from Basra to Baghdad by an Arab revolt.

While awaiting the consul's return, Michaux traveled a day's journey south of Baghdad to the ancient Parthian city of Ctesiphon,[9] where, on the east bank of the Tigris, at the site known as the Garden of Semiramis, the legendary queen of Babylonia, he discovered a monument among the ruins of the palace. This stone, which was shipped to Paris, is in the form of a pear, a little flattened on two sides, a foot and a half high and a foot broad, weighing forty-four pounds. It is ornamented with carving on the two flat sides; on the upper part are various symbolic figures and below is a long inscription on two spaces, one of twenty-five and the other of twenty-six lines.[10]

This sculptured monument, belonging to the period between 1300 and 900 B.C., belongs to a group described by scholars of Assyrian antiquities by the Babylonian term *kudurrus,* or boundary stones, inscribed with titles of property or charters of franchise, and placed in fields and temples. Michaux's discovery was the first of a series of forty such stones now known to exist, of considerable juridical and mythological significance in the study of Assyriology.[11]

A few days after Rousseau's return to Baghdad, Michaux, bidding farewell to his friend, set out (on New Year's Eve, 1784) on the long journey westward. On the last day of January 1785 he was once more in Aleppo. From there he wrote to Lemonnier: "I have a little collection of liliaceous plants in bulbs, which I have collected in Persia, and they are still in good condition in spite of cruel frosts that our caravan has experienced in the neighborhood of Teibet and Palmyra. Some camels were left on the road and several of our Arabs have been on the point of perishing. But we found a favorable temperature as we approached here."[12] In a note attached to this letter, the botanist added that he had among his liliaceous bulbs an *Amaryllis* "more precious than the others" which he had wrapped separately in parchment.

At Aleppo the customs officials, searching for smuggled pearls and precious stones, seemed to the botanist particularly destructive in their inspections, as did the sanitary inspectors who slashed open all correspondence before passing it through damaging solutions of vinegar and perfumes.

Michaux had hoped to return to Paris via Constantinople and the Black Sea, with opportunities for research in the rich regions along the way, but, as this plan proved impossible to effect, he set out to return as he had come, via Cyprus, where he discovered, during his brief stop-over on the island, a beautiful shrub of the genus *Stellaria.*

The ship, *La Levantine,* on which he embarked from Cyprus on April 13, dropped anchor in the harbor of Marseilles on May 23, but the sea-weary travelers were forced to wait out a quarantine imposed on all ships arriving from the East. Michaux had plenty of time to shake from his shoes the sand of eastern deserts before, at long last, as June neared its close, he arrived in Versailles, after an absence of three years and five months, to scenes of welcome and the well-earned honors that awaited him.

He had brought back from the East a magnificent collection of seeds and plants, tangible evidence of his professional prowess as a naturalist explorer and collector in foreign lands. That he had the physical stamina, courage, adaptability, and perseverance essential to the pursuit of such a demanding career had been well demonstrated by the success with which he had surmounted the challenges of his perilous mission. For him, as for most explorers on all frontiers, difficulties, hardships, and dangers seemed to act only as stimulants to greater efforts. Thus it was that he now looked forward eagerly to a return to Asia to extend his work into regions east of the Caspian Sea and into Tibet and Kashmir, unaware that the winds of his destiny were now blowing westward.

CHAPTER 4

✑ King's Botanist, Mission to America, 1785

THE PREVAILING MOOD in Paris in 1785 still reflected the jubilation of victory over Britain in her war with her American colonies and the return of peace. Louis XVI had never been more popular. Yet the state of the nation was far from healthy. Participation in the "American War" had pushed the already overburdened treasury very near bankruptcy. Severe droughts and widespread crop failures had further weakened the economy and increased the misery of the poor. Long dormant seeds of discontent began to stir in fertile soil.

The government acted wisely, if too late, to secure the fruits of victory and relieve distress by much needed reforms. Every effort was made to stimulate agriculture, industry, commerce, and the arts. Louis XVI resolved to send forth research expeditions and explorer-naturalists to the far corners of the earth in order to add to scientific knowledge, to enrich the country's agriculture with new plants and new methods, and to restock and strengthen the national forests, badly depleted by the demands of shipbuilding in the long years of struggle with Britain for the control of the seas. One such mission, known as the La Pérouse Expedition, outfitted on a grand scale and carrying a full complement of scientists, embarked from Brest on August 1, 1785, on an ambitious "round the world" research voyage.[1]

For Michaux there were other plans. Enthusiastically welcomed on his return, with gratifying recognition of his achievements, the botanist received, a few weeks after he arrived back, indisputable proof of the king's favor: a commission as king's botanist, attached to the royal nurseries under the direction of comte D'Angiviller. Michaux's brevet, or commission, signed by His Majesty himself, reveals the scope of his assignment:

> *Today, the eighteenth day of July, 1785, His Majesty, being at Versailles, and having fixed his ideas on the desire . . . to introduce into his kingdom and to acclimatize there, by an intelligent and consistent culture . . . all the trees and forest plants which nature has given, up to the present time, only to foreign lands, but which are of the greatest interest for works of art as well as for carpentry construction, His Majesty has felt that the success of his designs depends necessarily on his choice of a subject who combines intelligence, ripened by experience, with the faculties and strength necessary to travel in any country whatsoever to study the productions and collect with care for His Majesty plants, seeds and fruits of all trees and shrubs, even of herbaceous plants suitable for increasing the species of forage . . . for cattle; to embrace, moreover, all the researches which relate to botany, and to establish correspondence by means of which the director of buildings can continue the researches and the advantages which they should produce; and His Majesty, being informed of the profound knowledge which le Sieur André Michaux, born at Versailles of a family devoted to agriculture, has acquired and who, inspired by his love for the sciences, has not*

*ceased up to the present time to expose himself to the most painful
and the most useful journeys into various climes, notably into
Persia, where he has just made . . . a sojourn whose results attest
to all that one could hope for, in new studies, which he is disposed
to attempt everywhere that interesting productions of nature can
give material for them. His Majesty has resolved to attach him especially to his service . . . with the title and office of botanist attached to the nurseries cultivated under the orders of the director
and manager-general of the Buildings of the king.*[2]

This comprehensive and enlightened program, of which Michaux was to become so effective an instrument, dominated the rest of
the botanist's professional life. That he succeeded in carrying out his
task so triumphantly through all the years of his labors often against
seemingly overwhelming odds may be partly explained perhaps by the
fact that this mission, in the larger sense, as perfectly fulfilled his own
ambitions and hopes as his character, talents, and abilities matched the
demands of such a challenge.

Not only did this appointment represent for the botanist an
opportunity to realize his cherished dreams. It automatically conferred
also professional and social prestige, as Michaux was instructed to
present himself and to live "on a par with all ambassadors, ministers, . . . consuls, vice-consuls, chancellors . . . and all other agents for
France, public or private, under the protection and immediate safeguard of His Majesty." Consequently, all such agents of all ranks were
instructed to give "all support and assistance, even financial . . . as
much in health as in sickness" to safeguard the king's botanist and
facilitate his work.

On the practical side, the botanist was to be awarded an annual
salary of 2,000 livres while all travel and other just costs were to be at
His Majesty's expense, paid from funds administered by comte D'Angiviller, whose signature, with accompanying list of exalted titles, and
embellished by his seal in red wax, confirmed his royal master's decree.[3]

Michaux had hardly time to accustom himself to his royal mantle
before receiving his first assignment as king's botanist: not to expand
his eastern travels farther into Asia, as he may have hoped and expected, but to cross the Western Sea to North America.

Plant exchanges between the Old World and the New had taken
place in some form from the time of the first explorations of the
western continents. But planned and systematic botanical exchange
and research received tremendous impetus in the eighteenth century

when, as a facet of the scientific renaissance of the Enlightenment, interest in natural history became a passion. Research and exchange among the European nations and the western colonies proceeded in an almost arcadian atmosphere of reciprocal sharing that for many years transcended political enmities. In this enlightened policy governments necessarily played no small part. Their emissaries at every level often initiated as well as encouraged and supported the work of field naturalists. For example, Conrad Gérard, first French envoy to the American Congress, was charged with the misson of establishing connections with botanists and horticulturists in the United States, with a view to botanical exchanges.[4]

In consideration of the latter process, one should not neglect to mention the versatile and talented Frenchman, J. Hector St. John Crèvecoeur, who spent in all nearly thirty years on the American continent as, in turn, soldier, farmer, fugitive, and, from 1783 to 1790, consul of France to the United States.[5] Crèvecoeur not only introduced into this country useful agricultural plants, among them alfalfa and a variety of vetches, but actively promoted botanical exchanges between his native France and the United States and urged the appointment of an official French botanist to implement this policy.

Fortunately, the American colonies and subsequently the United States were represented in Europe, during and immediately following the struggle for independence, by two men of genius who personified the spirit of the Enlightenment, Benjamin Franklin and Thomas Jefferson, each of whom played a vital role in promoting a healthy intellectual and scientific exchange between America and Europe.

Throughout most of his long and productive career, Franklin was intimately associated with American and European botanists actively engaged in reciprocal sharing of seeds, plants, and scientific research. Even a cursory glance at the correspondence of the Pennsylvania botanists John and William Bartram and Humphrey Marshall, with their European colleagues, among them Peter Collinson, Dr. Fothergill, Linnaeus, and others, reveals the pervasive presence of the versatile Franklin, sometimes as participant—"a few seeds of Swiss barley"—often as resourceful mentor.[6] During the long and challenging years of his diplomatic service in England and France, and even when the fortunes of war threatened to interrupt the transatlantic botanical exchanges, Franklin contrived to aid scientists on both sides of the sea to continue their fruitful traffic.[7]

It was midsummer of 1785 when the aging Franklin, frail but triumphant, bade farewell for the last time to the City of Light. Perhaps

André Michaux, only recently returned to Paris from the East, witnessed the affecting scene as the old patriarch, revered and beloved throughout France, was carried slowly through the streets of Paris in a royal litter provided by Her Majesty, and, escorted by weeping crowds, out along the roads through the lush green countryside of Normandy to Le Havre.[8]

Franklin's unassailable place in the hearts of the French people made his years of service in Paris a difficult act to follow, even for Thomas Jefferson, his brilliant successor, as minister from the United States to the French Court, who presented his credentials to His Majesty at Versailles on May 17, 1785. As Jefferson later confessed to a friend, "The succession of Dr. Franklin at the Court of France was an excellent school of humility. On being presented to anyone as the Minister of America, the common-place question used in such cases was 'c'est vous, Monsieur, qui remplacez le Docteur Franklin?' . . . I generally answered 'No one can replace him, Sir; I am only his successor.'"[9]

Jefferson had arrived in Paris in August 1784 to serve as one of the commissioners, with Franklin and Adams, to negotiate trade treaties with European powers and was not appointed minister until the following spring. Thus he and Franklin had nearly a year in Paris together. The Virginian had brought with him from Monticello his eleven-year-old daughter Martha, a black servant, James Hemings, and the bulky manuscript of *Notes on the State of Virginia,* which he hoped to publish in Paris. It was probably Franklin who directed him to the French printer Philippe-Denis Pierres who published the *Notes* early in May 1785 in an edition of only 200 copies, intended by the author as presentation copies to friends on both sides of the Atlantic.

Among the first to receive a gift copy was Buffon, author of the stupendous *Histoire Naturelle,* greatly esteemed by Jefferson, who said of Buffon: "I think him the best informed of any naturalist who has ever written."[10] In response to the *Notes,* followed by the gift of a panther skin brought from America, Buffon invited Jefferson to dine with him at the intendant's house at the Jardin du Roi, where the ailing old naturalist resided in semiretirement. The garden with greenhouses, museums, and community of scientists became the scene of many happy hours for Jefferson. Among the warm and fruitful friendships he made there, none was deeper or more lasting than that with André Thouin, chief gardener, who, as long as he lived, sent a yearly gift of seeds and plants to Monticello.[11]

Jefferson's already keen interest in every aspect of natural history was deepened, and his dedication to international botanical exchange intensified, by his association with French botanists and horticulturists during his years in Paris. A few weeks after his arrival in France he visited the nurseries at Versailles and some time later the gardens of Malesherbes, who was said to know more about trees than any man in France.

Though we have found no record of a meeting between André Michaux and Thomas Jefferson during that summer of 1785, it seems probable that such a meeting took place by chance, or design, in the company of their common friend André Thouin at the Jardin du Roi. No American of his time did more than Jefferson to promote scientific exchanges between his own country and foreign nations, and one may safely assume that he enthusiastically endorsed the mission assigned by the king to Michaux.

On August 9, "Instructions to Le Sieur André Michaux, botanist to the king, for the exercise of the commission which His Majesty has been willing to entrust to him" were presented to Michaux at Versailles. Implicit in the program was the urgent need to alleviate the economic distress of the nation by reforestation and enrichment of the fields with new and invigorating importations.

Both useful and agreeable plants were desired, but the latter were to be subordinated to the useful. Plants used in medicine and not already cultivated in France were especially needed. Also wild animals, such as the wild turkey, to propagate in France, and all manner of game for the forests, as well as poultry and domestic animals.[12] Finally, the botanist was not to neglect to search out and bring back interesting and beautiful flowering shrubs and plants and all manner of fruit trees for the gardens and orchards.[13]

The "Instructions" left nothing to chance. The document emphasized the importance of establishing an adequate nursery for the sowing of seeds and the cultivation and protection of plants to be shipped at the proper seasons, but, mindful of the independent and democratic nature of the American people, the document urged the botanist to practice a wise economy, to keep his establishment within modest limits, and in this and all other ways to endeavor to win for himself the respect, goodwill, and cooperation of native Americans. He would be supplied with letters of recommendation to many persons, among whom he should single out Franklin, Washington, and Madison, to request their support in any negotiations that might arise. The "Instructions" further recommended that the botanical establishment be located on land adjacent to New York City for the convenience of shipping by way of packet boats to Le Havre and other French ports.

Furthermore, the botanist was requested to acquire knowledge of the qualities of fully mature, old trees of great height in the forests of America, and to send descriptions and samples of wood, with the bark on, or logs two or three feet long, so that it could be determined in France which woods were desirable for the king's needs.

It is clear that the government regarded this North American assignment as only the first of such explorations to be entrusted to the king's botanist, for "Monsieur Michaux, whom his commission destines to visit other countries," was directed to keep the resident ministers, as well as the gardener, who would live as overseer of the establishment, so informed, through discussions and correspondence, of the activities and progress of his undertaking as to establish and maintain a basis for continuity after his departure.

Nine days after the date of this formidable document, Michaux acknowledged in signed and sealed statement the receipt of "the general rule and principle of my operations." "I assent, in consequence, with all the zeal that I owe to the confidence of His Majesty and the good of his service."[14] Five thousand livres were allotted to the botanist immediately to settle his affairs in France to his satisfaction, and to buy clothing, books, equipment, and other necessities for his journey.[15] Six thousand were to be paid to him, "on account," upon his departure from Paris.

It appears that particular care was given to the selection of the journeyman gardener who was to accompany the botanist to America. The choice fell finally on Pierre Paul Saunier, age thirty-four,[16] native of St.-Aubin-sur-Gallon, in Normandy, an apprentice gardener at the Jardin du Roi, trained presumably under the watchful eyes of André Thouin.[17]

A document signed by D'Angiviller on August 14 was agreed to four days later by "Pierre Paul Saunier, engaged and retained in the service of the king, to go to reside in North America, and to form there, under the eyes and on the instructions of Le Sieur Michaux, botanist of the king, such an establishment as is found possible . . . etc." This nursery was to exist under the protection of His Majesty, and would be left to the care of Saunier when Michaux left America. Moreover, the gardener was to be paid an annual salary and to be provided with a modest sum with which to equip himself. He was to travel from Paris to Lorient with Michaux, there to embark on the king's packet boat to voyage at the king's expense to the United States where he was to spend all his time in the practice and labor of his employment and be at all times completely subordinate to Michaux. Finally, as in the instructions to Michaux, every important detail was provided for in Saunier's orders, even to the issuing of a selection of botanical works to improve his knowledge of his craft.[18]

When and for what reasons the decision was made for François André to accompany his father on his American mission are matters for speculation. As he was named in the botanist's ratification of his contract, as traveling with his father at the king's expense, it appears that the youth was officially included in the arrangements very early in the plan, probably viewed as serving as apprentice field naturalist. Certainly the American mission offered an ideal opportunity for Michaux to share with his son his love for the green world and the knowledge and skill he had acquired as an experienced botanical explorer. Also, the prospect of another separation for indefinite sojourn in a distant land, hard upon the heels of his long absence in the East, must have seemed unacceptable to the botanist, as well as to François André and their kinsmen, who had served as the youth's guardians. One can imagine with what delight the lad, just turned fifteen, anticipated the adventurous possibilities of a strange romantic wilderness, inhabited by fierce animals, exotic birds, and savage red men.

The two Michauxs, with their domestic servant, Jacques Renaud, and Pierre Paul Saunier, arrived at the port of Lorient, in Brittany, on the western coast of France, on August 30, 1785, expecting to set sail for America on September 1, but for four weeks the ship remained in port, awaiting favorable winds. The botanist occupied this interval in correspondence and in exploring the environs for plants and seeds, shipments of which he sent to Lemonnier and to D'Angiviller. Among his letters, one to the count's secretary, Cuvillier, requested his intervention with the customs officers to prevent their examination of his trunks, in order to avoid delay prejudicial to departure: three trunks, one entirely of books, the second of linen and clothing, the third of agricultural and botanical tools, equipment and supplies in medicine, mineralogy and physics.[19]

Writing to inform the count of the reason for the delay in port, Michaux gratefully acknowledged letters of recommendation, sent by the count, to the governors of French possessions in America, as well as to governors of the several United States. Reaffirming his eagerness to acquit himself well in his mission, he assured the count, "I shall have nothing to fear so much as leaving discoveries to be made by those who shall come after me."[20]

On the eighth the eager pilgrim, still stranded on shore, wrote to a friend: "I await with impatience my arrival in America to be able to give proof of my enthusiasm. . . . I imagine myself setting out to the conquest of the new world."[21] But not until the last days of September did the winds change. An elated Michaux dashed off a farewell note to the count: "The winds have changed, the north wind has been blowing since yesterday evening, and we are to embark today before seven o'clock in the morning."[22]

After a stormy passage of forty-seven days in frightful weather, *Le Courrier de New York* dropped anchor in New York harbor on Sunday, November 13, and on the following day the storm-tossed passengers stepped ashore on American soil. In compliance with the count's instructions, the botanist soon presented himself to the French minister, Otto, who welcomed him with particular pleasure.[23] Among the many duties imposed upon that busy chargé d'affaires had been the frustrating task of trying to satisfy requests from France for shipments of American flora and fauna by means of soliciting the great landowners, whom he found indifferent and unresponsive, or, alternately, by dealing with commercial botanists, who were "of an exorbitant dearness."

While Michaux was still upon the sea en route to New York, Otto wrote to the count, stressing the importance to France of sending a king's botanist to America. "Independently of the advantage which we could derive from such a commission, if it were given to an intelligent man, it would spread a great illumination over this part of natural history. Kalm, Carver, and Catesby have still only skimmed the surface of this material."[24]

Fortunately, Michaux and the French minister seem to have established an immediate rapport. After their first meeting, Otto wrote to D'Angiviller: "I have just had an interview with this individual, who seems to me the best possible person to carry out the purposes of the government. . . . I cannot express to you, Monsieur Le Comte, the satisfaction which the arrival of this botanist has caused me."[25]

Henceforth, Otto informed Michaux, all shipments of plants and seeds would be entirely under the direction of the botanist, who would address them to Otto in New York, to be promptly expedited to France. All captains of all packet boats in the service of the king had been instructed to give priority to the botanist and his shipments.[26] There was need of haste, Otto advised Michaux, if a shipment for France was to be aboard the next packet boat scheduled for departure in a few weeks.

CHAPTER 5

◦§ New York, Entrée and Establishment, 1785–1786

THE DELAY AT LORIENT had been costly, for seed and plant shipment season in New York was already far advanced and the ground already frozen. Yet, with his usual dispatch, Michaux was hard at work three days after landing, searching, with the help of day laborers, in the still abundant forests in New Jersey and on Long Island, for plants and seeds, establishing a pattern of indefatigable industry, endurance, and dedication that would persist throughout his career.[1]

In consequence, he was able to send a considerable shipment to France before the middle of December. There were five large boxes addressed to D'Angiviller, containing acorns of the red and the white oak, some American chestnuts—"truly a different species from those of Europe and, though small, agreeable to eat"; some Carolina potatoes, subject to frost; an abundance of vaccinium, including cranberries, "a fruit used for jam"; azaleas; tulip trees; more than six hundred shoots of liquidambar; and two of the evergreen mountain laurel, *Kalmia*, "the only one I have found so far." In addition he sent a shrub with scarlet berries, called "Red Berry." "It will make an agreeable and surprising effect next winter, if it is planted in the park of Rambouillet."[2]

Most of the shipments from North America to France were destined for this beautiful park, acquired by Louis XVI in 1783, where the king hoped to amass a huge central collection of foreign plants from which seeds, shrubs, and trees could be shipped wherever needed in the country. The more than 32,000 acres of varied terrain, including an extensive game-filled forest and innumerable waterways dotted with islands, seemed an ideal choice for the acclimatization of exotic flora and fauna.[3]

For the forests of Rambouillet, Michaux sent, with this first shipment of botanical treasures, a cage containing eighteen partridges "which differ in many respects from the partridges of Europe"; they "have the advantage of not being wanderers like the red partridges, and they frequent the green fields as well as the forests."[4] The botanist entrusted these little birds (quail), described to the count as dwarf partridges, "very good to eat," to a Canadian traveling by the same ship who was charged with their care not only on the ocean voyage but overland from Lorient to Paris as well. He bore a letter from Michaux introducing him to the count as the bearer of seeds and beautiful furs from Canada, and one well informed abut those rich northern lands, so regrettably lost by France.

The first shipments of seeds and plants reached Paris safely early in the new year. On February 6 Abbé Nolin, D'Angiviller's trusted director of Royal Nurseries, wrote to the count detailing ways to preserve and make the best use of each box destined for Rambouillet, where the Abbé was already overseeing the preparation of proper grounds, seedbeds, and greenhouses to receive all future shipments "tout de suite."[5]

But what had become of the partridges? Answer arrived next day in the form of a mournful letter from the woebegone Canadian traveler, stranded in the port of Nantes, with his seeds and his furs and his cage of little birds. Enclosing Michaux's introductory note to the count and confessing himself quite unable to make the journey on to Paris, he begged to be relieved of his little feathered charges, now reduced to thirteen, in spite of all the care he had given them.[6]

The necessity of meeting the packet-boat schedule had allowed the frantically busy botanist insufficient time to prepare for shipment the 4,000 to 5,000 trees of different species which he had painfully pried from the frozen earth of the forests not far from New York City, and which, perforce, had to be preserved in a hastily rented warehouse to await the next boat.

Begging indulgence for any shortcomings in his first offerings to cross the sea, Michaux confided to the ever-sympathetic Lemonnier, to whom he had sent, enclosed in the shipment to the count, a small box of "very interesting seeds": "It is now one hour after midnight, no fire; you will recognize in everything the haste and confusion which have overwhelmed me. I was told this evening that it would not be surprising if the rivers are frozen tomorrow morning. . . . That often happens here."[7] In addition to the rough wintry weather, there were other difficulties constantly confronting him: his unfamiliarity with the country, resulting in futile journeys and disappointments; his lack of fluency in the English language; long distances to travel for, and to haul back, his collections; scarcity of the moss customarily used in France for packing plants, forcing the substitution of turf or earth, heavy and expensive to ship; no permanent lodging or workspace, no adequate depository for plants, and, to his amazement and chagrin, "the ill-will, indifference, and indolence" of even the poorest inhabitants, making it difficult to hire laborers at any price. "I am sure," he commented to the count, "if I were assisted, as one would be in France, by the laborers in the countryside, I could send every year several shiploads of interesting productions."[8]

The difficulty of hiring day laborers continued to plague the botanist, as he explained to Dutartre, treasurer of the King's Buildings and Gardens in Paris. "It is impossible to obtain day labor here for less than two dollars a day. If some few do content themselves with less, they will do only two hours of work. There are not, in fact, properly speaking, any day laborers; here each man works for himself and the service of others is done by Negroes."[9] As a practical measure Jacques Renaud, the domestic servant who had accompanied Michaux from France, was now pressed into service as gardener's helper, working under Pierre Paul Saunier, who, Michaux assured Lemonnier, "is a treasure, for his good will and his enthusiasm; he is intelligent and very industrious."[10]

Early in December, as we learn from his expense account, Michaux did succeed in hiring a day laborer capable of serving as interpreter as well, for whom he purchased a new pair of boots, apparently a profitable investment, for by March 1 of the following year, he felt confident enough, after purchasing *Le Grand Dictionnaire Anglais* for seven dollars, to proceed unassisted on the treacherous waters of the English language, and the interpreter and his boots disappear from the scene.[11]

The dizzying round of activities during these first weeks had made it impossible for the harassed Frenchman even to present any of his letters of recommendation to those to whom they were addressed, some of whom he hoped to see on the journey he planned to make as far south as northern Virginia, to collect trees and seeds "such as some magnolia and others which are not even known in New York."[12] However, of more immediate urgency was the necessity of establishing the proposed French botanical garden. He had come to realize its crucial importance during the past weeks of collecting. The seeds of some trees could not survive shipping and had to be planted and shipped later as seedlings; trees with tap roots required a period of conditioning by being replanted in soil before being packed for shipping; the daily collections of seeds, plants, and trees required a suitable way station for preservation while awaiting export. Otto was in full agreement on the importance of the garden. "We will have time, Monsieur Michaux and I," Otto had assured the count, "to choose during the winter, in the neighborhood of New York, a land suitable for the establishment of the gardens of the king."[13] And, indeed, in the first month of the new year Michaux announced to the count, with great satisfaction, not only the discovery of a desirable site for the garden, but also his shipment of "twelve strong boxes of interesting trees," consisting primarily of useful trees, all carefully packed in a new kind of moss—sphagnum moss—light, supple, and ideal for shipping, which he and Saunier had come upon amid the frost and snow.[14]

The enclosed catalog, characteristic of the precise statements that would accompany each shipment made by Michaux, listed the contents, with both common and botanical names, and observations, such as: "the first box: 150 *Cupressus thyoides* [now *Chamaecyparis thyoides*] white cedar; this tree grows in the most moist and even in submerged places; they are so close packed and crowded, one against another, that it is very difficult to penetrate. The wood is less heavy than that of the red cedar. As it combines lightness with other qualities good for construction, the best ship's boats [long boats] are made of this wood." And so on. A hundred red cedars also (*Juniperus virginiana*), varieties of pine, spruce, 130 tulip trees *Liriodendron tulipifera, Rhododendron maximum, Magnolia glauca* (now *virginiana*), the evergreen *Kalmia latifolia*, as well as the little *Kalmia angustifolia*, and many others.

The boxes, numbered ten, eleven, and twelve, contained, respectively, trees for the Jardin du Roi in Paris, a selection for His Majesty's pleasure gardens, and a variety of species for Malesherbes.

The land selected by Michaux and Otto as suitable for the King's Garden consisted of a rectangle of twenty-nine acres situated in Bergen (now Hudson) County, New Jersey, six miles from New York City, opposite what is now Fortieth Street. The property, bordering on great woods along the Hudson River at one end and a smaller forest along the Hackensack River at the other end, with private holdings on the two sides, was traversed by the main road from New York and Bergen to Hackensack. Its principle advantages, as Michaux explained to the count, were the proximity of great forests for collecting seeds and trees, the proximity to New York and the river for convenience in shipping, and the quality of the land, which included a hillside slope with substantial clayey soil, a central portion of meadowlands, sandy areas, and a low, swampy woodland, filled with "*Cyprès aquatica.*"[15] This "Cyprus forest" is so dense with trees, he wrote to Lemonnier, "that one can hardly penetrate. It is in the shadow of these cyprus trees, where the rays of the sun have no access, that one finds the magnolia and the rhododendron in all their magnificence."[16]

"This affair is not yet concluded," explained the botanist to the count. "There are some difficulties relative to the laws and customs because it is necessary to become a naturalized American to acquire property. I do not wish to act in this affair without the advice of Monsieur Otto and we are awaiting the response of the governor."[17] Governor Livingston[18] and the legislators could scarcely fail to be impressed by Michaux's credentials or by the "full powers" granted him by his royal patron "to import from France at the expense of the king every species of trees, plants, or vegetables which might be needed in this country," and "to establish a botanical garden, not only of plants from France and from America but also of productions from all over the world which can be found in the gardens of the king at Paris."

By an act of the General Assembly of the state of New Jersey, March 3, 1786, Michaux was permitted, as an alien, without the requirement of the oath of allegiance, to purchase any lands in the state of New Jersey not exceeding 200 acres, on the same terms as an American citizen, with the single condition that the land be used for the sole purpose of a botanical garden.[19] This generous concession seemed all the more gratifying to Otto, as he commented to his colleagues in Paris, "when I consider how difficult it is in America to obtain the least favor contrary to the laws and customs."[20]

By a conveyance of March 28, 1786, Michaux acquired title to the land at the price of 300 pounds, New York currency, a good investment, as Michaux assured the count, for the property, with the projected improvements, was sure to double in value in four or five years.[21] For the purchase money the botanist, with his usual scrupulous concern for economy, did not make use of the letter of credit on Robert Morris of Philadelphia, supplied to him on his departure from France, but on the advice of Otto, deposited his letter of credit with the French vice-consul in New York, who would supply him with funds at a better exchange rate than would Morris.[22] Though the land transaction was not completed until the end of March, Michaux paid for the land on February 8 and next day engaged a contractor to build a house on the site, giving him 400 dollars as half the price of construction.[23]

By May 1 the house was within three weeks of completion. It was, as Michaux described it, well situated and of pleasing design, with four rooms, two on the ground level, two above, and a granary. There was a small cottage nearby for the gardener, who had begun his residence on the site in May and was expected to produce from the land in the future not only his own subsistence but that of his helper and any daily workmen employed, as well as food for the horses. Though the requirement for so much productive farming may seem an extra burden for Saunier, in addition to his duties as gardener for the king's establishment, the privilege of cultivating some acres of land on his own was intended as compensation for the fact that, as Michaux pointed out to the count, his wages were proving inadequate to meet living costs in America.[24] Saunier's helper, Jacques Renaud, the erstwhile domestic, a young man whom Michaux had brought with him from France "because of his good will," had perhaps great need of that quality as he received no pay for his work as gardener-boy, except his maintenance, and "had no right to demand steady wages . . . because he is more fortunate here than at home; . . . because he has been expensive to be brought here and one will be able to recompense him in future if his good will persists."[25]

With this letter describing the garden property and the house, Michaux enclosed for the count a copy of the petition presented to the Assembly of the state of New Jersey, a copy of the title of the acquisition of the land, "the map of the land acquired in New Jersey at Bergen's Wood . . . a small hamlet, located six miles from New York . . . a drawing of the layout of the garden, and the design of the house."

He added a list of the plants shipped to the count in two chests, one to Versailles and the other to the Jardin du Roi, containing a variety of ornamental plants, including some for Monsieur—a trial shipment, so to speak, as their survival was uncertain so late in the season. The last included some of the loveliest "wildflowers"; dogtooth violets, *Erythronium*, "the flower resembles a tulip"; spring beauties, *Claytonia virginica*, "the root is like a little potato"; bloodroot, *Sanguinaria canadensis*, "the flower of this plant is pretty among the rocky crags"; two kinds of violets, "one with beautiful yellow flowers"; pitcher plants, *Sarracenia purpurea*, "whose leaf shape is extraordinary"; and many species of wintergreen, *Pyrola*, and bellwort, *Uvularia*, as well as a little orchis "whose flower I have not seen."[26]

Reading over these familiar names from Michaux's list, with his comments, one can easily imagine his delight in the experience of his first intoxicating spring season in America, with all the green and flower-spangled beauty of the northern spring unfolding before his eyes. But always for Michaux the far horizon beckoned. It was time to move on. The first six months had been well spent and a solid foundation established for the success of his mission. Summarizing the situation for Cuvillier, he described the new garden of the king, with its subsistence farm, its "elegant" house, fine greenhouse, two gardens enclosed with painted boards seven feet high, and a four-foot-high fence surrounding the whole property.

In a more expansive mood than usual, he attempted to respond to Cuvillier's request for a description of the characters of Americans.

Although protesting that it was too soon for him to make a profound analysis, Michaux noted his impressions that the settlers from the different nations of Europe in general retained the customs, costumes, virtues, and vices of their native lands. Those living in the environs of New York, who still spoke the Dutch language, for instance, displayed all the energy, diligence, solicitude, and exquisite cleanliness one finds in Holland. The Germans in Pennsylvania were industrious and hospitable. And so on. But the Americans of several generations, accustomed to abundance of game and fish, and too often demoralized by rum cheaply imported from the Islands, had become idle and did not even trouble to cultivate the fertile land, which would yield twenty bushels to one.

In Connecticut homes a stranger was hospitably welcomed only after he had been gravely inspected and only if he could answer satisfactorily such questions as "Who are you? Whence do you come? Where are you going? What is your business? What is your religion?" Those puritanical people allowed no work of any kind on Sundays, nor any travel, nor any but necessary speech and that in a low voice. To the Frenchman, familiar with the pleasure-loving Court of Versailles, where Molière was regularly performed and glittering balls were routine, these Connecticut farmers, who would not permit a reading of comedies or even a mention of whist, the quadrille, or the opera, were "prudes." Many were classical scholars of Latin, fond of learned discourses on religion, but, the botanist warned, "one must be careful not to oppose them for they are the best of friends but the worst of enemies."[27]

Eager to push on southward where a varied and richer vegetation would soon be ripening into summer, Michaux lingered on only for François, whom he had placed in the home of a minister, where only English was spoken, to acquire at least a working proficiency in the language. In mid-May, Michaux reported to Cuvillier, "I have not yet found him strong enough in English to translate it and to put French into English; as I intend to have him travel with me to work in botany and to collect, it is for this that I have delayed." But François, it seems, was still not proficient enough in English to accompany his father when he set out on June 3 for a journey south through Pennsylvania, Maryland, and parts of Virginia, with the purpose of calling on those prominent Americans to whom he had letters of introduction, and with the intention of reconnoitering for a later collection as the season was too late for shipping and too early for seeds.

However, he assured the count, "there is no day in which I do not find some plants that are interesting either because they are very rare in France, and even for the most part are not there at all, or because they are very pleasing and worthy to ornament the garden of His Majesty. I have discovered many which, shipped next autumn, will be in condition to make a show the following spring."[28] Although Michaux made no comment in his letters on the New Jersey landscape through which he passed, which Peter Kalm[29] had found so pleasing forty years earlier and which François André would admire years later, as the stagecoach rolled through the green and fertile fields of Pennsylvania, he noted with approval the productive farms of the inhabitants, German in origin. "There is not a more industrious people among the different nations which have come to form the United States."[30]

The City of Brotherly Love delighted him. "Philadelphia deserves to be compared with the best cities of Europe, after Paris. The first edge of it is very agreeable, for the regularity of the streets and for its situation. Merchandise from all parts of Europe is plentiful. There are more well-informed people and scholars than in any other parts of this continent." His enthusiasm seems justified. Philadelphia in the last quarter of the eighteenth century "ranked second among the English-speaking cities of the world. And this does not mean in population alone, or merely as a seaport, or commercially, or financially, but culturally as well—scientifically, artistically, and in the urbane intelligence and life of its inhabitants."[31]

Here "I have been very well received by Dr. Franklin" the botanist reported to the count, "and by all the persons to whom I have been addressed. Dr. Franklin has promised me letters of recommendation for Carolina and Georgia."[32] One may assume that the "old Patriarch," Francophile that he was, also saw to it that his guest from France was introduced during his stay to the scholars, artists, and fellow scientists who composed the stimulating intellectual community of the city.

But the high point of the first visit to Philadelphia for the Frenchman was probably his visit to that mecca for visiting botanists, the Bartram botanical garden, where Franklin may well have accompanied him.[33] There in his father's old home at Kingsessing on the Schuylkill River, William Bartram presided over the famous garden and labored to complete his manuscript of his *Travels*. One can imagine the eager talk between the two botanists, especially about the luxuriant lands of the South, so well traveled by William in past years and so soon to welcome the Frenchman to their richly forested wilderness. Again and again during the years of his American mission, Michaux would return to the Bartram household, always coming away enriched and refreshed. On this occasion, he saw for the first time "an interesting and new tree, *Franklinia*."[34]

Journeying south from Philadelphia, the botanist found little to appeal to him in Maryland, where the soil seemed sterile and even rye seemed to grow only with difficulty. More pleasing to him was Virginia, where he traveled as far as "Fredericktown" (Fredericksburg) on the Rappahannock, with its rich and fertile soil, but he noted that the land was largely divided among large landowners with great estates "cultivated only in proportion to the number of slaves."

On Monday afternoon, June 19, Michaux paid his long-delayed call upon George Washington at Mount Vernon, affording him the opportunity to observe firsthand the complex operation of a large Virginia plantation. The general, according to his Diary, had spent the morning riding over the farm, overseeing the workers in the fields and the artisans in the shops before returning to the mansion where he found eight guests arrived for dinner, including a distinguished visitor from France. "A Monsr. Andri Michaux—a Botanest sent by the Court of France to America (after having been only 6 Weeks returned from India) came in a little before dinner with letters of Introduction & recommendation from the Duke de Lauzen,[35] & Marqs. de la Fayette to me. He dined and returned afterwards to Alexandria on his way to New York, from whence he had come; and where he was about to establish a Botanical garden."

The king's botanist had not come empty-handed to Mount Vernon, as one learns from Washington's diary records during the next ten days:

> *Thursday [June] 29th. . . .*
>
> *Planted in one Row, between the Cherokee Plumb, & the honey locust, back of the No. Garden adjoining the green House (where the Spanish chestnuts had been placed and were rotten) 25 of the Paliurus, very good to make hedges and inclosures for fields. Also in the section betwn. the work House & Salt house adjoining the Pride of China Plants, & between the rows in which the Carolina Laurel seeds had been sowed, 46 of the Pistatia nut in 3 rows and in the places where the Hemlock pine had been planted and were dead, Et. & W. of the Garden gates, the Seeds of the Pyramidical Cyprus 75 in number—all of which with others were presented to me by Mr. Michaux Botanist to his most Christn. Majesty.*

Saturday [July] 1st. . . .
    *Planted 4 of the Ramnus Tree (an ever green) one on each
side of the Garden gates—a peg with 2 Notches drove down by
them (Pegs No. 1 being by the Pyramidical Cyprues). Also
planted 24 of the Philirea latitolio (an ever green shrub) in the
shrubberies by Pegs No. 3 and 48 of the Cytise—a Tree produced
in a cold climate of quick growth by pegs No. 4. All these plants
were given to me by Mr. Michaux.*[36]

This first meeting between Michaux and the future President of the
country to which he was an envoy had apparently been cordial and
mutually advantageous.

"General Washington," Michaux reported to the count, "has offered to allow me to send my collections to his home on deposit, and I
will take advantage, on every occasion, of the offers which have been
made to me." The botanist was back in New York City by July 1. The
journey south seemed, on the whole, to have fulfilled its purpose. "I
have gathered a great many interesting plants," he assured his patron,
"but did not remain because the essential purpose is to gather seeds. . . .
I shall set out before the 15th of the next month for Carolina and
Georgia so that by arriving soon enough for seeds I can reap every
advantage possible from the journey."[37]

As it was, he did not leave until the first week of September. July
and August went by in a flurry of activities, weeks of botanizing in New
Jersey with Saunier, who was to be left in charge of the garden and
responsible for shipments of northern plants to France during Michaux's absence. He arranged for the completion of the fencing of the
property, settled accounts with contractors and carpenters, purchased a
"complete American Atlas" for $13 and three horses for a total of $113,
two horses to take with him and one to remain on the plantation.[38]

In a final letter to D'Angiviller before departing, he explained
that, anticipating an absence of at least six months in Carolina and
Georgia, he had drawn on the Treasury in France for 5,000 livres, being
informed that there was in Carolina only paper money with no negotia-
ble value in other states. He was sending to Lemonnier a detailed list of
everything collected since spring, and to Abbé Nolin the detailed descriptions of all trees and plants collected, ornamental or otherwise,
promising to send similar reports from every state he should visit.
Moreover, he had arranged with Saunier to ship in the autumn, in
addition to plants and seeds, the seventy partridges, more females than
males, requested in the count's last letter.[39]

One is impressed, in Michaux's letters to the count and his colleagues, by his intelligent, orderly, conscientious conduct of his royal mission. He himself was singularly fortunate, as he was aware, in the characters of the men to whom he was chiefly responsible, such as Abbé Nolin, Lemonnier, and the count, to whom he confessed in this long, comprehensive letter:

> The confidence with which you have been willing to honor me, Monsieur Le Comte, would be more than sufficient motivation, if it were possible for me to have even more enthusiasm and gratitude. I confess that I cannot desire a situation more fortunate than that of having an immense country to visit, immense collections to make, for which I would devote all my life, my time, my fortune. . . . I experience with the greatest satisfaction the fatigue which results from this labor, and the least botanizing procures for me collections for which botanists would go from one end of France to the other.[40]

His satisfaction was only qualified by the realization that he could accomplish ten times more had the inhabitants of this country the same inclination to work as those of France. The perennial shortage of labor was aggravated, he observed, by the spirit of migration infecting all thirteen states—"the many who are idle seek more abundant game and richer lands beyond the Appalachian Mountains, while the ambitious and industrious think to grow wealthy there on lands selling for one shilling an acre. In Kentucky there is almost no more to sell." Passing on to the count a rumor that France was on the point of acquiring Florida from Spain, he foresaw, in this possibility, a French Florida flourishing with a multitude of French emigrants from Canada and Louisiana, with communications as far as the Southern Seas, which would benefit the United States, but chiefly, he hoped, his native land.

Shortly before his departure by sea for Charleston, Michaux made a flying trip to Philadelphia, probably to pick up letters of recommendation for Carolina and Georgia from Dr. Franklin and William Bartram, both of whom he visited, and to seek last minute travel advice from the latter.[41] He took time also to call upon Bartram's Schuylkill neighbor, William Hamilton, whose elegant estate, Woodlands, contained a famous collection of rare plants.[42]

Finally, on September 6, accompanied by his son, their servant, and the two horses, Michaux set sail from New York and arrived in Charleston on the twenty-first. He congratulated himself on having come by sea, for another French traveler, who arrived in Charleston the same day, had set out from New York on August 3 but was so impeded by floods, which drowned out roads and destroyed bridges, that he was forced to embark at Wilmington to make the rest of the journey by sea.[43]

CHAPTER **6**

≈§ Carolina, 1786–1787

THE CITY OF CHARLESTON, which would become the botanist's home, insofar as he had a home, during his remaining years in America, was slowly recovering from the ravages of war and the bitter years of British occupation.[1] "In 1783, the town and the parishes were alike in ruins," according to General Moultrie, who described his ride from George-town to the Ashley River, following his release in the prisoner-of-war exchange in Philadelphia, as

> *the most dull, melancholy, dreary ride that anyone could possibly take, of about one hundred miles through the woods of that country which I had been accustomed to see abound with live stock, and wild fowl of every kind, now destitute of all. . . . not the vestige of horses, cattle, hogs, or deer, etc. were to be found. The squirrels and birds of every kind were totally destroyed. The dragoons told me that, on their scouts, no living creature was to be seen except now and then a few camp scavengers (viz. buzzards) picking the bones of some unfortunate fellows who had been shot or cut down and left in the woods above ground.[2]*

Yet so swift are the healing powers of nature in these kindly latitudes that Michaux, arriving only four years after the fighting had ceased, found the forests again full of birdlife. From his first weeks in America he had longed to see for himself the well-nigh legendary variety of flora and fauna of the southern states, a hunger stimulated, one assumes, by the rapturous descriptions of William Bartram. Now, after a day dutifully devoted to official visits to the French consul[3] and General Moultrie, the governor of the state,[4] the newly arrived naturalist, as he wrote to the count nine days after landing at the port city, had spent every day in the forests where he had "already recognized a great part of the most interesting indigenous trees and a great many others."[5] He also told of seeing many kinds of birds that could be naturalized and bred in France, in addition to wild turkeys, dwarf partridges, and American swans. The bird he was most certain could thrive in France was a particularly beautiful duck, known to Buffon as *Beau Canard huppe* and to Catesby as the crested summer duck, (*Aix sponsa*), because it remains in these regions all summer; but most Americans call it the wood duck, for it loves to alight on branches and nests in hollow trees. He had been promised five of these ducks that year and several dozens next year.

As was to be expected in the Charleston society of long-established and wealthy landowners, with a strong flavor of French culture from the influential Huguenot community, Michaux was made "most welcome" in the city and offered every assistance, with invitations to visit town houses and plantations, and even the loan of slaves to guide him. But however agreeable the Charleston milieu, it was soon clear to the botanist that he could afford neither the money nor the time to live in the city, where living expenses were "ten times greater" than in the country and where, as the forests were several leagues away, it was often necessary "to go ten leagues distance for certain species of trees."[6]

He had made every effort possible to profit by a ship leaving Charleston on November 12, as he told the count in a long and enthusiastic letter, dated the day the ship sailed. "Even now the captain is leaving the harbor for the open sea." Though a great part of the seeds he had gathered were not yet in condition for shipment, he had managed to send to France this time an astonishing variety of seeds. He looked forward confidently to abundant shipments in future, including animals, especially summer ducks for the waterways of Rambouillet, wild turkeys, which must be captured young, as well as deer for the forests.

Again, and even more urgently than in New York, because of the prospects of much larger collections, he realized the necessity of establishing a rural nursery and garden. He confessed that he had already rented a house in the country, three leagues from Charleston, "in the midst of a forest but in the neighborhood of honest people, which is important." The house carried with it 111 acres of land, more than 80 of it in forests, the remainder in pastures and farmland, the entire property for sale for only 100 guineas, a sum sure to be repaid in economic benefits accruing.

The balance of this letter was a persuasive plea for the count's

View of the harbor of Charleston, S.C., c. 1800. (Courtesy of the South Caroliniana Library of the University of South Carolina)

approval of the purchase of the house and land, to serve as the garden of the king in the South.[7] As he poured forth his arguments in a rush of words, his eagerness and the urgency he felt are revealed in emphatic underlinings of whole paragraphs, a rare departure from his usual restraint. "There is an infinity of advantages which this residence combines where I am going to establish the home of my son and the servant I brought with me, and my home, when I shall not be traveling into other parts of the continent." These advantages included a spring of pure water near the house, space for nurseries and greenhouses, an ideal situation for raising the lovely summer ducks he was so hopeful of sending to Rambouillet, the wild turkeys, partridges, American deer, and every other species suitable for breeding in France, but not yet known to him. Naturally, he did not fail to underscore the great economic benefits to be derived from such a self-contained establishment, with subsistence farming to maintain man and beast, forests to provide wood for boxes, garden frames, fencing, wagon carts, and the like, and, above all, the means of making "more abundant collections than you can imagine" and for very little extra expenditure.

"It is necessary," he reminded the count characteristically, "to be in a position to be independent of others."[8] In this rare mood of euphoria, he declared that he could, with the benefit of such an establishment and a packet boat at the right seasons, ship two hundred boxes and more, including samples of wood of the interesting and beautiful kinds produced in Georgia and along the Carolina riverbanks, satinlike woods of different colors; he promised to prepare for the count some wood of the *Magnolia grandiflora* with which to have furniture made. His enthusiasm embraced even the buffalo, "an interesting animal to become acquainted with for a nation which concerns itself more than all others with extending knowledge." He was confident of readily obtaining a supply of the great, shaggy beasts from St. Augustine or from North Carolina, and of easily taming, breeding, and shipping them to France.

Unhappily, his elation did not extend to his personal life. "When I speak of placing my son on this plantation," he confided to the count, "it is because I do not recognize in him either the energy or the disposition for any kind of knowledge and, being obliged to work for a living, he will learn the necessity for it, so much the more as I will not supply him with any other help than that of establishing him on the place."[9]

Ironic as this confession of paternal discouragement may appear to us, who are aware of his son's brilliant destiny, it seems, from the reserved botanist, a veritable *cri de coeur.* Dedicated scientist that he was, wholly absorbed in his mission, he was scarcely the man to take into account the emotional burdens of a youth flung into a strange way of life in a foreign country, in the company of a demanding and formidable father, from whom he had long been separated. And the boy, then barely sixteen, was doubtless subject to the moods and tangential behavior that commonly possess boys of that age, while the elder Michaux was, himself, obviously much too impatient with the ungainly lad as he hesitated on the threshold of manhood. He could ill restrain his anxiety to see his son reach the fruition he envisaged for him: that he should readily and enthusiastically follow in his footsteps and carry on beyond his own mortality as an extension of his dedicated life. Nor did all Michaux's wisdom and experience give him the insight to perceive, behind the shell of the immature, inarticulate boy, the hidden promise of distinguished achievement.

In a final plea for the purchase of the establishment the letter concluded: "As for what concerns the service of the king, for which you have sent me, Monsieur Le Comte, it is of the greatest interest for performing it to have a station in the center of a country the most interesting of all of America, that is to say Georgia, South Carolina, and North Carolina, without speaking of the mountains which border these Provinces [and] of Florida, to which one can go from here in twenty-four hours by sea."[10] Thus he could bring together all the productions from these regions, cultivate and increase them, and remain for as many years as the service of the king required. With that sweeping and enticing prospect Michaux rested his case, only lingering to mention a new species of *Gordonia*, the beautiful Franklinia tree he had already seen in Philadelphia, a scarlet *Azalea*, and a new *Nyssa*, all to be found near the Savannah River.

Appended to this long letter was a "Liste des Graines de la Caroline," including names of all species of seeds shipped in the three large chests now en route to France, with comments on their habitats and lists of other seeds already gathered but not yet in condition for shipment—four pages of fruitful testimony to his newfound paradise. The species cataloged in this summary are many and varied, evocative of the myriad flora of the southern landscape. Fittingly enough, *Gordonia lasianthus*, known as loblolly bay, although a member of the Tea family, headed the list of those in the first chest though Michaux had not yet seen this queen of the southern lowlands in its spring glory, so memorably described by William Bartram, when "the thick foliage of a dark green color is flowered over with large milk-white, fragrant blossoms."[11] Michaux described it only as a tall tree, growing in very wet places, which should probably be planted in a greenhouse with a continual supply of water, though perhaps it would thrive out of doors in the most southern regions of France. The *Diospyros*, or persimmon tree, the fruit of which is very good to eat, "can be cultivated like a plum or even espaliered." He had also sent seeds of *Callicarpa*, called beauty berry, for its pink to lavender berries; *Hamamelis*, or witch hazel; *Halesia*, the delicately lovely silver bell tree; *Clethra*, the sweet pepper bush, and *Sarracenia lutea*, a curious, insectivorous yellow trumpet of the bogs, now *S. flava*.

Not forgotten were the seeds of the climbing *Gelsemium sempervirens*, yellow jessamine, which Michaux called *Bignonia sempervirens*; the thorny, tiny ground *mimosa*; the dainty *Mitchella repens*, or partridge berry, whose light red berries gleam through the leaves of the forest floor in winter; the *Yucca gloriosa*, or Spanish bayonet; the *Baccharis halimifolia,* groundsell bush, or silverling, whose silken seeds, like those of the milkweed, shine like spun silver in the autumn sunlight; the *Cyrilla racemiflora,* titi, or leatherwood, thriving in low, moist places; and the vivid, exotic-seeming *Passiflora,* the passionflower bearing large, green, egg-shaped fruit that pop when pressed—hence maypops to children.

He had, he believed, already identified eight species of *Quercus,* or oak, but could ship at this time only the acorns of the chestnut oak, *Quercus prinus,* which seemed to him the largest, the best, and the rarest of the oaks. And, as if inspired by the generous prodigality of nature all about him, he wrote that he hoped to send before the end of winter fifty bushels of seeds of *Cupressus distichia* (*Taxodium distichum*), bald cypress. As for the seeds of *Nyssa montana* (probably *N. sylvatica,* black gum) and *Ilex cassine,* or cassina tree, he had already gathered four bushels of seeds of each of these species, which were still too fresh to send at that time. Indeed, as the *Nyssa montana* seemed to him one of the most useful of American trees, for the hardness and elasticity of its wood, and, as the seeds were difficult to preserve, he hoped to send next year several thousand plants of this valuable tree, as well as more than twenty thousand plants of *Ilex cassine.*[12] As an experiment he had stripped away the outer covering from some of the seeds of the *Ilex cassine,* the *Nyssa aquatica,* the *Nyssa montana,* and the *Magnolia grandiflora* before shipping, to see if they were preserved better thus.

Because the inhabitants burned over most of the forests every year, one had to seek out the old forests that had escaped this pernicious practice "in order to find *Magnolia grandiflora,* some of which, in these 'vielles forêts' are more than eighty feet high." There too grew the fragrant sweet bay, the *M. virginiana,* which Michaux called *M. glauca.* He was sending some seeds of the *grandiflora* packed in moss, as well as those of the chinquapin, a shrub species of American chestnut. Of the *Lauraceae,* he included seeds of the *Laurus aestivalis* (now *Litsea*) and of the *Laurus borbonia* (now *Persea borbonia*), the red bay, the first to be planted in continually submerged locations, the second in very wet places, and a third *Laurus,* unidentified but thought by the botanist to be a new species, also found in submerged regions.[13]

Michaux remained at his Charleston place for over a month more.[14] By that time the hardships of continual journeys from town to forests, often far away, and back again, loaded with trees and plants, was proving exhausting, not only for the botanist and his son, but also for the horses, who fell sick from fatigue and exposure. Constant vigilance was necessary to detect the precise moment for collection of seeds of different species, which ripened successively, and it was often a race to gather the seeds ahead of the ravenous flocks of birds. "The forests are full of a multitude of birds of different kinds," he reported to the count, "in the proportion of a hundred to one in Europe. They take away the seeds and fruits from certain kinds of trees, even before maturity, so that three or four days' delay can no longer be made up for and so, notwithstanding the rains and floods to which this region is susceptible, it is necessary to go and collect." [15]

The plantation he had rented ten miles from Charleston offered such a sensible, practical, and economical solution to his difficulties, on all fronts, that he continued to reiterate to the count the "infinity" of advantages to be derived from its purchase. The decision to acquire ownership of the land selected by Michaux for his rural establishment became urgent when the proprietor threatened to sell the property to a prospective buyer. Confident of the count's approval of an acquisition so essential to the American mission, and aware of the three months, at best, required for a reply to reach Charleston from Versailles, Michaux resolved to purchase the property on his own. [16]

His expense account for the last month of 1786 reveals the complex activities involved in setting up a working establishment on the land: the purchase of hatchets, axes, scissors, sickles, pickaxes, saws, augurs, files, gimlets, carriage, axletree, large saw, nails, dishes, 320 feet of boards, 10 bushels of potatoes, rice, rye, and wheat, 12 bushels of corn, a barrel of ship's biscuits, 123 pounds of pork, and transportation for all these, as well as for the accumulated possessions of his son, their servant, and himself. There is no more complaint of a shortage of manual workers, four of whom he had hired for a month and a half at thirty-two dollars. [17]

For the first time in many years father and son began to share a home with some prospect of relative permanence, and the effect on both seemed salutary. Michaux, perhaps recalling his disparaging remarks about his son in an earlier letter, now assured the count. "Thoughtlessness aside, I am content with him, for he seems to do all that he can, and to be interested in our affairs, and this is what I principally desired." [18] How deeply interested time would amply prove. At the moment it was satisfaction enough for the botanist to have gained his son's helpful and willing assistance.

One constant disadvantage in the otherwise highly pleasing situation in Carolina was, as Michaux repeatedly pointed out to the count, the lack of regular packet-boat service direct from Charleston to France. As it was, shipments had to undergo a much longer voyage than necessary because, except on the rare occasions when a vessel bound for France stopped by the Charleston port, the boxes of trees and plants had to be placed on board a packet boat for New York, there to be transferred—after who knew what delays—to a ship destined for a French port. The prolonged journey was often damaging, sometimes disastrous, to the plant and seed shipments, and frequently fatal to the bird and animal travelers. As 1786 drew to a close he was again explaining that the scarcity of ships had prevented any shipments "until this moment. I profit by an American packet boat to send you thirteen boxes of trees and three of seeds, one box intended for the Jardin du Roi in Paris, and one little package of seeds for Monsieur Thouin." He had instructed the gardener in New Jersey to meet the boat and take precautions so that the shipments would not freeze if delayed in New York. Once again Michaux urged the sending of a French ship to Charleston, next year if possible, to carry shipments direct to France.[19]

If that was done, he hoped to be able to send not only more abundant botanical shipments without danger of freezing, but animals and birds as well, wild turkeys, which were very delicate, and summer ducks, perhaps a kind of *Biche blanche,* white doe, rare in this country, ten more patridges, bred in captivity from eggs brooded by hens, and even—it may be—the buffalo, useful for its skin and said to be excellent to eat, though the oriental buffalo, which he saw in the East, was poor food, eaten only by the most miserable Arabs in Baghdad. Having observed the effect of frosts and freezes on *Magnolia grandiflora, Gordonia,* and other trees, Michaux suggested the advisability of constructing "a kind of large orangerie" at Rambouillet, where such species could be planted directly into soil but sheltered from the worst cold spells. One might even have two orangeries, one ornamental, one a nursery.[20]

Next year, he assured the count, he would be in these southern regions at the right time to observe and identify trees before their leaves fell, for, stripped as they were of foliage, it was more difficult to recognize them. Yet he had made another abundant collection. An attached list of the contents of his late December shipment contained over 100 varieties of plants and seeds. The majority were species already sent on November 12, but the botanist had now adopted a policy of shipping desirable species again and again, whenever possible, in an effort to compensate for the high toll exacted by the hazards of the long journey from America to France. Among the most interesting of the species included for the first time were the forty *Magnolia tripetala,* or umbrella trees, of which Michaux had found no specimen with a trunk thicker than his wrist, leading him to conclude that he had

Camellia, "Reine des Fleurs," Middleton Gardens, Charleston, S.C. One of the ancient, surviving camellias presented in 1786, according to family tradition, to the Middleton family by André Michaux. (Courtesy of Middleton Place, Charleston)

Crape myrtle, Lagerstroemia indica, *Middleton Gardens, Charleston, S.C. Ancient surviving plant presented to the Middleton Family by André Michaux, c. 1786. (Courtesy of Middleton Place, Charleston)*

Drayton Hall (1738–1742), country seat of the Drayton family of Charleston, S.C., one of the plantation homes along the Ashley River periodically visited by the Michauxs. (Courtesy of Drayton Hall; photograph by Jane Isley)

not yet seen these trees in places best suited to their growth, and that those he found were perhaps brought by birds; the three *Stewartia malacodendron*, or silky camellia trees, whose monstrous twisted roots prevented him from sending many of their plants; the twenty-five *Azalea* plants, identified only as two species growing in wet places; and the *Sabal palmetto,* which he called *Chamaerops caroliniana, "Palmetto de Caroline."*[21]

The steady industry always characteristic of Michaux took on an extra dimension during the first three months of the new year as the process of converting the rural property into a productive plantation and nursery competed for his time with his regular duties of collecting and shipping. Here Michaux's boyhood on the Satory farm served him well. His heart must have warmed with memories as the Carolina establishment began to hum with life, to take on the sights, sounds, and smells of a working farm, with a fourth horse added in January, three sows and eleven little pigs three weeks later, two summer ducks for breeding, and ten hens.[22]

There were other new sounds as well: the ring of axes, the sharp staccato of hammers and the voices of hired carpenters and other artisans.[23] The old building on the site was repaired and a new four-room house constructed. An acre and a half of garden was fenced with rough boards; one enclosure for wild turkeys, partridges, and other fowl was made, and another provided for a fifteen-acre field to be sown in maize and potatoes for the nourishment of men and beasts. A new road had to be built across a marsh and the stream bridged. Finally, several acres of good land had to be cleared and cultivated for the nursery garden.[24]

Michaux worked, himself, and expected others to work as though time were running out. But whatever the demands on his attention, he never failed to give priority to the duties of his mission, traveling repeatedly, often great distances, to dig up plants or to collect seeds, in spite of inclement weather, and getting off shipments to France at every opportunity. In February he sent to France the first specimen of the water chinquapin, the American lotus, *Nelumbo lutea,* which he called *Nymphea nelumbo* and which he would later ship in quantity. "I am sending to you, Monsieur le Comte," he wrote, "an aquatic plant which seems to me new, whose fruitification is different from that of other plants. The receptacle of the seeds resembles a honeycomb made by bees, except that this plant grows in watery places among the *Nymphaea."*[25]

During the first three months of the year the largest shipment consisted of twenty-two chests of plants and seeds, sent on March 10, including a variety of beautiful and useful species, some in astonishingly large quantities, such as 525 red maples, *Acer rubrum*; 190 *Magnolia grandiflora*; 260 hickories, of two varieties; 112 silver bell trees, *Halesia carolina*; 100 *Ilex virginicus* (probably *Ilex opaca,* holly); as well as, in lesser amounts, sweet gum trees, *Liquidambar styraciflua*; mulberries (*Morus*); sweet buckeyes (*Aesculus octandra*), called by Michaux *Pavia lutea*; fringe, or graybeard, trees, *Chionanthus virginicus*; lindens, *Tilia caroliniana*; paper birches, *Betula papyrifera*; and many more too numerous to list here.[26] Along with these botanical treasures shipped on the American vessel *Adriana,* Captain Clark in command, bound for Bordeaux, Michaux longed to send some partridges for Rambouillet. "But," he lamented, "I do not dare to trust them to the Americans. I have learned that the summer ducks I sent to you last November perished two days after embarkation."[27]

Nevertheless, so great was his desire to establish the beautiful *Canards d'été* in the forests of his native land, he did, a month later, entrust five of these vivid birds, three females and two males, to an American ship, *Olive Branch,* under Captain Robert Beck, leaving Charleston early in April for Le Havre. No doubt he was somewhat reassured by the presence of a French sailor on board, in whose care he left his little feathered voyagers. The botanist's solicitude for the survival of his birds followed them across the sea with suggestions to Cuvillier as to their transport from the port of Le Havre to Versailles "making use of a little conveyance, because all birds accustom themselves to the use of a carriage when it is regulated, not neglecting to give them a little mixed wheat and rye twice a day, and water three times, and, upon their arrival, to place them in a body of fresh water, . . . preferably surrounded by trees and shrubs very thickly, to protect them against the cold northeast winds."[28]

The botanist's tender concern for the well-being of these beautiful birds is characteristic of his habitual care for all living things, animal or vegetable, which he undertook to transplant from the New World to the Old. Often his efforts were to no avail, but his care was rewarded in the case of these ducks, which we are able to follow through their arrival at Le Havre in late May, and their dispatch from there to Rouen, not in a carriage, but in a river barge on the Seine, en route to Versailles.[29]

CHAPTER 7

❧ Botanizing in Carolina, 1787–1788

BY THE TIME those summer ducks reached Le Havre, Michaux was far from Charleston, traveling with his son on a long-planned journey that was to take them, in less than three month's time, through a large part of Georgia and into the country of the Cherokee in the Appalachians as far as the sources of the Tennessee River and across South Carolina from west to east on the return journey back to Charleston.

This fruitful exploration was the first extensive and prolonged expedition of botanical research the botanist had thus far made in America. Though he would make many such journeys during his eleven years in this country, some of far greater range, this journey seems significant as his first real introduction to the American wilderness, his first collecting trip of any length with his son, and his first association with the greatest natural garden in the temperate zone, one to which he would return again and again—the southern Appalachians, "les hautes montaignes de Caroline."

It was with this journey that Michaux began the first surviving notebook of his "Journal de Mon Voyage," the account of eleven years of exploration and research in the still virgin wilderness of eighteenth-century America. Recorded day by day in his neat, legible script, in a series of pocket-size notebooks, or *Cahiers,* written by the light of campfires or "au claire de le lune," often in conditions of fatigue, loneliness, and danger, they furnish moving testimony of one man's single-hearted dedication to the natural world. Many of the entries are simply the conscientious scientific notes of his daily activities, as terse in style and spare of words as the author was said to be, with none of the literary flourishes or romantic reflections of William Bartram's *Travels.* Yet the careful listings and botanical descriptions of hundreds of plants have a beauty of their own, illuminating the pages with an almost daily litany in celebration of the green kingdom.

As Michaux was at heart a horizon-bewitched seeker with an insatiable passion for discovering unknown plants, his journal blazes a trail of botanical adventure across the face of America from Florida to Hudson Bay. Most memorable are his descriptions of the challenges and dangers of his many well-nigh incredible expeditions recounted with his customary restraint, but none the less impressive for that. As in his Persian journal, he included also meticulous observations on the geology and geography of landscape and terrain, as well as practical notes on mileage, weather, conditions of roads and rivers, and even, as an aid to later travelers, on the availability of inns—rare and usually execrable.

Solitary traveler though he often was, his range of association with his fellow men was surprisingly wide, as the journal reveals in comments on fellow travelers or other folk met on his journeys, sometimes comments enlivened with flashes of his characteristic dry, sardonic wit, or sometimes appreciative references to the beauty and gracious manners of women in whose homes he found a hospitable welcome. As envoy of the French king, he had, in addition to his scientific duties, social obligations he scrupulously observed, paying his respects to persons of official or intellectual prominence wherever he found them. Not the least impressive of the personal qualities reflected in his journal is the grace with which he could move from weeks in the forest in the company of Indian guides to the elegant society of a president, a governor, or an ambassador, at ease wherever his mission led him.

The first portion of the journal was lost at sea, when the author was shipwrecked off the coast of Holland in 1796 on his way home to France.[1] The remaining manuscript notebooks, beginning with April 1787 and extending through Michaux's return to France and his first weeks in Paris, survived.[2] Stained with seawater and the sweat of travel, they remain an enduring personal record of an enthralling odyssey.

We take up Michaux's story again with the journey, recorded in the first of his surviving notebooks,[2] along coastal Carolina and Georgia, and up into the mountains, beginning on April 19, 1787, when he set out from his Charleston plantation, accompanied by his son, then in his seventeenth year, and by a Scottish botanist by the name of John Fraser.[3] The three made their way across the Carolina lowcountry toward Two Sisters Ferry on the Savannah River, following the route taken in 1765 by John Bartram and his son William on Bartram's expedition into Florida as botanist to King George.

"Our journey led always through forests," Michaux noted in his journal, "but forests varied enough in soil and terrain to promise a rich harvest of plants."[4] Stretches of grassy pine flats, where white and graceful sprays of flowering dogwood gleamed beneath the deep green canopy of towering pines, were interspersed with savannahs bright

me dirent que les feuilles avoient
bon gout étant machées et que
l'Odeur en etoit agreable en
les froissant, ce que je trouvai
effectivement.

Direction pour trouver cet arbuste
La Tête de Rivière est la jonction de deux
Torrens considérables qui coulent par
Cascades des hautes Montagnes. qui ~
Cette jonction se fait dans une petite
Plaine ou il y avoit autrefois une rit
ou plutot un Village de Cherokies
En descendant au travers de la jonction
ces deux Torrens ayant la riv. a droite et les
montagnes qui regardent le nord a mex
Droite on Trouve a env. 30 a 50
toises de ce Confluent un Sent
formé par les Chasseurs Sauv
il conduit a un ruisseau ou lo
reconnoit les vestiges d'un Villag
de Sauvages par les Pêcheurs qui
subsistent au milieu des Brous
En continuant ce Sentier on arrive
aussitot sur les montagnes et l'on y
Trouve cet arbuste qui couvre la sol

Two pages from the notebook journal of André Michaux, reporting his 1788 Keowees expedition and giving directions for finding the long-lost Shortia, *and ending: "I wrote in my journal by the light of the moon." (Courtesy of the American Philosophical Society)*

avec l'Epigea repens

Le 12 Decembre 1788 je
visitay les Montagnes exposées
au Sud en revenant, car les
provisions étoient si avancées qu'il
y eut un Déjeuner très sobre
Je recueillis beaucoup de Magn
cordata en en meilleur état que ceux
des jours précédens

Nous cotoyames la riv. et nous
vimes plusi. Troupes de Dindons
Sauvages. Notre Guide sauvage tira
dessus mais le fusil qui avoit pu
être garanti de la pluye qques jours
apparav.t manqua a plusi reprises
Ainsi notre souper fut de qques
Chataignes q. notre Sauvage avoit
reçu d'un autre dénomination
Notre Marche fut de dix huit Milles
le Temps fut très clair ja la gelée se
fit sentir des le soir même et apres
avoir Demandé a mon Sauvage les
noms de plusi Plantes dans son langage
j'écrivis mon Journal au clair de la Lune

with the yellow blossoms of the *Sarracenia* swaying on their slender stalks above the curious green-gold trumpets of their leaves, sweet insidious traps for unwary insects.

In sharp contrast were the rich and somber swamplands along the rivers with their haunting Indian names, Combahee, Ashepoo, and Edisto, where magnificent, moss-draped live oaks cast gloomy shadows and the fern-leafed cypress trees spread their flaring trunks in still pools of black water.

In humid but less profoundly boggy lands the regal *Gordonia lasianthus* pushed its steeple top high above sweet bay, red bay, black gum, yellow birch, sycamore, and water locust.

Near the Savannah River, in a forest bordered by hills, Michaux rejoiced to gather a new *Azalea* with deep pink flowers, *Rhododendron nudiflorum*, popularly known as the pinxter flower; as well as a new *Kalmia;* the delicate crimson *Silene virginica*; fringe trees, *Chionanthus virginicus*; and a magnolia with flowers the shape of those of the *Magnolia tripetala* but agreeably fragrant, as those of the latter are not.[5] Where the nearby sand hills were bright with vivid spears of lupin, he gathered two varieties, the blue and the purple, as well as two kinds of verbena, two of milkweed, and a species of pawpaw.

Beyond Two Sisters Ferry the roads became so nearly impassable the travelers could make only two miles in five hours, the horses often bogging deep in mud or water and on one occasion even being forced to swim. Nor were bad roads the only hazards. This Eden of green shade, brilliant flowers, and seductive fragrance had also its serpents, viewed by the Frenchmen with caution and in the case of the rattlesnake with sensible dread. In the course of one day's travel the botanist records that he killed "a very beautiful snake with yellow, black, and red bands, the colors very vivid and well marked"[6] and three moccasins, one over three-feet nine-inches long and eight inches around, while his son accounted for a "serpent noir"; a blacksnake.

However, neither wretched roads nor snakes could dampen Michaux's pleasure in the open woodlands flaming with the glorious red azalea "the color of fire, deep red in all parts of the flower and even more vivid in shady spots," now commonly known as the flame azalea, *Rhododendron calendulaceum.*

In low-lying woodlands thick with birch trees with a little river flowing among them, not far from the hamlet of Ebenezer, Michaux gathered exquisite wild orchids, rose pogonias, grass pinks, bog roses, and an unidentified new species. The discovery of a species of silver bell, *Halesia,* in forests belonging to a Dutchman, who provided provisions for their journey along with the hospitality of his plantation, rounded out this fruitful day, April 27.

The last day of the month found the travelers in Savannah, a well-laid-out town of about 150 houses, situated on what seemed high sandhills piled up by the winds. Michaux spent the first morning botanizing, discovering a palm different from the "Chamaerops of Carolina," the palmetto, and the rest of the day paying visits to prominent citizens, an essential part of his mission. Lingering next day only long enough to replenish supplies, the companions rode on southward toward the Ogeechee River through forests abounding in *Magnolia grandiflora* and tupelo and bright with spiderwort, *Tradescantia rosea,* aptly known as dayflower.

When they reached the river, Michaux gathered along its banks the rare *Nyssa ogeche,* the Ogeechee plum discovered by Bartram, and the fragrant spider lily, and among the reeds along the shores, *Zizania palustris,* wild rice, a favorite food of the Indians of the lake regions of the Northwest. Hardly a day passed without its harvest of plants, too numerous to list in full, but including, as they neared the coast, a new species of *Kalmia* and the wild calla, or water arum, which he called *Calla palustris* (probably *Peltandra sagittaefolia*) with its spathe as white as the flower of the lily.

At the old (now abandoned) seaport of Sunbury, Georgia, reached on May 6, they found it impossible to carry out their plan to go on to Florida, as they had hoped. For a few days the party separated. François André, with two companions, set out to visit the fertile shores of the Altamaha River, the region of the discovery by the Bartrams of the rare and beautiful plants *Franklinia* and *Pinckneya*. Michaux père remained at an inn near Sunbury to recover from a leg injury caused by the bite of an insect the day before and inflamed into an abscess by the continual friction of the horse against the wound. He found this convalescent period a useful interval in which to set his herbarium in order and write up his discoveries. However, a few days later when François André and his companions returned, he was sufficiently recovered, and the season far enough advanced, for the company to set out for the mountainous country of the Cherokee, by following the old Indian trail along the southwest bank of the Savannah River to Augusta. Near the trail, about twenty-one miles from Savannah, after setting up camp for the night, Michaux collected a hawthorne with bright red fruit, *Crataegus aestivalis,* and in the lowlands, along a little river, the swamp cotton-wood, *Populus heterophylla,* the thorny water locust, *Gleditsia aquatica,* and a special prize, a rare species of silver bell, *Halesia diptera,* "whose existence," he noted, "I have doubted until now," and in the stream itself, quantities of wild rice.

On the morning of May 15 Michaux discovered to his dismay that his horses were missing, stolen or strayed away during the night, the first of many similar losses he was to suffer during his eleven years in America, as he usually followed the prevailing custom of turning the horses free to graze when he camped in unpopulated areas, after equipping each with a bell. But on this occasion he made use of his misfortune as an excuse to rid himself of the company of John Fraser, who had become increasingly a thorn in the side of the Frenchman.

As he confided to his journal, Michaux had accepted the companionship of the Scot, who had vowed to follow him wherever he might go, in the hope that Fraser, being British, might be helpful in obtaining supplies and other needs in sparsely settled regions. "I always traveled with him in good faith," Michaux asserted. But, as Fraser proved to have small knowledge of natural history and insisted on loading the party down with great quantities of common plants of little value, all the while wasting precious time on trifles and irritating the taciturn Frenchman with chatter and foolish questions, Michaux seized upon the loss of his horses to send the garrulous Scot upon his way alone, leaving the others to linger in the neighborhood for several days in a vain attempt to find the missing animals. At last they were forced to continue their journey on foot, trundling a little cart loaded with supplies and collections. They became convinced their horses had been stolen when they met on the road a group of armed men pursuing a certain "Captain" known to be a horse thief, and when, a few days later, they learned this Captain had been caught and shot, though his accomplices had fled with the stolen horses into the country of the Creek Indians.

Their slow progress on foot became even more difficult when a wheel broke off the cart, an accident redeemed in part by the discovery in that area of an exquisite trillium, the yellow-flowered lady's slipper, *Cypripedium calceolus,* as well as the sweet-scented Carolina spicebush, or sweet shrub, *Calycanthus floridus,* whose dark red, cup-shaped flowers exuded an enchanting perfume. In one place along their road where they were forced to cross a deep stream by means of a fallen tree at water level, Michaux feared there was a risk of being attacked by alligators "which," he noted, "abound in the streams, creeks, and swamps of Georgia and even of Carolina." Fortunately, there seemed to be none of these frightening reptiles in the stream near Augusta, where they were forced to stand for three hours in the water to repair a broken bridge.

Arriving in Augusta on a Saturday, May 26, the impatient botanist was forced to spend all next day resting, for, he complained, "They are so scrupulous here in America, one doesn't dare go out or even take a walk on Sunday in the large towns." Augusta, then a community of 120 houses, though agreeably situated on the Savannah River, was little to his liking, inhabited largely by idlers and gamblers, addicted to rum, drunk to excess in America.

In pleasing contrast was his visit on Monday to the home of Colonel Le Roy Hammond, three miles on the South Carolina side of the Savannah River.[7] Though the colonel was not at home, the botanist was graciously welcomed by the "amiable" ladies of the house, as well as by a visiting lawyer, who gave him a letter of introduction for the district of Keowee. "This home," commented Michaux gratefully, "seemed to me very distinguished in every way, by good manners, wealth, and elegance."

Augusta, on his return there, seemed even more inhospitable. Unable to find anyone willing to sell even the most essential provisions for their journey, Michaux and his son set out without bread and cornmeal, and without any corn for their newly purchased horse. Fortunately, after crossing the river, their road to the Cherokee Nation soon led them through a region of French settlers, one of whom generously supplied them with milk and other provisions, "because we are French," explained Michaux, who was pleased to observe that the French settlers were generally esteemed for their honesty and good morals.

For the next few days they followed a trail, at times hardly distinguishable, through forests of pines, oaks, and persimmon trees, where Michaux killed two black squirrels, a magpie, and a grosbeak finch with bright yellow plumage. After days with no sign of habitation but abandoned farms, they came upon a poor farm whose hospitable mistress not only sold them three pounds of butter but treated them to milk and baked for them bread of cornmeal, wheat, and leavening—as rare a luxury in their austere daily fare as, perhaps, were visitors in the lonely life of their hostess.

A few days later large groups of people, returning from a church on their road, assured them that they were approaching thickly settled areas of "honest people," which proved true, for on June 5 the weary Frenchmen arrived at the plantation of General Andrew Pickens, for whom Michaux had a letter of introduction from Colonel Hammond.[8] There, graciously received in the Pickens home, Hopewell, the Michauxs spent a comfortable night, a most welcome contrast to the previous night when torrential rains had forced them to sleep beneath their cart. Before leaving Hopewell, they had the further satisfaction of arranging with a Captain "Middle," a neighbor of Pickens, to obtain some wild turkeys which he promised to have ready on their return. Taking to the trail again, they found as they neared Seneca that the soil changed to clay mixed with granite, shale, mica, and iron minerals. A great owl, shot by Michaux, plummeted down, to their amazement still clutching in its fierce talons a blacksnake of the coachwhip species, "fouet de cocher" to the Frenchmen.[9]

Along the shores of the Keowee River[10] grew masses of *Kalmia latifolia,* almost ubiquitous in those mountain regions. Michaux observed also the trailing arbutus, *Epigaea repens,* whose star-shaped, sweet-scented, pink and white blossoms would have been very scarce so late in the season, as well as the wild hydrangea, *Hydrangea arborescens,* with its rounded umbel-shaped clusters of creamy-white flowers, and the rare, alternate-leafed dogwood, *Cornus alternifolia.* But perhaps the most intriguing plant the botanist found at this time was the curious ginseng, *Panax quinquefolium,* whose umbels of small, greenish yellow or greenish white flowers, with a faint but unmistakable lily-of-the-valley fragrance, rise from a circle of leaves, a plant whose modest appearance gives no hint of its fascinating history going back for centuries of fact and legend. Michaux was undoubtedly already familiar with the extraordinary medical properties attributed to the ginseng root in Asia, especially in China and Japan, where for centuries it has been treasured as a miraculous restorative and tonic, a potent panacea for all human infirmities—hence the name *Panax*—and, as such, a commodity of high commercial value. New France (Canada) had exported a large quantity of ginseng to the East in the eighteenth century, but the American colonies did not enter the market until after the Revolution. The first boat to ply the trade, the *Empress of China,* sailed from New York to Canton in 1784, with a cargo of wild ginseng to exchange for silk and tea.[11]

On June 8 the Michauxs reached Seneca, a frontier village and trading station on the threshold of the Cherokee Nation. An old Indian town lay mostly on the west side of the lovely Keowee River, on whose eastern bank the settlers had established their cabins and fort, once known as Fort Seneca but at this time called Fort Rutledge. This was the last outpost for travelers venturing into the mountains, whose ragged outlines had loomed on the horizon for days, a shifting, haunting blue mirage, slowly taking shape as a solid wall of forested peaks.

They were a dramatic scene for Michaux, who was about to

explore for the first time a region of surpassing beauty that would enthrall him with the wealth of its flora, unmatched in abundance and variety in all the temperate world.

Something of their prospect he had no doubt gleaned from his visits to William Bartram, who had botanized in these mountains twelve years earlier all the way to the transmontane Indian towns in the Tennessee Valley, the only botanist before Michaux to have explored these ranges. Certainly, Michaux knew or guessed enough about the formidable difficulties and dangers of exploring an unmapped mountain wilderness to recognize the need for a guide. William Bartram, it is true, having failed to find a guide, had made his journey alone, an incredible venture for anyone but William Bartram, whom Indians everywhere revered, sensing perhaps, with the instinct of primitive people, the essentially peaceful nature of the gentle naturalist-artist, whom the Creek Indians in Florida called "Puc Puggy," the "Flower Hunter."

For the second day after their night at General Picken's plantation, Michaux's journal has this entry: "On June 9th we went to see a Frenchman named M. Martin who had settled in the area as a planter. We wished to hire two Indians to guide us in the mountains which separate the state of Carolina from the Indian Nations of the Cherokee, Creek, Chickasaw, etc." This journal statement and what we have learned from different sources of other activities of Michaux's on this day, of considerable interest but unmentioned in his journal, reveal again how very strictly this daily diary confines itself to the business of his mission, eschewing all irrelevant matters. From other leads we know that the Martin that Michaux visited on June 9 was Louis D. Martin, at that time a deputy surveyor of South Carolina, whose business included laying off and platting unclaimed lands being purchased from the state, and that when Michaux visited him he arranged for him, probably at the suggestion of Pickens, to select, lay out, and plat three tracts of land on the West Fork of Cane Creek, a tributary of the Keowee, coming in from the west, near Martin's place. Two weeks later, on Michaux's return from his excursion into the mountains, Martin delivered to him plats delineating three tracts, one containing 888 acres and the other two of a thousand acres each. After his return to Charleston, "Andrew Michaux" secured conveyances of those three tracts executed on behalf of the state by Thomas Pinckney, governor.[12]

As recorded in his journal, with Martin's aid Michaux managed to engage two Indians to accompany him and his son into the mountains. But they were hard to persuade, and when they understood that he wished to visit not only the sources of the Keowee and Tugaloo rivers but also those of the Tennessee, which flows into the Ohio, and to go on to the Tennessee Indian towns as well, they demanded a blanket and a petticoat apiece, as well as the value of six dollars each for the twelve days the journey was expected to last, half of the payment to be in advance, for they said they had too often been cheated by white men. To all their requests, Michaux agreed, adding that he would "fill their bellies with rum" on his return should the journey prove satisfactory.

The expedition aroused considerable interest among the established settlers of the Seneca region, who supplied the travelers generously with bread, cornmeal, corn for the horses, and even the loan of a cart. On Monday, June 11, Michaux and François André, accompanied by a young man who had lived for some months among the Indians and understood a little of their language, set out with the two Indian guides, who had been provided by the botanist with powder and shot.

Over steep mountain trails, through deep valleys, and across rapid streams the sure-footed savages led them with such speed that they arrived the same day at Little River, which, to Michaux's dismay, they had to cross on sloping rocks, a foot or two under water and covered with slimy moss. He feared that their horses would lose their footing in a current so swift that "anyone but an Indian would have been dragged under," but there was no other way, for, notes the journal, "Indians are not inclined to listen to one's protests under such circumstances." Their bread supply was soon gone, and, though the Indians went hunting daily, they killed nothing. Their diet was reduced to cornmeal boiled or simply soaked in water, the delicious water of the mountain streams, said by their guides to be the purest and best in America. During this first portion of his journey, neither the dangerous trail nor the austere fare disturbed Michaux as much as the disappointment of not having yet come upon the many interesting new plants he had anticipated, so that he was haunted by the dismal possibility of a fruitless journey.

Still they struggled on, climbing over steep and rocky trails, down into valleys, through deep streams or swamps filled with horribly thorny smilax, which wrapped itself continually about the face, body, and legs, coming at rare intervals to lush and fertile meadows along the river where the guides pointed out the remains of Indian villages now abandoned to the wilderness. They continued to ascend the river against the current and at last on June 13 the hunters redeemed themselves by shooting both a wild turkey and a bear, while the botanist, too, was having a fruitful day. He had found a dioecious shrub whose seed in the shape of a pear was not yet ripe but sufficiently formed to be identified as a nut,[13] and some cucumber trees, the first he had seen in America, *Magnolia acuminata*. While the Indians prepared the long-awaited feast for the famished travelers, the botanist visited the riverbanks covered with glorious masses of the pink and white flowers of the great laurel, which some call rose bay, *Rhododendron maximum*, and the equally beautiful mountain laurel, *Kalmia latifolia*.

The festive and bountiful meal of wild turkey and bear that followed was well-timed because they soon had need of all their strength, as the journal records:

> *The 14th of June we went on, always following the river, first on our right and then on our left; we had to scramble over boulders, straddle high trees which had fallen across thickets of undergrowth, where one could hardly see one's way because of the density of the shrubbery, the lofty mountains now shutting us in, and the gloom brought on by the somber weather and the mists which seemed to enclose us in darkest night. The turmoil and confusion were increased by the noise of the river rushing over rocks and the sound of the torrents that we had to cross, up to our knees in water.*
>
> *I was continually in dread of stepping on snakes and terribly frightened when we had to cross over great logs so rotten that they gave way under foot and one was half-buried in the bark and vegetation around them.[14]*

This kind of travel was hardly compatible with collecting, but eventually, after crossing the river at a shallow ford, they arrived at a lovely peaceful spot, a wide, semicircular plain surrounded by high mountains where the Keowee River begins its bed. There they rested thankfully, feasting on the abundant and delicious wild strawberries, so delectable that Michaux collected roots of their plants to take back to France, where they thrived.[15] Perhaps the flavor of this wild berry had already been described to Michaux by William Bartram, who, on a hillside in this region in late May 1775 had come upon a group of Cherokee maidens who shyly approached him and his companion and, related William, "with native innocence and cheerfulness, presented their little baskets, merrily telling us their fruit was ripe and sound."[16]

Though Michaux and his companions saw no charming Cherokee maidens nor any of their nation in the forest paths they followed, signs of their former presence were everywhere visible in their now deserted villages. Once the travelers sheltered through a night of heavy

rain under a tree bark shed, left by Indian hunters, whom they identified as such by the remains of their scaffold for roasting and the bones
of the animals on which they feasted.

On June 15 they reached the headwaters of the Tugaloo, after
traveling all day in a blinding rain over high mountain trails. A few days
earlier Michaux had discovered the five-leafed white pine, *Pinus strobus,*
and a magnolia which he called *Magnolia hastata* (*magnolia fraseri,* the
umbrella tree), as well as the curious climbing vine of the Dutchman's-
pipe, *Aristolochia macrophylla,* with heart-shaped leaves and bizarre
yellow or white flowers, once used as an aid in childbirth. In spite of
continual rain he also discovered there a new species of sweet pepper-
bush, *Clethra acuminata,* very tall, with a stem four inches in circumference; and a violet with lance-shaped leaves, *Viola hastata,* whose seeds
he gathered.

After two more days of toiling over trails so deep within the high
mountain ranges "one hardly ever saw daylight," they came at last to
the watershed where the rivers flowed into the Tennessee. During
three days of botanizing in a steady rain, Michaux, who had noted only
an abundance of umbrella trees, an "arbutus" much fancied by bears,
and an azalea with yellow flowers, determined to push on to the Tennessee River, without tarrying along its tributaries.

But that was not to be. When he announced his decision, his
young companion, who understood a little of the Cherokee language,
now warned Michaux that the guides confessed they no longer recognized the trails. As under those conditions it was impossible to continue
any farther in the mountains, they turned aside to seek an Indian
village where they might buy cornmeal, but instead, luckily, they stum-
bled upon a path made by fur traders, along which they resolved to
return. Journeying homeward over gently sloping trails, they enjoyed,
Michaux noted in a rare aesthetic comment, "beautiful weather for the
first time, and the luminous clarity of the air created charming effects
on some of the mountains."[17] Traveling rapidly, in spite of flooded
areas, they reached Seneca on the evening of June 18, exhausted. Next
day, as they rested and prepared to return to Charleston, Michaux
confided to his journal his disappointment in finding so few rare plants
in the mountains, compared to those gathered in Georgia, and in not
seeing one single interesting bird.[18] Nevertheless, the two months'
journey had been valuable if only as a reconnoitering trip for future
expeditions he hoped to make in seedtime, provided no outbreak of
frontier hostilities disturbed the uneasy peace between the Indians and
the settlers. He had observed that the lands owned by the Cherokee

were invariably superior to those owned by the white settlers who viewed the fertile grounds of their red neighbors with covetous eyes. The Cherokee were the most numerous Indian tribe of the region except for the Creek, whose nation extended over a wide area south and west of Carolina, and the settlers, who feared a union of these powerful nations, were already constructing a fort in which to take refuge in case of attack.

The remainder of Michaux's journey homeward, approximately 250 miles to Charleston,[19] was relatively uneventful, save for the loss of one of the horses, which strayed away just as they reached the Pickens plantation. No wild turkeys awaited them there, but the Captain, this time called "Captain Veddle," promised to enlist the help of all the neighbors in obtaining some of these great and wily birds.

Back at home in mid-July, the botanist found awaiting him the long-delayed letter from comte D'Angiviller, dated at Versaille February 7, giving official sanction for the acquisition of land for the garden of the king, and a letter from Abbé Nolin as well, commenting on the condition of shipments received in France from Michaux and enclosing a list of the plants most desired. Those letters resulted in four hectic days as the botanist concluded his formal purchase of the property, put in order the affairs of the plantation, packed a shipment of seeds, and prepared for his scheduled journey to New York, via ship to Philadelphia, and on by stagecoach the remainder of the way.

Arriving in Philadelphia at the end of July, Michaux spent but three days in the capital, where he dined with the French consul, Marbois, and visited the Bartrams in Kingsessing, where he doubtless found an attentive audience for tales of his recent expedition. Continuing on to New York, he divided his time there between the city, where he dined with the chargé d'affaires, and received his allotted funds from La Forest, and the New Jersey establishment, where he paid the gardener, Saunier, his wages, conferred with him on the fruit trees and other species to be shipped to France, and packed his books and herbaria to send to the Carolina plantation, now firmly established as his American home.

It was not until near the end of his New York stay that he at last found the leisure to write to the count a full report of his journey to the Carolina mountains, including a list of the principal plants and the interesting trees he had identified. "Among the Indians I found three very interesting new trees," he wrote, "which are not found in Georgia," adding, with more satisfaction than he had expressed in his journal, "In all respects this journey has been one of the most advantageous for the abundance of things collected and for the use of my time," a statement confirmed by the enclosed list of approximately 150 "trees and plants identified on my journey into Georgia and other western regions."[20] In further confirmation of his retrospective view of the expedition is the box of seeds gathered in Georgia and Carolina before his departure and brought with him to New York to await shipment by the first packet boat, containing "about thirty-five different species and a great quantity of a very pretty shrub called *Fothergilla*," a witch alder closely related to witch hazel.[21] In addition, there were, among others, lupines, *Lupinus perennis* and *L. diffusus*; the sourwood tree, *Andromeda arborea* (now *Oxydendrum arboreum*); water locust, *Gleditsia aquatica*; wild larkspur (probably *Delphinium tricorne*, called by Michaux *Delphinium lazuli*); and a tall variety of *Sarracenia*, called by Michaux *Sarracenia tubifolia*.

The remainder of Michaux's letter to the count consisted of a reply to the latter's proposal, approved by His Majesty, that François André be permitted to cultivate the plantation land for his personal profit, a generous and kindly intentioned offer, which, however, indicated how little this noble patron, three thousand miles away in the elegant court of Versailles, comprehended the profound dedication of the king's botanist to his mission.

"I am very grateful to His Majesty," replied Michaux, "but I will observe to you, Monsieur le Comte, in my present circumstances I cannot turn over this plantation to my son to cultivate for his own advantage productions which have nothing to do with the commission entrusted to me. I would like very much to be able to explain to you the necessity and many advantages together involved in making this establishment serve only the interests of the department."[22] The land was essential, he pointed out, first, for the maintainence of trees collected over a period of time and forced to be kept waiting for a ship destined for France, and in the same way essential for the growing of trees that had to be shipped as young plants because the seeds would not remain viable throughout a long sea voyage; second, the land was needed for the pasturage of the horses necessary for collecting over long distances and often in opposite directions for such plants as *Magnolia acuminata*, *Calycanthus*, *Gleditsia aquatica*, as there was no vehicle or transport to rent. In further explanation of his position, he added:

> There are few or no inns and few inhabitants, and there are
> spaces so uninhabited that during three months at the time of my
> last journey we have slept more than sixty nights in the woods.
> Thus the great forests in the neighborhood of this establishment
> save a great deal of time in gathering more abundantly, and sur-

mounting more easily two great obstacles of this country: the warmth of the climate which makes the maturity of seeds pass rapidly, and the depredations of birds which destroy them before maturity.

The imminent approach of the seed harvest in Carolina and the pressure of its short duration now hastened the botanist's departure from New York, which he left on August 10, pausing in Philadelphia only long enough to obtain funds from Marbois, the French consul, before embarking for Charleston. His haste was to no avail as storms and furious gales, succeeded by days of breathless calm, prolonged the voyage for eighteen days.

His first day back in the port city was spent writing letters to the count, to Abbé Nolan, to Marbois, and to Saunier. As the uncertainty of sea transport made it expedient to follow up all important communications with at least one repetition, Michaux referred briefly, in this letter to the count, to his mountain journey and to his two bills of exchange for 3,000 francs,[23] matters already related in a previous letter, and again pointed out the need for direct transport from Charleston to France at the right season for shipment as there was no longer any regular packet-boat service between New York and Charleston. "I would like very much to have a packet boat from France in January or February," he wrote, "or merely a French merchant ship between Charleston and Havre de Grace [Le Havre], whose profits would be considerable, receiving here its cargo of rice, and arriving in the port of Havre de Grace a little before Lent."[24]

For two more days Michaux remained in the city before returning home to the plantation where François proudly displayed the collections he had made during his father's absence, which together they sorted and labeled. Since sharing the hardships and dangers of their mountain journey, the affinity between father and son seemed to have deepened. The journal records a more constant partnership through the swiftly passing days of harvest and seedtime, a crowded, exhausting, but exhilarating season for both. They bought another horse for collecting journeys, ploughed the rich land to receive the seeds gathered, acquired seven sheep to furnish fertilizer for the garden, and built a granary for seed storage when needed. Sometimes their search for seeds took them across the Cooper River, sometimes up beyond Dorchester and Moncks Corner or farther into the interior, and sometimes for long days of gathering in the dense forests surrounding the plantation.

As the work progressed, one can imagine with what quiet satisfaction Michaux included in his terse record of each day's activities the phrase "avec mon fils." Throughout the autumn months they collected together a vast quantity of seeds, fascinating in the infinite variety of size, color, and design: round, shining seeds of the palmetto, *Sabal palmetto*; long, blackish pods of the honey locust, *Gleditsia triacanthos*, its seeds embedded in sugary syrup; large, greenish brown cones of *Magnolia grandiflora*, bursting with bright crimson seeds; and hundreds of others. After harvesting came the essential task of drying the seeds, some to be labeled and carefully packed for shipment to France, others to be planted for later shipment as seedlings. For days at a time journal entries consist only of the words "plowed and sowed" or sometimes merely the word "sowed," as father and son through the long golden autumn season gave back the seed to the waiting earth, participating together, with every son of Adam, in the miracle of creation, the age-old ritual, the source of man's bodily nourishment and symbol of his spiritual faith.

There were interruptions in this absorbing work, such as a trip to Charleston at the end of September to place on board a ship bound for Bordeaux two chests of seeds and eight summer ducks.

Michaux's letter to the count announcing this shipment explained that the care of the ducks during the sea voyage was being entrusted to a poor Frenchman, Bertrand, a former soldier who longed only for a quiet life and begged that, in exchange for his care of them, the count would recommend him for a job on the Island of St. Dominique.[25] Also, it is in this letter we find his first reference to Jean Jacques Himely, with whom the botanist and his son were to be closely associated, mentioned on this occasion as the Charleston friend who had handled for him a draft of 3,000 francs until his funds should arrive from Philadelphia.

Michaux attached to this letter a list of seeds contained in the shipment, including, among others, two species of magnolias, *fraseri* and *tripetala*; Hercules'-club, *Zanthoxylum* (*clava-herculis*); *Stewartia malacodendron*; and *Sassafras*; with a promise to send more later in the winter, adding, "As for those I identified in the country of the Indians, there may perhaps be some difficulties because war has been declared by the Georgians and the Carolinians against the Creek, Cherokee, and Chickasaw united."[26]

Though Michaux was handicapped by rheumatism and both he and François endured a siege of fever lasting through the last two weeks of October, they somehow managed to have ready a shipment of seven chests of seeds and a cage of eight summer ducks to embark in early

November on a ship bound for Le Havre, the port to which he had recently been instructed to direct all shipments.

Plant traffic was not all one-way. Michaux was in Charleston on November 18 and 19 to receive shipments of plants from New York, probably from France via the New York port, as part of the botanical exchange agreed upon in the terms of his royal commission. As they were sent to Charleston, they would have been plants suitable for southern regions, such as *Camellias*; sweet olives, *Osmanthus fragrans*; and crape myrtles, *Lagerstroemia indica*; all of these are plants introduced into this country by Michaux. He spent the following week planting these imported offerings in the king's Carolina garden, to be presented to appropriate persons or nurtured to provide seeds and seedlings for the future enrichment of the gardens of his host country.

Though the botanist's mission concerned the export into France of game birds and animals as well as plants, he had so far been able to send only ducks and partridges, though he had made unsuccessful attempts to obtain wild turkeys. Now he determined to try to send over the sea for the forests of Rambouillet some of the graceful and beautiful Virginia deer he so much admired, which he called dwarf deer *"les cerfs nains,"* because of their small size compared to the European stag, and for this purpose he fenced in an area in the hope of keeping the deer in captivity until they could be shipped to France.

Three more shipments of plants were sent from the plantation before the end of the year, one on December 12 of particular interest as it consisted of "the most choice seeds" which Michaux explained he was forced to send via New York after waiting in vain for over a month for a vessel direct to LeHavre.[27] The two chests contained seeds of some of Michaux's favorite and most admired plants, including among them that stately denizen of the forest, the tulip tree, *Liriodendron tulipifera*; the sweet gum, *Liquidambar styraciflua*; as well as persimmon, *Diospyros virginiana,* a relative of the tropical ebony tree; and, for more humid areas, cypresses, tupelos, and the elegant *Gordonia lasianthus.* He sent also seeds of the Virginia willow, *Itea virginica,* a graceful ornamental shrub for landscaping near the waterways of Rambouillet; and, again, he sent the acornlike seeds of the fascinating and beautiful American yellow lotus, *Nelumbo lutea* (which he called *Nymphea nelumbo*), to be planted in the lakes of the royal gardens.

Scarcely had the ship bearing the choice seeds cleared the harbor before Michaux was off again, on December 15, on a collecting journey into the Carolina interior, spurred by news of the imminent arrival in port of a ship destined for Le Havre. From this day right through the

Christmas season he was absorbed in the arduous task of collecting, preparing, and shipping six boxes of trees, five chests of seeds, and eight ducks contained in a cage, which, he wrote to the count, "I have constructed on a model sent from London, which will protect them from injuries from weather and the sea. . . . The war between the Americans and the Indians," continued the letter, "is about to be concluded. They are busy naming commissioners from the southern states to go to settle their differences."[28]

CHAPTER **8**

✒ Florida, 1788

HOPE OF PEACE on this occasion, as on so many others, proved illusory. Michaux, not daring to return as planned for seeds to the country of the still hostile Cherokee, turned his thoughts toward Florida. It was unlikely that such a journey would yield any new species of plants suitable for naturalization in France, which had no area comparable to humid, subtropical Florida,[1] but as a naturalist he could not resist the lure of the lush and fertile land so glowingly described by William Bartram, and he hoped to advance the science of botany by new discoveries in that verdant wilderness.

On St. Valentine's Day 1788, accompanied by his son and a "little Negro" purchased for fifty pounds, he embarked for St. Augustine, Florida. Their ship was delayed in the harbor for ten days by a series of frustrating circumstances, contrary winds or none at all, followed by storms so severe the ship was forced to seek shelter near Sullivans Island. Going ashore on the island to botanize, Michaux found nothing of value, commenting that the English had cut down all the tall palms during the last war and the American custom of burning woods each year had destroyed the rest of the trees. As a final contretemps the ship's anchor proved to be so deeply embedded in the bottom of the sea as to require the aid of a stronger vessel to disengage it before, at last, on Sunday, the twenty-fourth, they were wafted by a light but favorable wind out into the open sea.

Four days later their ship entered the port of St. Augustine, then in Spanish hands. Only a few years had passed since England had ceded East and West Florida to Spain, and the zealous port officials questioned Michaux suspiciously on the object of his visit. Since the botanist had wisely obtained a permit in advance from the Spanish governor, whom he had assured of the scientific purpose of his visit, suspicion changed to cordial welcome and offers of assistance in his study of the natural history of the province.

Michaux planned to explore first the eastern coast of Florida as far south as proved practical. Taking time out only on Sunday, when he and François André attended Mass in the church (where most of the population as well as Governor Céspedes were present), the botanist spent the week in preparation for the journey, studying maps and guidebooks of the region, buying a large canoe, hiring two oarsmen, and laying in a supply of food, and powder and shot for hunting game in the wilderness inhabited only by Indians. The canoes used there by Indians and settlers alike were made from the hollowed-out trunks of large cypress trees averaging about twenty-two feet long and three feet wide, but only two and a half feet deep, and, though two persons could not sit abreast, there was still room for the Michauxs, their black, the two men using paddles, and with space left for plant collections.

On Wednesday, March 12, they made an inauspicious start, with winds favorable but so strong they whipped the seas into high waves that threatened to swamp the boat, forcing them to seek refuge on the barrier island of St. Anastasia at the house of a venerable old man, a resident there for fifty years. "This hard-working old man, the most industrious in all Florida," commented Michaux, for whom diligence was a cardinal virtue, "had made his abode a paradise, notwithstanding the various ravages of pirates he had endured, and the revolutions he had twice experienced through changes of government, as this province passed, during his sojourn, into the power of the English, and again into the power of the Spaniards."[2]

Here and there on the island grew groves of fantastic mangroves. These strange trees, whose floating seeds "shaped like elephant tusks, anchor themselves in shallow places, rise from tide-washed sand flats where, with their exposed perpendicular roots, they give the impression of a forest marching on stilts."[3] On other parts of the island grew the Florida arrow root, *Zamia,* of the sago palm family, which the early Seminole Indians called *Conti Hataka,* or breadroot, using its roots for making bread.

On the evening of March 13 they arrived at Fort Matanzas, on the inlet at the southern end of St. Anastasia, an area of somber and tragic association. Nearly two centuries earlier, several hundred Huguenot settlers who, under the leadership of Jean Ribaut, had established a frail foothold there for their native France and freedom of religion, were massacred by the Spanish commander and founder of St. Augustine, Pedro Menéndez de Avilés, in the name of God and King Philip of Spain, thus at once destroying heretics and a rival claim to Florida.

The following morning Michaux and his party struggled in vain to cross the bar of Matanzas Inlet against strong winds from the sea and were at last driven to stop at the home of a Minorcan settler three miles from the mouth of a little tidal stream called Northwest River. Botanizing in the surrounding countryside, Michaux found the woods filled with trees well known to him in Carolina and Georgia, such as *Magnolia grandiflora*; willow oaks, *Quercus phellos*; loblolly pines, *Pinus taeda*; hickories and wax myrtles, *Myrica cerifera*; and the air sweet with the familiar fragrance of yellow jessamine already in bloom.

As the winds continued unabated, Michaux resolved to leave the two oarsmen and the black with the canoe to wait for a propitious moment for crossing the bar, while he and François André, with a hired horse and a guide, ascended the Northwest River. Along its shores, mingled with familiar forest trees, he noted *Gordonias* just coming into flower and sourwoods shaking out their pearly tassels, but also new species of familiar genera—pawpaws, silver bells, viburnums, and a plant of the heath family with straight, hollow stems, which the Indians told him they used to make their calumets. "I did not see it in flower," noted the botanist, "but I believe it is the one that Bartram described to me under the name of *Andromeda formossissima*."[4] Here and there, where the sun's rays flickered through the leafy canopy overhead, the travelers noted the sky-blue candles of lupines brightening the forest floor, and the crimson, scimitar-shaped blossoms of *Erythrina*, a strange legume, commonly known as coral beans, flashing in the sunlight, the swordlike seed pods still filled with last year's seeds, a rich harvest for the botanist.

Returning to the site of their rendezvous with their companions in the canoe, they learned from a soldier from Fort Matanzas that their Indian rowers had seized the opportunity of a momentary calm in the winds to cross the bar safely, but had been swept onward by the sea with no chance to fire off the agreed-upon signal shot.

Michaux and his son immediately set off in pursuit, with their Minorcan host, who not only furnished horses but came along as guide. All day they rode without stopping, through "the most arid region of

Florida," varied only by the sight of an abandoned plantation once the property of Governor Moultrie.[5] At the mouth of the Tomoka River, "forty miles from St. Augustine in a straight line," they stopped for the night on the shore of a lagoon.[6] The signal shot they fired off was immediately answered by another from their Indians, who had arrived the day before, having suffered no worse disasters than being flung twice into the sea when waves overturned their canoe.

Bidding farewell to their generous Minorcan companion and guide, the last person other than those of their own party any of them would see until their return from their month-long exploration down the coast, the Michauxs, with their Indians and black, set out on their southward voyage. Along the way the ruins of many an extensive plantation abandoned by the English lent a desolate and melancholy air to the landscape,[7] relieved for the Michauxs to their delight by their first view of orange trees, not set out in hothouse pots as at Versailles, but in grove after grove of leafy trees loaded with fruit, and by the discovery of "many interesting plants," including the exotic *Carica papaya,* introduced into Florida from the West Indies by the Spaniards and valued for its melonlike yellow fruit.

On Easter Sunday, March 23, a favorable wind brought them as far as New Smyrna, where they camped on the ruins of the short-lived colony, established by the English nearly twenty years earlier, backed by the British government, who had given over 100,000 acres of land to the settlers, and directed by a Scottish physician, Dr. Andrew Turnbull, who, Michaux declared indignantly, "had seduced and led away from their native shores more than 1,200 persons, men, women, and children, the majority from Minorca. The harshness and oriental tyranny with which this [Scottish] barbarian managed his colony was still the subject of conversation among the inhabitants of St. Augustine when I was there."[8] Michaux observed the evidence of more than 400 destroyed houses on this site, only the chimneys remaining, as the Indians who came to the place for oranges had carried away all the wood of the houses for fuel. There was little to excite the botanist in the next four days of navigation, by the Isle of Mangroves, and a hill called Mount Tucker, where he found a few tropical shrubs and plants, and on to the fertile swamplands where they camped at Captain Rogers's abandoned sugar plantation, the southern extent of English settlements.

Four days after leaving New Smyrna, they awoke to the realization that Mosquito Lagoon (now Indian River Lagoon) was, in fact, a cul-de-sac. They were faced with a choice between reversing their course or making a portage across the western shore of the lagoon into Indian

River, "which," explained Michaux, "is not a river at all but an arm of the sea," enclosed from the sea like all the others by a broken chain of islands.

They resolved to attempt the portage, for by this time the whole party, devoured by mosquitos and with only salty water to drink, was eager to return, including the botanist, who had found nothing of interest save a new species of fig, a new *Sophora,* and two unidentified plants, and the Indians, whose supply of rum was exhausted. Discouraging, too, was the portage, which proved far more difficult than anticipated. A passage of more than a mile had to be cut for the roller logs across the sandy isthmus covered with cones, briars, and saw-toothed palmettos, whose vicious blades sliced legs and boots and whose tough, rampant stems, resistant to even the sharpest blades, were often intricately tangled with equally thick stems of neighboring plants. At last, on the evening of Sunday, March 30, the exhausted workers, with canoe and baggage, came to rest on the shore of Indian River, only to be confronted with a new challenge. The river at this spot was almost six miles wide and so shallow the canoe repeatedly stranded, even though Michaux and his son walked for more than four miles in water up to their knees. Yet when the river deepened and the two got back into the canoe, waves from strong adverse winds washed into the boat, soaking passengers, provisions, and baggage. As the immense marshes and mangrove swamps which formed the shore made camping impossible, they were forced to turn back to their resting place of the previous evening.

Next day the wind blew with even more violence, serving at least to dry provisions and baggage and affording a needed respite from travel. The Indians went fishing, bringing back to camp two fish weighing eighteen pounds each, a welcome addition to their diet of biscuits and rice. Michaux and his son explored the region, noting the number and variety of water birds, herons, egrets, gulls, ibis, and many others. On more than one occasion François André killed more than a dozen with one shot. Michaux observed two species of very unusual tree ferns growing on the giant palm trees, whose succulent hearts helped to supplement their diet, now reduced to two biscuits a day each.

On April 2 wind and sea had calmed sufficiently to allow them to cross the six miles of water separating them from the mainland. There Michaux discovered a great many necklace pod trees, *Sophora tomentosa,* which he described as "a beautiful tree. . . . I gathered a great many of its seeds, and a beautiful cluster of flowers convinced me that this was a *Sophora* with a very agreeable blossom."[9] Now "the hope of discovering new and interesting plants inspired me to overcome all difficulties," he confided to his journal, "even that of traveling constantly on foot to relieve the Indian rowers in their struggles against adverse winds." [10] The discovery on April 3 of two trees of the *Annona,* or custard apple, family, "one a new species with very large white flowers," was cheering, but the farther they advanced, the more he discovered trees and plants natural to the tropics and unsuitable to the climate of France. Thus, reluctantly abandoning his plan to go to the tip of Florida, Michaux resolved to turn back "at Cape Canaveral, a little below the latitude of 28 degrees, 15 minutes."

Profiting by the calm before the rising of the sun, they embarked before dawn on April 4, to cross the eastern bank of the river. Though they had been warned of possible dangers from hostile Indians, they had met no red men since leaving St. Augustine, but this evening they again saw by their campfire, as they had seen often before, the gleam of the fires of Indian hunters in the distance. Their guides advised them not to visit these Indians because they would be sure to beg for rum. Their own Indians, Michaux noted, were fortunately unusually moderate in this respect.

The return journey, retracing their route, was relatively uneventful. Leaving the Indians to cross the bar of Matanzas as before, Michaux sent his servant to procure horses from the Minorcan plantation, while he and' his son spent the interval botanizing and carefully packing the rare trees and shrubs he proposed to carry with him to Charleston "at all costs." But when the time came to rejoin the Indians, they found their way blocked by forest fires, set the previous day and still burning. The wind was blowing in their direction carrying the flames toward them with frightening speed, forcing them to detour widely over thorny palmetto barriers. "One has no idea, in Europe, of the considerable extent of forests which are burned annually in America," wrote Michaux, who strongly condemned this pernicious practice, "either by the Indians or by the Americans. Neither the one nor the other has any other motive than to have, by their fires, a new grass crop free of the stubble of the previous year. I am convinced that this is the principal reason for the decline in the numbers of deer for hunters and the decrease in food for all forest creatures." [11]

Back in St. Augustine, the botanist, as protocol demanded, lost no time in calling upon the Spanish governor, Señor Vincente Manuel de Céspedes, who was now inclined to treat the Frenchman with great respect since he had observed on letters addressed to Michaux from Charleston his distinguished title "botanist to the king of France."

"Sunday, April 20," Michaux recorded in his journal, "I received a visit from the governor, who came to see my plants and other collections I had gathered on my journey, birds, etc. I was engaged to dine at his home and the afternoon was spent in his Excellency's gardens with the amiable ladies of his family."[12]

It seems probable that the governor found himself as much impressed by the man Michaux as by his royal soubriquet. By all accounts the botanist, though reserved, was a person of great social charm for whom the language barrier seemed hardly to exist. Certainly the governor had reason to remember his visitor's generosity. Michaux had noted in St. Augustine a female date palm forty feet high, which had never borne fruit, for lack of a male tree in the vicinity, a lack which he volunteered to remedy by sending some young male date palms to the city. Also, recalling with pleasure his visit to Spain many years ago, he presented to the governor, on his departure from the city, a box of choice seeds to be sent to the gardens of Madrid. But surely the tribute most valued by Señor Céspedes was Michaux's naming of the bush clover for his Spanish host—*Céspedeza,* which became, through a printer's error, *Lespedèza* and has so remained.[13]

Delightful as visiting in the gracious old Spanish city must have seemed to the travel-weary Frenchman, he allowed himself only a brief respite before resuming his journey. He had yet to see for himself the scenes of William Bartram's most rapturous descriptions, the region of the legendary river St. Johns and Lake George. Before setting out to explore those waters, he lingered in St. Augustine long enough to consult a Mr. Leslie, agent for Indian affairs, on the voyage he wished to make on the St. Johns among the Indians of the interior, to write his report to the count, and arrange for a draft to replenish his funds and provide for Saunier and the New Jersey garden, and to make a methodical listing and description of what he had so far collected on this journey: "in all 105 trees or plants from the first of March up to this day, Sunday, the 27th of April."[14]

Two days later he and François André set out for the St. Johns River. Forty miles by land from St. Augustine, at the plantation of a Mr. Wiggan, they had arranged to rendezvous with the Indian caravan and a canoe previously engaged,[15] and on May 2 the two Frenchmen, the black, and their Indian guides began the ascent of the river aiming for Lake George. Two days of navigating against the current and adverse winds brought them to the entrance of the great lake where they camped on an island, opposite Alligator Point, near groves of very bitter oranges.

On entering Lake George next morning they came upon a river flowing into the northwest corner of the lake.[16] On ascending this river, they found the mouth so filled with sand they had to drag their canoe a distance of "twenty-five to thirty fathoms. Immediately after, one finds a depth of 15 feet, the water is salty and more disgusting than that of the St. Johns River or Lake George. After ascending for more than three miles we found the source, which bubbles out of the earth, rising more than one half foot above the surface of the water. It is so clear one can see the bottom more than 30 feet below. Around the basin formed by the springs we recognized the *Illicium*."[17]

Here indeed were "the odoriferous Illicium groves" of Bartram's rhapsody. Among the *Illicium*, in the sandy soil blackened and enriched with rotting vegetation and shell debris, grew magnolias, *grandiflora* and *fraseri*; cassinas, *Ilex cassine*; wild olive trees; and red bays *Laurus borbonia* (now *Persea*). The brackish water was alive with fish, which hurled themselves against the boat as it pushed forward, but fresh water was now the need of the thirsty voyagers. Fortunately, Michaux, exploring on foot next day, came upon, only a mile from the mouth of this salty river, a spring of the purest and best water he had yet tasted in Florida. Here, too, and indeed here and there everywhere in the area of Lake George they observed the *Illicium*, especially abundant near the southern tip where grew also swamp lilies, *Crinum americanum*.

Entering the St. Johns to continue upstream beyond Lake George, they camped in an orange grove but soon found that there was little hope of botanizing there as fierce storms forced them to huddle under their hastily constructed shelter of wild palm leaves. Next day they pushed on for ten miles in an even more severe storm. There is a rare and revealing touch of self-portraiture in an incident described by the botanist in his journal entry for May 8:

"We came upon a place frequented by savages. There was a canoe belonging to them on the bank of the river and a cooking pot. I put some biscuits, some beans, and some sweet oranges in this pot, and we went on our way. We heard two shots in the distance which proved that Indians were hunting nearby."[18]

Continuously contrary winds and the opposing current had made progress upstream very slow in spite of the steady labor of the Indians. Now they found themselves inching along between shores lined with alligators, "whose horrible appearance is accentuated by their enormous size. Their shape is that of a lizard, but they are black and armed the whole length of the back with great spines which bristle when they are angry."

The botanist, like Bartram and many another traveler, found these reptiles a source of irresistible, if horrid, fascination. He observed that

these creatures have a nose like a pig and eyes close together at the top of their flat heads; they have 72 teeth in their jaws and easily swallow dogs, pigs, and young calves, but, at the least movement of a man, throw themselves into the water with a terrible noise and commotion. They are amphibious and come every morning to pay us a visit in search of the remains of the fish we had caught in the river. We were also treated to their music, a stronger and more continuous roaring than the bellowing of a bull in a valley half a mile away.[19]

Perhaps to escape from such formidable neighbors, Michaux and his companions turned aside to ascend a tributary as far as its source, a day's journey away. The water, though so clear one could see the bottom fifteen or twenty feet below, was salty "with an unbearable odor" and filled with trees which often impeded their progress.

Sunday, May 11, was marked by the discovery of a moonflower, *Ipomoea Bona-nox* (now *Calonyction aculeatum*), "whose blossom was perfectly white and its tube six inches long," and by Michaux's decision to turn back as the river seemed about to lose itself in marshes. Now, with wind and current in their favor, progress was swift. Camping on May 13, on the banks of that stream whose water was so agreeable and pure, Michaux again delighted in gathering *Illicium*. "It is worth remarking," he observed, "that this tree is found in places where grow *Magnolia grandiflora, Annona grandiflora, Olea americana, Ilex cassine*, etc., etc., but most especially where one finds also *Aralia spinosa* and a grass called canes which grows to ten feet in height, always an indication of good soil, but sandy and moist."[20]

They arrived back in St. Augustine in the early afternoon of May 16, having picked up their horses at the Wiggan plantation; and, after ten busy days in the city, paying visits, putting the collections in order, preparing for the governor a detailed statement of the observations made in Florida during their stay in the province, Michaux and his son took their leave of his Excellency and "many persons of distinction who had welcomed me graciously."

They returned to Charleston by canoe as far as Savannah, cruising along the channels of the present-day Inland Waterway, between the beautiful and romantic Sea Islands, with their moss-draped live oaks and legend-haunted shores, and the green and golden marshlands of the coastal mainland. On Cumberland Island they found many refugees from Georgia fleeing the ravages of the Creek Indians, who had destroyed their cattle, burned their homes, and killed a great many of their people, a grim reminder to the Frenchmen of the dangers they had escaped. They stopped again at a town called, in the journal, Fredericktown, which is almost certainly Frederica on St. Simon's Island, where Michaux "delivered letters to various people," probably from William Bartram. "I dined with my son at the home of Mr. Spalding, where were gathered the ladies of General MacIntosh's family and several other persons of importance,"[21] he noted in the journal, an occasion worthy of mention as another tie with William Bartram, who knew this region well and whose companion on one of his botanizing journeys had been General MacIntosh's son, John.

At Savannah they took passage on a commercial vessel bound for Charleston, where they landed on Sunday, June 8. "The journey has been very successful," he reported to the count, "in the large number of new and rare plants procured. I have received on the part of the governor and from all the civil and military officials of the government the most favorable reception."[22]

After an absence of nearly four months, he plunged into work on the plantation. The most urgent task was that of unpacking and setting out in the garden the trees and plants brought back from Florida, as well as of sowing the seeds from Florida and a great quantity previously collected. He and François André went several times up to Camden and over to the Santee and Cooper rivers, in search of *Stewartia* and other plants, and, with several hired blacks, they gathered an abundance of *Fothergilla gardenii,* or witch alder, four bushels in one harvest, perhaps for medicinal uses similar to that of its relative, witch hazel.

There were always the shipments to be prepared and embarked, with accompanying lists and letters of description. A third chest of seeds from Florida went off on July 1, though, as Michaux explained to the count, the journey not taking place in seedtime had produced few seeds "in comparison with the different kinds of rare and interesting trees I will be able to send you at the appropriate time.[23] I am planning another journey whose success is already almost assured since it has for its purpose the collection of the discoveries of last year." This was to be the customary follow-up journey to collect seeds and plants identified in flower the previous spring. "The war is ended with the savages of Georgia, and we will set out before the end of the month," he predicted confidently on August 2.[24]

But it was to be November before Michaux could travel again.

Stricken on August 15 with an attack of malarial fever so severe and persistent he was forced to seek medical aid in Charleston, he remained in the city slowly recovering through the month of September, with only brief visits to the plantation.

Nevertheless, he somehow managed, with his son's aid, to send off a shipment to the count early in October, via New York, only two chests and a "small box of the most choice seeds. . . . I will make larger shipments by a vessel setting out from here direct for France."[25]

The list included, along with the old favorites, such as magnolia, silver bells, and fringe trees, some seeds of the American linden, *Tilia carolinia.:a*; of hibiscus, rose of Sharon; *Gerardia lutea*; the leather-flower, *Clematis viorna*; and a quantity of chinquapin seeds, *Castanea pumila.* These last would not stand a long delay in the New York port, he pointed out; if no ship was ready for Le Havre, they would have to be sown in the New Jersey garden.

Much precious time had been lost during the weeks of fever and convalescence, and the botanist now threw himself with renewed ardor into the work on the plantation. Totally absorbed once more in the fascinating business of seeds, he labored through the long blue and golden days of October, Carolina's loveliest month, when the heat and fever of summer have spent themselves and winter's frost is only a distant threat. One journal entry is typical of many: "October 18. Sowed seeds of *Magnolia glauca* (*virginiana*) or sweet Bay, and *Magnolia tripetala, Chionanthus, Stewartia, . . . Zanthoxylum, Styrax, Halesia, Fothergilla, Magnolia acuminata, Viburnum dentatum.*" A shipment of trees arrived for him from Philadelphia, probably more plants from France, and a day was devoted to setting these out in the plantation gardens.[26]

There were glass-covered garden frames to be built and a shelter constructed to protect the rare *Illicium* from "the winds out of the north and the rains from the northwest," and a ditch dug also, to drain away any excess water from this precious Florida plant. Those tasks done, Michaux and his son spent days gathering a great quantity of pine cones with the help of several black workers. Though it was a good year for pine harvest, he found that "a tree of a foot and a half to two feet in diameter produces only about a peck or at the most a half-bushel of cones." Finally, just before Michaux departed for his long-delayed journey, they arranged for the shipment of a collection of seeds especially requested by Abbé Nolin in his last letter, among them the cross vine, *Bignonia crucigera* (now *Anisostichus capreolata*), and the sweet pepper bush, *Clethra.*[27]

CHAPTER 9

⊷§ Temperate Mountains and Tropical Isles, 1788–1791

FINALLY, ON NOVEMBER 5, Michaux set out for Augusta, accompanied only by his black helper, who had become devoted to him. Warned by the French consul not to venture south of the town of Savannah, as the Indians were again on the warpath, he confined his botanizing within a wide area around Augusta, returning to the city from time to time with the fruit of his harvest. Before leaving for the mountains, he was able to crate and ship from Augusta, via Savannah to Charleston, 1,168 trees and plants, including a new species of buckeye, *Aesculus*; a new species of the plum family, *Prunus*; a new buckthorn of the *Rhamnaceae* family; as well as *Rhododendron, Kalmia,* and *Annona* (now *Asimina*).

During the last week of November he suffered so acutely from kidney pains and fever that he was obliged to stay in Washington, Georgia, for four or five days under the care of a French doctor "who gave me remedies and ordered me to rest." Before moving on, the botanist identified near Washington the mountain magnolia, *Magnolia acuminata,* which he had not seen since leaving Charleston.

On this second journey over now familiar territory, he seems to have found hospitality in many more homes than before when most often he had slept on the ground. The names of his hosts for a night's lodging illumine the journal's pages, and one may assume that the evening's companionship was no less welcome to the inhabitants in their far-scattered homes than to the solitary Frenchman, who is said to have been both a good conversationalist and an excellent listener. He had need of this last quality as well as of patience and good French manners when he stopped for the night at the home of a Mr. Freeman on a small tributary creek of the Savannah, not far from the confluence of the Tugaloo and the Keowee rivers: "I was received with a great deal of courtesy by the mistress of the house whose husband was away. This woman was young, beautiful, but very devout, and continually reflecting on the different ways of thought among the Methodists, Anabaptists and Quakers. Conversation on these subjects went on from seven until ten-thirty; I then became bored with it in spite of the kindness and charm of this woman, and I went to bed."[1]

We come now to a part of this expedition so integral to the Michaux story and so eloquently described in his journal that we quote his own account, in an unembellished translation with only a minimum of comment, beginning with his departure for the mountains:

> *December 2, 1788. I left the confluence of the two rivers, Tugaloo and Kiwi [Keowee] to go up the Tugaloo, and I slept at the home of Larkin Cleveland, Esquire, 19 miles.*
>
> *The 3d. I crossed the Tugaloo River at the only place used for fording. It was so dangerous that two of our horses narrowly escaped drowning. I had breakfast at the home of John Cleveland on the other side of the river. I was told that there were no other settlements, and I crossed through country completely covered with forests, like all southern provinces, but it was very hilly and in the evening I reached Seneca, where I slept on the ground. 19 miles.[2]*

The next morning he arose at dawn to find a hard frost and a thin film of ice on the ground. Nevertheless, he botanized on the shores of the river for two days, discovering a new species of rhododendron, as well as kalmia, spruce, silver bell, Carolina allspice, pawpaw, black maple, and alternate-leafed dogwood. Then, leaving his black companion to dig up the plants, he went in search of an interpreter and a Cherokee Indian to accompany him into the mountains inhabited by their nation.

> *December 6, 1788. I set out for the mountains and slept with my guide at an Indian village. The chief of the village received us cordially. He told us that his son, who was to return from hunting that evening, would guide us into the mountains to the source of the Kiwi. But he did not return and the old man, who seemed about seventy, offered to accompany me. This man, who was born in a village near the source of this river, knew the mountains perfectly, and I hoped that his son would not come back. He had a supper served to us of stewed deer meat and bread made of cornmeal and sweet potatoes. I ate with my guide, who, knowing the Indian language, served as my interpreter. The chief ate with his wife at another bench. The mother of his wife and his two daughters, one married and the other about fourteen to fifteen years old, sat around the cooking pot where the*

meat was being boiled. These ladies were naked down to the waist having no other clothing but a single skirt each.

Sunday, Dec. 7: The mistress of the house roasted some corn using sifted embers in an earthen pot. When it was a little more than half roasted, the corn was retrieved, then put into a mortar, and after it was pounded it was sifted to separate the fine corn-meal, which was put into sacks for us to carry. When one is tired, one puts about three spoonfulls in a glass of water, often with brown sugar. This drink, besides being very pleasant, is a restorative which immediately restores one's strength. The Indians never undertake a journey without a supply of this meal. . . . Our progress was about fourteen miles from seven thirty in the morning until six in the evening. We camped on the shores of the Kiwi at the foot of the mountains among rhododendrons of two kinds, kalmias, and azaleas, etc.

December 8, 1788. The nearer we drew to the source of the Kiwi, the more difficult became our way. Two miles before arriving there I recognized the **Magnolia** **montana**, *which has been named* **Magnolia** **cordata** *or* **auriculata** *by Bartram. There was in this place a little cabin inhabited by a family of Cherokee Indians. We stopped there to camp and I hurried to search for plants. I gathered a new plant with denticulated leaves spreading over the mountainside a little way from the river. The weather changed and it rained all night. Although we were under the shelter of a great white pine, our clothes and our blankets were drenched and soaked through. About the middle of the night I went into the Indians' hut, which could hardly hold the family of eight persons, men and women. Moreover, there were six great dogs who increased the dirt and inconvenience of this dwelling. The fire was set in the middle of the room without an opening in the ceiling for the smoke to escape but sufficient opening to let in the rain through the roof. An Indian offered me his bed which was a bear skin, and he took my place by the fire. But at last, disturbed by the dogs who continually fought for a place next to the fire, I returned to our camp, as the rain had stopped.*

This place, which is called the source of the Kiwi, is incorrectly named. It is the junction of two other rivers or large streams [the Horsepasture and the Toxaway] which come together here and have not been named except as branches of the Kiwi.

The 9th. We set out, guided by my Indian, to visit the high-

est mountains and to go to the source of the stream which seemed to be the most precipitous [theToxaway]. We had to negotiate cliffs and streams covered with [fallen] trees where ten times our horses plunged down and were in danger of perishing. We climbed up to a waterfall where the noise of the cataract sounded like distant gunfire. The Indians say that at night fires appear in this place. I wanted to camp there, but as it had begun to snow and a cold wind was blowing we looked for a more sheltered place at the foot of the mountain where there was pasturage for our horses. The night was horribly cold. There was pine wood to feed the fire but it burned badly because of the continually falling snow. Our blankets, covered with snow, became stiff with ice soon after being warmed.

All of the next day, December 10, Michaux spent in searching for and collecting *Magnolia cordata,* on the slopes and at the base of several neighboring mountains.

December 11. There was a hard freeze. The air was clear and very sharp. I noticed a range of high mountains which stretched from west to east where there was less snow and ice because of the southern exposure. I gathered a creeping juniper, which I had not seen before in the southern part of the United States. But it should be noted that I saw in these parts several other such northern trees as river beech, blue dogwood, white pine, balsam, etc. We traveled three miles through an unbroken grove of Rhododendron maximum. *I camped with my guides at the head of the Kiwi, and gathered a great quantity of the tooth-leafed plant found the day I arrived. I did not see it on any of the other mountains. The Indians here say that these leaves have a good taste and an agreeable scent when crushed, which indeed I found to be true.*

After a paragraph of detailed directions for finding this plant, the journal continues:

December 12, 1788. I visited the southern-facing mountains on the way back—our supplies were so depleted we had a very plain breakfast. I gathered a great deal of Magnolia cordata *in better condition than those of the previous day.*

We went along the river and saw several flocks of wild turkeys. Our Indian guide fired, but the gun, which had not been protected from the rain a few days before, twice misfired. So our supper was some chestnuts given to our Indian by another of his tribe.

Our journey was eighteen miles. The weather was very clear. The freeze set in early in the evening and, after having asked my Indian the names of several plants in his language, I wrote my journal by the light of the moon.

The 12th of December. I tried at daybreak to kill a wild turkey. There were many of them in this place, but I did not succeed and we broke camp without breakfast. Very hungry, we headed for a camp of Indian hunters and, although the mountains were now less steep, it was an hour after midday when we arrived there, after a journey of six hours, estimated at about fifteen miles of road. They cooked for us some bear meat, cut in little pieces and fried in bear fat. Although it was very greasy, we made a very good dinner of it, and, although I ate a great deal of the greasiest parts of this meat, I was not uncomfortable. The grease of bears has no taste and resembles olive oil. It has no odor, even when it is cooked with other foods, and it congeals only when frozen. After dinner we traveled for sixteen miles and arrived in the evening at Seneca.

Michaux paid off his Indian guide, wrapped and packed the collections to be carried on pack horses, bought two wild turkeys to be carried in cages on horseback, and set out on his return journey. Not surprisingly, the wild birds, whose struggles sent their cages careening from side to side on the horses, soon died, one after the other, one of them furnishing much-needed food for Michaux and his companion.

Michaux again spent a pleasant evening at the home of General Pickens but thereafter was less fortunate in his lodging for the night. Especially was this true on December 21 when, after fording twenty large streams in bitter cold weather, he sought shelter and warmth in the home of an American loyalist with no love for Frenchmen. "This American tory said to me on my arrival that he would kill me if I spent the night at his house," recounted the botanist, "and I told him I was not afraid of that because I was not fat enough nor my purse either! He wanted to badger me about my country but I was a match for him and he had to be content with making me pay dearly for my lodging."[3]

The next night was equally disagreeable as he stopped at the home of a Captain Baudet, where the inhabitants of the neighborhood were holding a kangaroo court for two suspected horse thieves, one of whom was set free and the other beaten. "The dispensers of frontier justice," commented Michaux wryly, "were all drunk on rum, and all night long I was disturbed and fatigued by this undesirable company."[4]

There was compensation in the hospitality next day of a very gracious host with whom he lunched and the discovery, appropriately enough on Christmas Eve, of a holly with small straight leaves near Givhans Ferry about thirty miles from Charleston, where they spent Christmas night. On the day after Christmas, never especially noted in the journal, Michaux and his faithful black, leading the pack horses laden with plants, arrived thankfully at the plantation.

Writing to the count to announce his return and to inform him of a draft of 3,000 francs on the treasury of France, the botanist reported with satisfaction his "large collection of new plants,"[5] a laconic summary of the fruit of his arduous winter expedition into the Carolina mountains that does not anticipate the great significance in botanical history of two of the specimens he brought back. These evoked in later years such intense interest among botanists that they call for a digression to underscore their importance here, in the context of their discovery, recorded in his journal entry for December 8. Both, one a tree and the other a small plant or herb, were destined to become the inspiration for botanical treasure hunts that would rival the search for the lost *Franklinia alatamaha* of the Bartrams.

The yellow-flowered magnolia that Michaux found near the source of the Keowee River on that cold December afternoon, and two days later collected on the slopes of neighboring mountains—"The day was spent most particularly in the search for this tree," which he called *Magnolia cordata*—was not found again growing in the wild for a century and a half, when it was rediscovered far to the south, near Augusta, Georgia. In the interval the specimens Michaux brought back from the mountains, and their descendants, remained the only source for this beautiful and ornamental tree.[6]

Far more dramatic were the consequences of his discovery that he described as a "new plant with denticulated leaves spreading over the mountainside," of which, three days later, he gathered a great quantity and which he considered so interesting that he wrote in his journal precise directions for finding this plant. Ironically, this same little "arbuste" was to prove the most elusive of all his discoveries, setting in motion a widespread and prolonged process of botanical detection of unprecedented scope.

The next act took place three thousand miles away, in Paris, more than three decades after Michaux's death. Two eminent American botanists, Asa Gray and John Torrey, in Paris in the Spring of 1839 in search of data for their projected *Flora of North America*, directed their quest to the Museum of Natural History at the Jardin des Plants, where the dried specimen of Michaux's little plant with denticulated leaves had been quietly gathering dust in his herbarium, along with the rest of his collection.

Among the plants in the herbarium labeled "unknown"—a challenging term to Gray's eager mind—was the little plant with leaves like those of a galax, whose provenance was said to be "les hautes montaignes de Caroline." As the first botanist to discover the dried specimen, Gray claimed the right to name the mysterious plant, which he called *Shortia* for Dr. Charles W. Short, a Kentucky botanist, and *galacifolia* from the resemblance of its leaves to those of the galax.[7]

He claimed also as his prerogative the privilege of launching the first searching expedition for the living *Shortia*, which he did in the spring of 1840, in the hope of finding the plant in flower. Misled by the herbarium description of the plant's habitat as the high mountains, Gray and his party searched for *Shortia* on the mountain heights, without coming within a hundred miles of the target. Yet all the while the missing clue in the treasure hunt lay, ignored by all, in the little notebooks of Michaux's journal.[8]

Undaunted, Gray continued his search three years later, still directing his steps into the highest mountains, following Michaux's trails to the top of Grandfather Mountain, Mount Mitchell, Roan Mountain, and other lofty peaks. All in vain. The mysterious, elusive *Shortia* remained lost, and its quest soon became a cause célèbre among American botanists, who roamed about the mountains like so many Sherlock Holmeses of the plant kingdom, sharing their hopes and their frustrations. All to no avail, for, after all, it was no learned scientist but a seventeen-year-old Carolina youth, George McQueen Hyams, who in May 1877 came upon some strange plants covering the ground beside the Catawba River, near Marion, North Carolina, and took a few home to his father, an amateur botanist, who in turn sent them, via a scientist friend, to Dr. Gray. *Shortia* had indeed been found again, though not where Michaux had discovered it.

But the search for the original site, too, was almost over. In the autumn of 1886 Charles Sprague Sargent of Harvard, using the directions in Michaux's journal as his guide, found the long-sought plant exactly where Michaux had first discovered it. The following spring, 1887, a member of the search party returned to the spot, where he found the *Shortia* in full bloom. "Masses of dainty little white, fringed bells, each swaying in the mountain breeze on its pink-tinted stem, rising about six inches from a rosette of glossy scalloped leaves."[9] A box of the flowering *Shortia* was sent to Dr. Gray. It is said that the old botanist, then in his seventy-eighth year, wept with joy.[10] As the place where Michaux discovered *Shortia galacifolia,* at an elevation of 1,500 feet, is in Oconee County, South Carolina, the plant is often commonly referred to as the Oconee bell.

Returning to our story in January of 1789, we find Michaux absorbed in unpacking and setting out in the plantation gardens the trees and seeds brought back from the mountains, and those sent back by pack horse and by ship via Savannah, arriving in a series of deliveries, the majority in remarkably good condition. Also, during the same month he prepared and sent to France at least two large shipments, one via packet boat to New York, one direct from Charleston to Le Havre, which included some birds. He remarked to the count that, since the cancellation of the regular packet-boat service had made shipments less frequent, he made every effort to make them more interesting.[11] Among the new plants from the Appalachian Mountains sent at this time were ten of *Magnolia cordata,* thirty of *Rhododendron minus,* both his own discoveries, and six of the new hollies.

It was well that he could not foresee the fate of these lovingly gathered and carefully packed plants. The good ship *Fanny,* Captain Hinbon in command, ran into two weeks of foul weather and "was continually struck by tempests" with the result that it staggered into the French port with its precious cargo thoroughly awash in seawater.[12] But all unaware of this misfortune, Michaux in Charleston was devoting his days to his voluminous correspondence, countless letters to a bewildering variety of persons, including the count to whom he wrote long detailed regular reports, Abbé Nolin and various French consuls, finance secretaries, and the like, as well as an assortment of French noblemen and American friends, such as William Bartram, not neglecting long newsy letters to his dear friends at the Jardin du Roi, Thouin and Lemonnier, for whom, with the count's approval, he often included in the shipments sent to Versailles little packages of choice seeds.[13]

In the middle of January 1789 André Michaux escaped from the pressure of work at the establishment to botanize for eight weeks in the balmy, flowering islands of the Bahamas. Although many of the plants found there were unsuitable for naturalization in France, he nevertheless wished to visit the islands, having in mind the hope of producing some day a complete *Flora* of North America from Hudson Bay to the tropics.

In the erstwhile pirate haven of New Providence he was graciously received by "My Lord Dunmore," the British governor of the islands, to whom he gave seeds to send to Sir Joseph Banks, president of the Royal Society in London and director of Kew Gardens. Observing that the soil and the climate would be appropriate for the culture of the vine and the date palm, Michaux suggested to the governor the cultivation of these plants and promised to send him some young date palms.

"I have recognized there," he wrote to the count, "all the trees cited by Catesby, with the exception of two or three species only; a very great number of those which have been described by Plumier, Jacques, and Sloane in the Antilles, and, finally, several new species. I have brought back more than 1,500 trees which I have planted to await the season for sending them to you."[14] From the sunny haven of the Bahamas, the botanist arrived back in Charleston in time for the spring flowering. In late May news of the April Riots in Paris reached him— the first storm warnings of the political tempest about to engulf the French capital. Uncertain what effect the situation might have on the continuation of his mission, he resolved, nevertheless, to go ahead with another journey he had planned into the mountains of North Carolina. He advised the count of his decision: "These mountains are the highest of all those which compose the Allegheny and the Appalachian Ranges, and their productions can thrive better in France than those of the southern parts of America. The temperature is so moderate there that I have recognized in the mountains of South Carolina trees of Canada and of New York State."

Michaux and his son set out from the plantation on May 30, accompanied by a black, probably the same devoted servant who had traveled with them in Florida.[15] Journeying on horseback, they followed the route of the Santee-Wateree-Catawba River system as far as Charlotte, North Carolina, noting, eighteen miles beyond Charlotte, a *Magnolia cordata,* "which appeared to differ, even from the *Magnolia cordata* discovered formerly; the leaves were of a glaucous or bluish color, very marked underneath."[16]

As Michaux's journal report of this journey is somewhat abbreviated, it seems useful to quote here the detailed account given by the botanist to his friend and biographer Deleuze, who recorded it:

> *Nearly three hundred miles from Charleston he took a guide with whom he plunged into the forests. At several days journey from every habitation of man the guide, having thrown himself upon a bear which he had brought to the ground, was severely wounded, and was in danger of being killed.*
>
> *Michaux takes occasion to observe that in these solitudes it*

*is essential to have two guides, there being various accidents by
which one may perish, and it would be almost a miracle for an
European to find his way back alone. He cannot follow the bed of
a torrent interrupted by prodigious falls, the banks of which are
precipices of rock, undermined by the waters which, giving way
under the feet, precipitate the traveller into the stream.*

   *If he climbs a mountain to descry the nature of the country,
he perceives nothing as far as the sight extends but the summits of
similar mountains with intervening plains, covered with Rhododendron, Kalmia, and Azalea, above which large trees, here and
there, rear their lofty heads. These woods are impenetrable to an
European; the Indian alone is able to discover tracks; the former
having no conception how he is to direct his course in these immense wilds.*[17]

Day after day Michaux and his companions forced their way
through tough jungle growth of Rhododendron and mountain laurel,
cutting a path with their tomahawks which, Michaux noted, "one must
always carry when travelling in the forest wilderness," even reaching
the summit of Yellow Mountain (now Mount Mitchell), "considered in
North Carolina and Virginia the highest mountain in all North America."[18]

It had been their plan to go on into Kentucky, but when they
arrived at the Block House about fifty miles from Mount Mitchell, a
rendezvous point where travelers going into Kentucky often joined
forces for greater safety, and there learned that the preceding week
several travelers returning from Kentucky had been massacred by
Indians, Michaux resolved to continue on into the mountains of Virginia and from there on to Philadelphia and New York, where he could
inspect the New Jersey Garden and where he anxiously hoped to obtain
the latest authentic news from Paris.

After passing the last of the southern mountains and moving on
into the Alleghenies, the botanist noted a yellow buckeye he called
Pavia lutea (now *Aesculus octandra*) three feet in diameter; and on the
steep rocky cliffs of the Roanoke River the *Thuja occidentalis* on the
northern exposure.[19] However, the botanist, always less interested in
stone than in things green and growing, had only a passing comment
on the Natural Bridge, near Lexington, Virginia, which inspired
Thomas Jefferson to rapture.[20]

On July 14, 1789, the date of the storming of the Bastille in Paris
by an angry mob, the Michauxs were passing through the beautiful and

pastoral Great Valley of Virginia, by Winchester, then a little trading
center on the overland route to the West, connecting the frontier
settlements of Kentucky with the establishments of Philadelphia, Alexandria, and Baltimore. Serenely unaware of the fateful events taking
place in Paris, Michaux père, the erstwhile farmer from Satory, observed admiringly the agricultural wealth of the limestone regions of
Virginia: "The country is rich, producing a great deal of grain, cattle in
abundance, and grass all year round, vigorous horses and people
enjoying the best of health." The wheat yield had been known to reach
twenty bushels an acre.[21]

Crossing the Potomac into Maryland and traveling on through
the predominantly German settlements of Pennsylvania, whose German farmers impressed Michaux with their industry, they arrived in
Philadelphia on July 21, where they remained for a week, occupied in
laying in essential supplies for the plantation, not available in Charleston, and in a round of visits, one to William Bartram and, most essentially, one to the French consul, Marbois, who could be expected to have
the latest news from France.[22]

For some time now, in the face of the uncertain and ominous
rumors from abroad, it had been increasingly difficult for Michaux to
obtain funds necessary for the maintenance of the New Jersey and
Carolina establishments and for financing the journeys essential to his
mission. We are not told what news from Paris Michaux learned from
Marbois, but it seems certain he received little reassurance as to the
stability or economic soundness of the royal government they both
served.

In the hope of consulting the ever-resourceful Otto, chargé d'affaires to the United States from France, Michaux hurried on to New
York, only to find this friend and advisor absent from the city. Fortunately, La Forest,[23] French consul in New York, seems to have given
him some financial help, for he settled his accounts with Saunier at the
New Jersey garden, which he found in good condition, and, as usual,
conferred with him as to the selection of trees, plants, and seeds for the
customary fall and winter shipments to France. Still, his money problems were far from solved. Back in Philadelphia, the harassed botanist
spent the better part of a week endeavoring to place his bills of exchange in order to obtain even enough money to pay the expenses of
his journey and of his return to Charleston. His efforts must have
partially succeeded, for he bought a horse for seventy dollars to replace
one gone lame.

Then, for a brief respite, he shared with his son a few leisurely,

delightful days visiting the famous gardens in the environs of Philadelphia, notably Woodlands on the right bank of the Schuylkill River.[24]
Across the river from Woodlands lay the Bartram farm and garden,
where Michaux was accustomed to leave his horses while in the area,
saving the expense of boarding animals in the city and at the same time
insuring for himself the pleasure of at least two visits with the Bartram
family. Stopping by to pick up their horses for the journey south, they
were detained for two days by heavy rains, a welcome interlude for the
Michauxs and their friend William Bartram, now nearing the completion of the manuscript of his long-awaited *Travels*.

There was little worthy of comment on the homeward journey
(which took them through Wilmington, Baltimore, Alexandria, Richmond, Petersburg, then, veering over to the coast, to Washington,
North Carolina, and Wilmington to enter South Carolina at Little
River) except the discovery, on the sandy, humid flats in North Carolina
of the tiny but fascinating insectivorous plant *Dionaea muscipula*,
known as Venus's-flytrap.

After sleeping for two nights on the marshy shore at the mouth of
the Santee River waiting for the winds to calm down enough for the
three of them and their three horses to cross, by ferry, the five-mile
stretch of brackish water, they finally reached the Cooper River crossing and, soon after, their home place, from which they had been absent
for well over three months.

There was hardly time to rest from their exhausting journey and
catch up on their mail before disaster struck. François André, walking
along the road near the plantation, on Sunday, September 20, 1789,
was wounded in the eye by a shot fired by a hunter aiming at partridges.

Next day the wounded youth was bled in the arm, according to the
barbarous medical practice of the day. As the eye, not surprisingly,
failed to respond to this remedy, Michaux resolved to place his son in
the care of a doctor in Charleston. But during the following week the
condition seemed to grow worse day by day, while the distracted botanist shuttled between the plantation and his son's bedside in the city. At
last, following an incision by the doctor and a regime of cold compresses
applied by Michaux père, the eye showed marked improvement.
Though the experience had been a ten-day ordeal of anxiety and
suffering for both Michauxs, one suspects that the father, stoical and
reserved by nature, may have failed to realize the intensity of his son's
fears of the effect of the accident on his vision. "The grief to which he
abandoned himself," Michaux wrote in his journal, "served to aggra-

vate his trouble."[25] It seems probable that the injury contributed to the failure of eyesight suffered by Michaux fils in later years.

By October 1 work on the plantation resumed its normal course, but then follows a gap in the journal of over five weeks, up until November 8, when the Michauxs again set out for another winter collecting journey to the mountains of North Carolina.[26] On the second night out they slept at Eutaw Springs (which Michaux called Youta-Spring), an exceptionally beautiful area where a powerful spring forced its way to the surface, appearing and disappearing and reappearing like a fountain, forming a deep, oval-shaped basin thirty feet in diameter from the volume of its flow. The pool was so translucent one could see the sandy bottom far below, but the water appeared blue from the clear reflection of the sky. Reflected also were the dark green of the leaves and the subtle shades of gray and brown of the limbs of the magnificent live oak trees surrounding the basin. In the fertile soil of the limestone hills, rising in gentle slopes around the pool throve many other varieties of oaks (Michaux lists five in the area), tupelos, black gums, cedars, and hawthorns.[27]

The region along the Santee River surrounding this idyllic spot was partially inhabited by Huguenots who had expanded northward from their settlements on the lower reaches of the river known as French Santee, and their comfortable homes and fertile farms were now intermingled with the plantations of English neighbors. Only eight years earlier the peaceful calm of this pastoral scene had been violently shattered by the opposing guns of the British and the American soldiers, engaged in the last battle of the Revolution before Yorktown—the Battle of Eutaw Springs, September 8, 1781.

A day's journey away the travelers stopped for the night at an isolated highland, on the north side of the river, where its hills of red soil served as a health resort for the French planters and their families and became known as "the High Hills of Santé." Here the forests took on a somber, romantic aspect from the festoons of gray moss, draping the branches of the live oaks, moss commonly seen in the lowcountry forests but rare at the elevation of this highland.

In contrast, in the Piedmont area beyond Camden they came upon an unusual outcropping of large, irregularly shaped granite boulders tumbled about the hillsides at random, an area that takes its name from a huge and seemingly precariously balanced slab, Hanging Rock, which gave its name also to the battle between rebel forces and British dragoons on August 6, 1780, witnessed by young Andrew

Jackson, age thirteen, in his capacity as mounted messenger for the American troops.[28] Farther along the road, now following the Catawba River, in the fields along their route Michaux observed with a farmer's eye the wheat, rye, and corn crops wherever they appeared. Near Charlotte he noted that, with the exception of the soil along the river-banks, the pasturelands were, for the most part, only a little better than those in most of South Carolina, the sheep "not very handsome" and the cattle as well.[29]

On November 16, two miles before crossing the Catawba at "Tack-a-sagee" ford, he found, near the banks of a little creek, hollies and mountain laurel and a tree he called *Magnolia glauca,* not as tall as other known species.[30] As they pushed on toward the high mountains, the weather grew steadily colder. White frost covered the ground each night. Between Morganton and Turkey Cove they gathered a new *Astragalus,* vetch; a moonseed with black fruit, *Menispermum canadense*; *Magnolia cordata*; butternut, *Juglans cinerea*; and, on the forest floor, wintergreen, the little, red-berried and evergreen plant of which oil of wintergreen is made, *Gaultheria procumbens,* all of whose parts, when crushed, release a pungent, refreshing fragrance.

For more than two weeks they made their arduous way over the rugged Blue Ridge Mountains, sometimes impeded by snowfall and ice underfoot, but collecting, always collecting—among other things, acorns of a mountain oak Michaux identifies simply as *Chêne glauque,* masses of flame azalea, and a new species of azalea as well, mountain laurel, rhododendron, cucumber trees—on and on, at one point stopping to measure and marvel at a sourwood tree, *Andromeda arborea* (now *Oxydendrum arboreum*), with a circumference of forty-nine inches.

At last, on December 5, the Michauxs turned homeward, laden with their carefully packed harvest, "about 2,500 trees, shrubs, and plants, seven chests in all."[31] One wonders whether, as they made their way homeward, François André was aware that this was his farewell journey to the high mountains of North Carolina, for many a long year, and whether Michaux père was haunted by the thought that this might be his last journey in the American wilderness in company with his son. Perhaps the decision had already been made, before their departure for the mountains, for François André to return to France, or perhaps was made soon after their return to the plantation. At any rate, the decision was obviously a wise one, considering the urgent need for the youth, already nineteen years old, to begin his formal and long-deferred scientific education either to pursue a medical career or to follow in his father's footsteps.

It had now been long evident that Michaux père, after a not uncommon interlude of discouragement with his son's progress during adolescence, had come to appreciate the young man's latent abilities and to recognize the necessity of academic training for his future career. In Paris he would have not only the support of his family but the guidance of the savants of the French scientific community who were his father's friends and teachers. Even had the botanist considered the possibility of sending his son to an American institution for scientific training, the shortage of funds now available to him would have prevented this course. Indeed, in view of the precarious condition of Michaux's finances, the presence of François André in Paris to look after his father's estate might well have seemed a prudent measure, in case of a further decline in the French economic situation, though Michaux could hardly have foreseen how chaotic that situation would soon become.

It seems probable that the departure of Michaux fils was hastened by the injury to his eye, which made the advice and long-term treatment of competent physicians desirable as soon as possible. The precise time of his departure from America is a matter of speculation, but we know that he had arrived in Paris by the spring of 1790, as Abbé Nolin informed the count. "The son of Monsieur Michaux has arrived from Charleston," wrote the Abbé to D'Angiviller. "His father has sent him back to France because of the difficulties he is experiencing in that country.[32] He wishes to have the honor of visiting you, and paying his respects to you. If I am informed of your wishes in this matter, I will have the honor of presenting him to you on one of your journeys to Paris or to Versailles."[33]

Possibly the youth embarked on February 5, 1790, from Charleston on a ship bound for Le Havre which carried, we are told, a shipment containing the harvest of the journeys he had made with his father during the last months in America: "fourteen chests, four containing trees, the fifth, sixth, and seventh, seeds, the eighth trees for the Jardin du Roi in Paris; in addition, six chests of acorns of different species of oaks";[34] or possibly it was a few weeks later that he sailed with two more chests of trees and a cage with two little deer, on a ship that left Charleston on February 23, bound for the little port of St.-Valéry-sur-Somme.[35]

Whatever the date or the port or the ship, one can imagine the mingled emotions of sorrow and hope with which the botanist bade farewell to the son who had been his almost constant companion during four and a half arduous years in a foreign land. Ahead for the youth lay

a long, perhaps perilous sea voyage with unforeseeable struggles awaiting him in his native France—for the father, a long period of anxiety
before he could hope to receive from France a reassuring letter from his
son. Letters were often nine months in transit across the Atlantic and
many did not arrive at all. To add to his anxiety about his son, Michaux
had the daily and pressing problem of obtaining money, as he wrote to
the count: "Mr. Petry charges me to inform you that he can no longer
endorse letters of exchange. [La Forest] made the same difficulty when
I was in New York, and, since then, these Messieurs have told me to
cease from traveling."[36] No doubt this dictum seemed to "these Messieurs" a reasonable and even necessary measure under the circumstances, but it threatened to frustrate Michaux's hopes of further exploration and discovery while he awaited with apprehension the count's
response, which could hardly be expected for many months. Meanwhile, he curtailed the operating expenses of the plantation as much as
possible, except for the cost of shipments, and he warned Saunier to do
the same in New Jersey, threatening, otherwise, to turn that garden
over to the French consul in New York.[37]

Unable to travel far afield for his collections, the resourceful
botanist obtained from sea captains engaged in the China trade seeds of
Asian trees which he planted in the garden to naturalize for the enrichment of this country and of his own. He had become a member of the
Charleston Agricultural Society, with whose members he shared the
results of some of his researches and plant experimentations, notably
his study of the proper preparation of the ginseng plant. He had
gathered large quantities of the ginseng on several of his mountain
expeditions and had learned how to treat it so as to preserve the
qualities that made the plant so valued in China.[38] And, moreover,
throughout 1790 he continued to make short collecting journeys in the
vicinity, and, once at least, into Georgia, probably in late summer, for he
wrote to the count in the autumn announcing a shipment of "a great
many new plants from Georgia, recognized there three years ago,
which the end of the war with the Indians has made it possible for me to
send you."[39]

The old year went out in a heavy snowstorm, laying down six
inches of snow in the city and eight in the country, covering the ground
for days. Despite that winter storm, on New Years Day 1791 a com-
patriot, Godart, chancellor of the Consulat in Charleston, rode out to
the plantation to spend three days with the botanist, bringing the latest
news from the city and abroad. But it was not until January 17 that
Michaux received the first anxiously awaited letter from his son.[40]

Neither this letter, dated the previous April, nor any subsequent letter from François André to his father has survived, so far as we have been able to determine, but one may assume that the youth gave his father, in addition to family news, his impressions of the political, social, and financial situation in the French capital. He had arrived in Paris after the turbulent events of 1789 were over; the April riots, the July storming of the Bastille, the riotous march of the Parisian mob to Versailles, in October, to forcibly escort their reluctant sovereign and his family to Paris. Two years of comparative quiet had followed, the lull before the storm, while the Assembly, in session in Paris, made serious efforts to draft a constitution and to consolidate the liberal reforms already initiated, the abolition of feudal rights and privileges, and the declaration of the rights of man.

During his five years in America, André Michaux had learned for himself the value of liberty and equality. He had been present in this country during the formation of the American republic, the election and inauguration of the first president, the meeting of the first Congress, and the ratification of the Constitution and the Bill of Rights, all peacefully accomplished by a free people. There now seemed to him reason to believe that his own country was moving in the direction, if not of a republic, of a society of liberty and equality under a constitutional monarchy.

Though by the end of 1790 sufficient economic improvement had been made in France to relieve the worst distress among the poor, the financial state of the government remained too unstable for the restoration of normal credit in foreign commerce. In this situation Michaux badly needed assistance and instructions from the count, from whom he had not heard for over two years. In a final attempt to learn his patron's wishes, the botanist wrote to his son in December 1790, asking him to deliver in person his request to D'Angiviller and to ascertain his orders, if possible, and at the beginning of the New Year he wrote to inform Abbé Nolin that he would be forced to return to France unless he could obtain money.[41] He spent most of the next three months preparing for such an eventuality. Always a meticulous manager, he now set about putting all his affairs in perfect order and overseeing the repairs of all buildings as well as the fences, which had constantly to be maintained to enclose the cows, goats, horses, and whatever wild animals might be in temporary residence awaiting shipment overseas.[42] His most time-consuming task was the organization of all his plants and trees, according to a systematic arrangement, some grouped by geographic provenance, some by botanical classification. Day after day he worked to bring his herbarium up to date and to complete his descriptions of new plants, in preparation for his projected *Flora Boreali-Americana.*

Spring came early in the year 1791. The scarlet peach of Persia and the Chickasaw plum blossomed in the garden in February.[43] He had retained his interest and his special skill in grafting, which he now applied to grafting buds from his Persian peach trees, probably trees grown from seeds brought by him from Persia, on the common peach of Carolina, the variety brought into this country by the early Spaniards and widely naturalized over the eastern states. He grafted also several species of viburnum, particularly *Viburnum cassinoides.*

A pleasant interruption in his busy schedule was afforded by a visit from Moses Bartram, the sailor brother of his friends William and John Bartram, Jr. Moses brought Michaux "a package of valuable seeds from China," sent by his brother John but perhaps brought back from Asia by Moses himself from one of his long sea voyages.[44] Another, less congenial visitor to the plantation was the Scottish botanist John Fraser, who had returned once more to America. "It seems that the good reception given him in France has made him more courteous," commented Michaux wryly. "He was very well received in France. He asked me to tell him about the new plants I had discovered and he wanted me to share them with him but, aware that his intention is to sell them, I gave him nothing and contented myself with receiving him as courteously as possible.[45]

Meanwhile in Paris, François André had received his father's request, dated the previous December and, after several attempts to see the count in Paris and in Versailles, he had resorted to a letter to convey his father's message to D'Angiviller. "He asks me to tell you that he is practicing the greatest economy in all his operations," wrote the youth, "and curtailing his journeys, and he estimates that the nurseries of New York and Charleston can be maintained thus for the sum of eight or ten thousand francs."[46] His father was most anxious to learn the count's wishes, which François André offered to convey "if you deem it appropriate," by way of a ship then at Bordeaux, destined for Charleston; at Bordeaux he had a correspondent who would entrust his letters to the captain of that ship. The son had proved to be a faithful emissary, but the count had already written fully to Michaux père the previous December, a letter that only reached the botanist in mid-April 1791, a letter that, we can infer from Michaux's reply, reflected the count's full recognition of the gravity of the political situation of the monarchy in

France, and his deep personal concern for the welfare of the royal botanist in America. With these considerations in mind he proposed the termination of the botanist's mission in the United States and the sale of the gardens, as soon as practical.

Michaux's reply was prompt and decisive. "I am, Monsieur le Comte, preparing for my return. As arrangements are already made with the laborers and expenditures have been contracted, the service of the department will continue, necessarily, until the end of the year. At that time when the season is favorable I will send you a selection of all the rarest trees, plants, and seeds in my collection."[47] He feared it would be difficult to sell the New Jersey establishment for a profit, because Saunier had not carried out his instructions for improvements, had persistently cultivated the garden for his personal advantage, and refused to recognize the authority of Michaux, 400 leagues away in Carolina. The garden in Charleston, on the other hand, could be sold advantageously at any time and for a large profit.

He hoped to send some wild turkeys before the end of the year, at which time he would dismiss his laborers and send home to France a full financial statement. "I will consider my mission finished."

Though he allowed himself to express genuine regret at having to leave to Americans the collection of new and interesting plants and trees in the garden which "they do not know how to appreciate here," he was swift to reject the suggestion made by the count that Michaux himself should remain permanently in America, as indeed Saunier was to do. Michaux, no less than the proverbial Scot, had a wandering foot but a home-loving heart, and his loyalty to his native land, for whom his mission was undertaken, was unswerving. He longed only to extend his botanical research and collection worldwide—for France. "Your Kindness, Monsieur le Comte," he wrote, "in consulting my wishes, encourages me to reveal to you that I would have the greatest aversion to settling myself in America, and that I desire to return to Persia."[48] But he resisted any quick termination of his mission. The middle or the end of the year 1792 seemed to him a likely date for his return to France. He had still to finish the descriptions of all the new plants he had discovered and to complete his herbarium before leaving America. Then there was a little business affair, a sum of money owed to him in Boston to be collected, payment for an investment he had made in a shipment of guns to the American "insurgents," as he called the patriots supporting the American Revolution.

With this decisive exchange of letters with his noble patron completed, a plan of action set up for the remainder of his mission and home in sight, the botanist resolved to permit himself another, more limited botanizing journey to the Georgia coast and Cumberland Island, a journey that lasted five weeks, from mid-April until late May.[49]

The most exciting discovery of this expedition was that of the very rare *Pinckneya pubens,* first found by the Bartrams in 1765 on the shores of the Altamaha River and first described and named by André Michaux. The *Pinckneya* is a striking monotypic genus, with *pubens* its only species, and is only found in southeastern United States. Many years later his son recalled: "My father found it for the first time in 1791 on the banks of the St. Mary. He carried seeds and young plants to Charleston and planted them in a garden he possessed there. Though entrusted to an ungrateful sod, they succeeded so well that in 1807 I found several of them 25 feet high and 7 or 8 inches in diameter."[50]

A member of the madder family Rubiaceae, and a relative of Cinchona from which quinine is derived, the *Pinckneya,* commonly known as the fever tree, was used by the inhabitants as a cure for fever. Sent to France by André Michaux, it was successfully cultivated in the gardens of Cels and in the Jardin du Roi. Michaux named the plant for his friend Charles Cotesworth Pinckney as a mark of gratitude and respect for this American statesman, "from whom," said Michaux fils, "my father and myself, during our residence in Charleston received multiplied proofs of benevolence and esteem."[51]

For the next ten months, after Michaux returned to Charleston on May 22, 1791, there are no entries in the journal, nor have any letters to or from the botanist, covering this period, come to light. During that period events in France were moving inexorably toward a climax. On June 20, 1791, Louis XVI and the royal family made an ill-advised and desperate attempt to escape from Paris to the frontier. Recaptured at Varennes and ignominiously brought back to the city, they remained nominally free but were virtually prisoners in an atmosphere of mounting hostility.

An immediate consequence of the king's humiliation was the exodus from France of many noblemen close to the throne. Among those who succeeded in escaping was the comte D'Angiviller, Michaux's friend and the director of his American mission, and Monsieur, brother of the king, thus removing from France Michaux's two strongest links with the royal regime. After fleeing from France, Monsieur, le comte de Provence, lived in exile in a succession of European countries, until his return to France after the fall of Napoleon to occupy the throne as

Louis XVIII. D'Angiviller found refuge in Russia under the protection of the empress, Catherine II. In later years he retreated to a Catholic convent in Germany, where he died in 1809, revered for the nobility and generosity of his mind.

CHAPTER **10**

ᵉᔆ The North Woods to Hudson Bay, 1792

FACED WITH THE CONFUSION of the times and, with only uncertain and belated news from France, André Michaux feared he might be recalled before he had an opportunity to complete his *Flora Boreali-Americana* or to complete the basic research necessary for a project he had long had in mind, a botanical geography of eastern America, significant to botanical science, which would necessitate another expedition to determine the regions where each species of the various forest trees of eastern America grows in the greatest number and to the largest size, and at what latitude each species disappears entirely. He had made such observations southward into Florida. He still wished to carry his research in botanical topography northward into Canada. His decision to go home at the end of the year seemed to have been abandoned in the intensity of his ambition to continue his botanical researches.

Before he had completed his preparations for this extensive and formidable expedition, Michaux received orders from the comptroller of lists in France to sell the Charleston establishment.[1] Though he had more than once mentioned to the count the eventual sale of the plantation, the botanist was by no means ready to dispense with his home and the garden, which contained the carefully nurtured trees and plants laboriously gathered on many arduous journeys through the years and which he still thought necessary as a depository for future collections.

Despite those reservations, in compliance with instructions, "the Carolina plantation was sold, on March 27, 1792, at public auction, for the price of 53 guineas or 247 dollars." The purchaser was Jean Jacques

Himely, Michaux's Charleston merchant friend[2] who, probably in accordance with a previous agreement, ceded the property back to Michaux some months later: "Desiring to preserve this depository of a great number of previously unknown plants," explained Michaux, "precious by virtue of the incredible dangers and fatigues of their acquisition, I, myself, became the proprietor of this establishment by the retrocession which the purchaser made of it to me."[3]

Moreover, in spite of orders from France to curtail his traveling, Michaux was now obviously resolved to continue his botanical research in North America and his service to natural history. "In order to continue my researches in natural history," he recorded, "I sold three of the blacks, acquired with my own money, in order to pay the expenses of a journey to Canada."[4]

His first stop on this northern journey was Philadelphia, where he arrived by packet boat from Charleston on April 25, 1792. Since his last visit to the city nearly three years before, Philadelphia had lost its bright luminary, with the death of Benjamin Franklin in April 1790.[5] In December of the same year it had become the nation's capital.[6] Unquestionably at this time the political and cultural center of the country, it was soon to become as well the city of refuge for hundreds of exiles from Revolutionary France.

Even a partial list of the persons visited by Michaux during his month in Philadelphia suggests the scope of his interests and associations at this time. The minister from France to the United States, Ternan, had priority, followed by the French consul, La Forest, with whom the botanist concluded the account with which the consul had been entrusted for advances to the New Jersey gardener, Saunier. As the consul was still unwilling or unable to accept French bills of exchange, Michaux was forced as a last resort to draw upon his personal patrimony through the managers of his estate in France.

Happily, Michaux was as usual able to find a welcome respite from financial worries a few miles from the city, at the Bartram garden on the Schuylkill, in the congenial company of the Bartram brothers, John, Jr., and William, whose *Travels* had at last been published,[7] and across the river at Woodlands, where William Hamilton often had some new and rare plants on display. Perhaps it was Hamilton or the Bartrams who recommended that the French botanist visit Dr. Barton, a brilliant young physician and naturalist, whom Michaux called on at this time.[8] Nor did he neglect to visit, as well, southern friends whom diplomatic and political appointments had brought to the capital. Among them were Ralph Izard,[9] prominent Revolutionary patriot and diplomat who had left his beautiful estate near Charleston, The Elms, to serve in the Senate, and Maj. Thomas Pinckney,[10] Charleston attorney and former governor of South Carolina, in Philadelphia that spring on the eve of his departure to London to take up his post as minister to the Court of St. James's.

Probably the most absorbing and interesting of Michaux's encounters during this month was his visit, on May 4, with the French botanist Palisot de Beauvois. Though Baron de Beauvois was in Philadelphia on a commission for the colonial government of Haiti, he was, like Michaux, a dedicated naturalist who had also pursued his green mistress into distant lands, traveling from his native France in 1786 to Owara, West Africa, on the Gulf of Guinea, where after six months he became so ill with fever he was sent on a slave ship to recuperate in Haiti, leaving behind his extensive African collections which were burned by the British in a raid on Owara in 1791.[11] Perhaps Beauvois, who was soon to journey over much of the United States already explored by Michaux, used this occasion to question the latter about the American wilderness, and perhaps these two adventurous French naturalists exchanged tales of their scientific discoveries in far away Persia and Africa.

Certainly Persia seems to have been the chief topic of conversation during Michaux's visit to Dr. Benjamin Rush,[12] a prominent Philadelphia physician, who has left a description of their afternoon together, worth quoting in full as one of the very few first-hand reports of a Michaux conversation:

> *May 1st, Thursday.*[13] *This day Mr. Mecheaux a French botanist on a tour through the American woods, drank tea with me. He was recommended to me from Charleston by Mr. Bushe and Dr. Baron. He had spent 14 months in Persia. He says he found the* Triticum spelta, *the* Lucerne, *and clover wild in that country, also many fruits, but the peach never. He spoke highly of the fruits of that country, that they were very saccharine and nourishing. He said that he once ate 120 nectarines for a breakfast, without being cloyed by them; that fruits composed the breakfast of rich and poor in Persia, rice and a small quantity of meat the dinner and supper. That the musk melons were preserved from September til May upon high and dry shelves, and always retained a good deal of their flavor. This he ascribed to their being raised in a loose, sandy, and dry soil, and to the great quantity of saccharine matter in them. That water was scarce in Persia and brought 60 leagues in some cases to supply their towns and*

gardens by means of aquaducts. That he once eat a grape in Per-
sia that had neither seeds nor stones. That he brought the seed of
a plumb tree from Persia to Charleston which flourished there, al-
though no European plumb had been known to thrive there. He
said that the seeds of all plants declined the first, but thrived the
second year after being transplanted. That the venereal disease
was universal and incurable in Persia. That he once had a
pleurisy in Persia from drinking sour milk when he was very
warm. He said that Chardin had published the best account of
Persia. [14] *The fig and the grape, he said, never rotted or became*
sour on the tree or after they fell but dried, became candied, and
still retained their sweetness. [15]

Not until the last week in May did Michaux leave Philadelphia to
begin his long journey northward to the Canadian wilderness. After a
visit to the New Jersey establishment and a few days of botanizing in the
verdant environs of New York, fragrant with the flowers of late spring,
he traveled on to New Haven and, on June 4, to Milford, Connecticut,
to consult Peter Pond, a former soldier, veteran explorer, and fur
trader, who had spent nearly twenty years in the Canadian wilderness.[16] Pond had penetrated into the Canadian northwest as far as
Great Slave Lake and had established a trading post on Lake Athabasca,
being the first white man to explore this region and make contact with
the Athabascan Indians. He had made a map in 1785 based on his
explorations, copies of which he presented to the Canadian government, the Congress of the United States, and the empress of Russia.
Copies were made also for the archives of Great Britain and France.
Possessed by the dream of finding the long-sought Northwest Passage
to the Pacific, he died without obtaining support for the attempt, but
not without having inspired others with his vision, of whom André
Michaux was probably one; for it seems reasonable to assume that, on
the occasion of this visit to the old explorer, he received both inspiration
and encouragement for his own western dream.

Of more immediate relevance was Pond's warning that he had no
time to lose if he wished to carry out his plans to explore Canada as far
as Hudson Bay. Already, Pond told him, he was too late to join the
Canadian fur traders, accustomed by long tradition to leave Montreal
for the interior no later than the end of April each year. Hurriedly,
Michaux returned to New York, traveling all night in his haste. Embarking for Albany, on the evening of June 8, on the Hudson—Henry

Hudson's "Great River of the Mountains"—he sailed beneath the frowning palisades and beside the forested hills and valleys of the picturesque Catskills through what must surely have been, two hundred years ago, one of the most beautiful landscapes of a continent replete with natural beauty.

From this point on Michaux journeyed in country new to him, as far as we know, and he eagerly noted along the way at every opportunity both familiar and unknown species. From Albany he set out immediately for Quebec, traveling by boat, carriage, and canoe in turn as required by the route via Lake Champlain, the Richelieu River, and Montreal.[17]

Though pressed for time in order to avoid being trapped in the Hudson Bay region by the implacable Arctic winter, the botanist neglected no opportunity en route for thorough research of the terrain, not only to discover new plants but to note the continual appearance or the disappearance of familiar species or changes in size and numbers of various plants, and the like—data all pertinent to topographical botany. During the Lake Champlain voyage alone the journal lists well over 150 species observed, among others the firs, spruce, balsam, arborvitae, paper birch, white and red elms, lindens, ash—names evoking the magnificent hardwood and coniferous forests of New England. He remarked as well "wild flowers" such as *Impatiens,* the fascinating jewelweed with its explosive seed pods, violets, ginseng, anemones, hepaticas, and myriads more.

At Montreal, strategically situated where the Ottawa and St. Lawrence rivers meet, Michaux remained for ten days visiting and dining with various persons to whom he bore letters of introduction, among them a Captain Hughes Scott, an officer with the English regiment garrisoned in Montreal, who was an amateur mineralogist, but he spent most of his time botanizing on the mountains and in the valleys around the city where he found, among other plants new to him, a new species of *Oxalis* and a new azalea.

Sailing down the St. Lawrence from Montreal past Trois Rivières and Cap de la Madaleine, he arrived on July 16 at the walled city of Quebec, founded by Samuel de Champlain in 1608 on the massive gray rock pile of Cape Diamond. In the romantic old city which, in 1792, still retained its French ambience and language in spite of thirty years of British rule, Michaux spent two busy weeks preparing for the challenging journey to Lake Mistassini and beyond, taking time out to call on Governor Clarke and to explore the environs where he noted balsam, arborvitae, larch, paper birch, and, of particular interest here, *Sarracenia purpurea*, named for Dr. M. Sarrasin, royal physician in Canada, who first introduced this curious pitcher plant into Europe.

On the last day of July he again embarked on the great river, accompanied by a young man named Metis, who had lived for three years among the Indians and whom he had engaged as an interpreter. Sailing northeast down the St. Lawrence to the mouth of the Saguenay River, they arrived, on Sunday, August 5, at Tadoussac, fifty miles from Quebec, the oldest fur-trading post in North America, but still a miserable little village huddled on the river's shore beneath the shadow of the mountains. There he bought two canoes and engaged three Indians to man them and to serve as guides into the wilderness. These canoes, which weighed only fifty pounds but could each hold four men and their luggage, were made by the Indians of the bark of the paper birch tree, *Betula papyrifera*, and were a striking example of the ingenuity and skill with which the "children of the forests" adapted its products to their uses. In the spring they selected the largest and strongest birch trees, in whose bark they made incisions at measured intervals, so that, with the rising of the sap, the bark could be easily removed. Using an awl, they sewed the pieces of bark together with fibers of the roots of the white fir tree, *Abies balsamea*, boiled to remove the rind, sealing over the seams with its resin. Ribs made of thin strips of the wood of the white cedar, *Cupressus* (now *Chamaecyparis*) *thyoides*, completed the construction of the light, swift, durable river craft, ideally suited to navigate the rivers of the wilderness.[18]

On the morning of August 7, Michaux, Metis, and the three Indian guides embarked at Tadoussac to ascend the Saguenay River. Reputedly one of the largest of the rivers that hurl themselves into the St. Lawrence,[19] the Saguenay presented a formidable challenge, flowing between frowning walls of high precipitous mountains composed of sheer rock. Though there was no soil at all on these mountains, pines clung to the rocky cliffs, obtaining their only nourishment from the detritus of mosses covering the rocky face. For the first few days heavy rains and thunder increased the somber gloom of their passage but on the tenth, as they neared Chicoutimi,[20] violent north winds dispersed the clouds and they observed on the mountainous shores, now covered with sphagnum moss, various plants, among them Ledum, Labrador tea (called by him *Ledum palustre*); sheep laurel, *Kalmia angustifolia*; cranberry, *Vaccinium oxycoccos*; the round-leafed sundew, *Drosera rotundifolia*; and on the shores of the river the spurred gentian, *Halenia deflexa* (called by Michaux *Swertia corniculata*).

Chicoutimi, an Indian village and trading post, was situated on
the Saguenay where the tide from the sea ceases to ascend the river.
Here where their route forsook the Saguenay to ascend the Chicoutimi
River to Lake St. John, they provisioned the two canoes for the long
wilderness journey ahead: 300 pounds of flour, 155 of salted pork, 2
skins of "Loup marins" for shoes, 100 pounds of biscuits, 50 of bread,
10 of salt, 5 of powder for shooting, 10 of shot, 3 rolls of birch bark for
tent, 3 rifles, a supply of heavy wool cloth, 3 pairs of wool stockings, and
2 pairs of wool gloves were added to the supplies purchased at Tadoussac, including 26 pounds of salted pork, 50 of bread, blankets,
shoes, flints, tinder boxes, a large loin of beef, and a ham.[21]

Fortunately, they were able to engage the assistance of six Indians
and seven squaws for a portage, on August 13, of canoes, baggage, and
provisions to the place more than a league away where it was possible to
enter the Chicoutimi above the series of cascades by which it effects its
tumultuous descent into the Saguenay. The continual necessity for
such portages was to be one of the most exhausting aspects of their
arduous voyage in the weeks ahead:

> *This day we have had four other portages, most of about*
> *200 to 500 fathoms, in order to go overland from below the*
> *rapids to above them. Often, when the canoes arrive at the bottom*
> *of the waterfalls they are swept along by the violence of the waters*
> *which are always in these places hemmed in by enormous rocks.*
> *One must, in turn, either paddle forcefully or resist the current by*
> *prodding the bottom, though sometimes one provides oneself with*
> *poles to struggle against the water.*
>
> *In spite of the lightness of the canoes the Indians have to*
> *use all their strength and they are very skillful in evading the*
> *danger of being swept or crushed against the rocks or even over-*
> *turned, which sometimes happens. There is rarely any danger of*
> *perishing if one knows how to swim, because, if one allows oneself*
> *to go with the current, one is at once carried into a place where*
> *the water is calm and often less than two feet deep. Then one*
> *must try to save what one can, canoes, baggage, and provisions.*
> *These voyages are terrifying for anyone not accustomed to them,*
> *and I would advise the fops of London or Paris, if there are still*
> *any there, to remain at home.*[22]

During four days of continual rain and mist, during which, on
four occasions, they were forced to carry the canoes and their loads up
the precipitous slopes beside the river's rapids, they navigated at times

through mountainous terrain, where grew the common juniper, *Juniperus communis*; striped maple, *Acer pennsylvanicum*; cinquefoil, *Potentilla nivea*; and firs—and at times by river borders of marshy meadowlands filled with meadow fern, *Myrica gale*; bog rosemary, *Andromeda phylla*; winterberry, *Prinos verticillata*; and closed gentians, *Gentiana linearis*.

On August 17 the canoes entered Lake St. John and after a day and a half of navigation on this great body of water, so extensive it resembles a sea but so shallow the canoes often touched bottom, they reached the last trading post in these wild regions, a shop run by two Canadian commissioners, the Panet brothers, for the purpose of trade with the Indians of the Lake of the Swans and Lake Mistassini. Delayed by thick fogs and violent winds, they remained at the post for two days, an opportunity for Michaux to botanize in the environs, where he observed birches, *Betula pumila,* along the shores and yellow water lilies of several species in the lake. They resumed their navigation of the lake on the twenty-first and after five hours entered the mouth of the Mistassini River, which is very shallow where it enters the lake and for many leagues beyond, as it flows through elongated hills of unstable sand dunes.[23] The botanist observed that the arborvitae ceased at Lake St. John and were not seen again at all along the river, where he noted fir balsam, *Abies balsamea*; larch, *Pinus larix*; and balsam poplars, *Populus balsamifera*; as well as Labrador tea, *Ledum palustre*.

The river, which had been three to four miles wide, narrowed as they continued their ascent, and great, jagged rock impeded their progress through the mountainous terrain, necessitating nine portages before they came upon the magnificent spectacle of "the Great Cascade of the Mistassini," which Michaux had heard wonderful reports of. "Although one generally regards cascades as impressive natural phenomena, one would find it hard to conceive the majestic prospect of this one."[24]

> The river, divided into various branches, is in breadth about 200 fathoms and is precipitated from a mountain about 250 fathoms in height. This mountain has the form of an amphitheatre, on the steps of which trees are seen through the arch of water formed by the fall over their lofty heads. The torrent rushes down the steep wtih an awful sound, and breaking into myriads of particles, while the vapours rise like a cloud, wetting all the neighborhood to a great distance. The torrent, repelled in its fall by the opposite banks, forms wells, which, between two rapid currents covered with foam, leaves spaces in which the water is tranquil and navi-

gable through the windings of which the Indians dexterously guide their canoes.

One must go between the arms of the waterfall to make the portage and place the baggage and the provisions on the rock above the surface of the water. The danger is that the rocks beneath the water are usually covered with a kind of slippery aquatic moss preventing a firm foothold. My guide, wishing to leap from one rock to another only an inch under water, fell with his burden, consisting of a 50 pound sack of flour and the bag containing his own clothing.[25]

Next day in calmer waters Michaux found, on the shores of the Mistassini River, gentians; trailing arbutus, those lovely denizens of the forest known in Quebec as the fleur de mai; twinflowers, *Linnaea borealis*; wintergreen, *Gaultheria*; two species of trillium; meadowsweet, *Spiraea salicifolia*; and asters; as well as bog laurel, *Kalmia polifolia*; sheep laurel, *Kalmia angustifolia*; white pines; larches; birches; and elms. Here he noted that the larches grew to "a beautiful height" although all other kinds of trees had diminished in size.

On Sunday the twenty-sixth, exhausted from several days of poling the canoes forward against the opposing current, a struggle rendered more difficult by the resistance of violent winds from the north, the travelers found a brief but welcome respite at an Indian cabin on the shore where they feasted on boiled beaver meat, blueberry jam, and fresh blueberries. Michaux found "this very agreeable fruit of which a great quantity never disagrees with one" growing so abundantly on the burned-over portions of the mountain ranges north of Quebec that one could take one's fill of them in a quarter of an hour.[26]

On August 28 they left the Mistassini River, now a narrow current flowing swiftly between steep, rocky walls, in order to portage over the mountains to the rivers of a new watershed, en route to the region of the Lake of the Swans that appeared to Michaux to bear "a most frightful aspect" of low, sterile lands covered only with very small stunted trees. The cold was harsh and unrelenting. In this depressing situation they were forced to remain an extra day in order to dry out the collections of seeds and plants as well as the herbarium, which had been immersed in water when one of the Indians slipped with his burden as they emerged from the lake.[27]

Advancing steadily northwest, they soon found themselves in a watery world of many low mountains and hills connected with each other by streams between the hills, whose valleys were filled with innumerable lakes "for the most part nameless, even for the Indians who frequently hunt there."[28] But there were also long intervals of extensive marshes through which they were forced to portage, sinking up to their knees in the boggy substance always steeped in water, even in the driest weather. Disagreeable as these marshes were, they were not without interest for the botanist, abounding as they did in *Kalmia glauca* (probably *K. polifolia*); bog rosemary he called *Andromeda rosmarinfolia* (now *A. glaucophylla*); *Sarracenia purpurea*; and cranberry, *Vaccinium oxycoccos*; and in the less humid places, Labrador tea; sheep laurel; trailing arbutus; and some species of pine. Occurrence of the balsam firs ceased at the Lake of the Swans except for a few in bush form, and, indeed, all the vegetation gave "the impression of decrepit pygmies" because of the sterility of the soil and the harshness of the cold. On the last day of August the bitter cold intensified as rain "like melted snow" began to fall. Drenched with icy water from the rain and from the sodden marshes they were forced to wade through, they found themselves too chilled even to eat. The Indians shivered and trembled continually and one of them fell sick, while Michaux himself, even in his warmer clothing, could hardly withstand the penetrating chill. They decided to call a halt, build a fire, and remain until dry and warm again.

Although more rain accompanied by thunder and lightning ushered in the new month, they resumed their journey, the Indians as well as the botanist desperately eager to complete their journey before the Arctic winter closed in. Rain soon turned to snow and sleet. In that bleak and solitary landscape they were startled by a glimpse of a caribou in the distance too far away to be overtaken by the Indians. Two days later they embarked on a northward-flowing river whose favorable current carried them swiftly along to enter Lake Mistassini on the morning of September 4. Navigating for ten or twelve leagues on the lake, they camped on the left bank to feast on a black-ringed goose the Indians killed, and five fish, a foot and a half to two-feet long, caught in a net. In spite of the bitter cold, Michaux botanized on the wintry shores, noting twenty-six varieties of plants, most of which he had observed during the last ten days of their journey.[29]

Lake Mistassini discharges its waters toward the north and north-west by various rivers that flow into Hudson Bay—a four-day voyage from the lake by river, but requiring at least ten days for the return journey. Still hoping to reach the bay, in spite of ominous signs of deepening winter, they chose Rupert River, which flows into Hudson Bay at Fort Rupert, and followed its course for two days. They were no great distance from the bay when the Indians, fearful that the snows would cut off their retreat, insisted on turning back.[30]

Though disappointed in not reaching Henry Hudson's "Great Bay," Michaux had, in fact, accomplished his purpose.

He had ascertained the position of the regions and determined which were the points most elevated and what were the communications between the different lakes and Hudson's Bay. He had exactly marked at what latitude the trees ceased to grow. In these vast solitudes none but a dreary vegetation was found, consisting of black and stunted pines, which bore their cones at four feet from the ground, dwarf birch, and service trees, a creeping juniper; the black currant; the twinflower (Linnaea borealis); Ledum, *a small rhododendron known as Labrador-tea, and some species of* Vaccinium; *all the fine trees which grow in the neighborhood of Quebec had disappeared.*[31]

The return journey from Lake Mistassini to Quebec occupied about three weeks. Homeward bound and moving with the current the Indians drove the canoes along with incredible speed and dexterity, often able to negotiate the descent of the rapids without portage. Nevertheless, as he had planned, Michaux found the time necessary on the return journey to collect the trees and plants already noted in each region, and methodically record the locality where each first made its appearance. He listed the quadrupeds also, skinning those which he or the Indians were able to kill, and he employed the Indians to gather quantities of seeds and wrap the plants and trees in moss. At the end of September the travelers arrived back at Tadoussac, where the botanist bade farewell to the companions of his journey who had served him faithfully, zealously, and with the most complete honesty and courage through all the hardships and hazards of the voyage.[32]

At the same time that Michaux was still in the little riverside village of Tadoussac, events of enormous import were taking place far away in his native France, materially altering his situation and prospects. The French National Convention, meeting in Paris in September 1792 formally abolished the centuries-old monarchy and officially proclaimed the republic of France, "one and indivisible."[33]

The impact of this tremendous news, which probably reached the ears of the botanist before he arrived in Philadelphia, must have been electrifying for him. Though he made no direct comment in the journal, it had long been obvious that seven years in the vigorous young American republic, exploring its fields and forests, mountains and shores, associating in a free society with political leaders and scientists, as well as planters, farmers, pioneers, and adventurers on the trail, had converted the loyal emissary of Louis XVI into an ardent republican.

The return journey from Tadoussac was relatively uneventful, and the triumphant naturalist found himself once more in Philadelphia, on December 8, after an absence from his Carolina plantation of almost eight months, three months of that time employed in the successful exploration of the Canadian wilderness from Quebec to the region of Hudson Bay. He had, as always, in spite of the hardships and dangers of the trail, drawn new strength from the solitude and beauty of virgin lands and the challenge of the wilderness. "My health has been completely restored," he asserted on the return journey.[34] With renewed confidence in his own powers he looked forward with undiminished ardor to further expeditions. Thus it was a bitter blow to learn, when he reached Philadelphia, "by letters dated at Paris last August that the report made to the legislative Assembly in the preceding January had not been placed on the agenda." In consequence, he foresaw his whole career in jeopardy. "Uncertain of being continued in the service of the republic and unable to get my drafts on my back salary accepted, I found myself more than ever destitute of means and threatened with losing my time."[35] "Loss of time" was an unacceptable sacrifice, a waste of a precious resource to a naturalist whose dedication to his chosen science was as intense as a religious vocation. Always he seemed driven to use every waking moment, every ounce of strength, in the service of his mission, aware of how much of the green kingdom of the world, as yet unexplored, awaited him.

CHAPTER 11

∽§ All Eyes on the West, 1793

HE NOW MET this new challenge with characteristic resilience, as he explained: "To remedy these difficulties, I communicated to several members of the Philosophical Society of Philadelphia my observations on the usefulness of a journey to the sources of the Missouri for geographical knowledge."[1] He was prepared, he told them, to explore

State House Square, Philadelphia, c. 1800. Birch Print, focusing on the State House (Independence Hall) and showing the American Philosophical Society Hall in the background. (Courtesy of the American Philosophical Society)

the regions west of the Mississippi, and even to seek out those rivers which flow into the Pacific Ocean, on the condition that the society endorse his drafts for 3,600 francs.[2]

The American Philosophical Society included in its membership an outstanding segment of the nation's leaders, well qualified to appreciate the potential significance of such a proposal. Many of the members already knew and esteemed the ardent Frenchman, notably George Washington and Thomas Jefferson, with whom he had associated in his official capacity as botanical envoy from the French Court. Michaux had a friend and advocate as well in another member of the society, the indefatigable Dr. Benjamin Rush, whose lively pen gives us one more glimpse of the naturalist shortly after his return to Philadelphia. He had found in him a congenial friend:

Mr. Michaux, a French botanist, drank tea with me. He had just returned from a journey . . . to the north of Quebec in search of plants. He found there many of the plants of similar latitudes in Europe, among others the Labrador Tea. He says that the scattered French people whom he found in that cold country had coarse skins from scorbatic complaints. They lived chiefly on salt meat and seals. . . . The Indians who eat wild fruits plentifully escape the scurvy.[3]

A colleague of Dr. Rush, and a fellow member of the society, Dr. Benjamin Barton, whom Michaux had met a year earlier, interested himself personally in his proposed western journey, as his letter to Thomas Jefferson on January 4, 1793, indicates, a letter valuable for its insight into Michaux's attitudes and intentions at this stage of the project, when he seemed ready to set forth at once:

In consequence of your note, I have waited on Mr. Michaux. He assures me that he will relinquish all thoughts of his journey to South Carolina and that he will engage in his scheme as soon as you think proper. He seems much pleased with the prospect of having so valuable a guide to Kaskaskia as the one you have pointed out, and I will be happy to have the opportunity of conversing with the Indian whenever you shall appoint a time for this purpose.

I have ventured this morning to be very explicit with my friend on the pecuniary head. He seems content to undertake this arduous task (for such it, undoubtedly, is) with a very moderate assistance in the off-set. This assistance he does not even ask for until his arrival at Kaskaskia where, he thinks, it would be [expedient?] that he should have the "power" of drawing for the sum of one hundred guineas. Upon his return, he supposes (provided he shall make discoveries of any interesting importance) he shall be entitled to something handsome. In consequence of some conversation I had with my uncle (Mr. Rittenhouse)[4] last evening, I ventured to tell Mr. Michaux that I did not doubt his expectation would be gratified.[5]

The recipient of this letter, Thomas Jefferson, then secretary of state, was, perhaps, of all the members of the Philosophical Society, the most deeply interested in Michaux's proposal. Probably more than any of his contemporaries he recognized the immense importance to the nation's destiny of the Louisiana Territory and what lay beyond. No doubt he was familiar with Peter Pond's 1785 map of his travels in the west and aware of Pond's representation to Congress. When he was in Paris serving as American minister to France in 1786, Jefferson had befriended the ill-fated adventurer John Ledyard, obsessed with his dream of establishing a thriving American fur trade on the northwest coast of America and finding an overland route across the continent in the latitude of Missouri.[6] After the failure of Ledyard's attempts, Jefferson's interest in the search for a transcontinental route persisted. Moreover, it was an interest shared to some degree by most of his colleagues. Indeed, throughout the land one could sense the stirring of a continental consciousness as migrations over the mountains increased from year to year, stimulating a nationwide curiosity in the mysterious wilderness beyond. That the time was ripe for such an undertaking as Michaux proposed seemed evident in the swift and favorable response from the members of the Philosophical Society. By a fortunate chance the original document of their response has recently come to light at the American Philosophical Society, a document of extraordinary historical interest, which merits quotation in full:

> *Whereas Andrew Michaux, a native of France, and inhabitant of the United States, has undertaken to explore the interior country of North America, from the Missisipy along the Missoury, and Westwardly to the Pacific Ocean, or in such other direction as shall be adviced by the American Philosophical Society, and on his return to communicate to the said Society the information he shall have acquired of the geography of the said country, its inhabitants, soil, climate, animals, vegetables, minerals, and other circumstances of note: We the Subscribers, desirous of obtaining for ourselves relative to the land we live in, and of communicating to the World, information so interesting to curiosity, to Science, and to the future prospects of mankind, promise for ourselves, our heirs, executors, and administrators, or his assigns, the sums herein affixed to our names respectively, one fourth thereof on demand, the remaining three fourths whenever, after his return, the said Philosophical Society shall declare themselves satisfied that he has performed the said journey, and that he has communicated to them freely all the information which he shall have acquired, and they demanded of him, or if the said Andrew Michaux shall not proceed to the Pacific Ocean, and shall reach the Sources of the waters running into it then we will pay him such part only of the remaining three fourths as the said Philosophical Society shall deem duly proportioned to the extent of unknown country explored by him in the direction prescribed,*

as compared with that omitted to be explored. And we consent that the bills of exchange of the said Andrew Michaux for monies said to be due to him in France, shall be received to the amount of two hundred Louis, and shall be negotiated by the said Philosophical Society, and the proceeds thereof retained in their hands, to be delivered to the said Andrew Michaux on his return, after having performed the journey to their satisfaction, or, if not to their satisfaction, then to be applied towards reimbursing the Subscribers the fourth of their subscription advanced to the said Andrew Michaux. We consent also that the said Andrew Michaux shall take to himself all the benefits arising from the publication of the discoveries he shall make in the three departments of natural history, animal, vegetable, and mineral, he consenting with the said Philosophical Society such measures for securing to himself the said benefit as shall be consistent with the due publication of the said discoveries. In witness whereof we have hereto subscribed our names and affixed the sums we engage respectively to contribute.[7]

Among the signatures are those of many of the nation's most distinguished citizens, including four presidents, George Washington, John Adams, Thomas Jefferson, and James Madison, as well as the national treasurer, Alexander Hamilton, seven members of the Constitutional Convention, and eminent scholars and scientists in various fields. Subscriptions begin with the maximum one hundred dollars subscribed by President Washington and vary down to a modest eight dollars.

Though this document is not dated, Michaux had apparently been notified, possibly by Thomas Jefferson, of the proposed subscription before January 20, 1793, as he refers to it in the "Statement of Conditions," noted in his journal entry of that date: "My proposition having been accepted, I have given to Mr. Jefferson, secretary of state, the conditions upon which I am prepared to undertake this journey."

This interesting communique from the botanist is divided into six articles, as follows—revealing his self-reliance, integrity, and foresight:

1. In order to be more free to act and to make decisions to which I may be forced by circumstances I prefer to undertake this journey at my own expense. My delicacy does not permit me to accept the proposed sum for an enterprise which it may not prove possible to carry out completely.

2. In order not to delay the journey and to alleviate the dif-

ficulties I now experience in drawing on the Administration, I would regard as a great favor the acceptance of my drafts up to the amount of three thousand six hundred pounds tournoes, on that of seventeen thousand, five hundred and twenty pounds due, for my salary and my advances, by the government. If Mr. Delaforest does not wish to endorse my drafts for the sum of 3,600 pounds, notwithstanding that he has been authorized to do so by the Minister of Marines, and if I am not assured of obtaining this sum before setting out from Philadelphia, I will not undertake this journey.

3. I will be given all the Letters of Recommendation necessary for negotiations with the Illinois, the Indian chieftains, etc.

4. All knowledge, observations, and geographical information will be communicated to the Philosophical Society.

5. Other discoveries in Natural History will be for my own immediate profit, and, afterwards, destined for the public good.

6. I will not undertake this journey until I have set my affairs in Carolina in order, and I request only three days after the reception of the letters I am awaiting from Charleston.

At Philadelphia January 20, 1793. A. Michaux[8]

Following this precise statement by Michaux, in response to the society's acceptance of his proposal and their offer of financial aid, one might expect the naturalist to set out upon his western expedition as soon as preparations could be completed. Instead there is a delay of three months before we find any further mention of the journey.

During this interval Michaux resumed his shipments to France, consisting largely of collections brought back from Canada, not only of seeds and plants but also boxes of insects and skins of birds and quadrupeds. While he awaited the formal confirmation he had requested from the government of France of his official status as botanical envoy from the French Republic,[9] his shipments seem to have been sent care of his scientist friends in Paris, two at least addressed to Louis Bosc, an accomplished and versatile French naturalist who had been a brilliant and dedicated fellow student with Michaux at the Jardin du Roi in Paris.[10]

In March or April, Thomas Jefferson submitted to the botanist a formal statement of "Instructions to Michaux for Exploring the Western Boundary," drawn up by Jefferson on behalf of the directors of the Philosophical Society.[11] "They observe to you," it stated, "that the chief objects of your journey are to find the shortest and most convenient route of communication between the United States and the Pacific Ocean, within the temperate latitudes, and to learn such particulars as can be obtained of the country through which it passes, its productions, inhabitants, and other interesting circumstances."

As the Missouri River was considered the preferred channel of communication and, consequently, a primary field of exploration, the society proposed to procure for the botanist a conveyance to Kaskaskia in the neighborhood of this river, in company with Kaskaskian Indians then in Philadelphia.

It is particularly interesting to note that many passages of this document are similar to the instructions given by Jefferson to Lewis and Clark a decade later on the eve of their great adventure westward. As for instance the following:

> You will in the course of your journey take note of the country you pass through, its general face, soil, rivers, mountains, its productions—animal, vegetable, and mineral—so far as they may be new to us and may also be useful or very curious; the latitudes of places, or material for calculating it, by such simple methods as your situation may admit you to practice, the names, numbers, and dwellings of the inhabitants, and such particulars as you can learn of their history, connection with each other, languages, manners, state of society, and of the arts and commerce among them.

As a veteran wilderness traveler Michaux may well have derived a wry amusement from the following suggestion, a modified version of which Jefferson also made to Lewis and Clark: "The method of preserving your observations is left to yourself, according to the means which shall be in your power. It is only suggested that the noting of them on the skin might be best for such as may be the most important, and that further details may be committed to the bark of paper-birch, a substance which may not excite suspicion among the Indians, and is little liable to injury from wet or other common accidents."

In spite of the courteous language of the Instructions, with expressions of confidence in the botanist's judgment, zeal, and discretion, and concern for his health and safety on the journey, Michaux inferred from the document that he was considered an alien employed only for the advantage of the Philosophical Society.

His response took the form of a characteristically candid and unequivocal statement of his priorities with reference to his obligations to his country, and implies a sober and realistic evaluation on his part of the odds against total success:

*Exposition of the basis on which I have resolved to under-
take the journey to the west of the Mississippi:*

*Bound by all manner of considerations to my country, I owe
to her my services, and the primary objective of my researches on
natural history is to fulfill my obligations in this regard; the second objective is to be useful to America.*

*The friendship which unites France and the United States
had led the old regime to authorize me to share (with the United
States) all the productions of the botanical gardens of Europe
and it is on this principle that I have introduced into Carolina
many trees and plants from Europe, from Asia, and from the
southern isles. Maintained in my mission by the French Republic
on the same plan of Instructions which had formerly been given
to me,[12] I am dedicated by duty and by inclination to the reciprocal benefit of the two nations and I will be happy to fulfill this
purpose to the best of my ability. But in accepting financial help
in advance, I would impose obligations upon myself, and in a
dangerous undertaking I wish to be free of such considerations
and to have no other impetus but the probability of success and
the honor of the achievement. On my return I will esteem as an
honor the merited marks of satisfaction and I shall receive them
with as much pride as gratitude.*

*Thus in order not to give rise to too high hopes I do not en-
gage myself to anything more than to make every effort to fulfill to
the letter the first, fourth, and fifth articles of the memoir remitted
the 20th of last January to Thomas Jefferson, Esquire.*

Philadelphia April 29, 1793 A. Michaux.[13]

*Further observations. It is in every sense of the word in
order not to give rise to too high hopes, and knowing how limited
is my information, that I desire to be free of obligations to fulfill;
but I will devote myself to this without reserve. April 30th.[14]*

These definitive statements by Michaux and his sponsors on the
last day of April sound very much like a parting exchange on the eve of
the botanist's departure for the West. Everything seemed settled, even
to the presence on the scene of the Kaskaskia Indian guides. It is easy to
imagine with what eagerness the horizon-obsessed naturalist looked
forward to this most challenging undertaking of his life. It is equally
easy to imagine with what mixed emotions he must have faced the
sudden alteration of his plans by the arrival on the scene—like a deus ex
machina—of the first diplomatic envoy to the United States from the

young French Republic—Edmond Charles Genet, minister plenipotentiary.[15]

It is difficult to describe Genet's character and actions at the time of his appearance in America without resorting to hyperbole, for he did nothing by halves. Young, handsome, talented, and intellectually precocious, he was in many ways an astonishing personality. By the age of twenty-five he had figured in one capacity or another in the most important courts of Europe. His social graces, linguistic brilliance, and revolutionary sentiments (in spite of his family's long association with the Versailles Court) made him seem an obvious choice for the important American post. As yet unrevealed were his rash impetuosity, arrogance, and fatal lack of judgment.

He had been instructed by the Executive Council of the French Republic to endeavor to strengthen the ties between France and the United States and to prepare a commercial treaty mutually advantageous to both parties. It was hoped by the French government that the people of the United States would form an alliance with their French ally "to encourage the liberation of mankind."

> *Such an alliance energetically supported by the people of France would not only pave the way for the liberation of Spanish America but also open the Mississippi to the inhabitants of Kentucky, deliver our brothers in Louisiana from the tyrannical yoke of Spain and perhaps add the glorious sites of Canada to the American constellation. However vast this project may be, it will be easy to carry out if the Americans wish it, and it is to persuade them that Citizen Genet must direct all his efforts.*[16]

It was assumed by the French Council that the Kentuckians, inflamed for a long time by the Spanish refusal to allow them free navigation of the Mississippi, would be able to support this objective without compromising the American Congress. In consequence, Genet was authorized to maintain agents in Kentucky and Louisiana. Moreover, he was entrusted by his government with blank commissions up to the rank of captain for Indian chieftains engaged in the French cause, and with letters of marque to be delivered to French or American privateers. The council authorized him also "to make whatever expenditures he shall judge appropriate to facilitate the execution of the project, leaving this to his prudence and loyalty." The loyalty of Citizen Genet was indisputable; it was prudence that proved to be lacking.

In view of these instructions from his government, it is not surprising that Genet conceived of his mission as a crusade to free Louisiana and the Floridas from the grip of Spain. The broad outline of his plans seems clear, though certain precise details remain cloudy. An army composed of soldiers and Indian warriors, recruited largely from Kentucky and led by officers chosen from among former Revolutionary leaders, was to attack the Spanish on the upper reaches of the Mississippi while a French fleet simultaneously assaulted New Orleans from the sea, thus insuring the "liberation" of all of Louisiana and Florida and possibly, eventually, even Canada. It was a vision of breathtaking proportions, in tune with the revolutionary and crusading fervor for *Liberté* still burning at fever heat in France.

Consequently, it was with this grandiose plan (like a time bomb ticking away in his diplomatic pouch) that the elegant young French minister appeared on the American scene and at once moved center stage. He had received his instructions as early as December 1792 but had been held in Paris by the Girondin faction, who hoped to save the king and the royal family from execution by sending them, with Genet as escort, into exile in America, where so many of their aristocratic subjects had already taken refuge. After the final defeat of this hope and the death of Louis on the scaffold, Genet left Paris immediately but was delayed for weeks in the port of Rochefort, awaiting favorable winds.

When at length on April 8, after a long and stormy voyage on the French frigate *L'Embuscade*, he reached America, he disembarked not at Philadelphia, as expected, but in Charleston, South Carolina. There he was warmly welcomed by the French consul, Mangouret;[17] and, in spite of the strong pro-British faction in the city, he was enthusiastically received by the governor, the erstwhile General William Moultrie, to whose sympathetic ears the French envoy confided something of his plans for the seizure of Florida.

As France had by this time declared war on both England and Spain, Genet hastened to outfit and arm four privateers in the Charleston port, apparently oblivious to the glaring impropriety of initiating such actions before being officially received, accredited, and given permission for these procedures by the national government of his host country, and apparently totally unaware that, in fact, the arming of French ships in the Charleston harbor could be and would be interpreted as a violation of American neutrality.

Leaving Governor Moultrie and Consul Mangouret to recruit soldiers and forward the plans for the assault on the Floridas, Genet set out, in a mood of self-confidence and optimism, for the overland journey to Philadelphia, traveling in a carriage drawn by four horses, purchased from General Pinckney, via Camden, Salisbury, Richmond, and Baltimore. Everywhere along his route he was feted and dined "by enthusiastic supporters."[18]

Meanwhile, the *Embuscade,* sent on ahead, sailed into the harbor of Philadelphia on May 5, bringing as trophy the British merchant ship the *Grange,* captured by the French ship in Delaware Bay.[19] Thomas Jefferson described the excitement in the city as the vessels came into view: "Thousands and thousands of the yeomanry of the city crowded the wharves. Never before was such a crowd seen there and when they saw the British colors reversed and the French flying above them, they rent the air with exultation."[20]

The welcome given to Genet on his arrival in the capital a few days later was no less heady. "My journey has been a continuous succession of public fetes and my reception at Philadelphia a triumph of liberty," reported the ebullient French envoy to his minister in Paris; "the true Americans are overwhelmed with joy."[21] There was a public reception on May 17 when a select committee, headed by David Rittenhouse, and followed, according to Jefferson, "by a vast concourse" of citizens, marched to the minister's lodgings to present an address of welcome, eloquently responded to by the elated Genet. For the next few weeks he lived, to use his own description, "in the midst of perpetual fetes,"[22] climaxing in an elaborate dinner for two hundred guests, who were serenaded by the *Marseillaise* sung in French by the guest of honor.

We can only speculate as to what part, if any, André Michaux played in this social whirl. With customary terseness his journal notes only: "arrived in Philadelphia Citizen Genet, minister plenipotentiary of the French Republic."[23] Yet in view of his ardent republican sympathies one may take for granted his enthusiastic sharing in the welcome accorded the victorious *Embuscade* and his attendance at the public reception for the minister.

Obviously a key role in Genet's plan for "liberating" Louisiana and Florida was that of courier and liaison agent between the minister in Philadelphia and the American frontier leaders, whose wholehearted support was essential to the success of the undertaking. It was in this crucial role that Michaux was now cast. As an intrepid and wilderness-wise traveler, and a renowned and respected botanist, he was the ideal choice for such a mission. His appointment had possibly been decided upon before Genet left Paris. In any case, it seems to have been fully confirmed on Genet's arrival in Philadelphia, for Michaux's journal records meetings with the minister on May 18 and May 22,[24] during which he presented "a memoir of observations on the French colonies in North America, on Louisiana, on Illinois, and on Canada," as well as an abridged memoir of his travels in North America,[25] and a financial statement of his expenses since leaving France, a large portion of which had still not been paid to him by the French government.[26] The first definite reference in the journal to his political assignment is undated but, sandwiched as it is between these last entries and his preparations for the mission, it would appear to refer to May 22 as the day on which he "consulted and conferred with Citizen Genet on my mission in Kentucky."[27] Reporting to the minister of foreign affairs in France, Genet described Michaux as "a man estimable in all respects, enjoying here a great regard; he is active, circumspect, loyal, and dedicated to the glory of his country; he speaks English, he knows the language and customs of the Indian nations. . . . As he is accustomed to travel in the hinterlands of America, his departure can be suspicious to no one."[28]

So much for the French attitude. But here we may well pause to wonder whether the botanist's acceptance of Genet's appointment entailed for him a great personal sacrifice, subverting, as it did, his western journey from one of independent scientific research to a military and political mission in which duty to the State must take precedence. But this would perhaps be to ignore essential elements of Michaux's character. Passionately patriotic, "bound by all manner of considerations to my country," as he had written to Jefferson, he must have welcomed the opportunity to play a significant part in what seemed an enterprise of enormous importance to France in the international power struggles of the day, and, fervent republican that he had become, he no doubt rejoiced to forward the cause of *Liberté,* and, not least, "to be useful to America," which he defined to Jefferson as his second objective. Nor did he appear to foresee any real conflict in combining the roles of naturalist-explorer and political courier. He had always confessed to serving two mistresses, for each of whom he felt an equal devotion—the science of botany and his native land. As we shall see, he continued botanizing whenever possible throughout the weeks of his political journey to Kentucky, and it seems clear that at this point he regarded his projected western expedition, sponsored by the Philosophical Society up the Missouri and beyond to the Western Sea, as merely deferred by his political appointment, not canceled.

Although in fact Michaux was never to realize his dream of following the setting sun to the blue waters of the Pacific, his idea proved a fertile seed, bearing fruit a dozen years later when Jefferson, as president, dispatched Meriwether Lewis and William Clark on their famous expedition along the way that Jefferson had projected for

Michaux, across the newly purchased Louisiana Territory to the Pacific Ocean.

After his late May conferences with Genet, Michaux devoted most of June to preparations for his journey to Kentucky, including the acquisition of letters to some twenty prominent western leaders, most significantly General George Rogers Clark, who had been selected by Genet as the military leader of the western forces.[29]

By a surprising coincidence, Clark, unaware of the French government's intentions toward Louisiana, had written a letter in February 1793 from the falls of the Ohio to the French government which Genet found awaiting him when he reached Philadelphia, offering to recruit an army of 1,500 men to take over Louisiana from the Spanish garrison, asking only for financial support and two or three frigates from the French government.[30]

Genet's response to this letter was entrusted to his emissary, Michaux, for whom Genet had obtained a letter of introduction to Clark from Senator John Brown of Kentucky, who described Michaux as "a worthy character and a man of Science" with considerable reputation as a botanist whose sole purpose in journeying westward was that of examining the plants and natural productions of the region.[31] It seems likely that the obliging senator was not wholly unaware of the dual purpose of the botanist's journey and perhaps not entirely unsympathetic with its political motivation.

In fact, it is difficult to analyze the effect of Genet's activities on his American associates as the full extent of his intrigues only very gradually became recognized. From the beginning the attitude of the Washington administration, as represented by that of the chief executive, was cautious, in sober contrast to the enthusiasm of the pro-French faction in Philadelphia or the jubilation of the crowds. The president remained sympathetic to the idealistic aims of the French Revolution, but the escalating violence of the movement and the execution of the king had considerably altered his views. He was prepared to recognize the new republic as the legitimate government of France and, consequently, to receive their minister. Nevertheless, when it was thought that the French envoy might arrive in the capital during his absence at Mount Vernon, in March, he instructed the secretary of state "to receive the minister without too much warmth or cordiality."[32]

On April 22, 1793, President Washington issued his Proclamation of Neutrality, committing the nation to a policy of friendly and impartial conduct toward all the warring powers.[33] Thus the French minister, who was presented officially to the president on May 18, could have been in no doubt of the administration's determination to protect the United States from any involvement in the European conflict. Yet Genet proceeded blindly on a collision course with the administration, with the singular obtuseness that had permitted him to pursue the political purposes of France on the soil of the United States for six weeks before he had even presented his credentials to the president of his host country.

The French minister angrily protested the administration's ban on the arming of privateers in American ports and reacted furiously to the seizure of ships illegally armed by the French consul in the port of New York. In reckless defiance of the administration's ruling, he sent to sea the *Little Democrat,* a captured British ship partially armed in Philadelphia.[34] In immoderate language he passionately protested the refusal of the administration to accede to his request for payment of the nation's debt to France before the due date or to immediately expedite a new and favorable commercial treaty with the French Republic, loudly denouncing the administration's decision as designed "to destroy by famine the French republicans and liberty."[35] Both his exaggerated self-confidence and his venom overflowed in his letters home. Weeks before his agent Michaux had even departed to set in motion the western plans, Genet informed his superiors in Paris: "I am inciting the Canadians to throw off the yoke of England; I am arming the Kentuckians, and I am preparing an expedition by sea to support the descent on New Orleans," boasting that his success with the American populace was in spite of "Old Washington" who had hindered his progress "in a thousand ways."[36]

The escalating hostility between the Washington administration and the French minister was particularly distressing to Thomas Jefferson who, strongly pro-French and pro-Republican, had been disposed to welcome any envoy from the country where he had spent some of the happiest years of his life, and he tried in vain to persuade Genet to moderate his conduct and to cease his harsh criticism of the American government. "Never, in my opinion, was so calamitous an appointment made as that of the present Minister of F. here," he wrote to Madison on July 7. "Hot-headed, all imagination, no judgment, passionate, disrespectful, even indecent towards the P. in his written as well as verbal communications, talking of appeals from him to Congress and from Congress to the people, urging the most unreasonable and groundless propositions and in the most dictatorial style."[37]

Two days earlier Genet had called on Jefferson, "not as secretary of state but as Mr. Jefferson." According to Jefferson's minutes of the visit, he revealed his plans for Kentucky, confided his instructions to Michaux, and read to Jefferson his addresses to the inhabitants of Kentucky and to those of Canada, encouraging them to revolt. He then explained that the troops would rendezvous outside of United States territories, probably in Louisiana, and, with the cooperation of two French frigates in the port of New Orleans, would succeed in liberating Louisiana, which would then become an independent state, trading with France and the United States.

"I told him," Jefferson recorded, "that his enticing officers and soldiers from Kentucky to go against Spain was really putting a halter about their necks, for that they would assuredly be hung, if they commenced hostilities against a government at peace with the United States, that leaving out that article I did not care what insurrection should be excited in Louisiana."[38] Jefferson further pointed out to Genet the particular importance of avoiding any action that might compromise the United States government, which was at present engaged in very delicate negotiations with the Spanish government on the question of the free navigation of the Mississippi.

After these reservations and warnings, Jefferson agreed to give Michaux a letter of introduction to Governor Shelby,[39] a letter he later amended at Genet's request so as to describe Michaux not only as a respected man of science but "as one having the good opinion of Genet." Commending him to the notice, councils, and good offices of Shelby, Jefferson concluded his letter: "His character here persuades me that they will be worthily bestowed on him and that your further knowledge of him will justify the liberty I take of making him known to you."[40]

In addition to all the letters of introduction, Genet provided Michaux with a formal commission, bearing the grand seal of the French Republic, charging him with "the important mission of Agent of the Republic of France to the inhabitants of Kentucky, Louisiana, and Illinois." His five-page Memoir of Instructions warned him to make every effort not to compromise the federal government of the United States, to carefully determine the disposition of the inhabitants of Kentucky, to confer with General Clark as to ways and means of procedure, and to determine the time when operations should begin so as to alert the frigates designed for the New Orleans assault, and to determine the strategy according to which "we shall break the chains of the inhabitants of Louisiana."[41] Furthermore, he was to cultivate the friendship of the Indians in the area by means of gifts and "to urge them to make common cause with us to free our Louisiana brothers, . . . who groan in the fetters of the tyrants."

He was entrusted with commissions *en blanc* up to the rank of captain for those Indian chieftains selected to join the cause, provisional commissions *en blanc* up to the rank of colonel, lieutenant colonel and adjutant general for officers selected by General Clark with a promise of the same rank in the French army, and a great number of commissions of undesignated rank, left to Michaux's discretion. General Clark would receive a provisional commission as commanding general of the expedition, with a promise of the rank of brigadier general in the French army.[42] In sum, Michaux was empowered to raise, in the name of the French Republic, outside of the territories of the United States, "an Independent and Revolutionary Legion which will combine with those honorable titles that of the Mississippi."[43]

Phrased in the confident and exultant rhetoric of the optimistic minister, it was an awesome assignment for a man of science, more accustomed to deal with the forces of nature than with the intrigues of men. Michaux could scarcely have failed to be stirred by the exalted description of his mission and the magnitude of his responsibility, but, as a man of thoughtful and deliberate judgment, the antithesis of the impulsive Genet, he was unlikely to have shared entirely in the minister's unqualified euphoria, particularly in the essential matter of finances. His own salary unpaid for many years, the botanist knew too well the dubious value of government promises. He may even have suspected on what a vulnerable financial foundation the whole enterprise rested, for Genet (frustrated in his expectation of supporting the expedition with money from the payment, in advance, of the United States debt to France, and unable to obtain funds from his own government, beleaguered by wars on every front and economic crises at home) was so short of funds he could supply his emissary with no more than 3,000 francs (about $750) to advance to Clark to form an army. Yet undeterred and "living always half in a world of fantasy," Genet pushed forward to launch his undertaking.[44]

CHAPTER 12

⤳ Two Missions West,
1793–1794

IT IS REFRESHING to turn from Genet's lush rhetoric to the austere simplicity of Michaux's journal: "On the 15th of July, 1793, I took leave of Citizen Genet, Minister of the Republic of France to the United States, and started from Philadelphia on the same date at ten o'clock at night to avoid the great heat, and to travel by the light of the moon."[1] He was accompanied by two noncommissioned officers of artillery, provided by Genet as escort for the botanist and potential aids to Clark. They are referred to by Michaux only once, and then, like Rosencrantz and Guildenstern, by surnames only: "The 16th, being in company with . . . humeau, and . . . Leblanc, we journeyed 40 miles."[2]

It was only after five days of traveling in this official company through the settlements of Lancaster, Carlisle, Shippensburg and into the foothills of the mountains that the botanist, whom no political mission could long distract from his absorption in his green world, responded freely once more to the rich vegetation about him, rejoicing in the familiar beauty of magnolias, azaleas, mountain laurels, beeches, pines, oaks, and walnuts, and, near the banks of the Juniata River, rhododendron, hydrangea, and trillium. The pages of his journal became once again dominated by the methodical, scientific listings of the naturalist in the field.

On July 27, the travelers reached Pittsburgh, a rapidly growing mining town of 250 houses, nestled in a beautiful valley where the Monongahela and the Allegheny rivers meet to form the Ohio, or Belle Rivière, the gateway to the Old Northwest. Here they spent almost three weeks, waiting for propitious conditions for their boat to depart down the Ohio. In Pittsburgh, Michaux presented the first of his letters of introduction, this one to Hugh H. Brackenridge, jurist and author, active in politics and a leader in the Republican party.[3] There was time also during those three weeks for the botanist to devote long hours to the geology and vegetation of the environs, where he noted among other plants, hickory, sycamore, red maple, dogwood, and linden trees as well as ginseng, lobelia, morning glories, sassafras, and cassina.

Finally, on August 14, he and his two companions embarked on the Ohio, probably on a keelboat, and two days later they crossed the boundary line between Pennsylvania and Virginia. The line was marked by a wide swath of felled forest on each side of the river, forty-five miles from Pittsburgh.

Just before reaching Marietta at the mouth of the Muskingum River, the botanist sighted several flocks of wild turkeys, and, as the boat glided down the current through almost unbroken walls of green, his eye delighted in the varied patterns of the forest trees, the scaly-white bark of the giant sycamores gleaming here and there among the rich foliage of a variety of maple trees, and the striking leaf patterns of the pawpaw and the horse chestnut.

Also on the right bank of the Ohio lay the ill-fated village of Gallipolis, where only a fourth of the unfortunate persons of the original settlement remained, still ministered to by the humanitarian Dr. Petit, "who," declared Michaux upon visiting him, "inspired me with the greatest respect by his good sense, his knowledge, and his virtue."[4]

After two more days of travel downstream through uninhabited wilderness, the travelers passed the first Kentucky settlements, known as the Three Islands, and arrived, on the evening of August 27, at Limestone (now Mayesville), an important port of entry into Kentucky where goods sent from Philadelphia were landed for the towns of the interior.[5] Here Michaux parted with his two companions, who went on to Louisville, leaving the botanist to visit the inland settlements.

At Mayesville, Michaux called on Colonel Alexander Orr, to whom he had a letter of introduction, and who offered to accompany him to Lexington.[6] He spent a week in this riverport, procuring horses and preparing for his journey inland. There was time, too, for several days of botanizing during which he noted among other plants the thorny honey locust, its long bean pods ripening in the late summer sun, ash trees, fragrant thoroughwort, and hawk's-beard. Before departing the town he dined with the politically influential General Henry Lee, a former Kentucky delegate in the Virginia House of Burgesses and member of the Danville Convention for organizing the state of Kentucky.[7]

As it was then possible to travel without danger the sixty-six miles from Mayesville to Lexington, Michaux took time along the road to examine the deposits of fossil shells and bones at Washington and Buffalo-Lick, a place characterized by bitter saline springs and soil so saline that vast herds of buffalo had come there regularly, up until a few years past, to lick the salt oozing from the earth.

At Lexington he presented two more letters of introduction to persons unnamed in his journal, before continuing on southward to Danville, located beyond the deep gorge of the Kentucky River, which flows at low water 100 feet below the level of the lands through which it passes. On the southern-facing parts of the steep cliffs rising from the river he noted several shrubs and plants, natives of Carolina, protected by that favorable situation.[8]

Although Michaux had called upon many influential citizens along his route to whom Genet had directed him and for whom he had brought letters of recommendation, it appears that his first high-level political contact as Genet's agent was with General Benjamin Logan, Genet's choice for second in command, whom he visited on September 11 near Danville, then the center of political activity in Kentucky.[9] Logan's reception of Genet's proposal was friendly but cautious, as the journal records:

> He told me he would be delighted to take part in the enterprise, but that he had received a letter a few days previously from J. Brown, which informed him that negotiations had begun between the United States and the Spaniards, respecting the navigation of the Mississippi and the Creek Indians; that a messenger had been sent to Madrid, and that any one of the United States that would venture to act in a hostile manner against the Spaniards before the return of the [messenger the] first of December next, would be disapproved by the federal Government.[10]

Logan added that he hoped General Clark would arrange further conferences after he had received Michaux's communications.

Two days later, on September 13, Michaux presented himself to the governor of the state of Kentucky, Isaac Shelby, to whom he had been recommended by both Jefferson and Senator Brown. He did not comment on the governor's reception of the plan, but the governor wrote to Jefferson expressing his opposition to Genet's project and later claimed that he was convinced all the time that the undertaking would "collapse of itself."[11]

It was not until September 16, a little over two months after his departure from Philadelphia, that Michaux reached Louisville and at last made his first official contact with the man chosen by Genet to head the expedition, George Rogers Clark, to whom he gave the minister's letter endorsing Clark's commission and confided his own assignment.[12] Although more than six months had elapsed since the date of Clark's letter to the French government proposing a similar expedition into Louisiana, Michaux found the old general still "very eager for the undertaking."[13] At a second conference, two days later, Clark agreed to send to Michaux, who was planning to return at once to Lexington, his reply to Genet's proposal, to be conveyed by him to the French minister.

On the way to Lexington, Michaux was delayed at the Kentucky River by his familiar mishap, the straying of his horse, and, as usual, he used the time spent searching for the animal to botanize freely, this time observing especially carpet-weed and bloodleaf on the sandy beaches of the river, alumroot and spleenwort on its rocky cliffs, leatherwood along the banks and, in the shady forests, red and sugar maples, honey locust, black locust, and ash trees.[14]

Michaux waited for one month for Clark's letter, shuttling between Lexington and Danville and sending reports to Genet whenever possible. Finally, in response to an urgent note sent by messenger to Clark, he received the old general's reply to Genet on October 21, 1793, which he had sent open to Michaux "for your perusal that our Letters may be common." As optimistic and confident as the French minister could have hoped, the general, after praising Michaux's ability and integrity, enthusiastically accepted his own appointment as commander in chief of the Independent and Revolutionary Legion of the Mississippi, and anticipated with pride the promised commission as brigadier general in the French army, pledging his support but advising caution and emphasizing the necessity for the cooperation of the French fleet in the lower Mississippi, with whose help success would be assured. In this happy vein the letter concluded with a flourish in Genet's own style: "I will surmount every obstacle and pave my way to Glory which is my object."[15] Clark had assured Michaux that he could get as many men as would be needed, but first boats and provisions must be obtained, and especially money—"without it our Scheams may be Ruined, and for so fair a prospect to meet with any difficulty of that nature would be lamentable."[16] To prevent this possibility, Michaux forthwith set about soliciting funds from sympathetic merchants in Lexington and Danville. "They have all promised to advance to me so much money as possible," he assured Clark, but for immediate funds "I shall be in the necessity to have recours to Philadelphia."[17]

In reply, Clark explained that a few hundred dollars would suffice to begin the construction of the boats. "Without them we can do nothing." He also thought it advisable that Genet send out guns and ammunition during the winter.[18] Further conferences with Clark convinced Michaux of the necessity of returning to Philadelphia for funds and consultations with Genet. With that intent he set out from Danville on November 10 for the long journey east.[19] Next day at Crab Orchard on the road southward toward Cumberland Gap, Michaux joined a group of a dozen persons "who had assembled at that place to pass through the woods inhabited and frequented by the Savages," and in their company he traveled safely the 130-mile tract known as the Wilderness Trail to Cumberland Gap and down to the Tennessee settlements on the Holston River. Before reaching the top of the Gap, he noted "a climbing fern covering an area of over six acres near the road."[20]

In his rapid journey from the Holston settlements down through Abingdon and the Shenandoah Valley to Harpers Ferry, and on to Philadelphia, there was little opportunity for botanizing, but his practiced eye observed the arborvitae and rhododendron on the northern hills of the little river he crossed in Tennessee and the cucumber trees where the soil was rich, and in Virginia, chinquapin, a variety of pines, mountain laurel, sourwood, and beech, as well as trailing arbutus.

On December 12, Michaux reached Philadelphia, after a five-month absence during most of which time he had been virtually out of touch with events in the East and abroad.[21] He found the city slowly recovering from a virulent outbreak of yellow fever of four months' duration which had subsided only with the first snows of December. Thousands had fled the stricken city, leaving government offices, newspapers, postal services, and businesses almost at a standstill or with their functions sharply curtailed. At the height of the epidemic in October the death toll was estimated at close to one hundred persons a day. Across the sea in France the Reign of Terror was taking its fearful toll, with the uncompromising Robespierre in control and the Law of Suspects in force, while savage civil war raged in the Vendée, and the embattled French army faced enemies on every front.

Genet had spent the past four months, up until mid-December, in New York, desperately attempting to commandeer for his Louisiana expedition the ships of the French fleet which had fled to the New York harbor following the terrible insurrection in Santo Domingo, and there in the American port had sought refuge and repairs. When his efforts failed and the ships returned instead to France, the chagrin and disappointment experienced by Genet was great but was as nothing compared to the shock he suffered on learning, at about the same time, of the administration's request for his recall. As early as the first week in August the Washington administration had reached this inevitable decision, based primarily on the grounds of Genet's repeated defiance of the United States government, but the official document, framed by Thomas Jefferson, did not reach Paris until October. Though the

Committee of Public Safety, already aware of their minister's indiscretions and offences, agreed without protest to recall Genet, he was permitted to continue in his diplomatic post until his replacement arrived. Genet's initial response to the news of the administration's action had been one of unrestrained rage, poured out in a furious letter to Jefferson, but by the time of his return to Philadelphia he had regained his composure and with it his irrepressible optimism, enabling him to welcome his returned political agent with enthusiasm for his mission and renewed plans.

Michaux's first priority on his return to Philadelphia had been to make his official report to Genet and deliver Clark's letter.[22] The minister informed him, he wrote to Clark, that "he persist always in the execution of the Plan you have proposed to him," though the operation would have to be deferred until spring, because of the difficulty in providing the back-up support of French ships. Michaux's letter to Clark written in English continued with an elated report of the successes of the victorious French armies in Europe, a passage worth quoting in full for what it reveals of the passionate devotion of this customarily reserved and taciturn man to the revolutionary cause of the Republic of France:

> As for the concern which you take to our success, I sent the most certain account we have from Europe.
>
> On the 10th of September the armies of the Republic have completely routed and driven the English and hanoverians from before Dunkirk. Adolphe one of the sons of George III is died of his wounds.
>
> The troops of holland headed by the Prince of Orange have been cut to pieces on the 6th of October.
>
> The Prince Saxe Coburg at the head of 80 thousand and Gen. Clairfait with 30 thousand men have been beaten from the 14th to the 18th of October, driven from before Maubeuge, have crossed the Sambre river and retreat from the french territories with a loss of more than 8 thousand men.
>
> The Spaniard in three different battles have lost baggage, Artillery, Military chest and they are in such situation that they will never be able to return in Spain. The french are now in Catalonia, etc.
>
> The King of Sardainia has lost the ¾ of his dominions. All the french vessels marchants in the seaports are taken to land in England an Army of 180 thousand Mens.
>
> The city of Lyons has been storm by the Republicans and 10

thousand Aristocrats put to the sword. All the insurrections in
Brittany, La Vendée, etc. are quelled.

By a late arrival from france has brought an account of the
retaking of Toulon; Valancienne Conde retaken; Ostend taken
and innumerable quantity of Provisions, Artillery, etc. etc. All
the Troops under Duck of York taken prisonners, only himself es-
caped in a fishing Boat.

Finally George III beging to speak of peace his tropps send
to quell the insurrections in many parts have joined the people
crying out, out! No War. The Queen of France paid for her trea-
sons of her head.[23]

After this decidedly bellicose and sanguinary account, the letter
concluded with a request for a receipt for the 400 dollars enclosed from
Genet, and is signed "Your fellow Citizen—A. Michaux," perhaps in
reference to General Clark's commission in the French army.[24]

There are indications in the journal entries for December 1793
and January 1794 that with the "liberation of Louisiana" postponed
until spring, Michaux felt free to concentrate on his natural history
researches and that he even had hopes of reviving plans for his exploration expedition to the Pacific. On December 14, the day after his
conference with Genet and two days after his return to the city from
Kentucky, Michaux visited Thomas Jefferson and David Rittenhouse,
president of the American Philosophical Society. Unfortunately, we
have no record of the substance of these meetings nor of his second
visits to Rittenhouse and Jefferson on December 26 and 28, respectively.[25] But it seems reasonable to assume that Michaux communicated
to Jefferson and Rittenhouse, representing the American Philosophical Society, geographical and scientific information obtained on his
western journey which might be relevant to their common concern with
western exploration to the Pacific, and that he discussed with them the
possibility of a revival at some future time of their mutually beneficial
contract for such an undertaking.

Clearly he was broadening his field of research. During the last
few months he had shown an increasing interest in ornithology, bringing to mind his predecessor Mark Catesby, whose dedication to natural
history, at first primarily botanical, widened during his years in America
to embrace ornithology and zoology.[26] In December and January his
journal records repeated excursions to observe and collect birds and
occasionally squirrels for study, and preparation of skins for shipment
to France along with the seeds he had brought back from Kentucky.

Always a scientific scholar as well as a field naturalist, he now borrowed from Dr. Barton a copy of the *Systema Naturae* of Linnaeus, from which he made an extract of the natural history classifications of mammals, quadrupeds, and birds, working steadily for three days to complete it.[27]

An interesting sidelight on Michaux's character is afforded by the journal entry of January 18: "Wrote a memoir for a proposal to make to the Society of the Friends of Liberty and Equality in Philadelphia to suggest ways to ameliorate the fate of French prisoners fallen into the hands of the English."[28] Perhaps his natural sympathy for his fellow countrymen was sharpened by memory of his own capture and imprisonment at the hands of eastern bandits.

In mid-January 1794 news of the recall of Citizen Genet by the all-powerful Committee of Public Safety in Paris reached Philadelphia. By this time also much of the material exposing Genet's rude and insolent conduct toward the United States government had been made public. Michaux made no comment in his journal on these developments. But he recorded a final visit to the minister during which he returned all the blank commissions entrusted to him and submitted a report on the state of the wheat harvest with relevance to provisions for France.[29] Genet, who had been given permission by the French and American authorities to stay on as minister until the arrival of his replacement from France, and who still had implicit faith in the feasibility of his military plans, consented in early February to Michaux's departure for the South, giving him instructions to confer with Consul Mangouret in Charleston on the Florida expedition, and adding that, on his return from South Carolina, he would send him on a mission to Kentucky, probably to forward plans for the spring expedition in Louisiana.

Michaux—after conferring, on Genet's advice, with the Kentucky delegation in Congress "on the dispositions of the federal government and the execution of the plan of General Clark," and applying in vain for reimbursement for the expenses of his Kentucky journey from the French consul, Citizen Bournonville, whom he found as unresponsive and evasive on financial matters as his royal counterparts in the past—was at last free to leave the confusions and dissensions of the city and turn, with a sigh of relief, southward toward home.

Following a stopover at the Bartram garden for a visit with William, who gave him a list of plants he wanted from the South, Michaux set out on February 9, in spite of a heavy snowfall, eager to return to his forsaken garden after an absence of approximately two years. Consequently, he was not on hand for the arrival, on February 21, of the new minister from the French Republic, Jean Fauchet, who headed a four-man commission sent to replace the incorrigible Genet. Nor was Michaux aware, until much later on, that Genet, who had requested, and been magnanimously granted, political asylum by President Washington, had slipped quietly out of the city at the end of the same month, for a refuge in the country.[30] Almost immediately the quietus was put upon Genet's Louisiana plans by Minister Fauchet. Responding to protests made by the administration, disturbed by wild rumors of large-scale military recruitments by Clark in Kentucky, Fauchet issued a proclamation on March 6, 1794, canceling all commissions conferred by the previous minister and instructing all French citizens to abide by the dictates of American neutrality. It was just as well, for, in any case, the ill-fated Louisiana enterprise was already collapsing of itself as Shelby had foreseen. Without funds General Clark had been able to recruit only a few dozen men and to gather a handful of flatboats for a rendezvous at the mouth of the Ohio by the time word arrived of Fauchet's proclamation, putting a decisive end to all further hopes.

Far from this forlorn scene of frustration and disappointment, Michaux had returned once more to his beloved plantation. He had journeyed on horseback down the old familiar roads from Philadelphia through Richmond, and Petersburg, to Wilmington, North Carolina, where he rested for several days, botanizing in the environs and cheered by talk with a group of French residents of republican sympathies, as well as with the innkeeper of the Great Taverne where he lodged, "a true friend of the Republic of France."[31]

After loading his collections of plants on a sloop bound for Charleston, on March 7 he set out, much refreshed, along the coastal route south. As always, on the trail naturalist Michaux had found much to observe and enjoy during the nearly five weeks of travel from Philadelphia to Charleston. More bird-conscious now, he noted with pleasure the variety of birds, as spring migrations were well underway, feeding on the abundant berries and last year's seeds: "mockers," cardinals, titmice, chickadees, bluebirds, and a species he does not name, feeding on last year's dried persimmons, but which he describes so accurately that it is easy to identify it as the exquisite cedar waxwing.[32] From the journal entries it seems evident that along the way he was methodically adding to his accumulated lore on the geographical distributions of plants for his projected work on this aspect of botany.

A single tall *Magnolia grandiflora* towering like a sentinel, near the border between the Carolinas welcomed him back as he rode into the small fishing village of Little River, where he visited "two French Democrats" and "had the satisfaction of hearing" the one called Jouvenceau boast of his fight with an American Tory who spoke slightingly of the French Republic.[33]

On March 14, 1794, the saddle-weary naturalist rode once more into the gracious streets of Charleston. At once he reported to Consul Mangouret, with whom he met and dined twice during the first week, conferring on the plans projected by Minister Genet for the conquest of East and West Florida. Fauchet's prohibition had obviously not yet arrived to put an end to all such hopes.[34]

Michaux seems to have spent the following weeks setting the gardens and nurseries of the plantation in order, planting the trees and shrubs shipped by sea from Wilmington, transplanting a great number of seedlings, pruning, trimming, and conferring with the gardener on future activities, but soon, restless for travel and botanizing, he was once more on the road, setting out in mid-July yet again for "les hautes montaignes de Caroline" on an expedition lasting three and a half months.[35] It was his first late-summer visit to the green wonderland of the Carolina mountains, and consequently his journal records the discovery of many plants new to him and some new to science. Again riding up the Santee-Wateree-Catawba River valley, he observed near Camden a new Kalmia, white wicky, *Kalmia cuneata,* "which," he wrote, "has not previously been described by anyone and probably has never been seen before." Also he collected a new *Stewartia* between Charlotte and Lincolnton, a lily of the valley on the mountain sides near Linville, where he measured a tulip tree twenty-three feet in circumference, a new flame azalea, white alder and mountain cranberry near Crabtree, *Diphylleia,* pixie-parasol, on Mount Mitchell, a genus with but two species, this one, *cymosa,* a discovery of Michaux, and one in Japan. On Roan Mountain he found several azaleas new to him and that beautiful miniature rhododendron sand myrtle, *Leiophyllum,* and false pennyroyal, *Isanthus,* a new species observed at the point where he forded the Catawba on his return trip.

On the trail to Roan Mountain, a particularly fruitful area, Michaux stopped at the home of Martin Davenport, "located near a spring not far from the Toe River."[36] Davenport, a well-known Whig of a prominent family, soon became his friend, his host, hunting companion and guide for his mountain journeys. On August 30 the two men climbed together to the summit of Grandfather Mountain which Michaux, misled by its dominant position among its neighboring peaks, called the highest mountain in all North America. There on its lofty crest the two companions, exhilarated by the altitude, the breathtaking beauty of the surrounding landscape, and their shared Republican fervor, "sang the *Marseillaise* and shouted 'Long Live America and the Republic of France, Long Live Liberty, etc., etc.'"[37]

The peripatetic botanist was back at his Charleston plantation by the beginning of October, where, from then until the end of November, he was occupied "in gathering the plants of autumn," but only under a heavy handicap. "About the tenth of October," he recorded in his journal, "the fever of the climate seized upon me." This seems to have been a severe attack of malaria which lasted nearly two weeks and from which he said, "I have been more than six weeks recovering."[38]

During this convalescent period much of his collecting was done in that rich area haunted by Catesby and other naturalists, the shores of the Ashley River, where we find him in early November, the guest of Dr. Charles Drayton, wealthy planter and physician, whose stately mansion, Drayton Hall, still overlooks that tidal stream. We learn from Drayton's diary that Michaux arrived at the Drayton plantation on November 10, and next day went in search of plants in the environs, only to suffer the misfortune of the death of his horse—Michaux seems to have been singularly unlucky in his horses! Readily supplied by his host with one for the return journey on November 12, he repaid Drayton's generosity by sending back the horse laden with rare plants and shrubs, a particular pleasure to the doctor, an ardent gardener and amateur botanist. This is only one example of many occasions on which Michaux repaid the hospitality of his American hosts with the enduring gift of rare and precious plants, particularly for the gardens of the opulent plantations, such as Drayton Hall, along the Carolina lowcountry rivers, where today many of these plants still thrive, keeping his memory green. Notable among these surviving gifts from Michaux are three beautiful and luxuriant camellias (presented to Middleton by Michaux, who supervised their planting) and a magnificent, many-trunked crape-myrtle tree which still, after two hundred years, grace the lovely gardens of Middleton Place on the Ashley River. Not only was the French naturalist a welcome visitor to the Carolina lowcountry plantations, but the Charleston planters and their families in turn often drove out to his establishment known as the French Botanic Garden, attracted by the variety and beauty of the hundreds of plants cultivated there. Along with exotics, a rich collection of choice native plants, collected by Michaux from every part of North America visited on his journeys, thrived in the garden under his care, including such rare native species as *Franklinia* and *Pinckneya*.

Dr. Drayton made rather frequent visits to the French garden over the years. On February 17, 1793, in company with General Pinckney and his family, he drove out to the establishment, failing to see Michaux who was still in Philadelphia, but finding, as Drayton records in his diary, that, early in the year though it was, yellow jessamine, red bud trees, and Chickasaw plum were in bloom. On a later visit, March 9, 1805, nearly three years after the death of Michaux, the Doctor recorded observing in the sadly neglected garden the sweet olive, *Osmanthus fragrans* (which Drayton called *Olea fragrans*), lending additional confirmation to the belief that André Michaux introduced into this country this much-prized native of eastern Asia, the haunting and pervasive fragrance of whose flowers has come to seem the very essence of southern gardens.[39]

CHAPTER 13

❧ West to the Mississippi and
American Finale, 1795–1796

IT WAS SPRING of the following year before the naturalist set out once more on a major expedition. Again he was forced to borrow on his estate in France in order to finance his journey, which would lead him across the Old Northwest Territory to the Mississippi and would prove to be the longest in duration—almost a year—and the last of all his journeys in the American wilderness. His journal records his departure, with the new style dating of the French Republican calendar: "The 30th Germinal in the 3rd year of the French Republic, One and Indivisible, (Sunday 19th of April, 1795) started to go and herborise in the high mountains of the Carolinas and afterward to visit the Western Territories."[1]

Following the familiar Catawba River route he headed north toward the mountains. Along the trail, near the High Hills of Santee he noted "very small Phlox with lance-shaped leaves," two different species, one with white, one with pink flowers, and five miles beyond Camden he found again "la nouveau *Kalmia*," probably the white wicky he had discovered in the same neighborhood the previous July, a plant now on the endangered species list. This time not yet in flower. Near

Hanging Rock his horse strayed away during the night—almost a sine qua non of his journeys—obliging him to spend a day searching for it, but as usual his search turned into fruitful botanizing; he noted especially the wild ginger, dogtooth violet, and rare shooting star.

His hosts for his nights' lodgings were often fellow Republicans, heroes of the American Revolution, such as Colonel James Crawford, uncle and foster father of Andrew Jackson, Colonel James Hill, owner of the most important ironworks in the state, and, farther on, beyond Morganton, Colonel Avery, a distinguished citizen of North Carolina, whose plantation home, Swans Pond, had welcomed Michaux on previous journeys.

But lingering nowhere, not even to take note of the splendid falls where the Linville River emerges from its sheer and narrow canyon, a rare phenomenon, he pushed on, arriving early in May at the home of his friend and guide Martin Davenport. With the Davenport house on the Toe River as his headquarters, Michaux explored the rich area of the surrounding mountains for over a week, a feast of color and fragrance. Along the valley of the Toe River, flowing its tortuous way between the wooded slopes of Roan and Yellow mountains, "All the lily of the valley were in bloom and the wild mandrake." Searching along the slopes and on the summits of the "Bleue Ridges," he noted an abundance of the "azalea with yellow flowers," observing that this variety was the only one to be found on the hills, but on the riverbanks one found generally "that with carnation and that with white flowers," while on the summits he found that most delicate of *Rhododendrons,* the *Rhododendron minus,* his own discovery, with its bell-shaped, shell-pink blossoms, and the exquisite yellow lady's slipper, *Cypripedium luteum,* both in flower.[2]

From Davenport's he set out to cross the mountains into Tennessee, a trail that "followed and crossed the Doe River 27 times" before reaching Jonesborough, the oldest town in Tennessee. He stopped at the home of yet another Colonel, lost his horse again, spent three days in futile search, bought another, and moved on to the newly settled village of Knoxville, where he botanized in the neighborhood, awaiting the accumulation of twenty-five westward-bound travelers, the minimum considered safe for travel on the Wilderness Trail toward Nashville, where it crossed territory only recently seized from the Cherokee and still in dispute. During his week of waiting, he listed in his journal the plants observed in the area, a practice he was to follow throughout this journey, as though taking a plant census, or making a topographical map of the plants east of the Mississippi. His "Plants and Trees of the

Territory of Knoxville and of the Neighboring Country" includes seven species of oaks, as well as varieties of elms, ash, persimmon, liquidambar, hickory, walnut, tupelo, sycamore, beech, magnolia, dogwood, birch, judas, in addition to varieties of wildflowers.[3]

So far his course had followed a fairly direct and familiar pattern, but his itinerary became more erratic as he roamed over the western territories, shuttling back and forth, often retracing his steps, combing the region as though eager to miss nothing. One is reminded of his confession to the count early in his mission: "I shall have nothing to fear so much as leaving discoveries to be made by those who shall come after me."

From the journal's detailed account of this yearlong expedition, we have space here only for the highlights. One of these must surely have been his passage through the wilderness toward Nashville. He set out on June 4 in the company of "15 armed men and more than Thirty women and children." As they crossed the low Cumberland mountains, "alternately ascending and descending," he noted in his journal a significant discovery: "*Magnolia petalis basi purpureis*," with no other comment. It seems highly probable that this was the rare *Magnolia macrophylla,* which he would find again the following April on his way home from the Carolina mountains, and would then describe in detail.

Thirteen miles from Nashville he stopped at the home of Andrew Jackson, at that time an obscure lawyer living at his plantation, Hunter's Hill, lying in fertile lands near the Cumberland River, where the botanist noted five species of oak, including the beautiful swamp chestnut, with very large acorns, later described by his son, for whom it is named, *Quercus michauxii.*

In the little village of Nashville, the capital of the Cumberland settlements on the river, Michaux lingered for a few days, herborizing widely over the countryside, recording a long list of trees—varieties of oak, maple, walnut, hickory, sycamore, sweet gum, elm, cedar, and mock orange—a significant observation for a soil-conscious collector of plants for introduction into the calcareous earth of France, as well as additional data for his topographical botany studies. Now his accumulation of plants and seeds shared space with his increasing collection of bird skins, including such commonly seen species of birds as robins, cardinals, fly catchers in abundance, and, of the rarer species, shrikes and woodpeckers. As for the quadrupeds, he contented himself with listing the species observed: muskrats, beavers, elk, dwarf deer, bears, buffalo, wolves, and small gray squirrels.[4]

On June 22, he set out from Nashville across the empty, still

Indian-haunted Barrens, where he "slept on the ground without a fire" and without allowing his horse to graze, for fear of the Indians. Stopping by Danville en route, he dined with Governor Shelby, whom he had last visited nine months before as courier and agent for Genet. Now free of this political involvement, Michaux perhaps discussed with the governor a proposition much more appealing to Shelby, the possibility of an overland journey to the Pacific. It may well have been in the interest of such a proposition that he visited a few weeks later, in Louisville, a wealthy and prominent merchant, a native of France but a longtime resident of the port city, in the hope of obtaining financial backing for an eventual expedition.

After two weeks of botanizing and compiling a list of "Trees, Plants, and Shrubs of Louisville Territory," mid-August found him on the banks of the Wabash on the Indiana side of the river, with no other company than "a savage and his wife hired for ten dollars," no doubt a wise precaution, as this region, only a year earlier, had been the scene of bloody battles with the Indians. However, the risk of losing one's scalp was not his only concern in crossing this inhospitable Indiana wilderness, a journey that seemed to the naturalist one of the most difficult he had made in his ten years in America, owing to the quantities of devouring flies, the thick brushwood through which they had to make their way, and the great number of trees overturned by storms and blocking the path. It was in attempting to leap over one of these that his horse fell, throwing the botanist a great distance, resulting in an injury to his left side where the trigger of his gun struck him in his fall.

During the three days of his convalescence from this accident, which had left him feeling almost ill, he botanized on the shores of the river. His "List of Plants Observed on the Wabash" included five species of verbena, six of sunflower, several oaks, and the Indian pink from which the Miami Indians of the region prepared a "Decoction of the root, a sovereign remedy for several diseases and for long continued venereal disease."[5] From the small military outpost of Vincennes on the Wabash, the naturalist and his Indians set out in the last week of August for the Illinois Territory on the Mississippi, traveling easily across the wide intervening prairie region, where he discovered a new species of *Gerardia auriculata,* with oval leaves and purple flowers. In this area, as yet unconquered by the white man's gun, they feasted on the plentiful and easily taken bear and deer, brought in by the Indian hunter. Michaux, who had at first welcomed the game, began to worry about the time lost in hunting and feasting—the Indians ate five meals a day—especially as they were delayed also by heavy rains, one of which had soaked his baggage, including four books of botany and mineralogy he had brought with him, fearing to expose them to the hazards of river transport, by which he had sent, via the Mississippi, "two trunks containing grey paper, Powder, Lead, Alum, Boxes for Collecting Insects, and all the articles required for making collections of Plants, Animals, Insects, and Minerals—a statement indicative of the scope of his project.[6]

By the end of August they had arrived at the village of Kaskaskia, "agreeably situated" two miles from the Mississippi River and one-half mile from the Kaskaskia River, a community of only forty-five families, chiefly descendants of Coureurs des Bois intermixed with Indians. Michaux found particularly distressing the plight of "these former Frenchmen living under the American government" but reduced to a state of idleness and poverty. "Nothing is to be seen but houses in ruins and abandoned because the French of Illinois country, having always been brought up in and accustomed to the Fur Trade with the Savages, have become the laziest and most ignorant of all men. They live and the majority of them dress in the manner of the Savages. They wear no breeches but pass between their thighs a piece of cloth about one third of an ell (in length) which is kept in place before and behind above the hips by a belt."[7]

During the whole of the following autumn, the naturalist roamed over western Illinois, traveling along the Mississippi northward as far as St. Louis, and downriver to the mouth of the Ohio and to Fort Massac, which General Wayne ("mad Anthony") had ordered erected in 1794 to prevent the projected attack on Louisiana, the promotion of which had first brought Michaux to Kentucky. The trail took him on through a series of villages with French names, strung along the river, a result of La Salle's dream of conquest and settlement, some reduced to a few families, Prairie du Rocher, St. Phillippe, Corne de Cerf, Bellefontaine, and by the once formidable Fort Chartres, abandoned and in ruins, victim of an assault by British forces and the eroding waters of the Mississippi. In the forests and along the shores of the rivers and in the rich soil of the prairies, his botanizing added long lists of trees and plants to his botanical tables, oaks predominating, with gum, locust, hickories, beech, elm, ash, birch, and, noted for the first time on this journey, catalpa and poplar—"called by the Americans Cotton tree."[8]

Game was still plentiful. "My guide killed an Elk called Cerf by the Canadians and the French of Illinois. This animal is much larger (twice as large) than the dwarf deer of the United States of which there is also an abundance in the Illinois country and which the French of these countries call chevreuil. Its antlers are twice the size of those of the European Stag." Two days later, he recorded, "My guide killed a Buffalo. . . . It seemed to weigh over nine hundred pounds . . . larger than any oxen in France, and to surpass them in length and size."[9]

From Fort Massac, Michaux set out in a canoe with two guides "to ascend the rivers of the territory of the Cherokee Savages," the Cumberland River and the "very great and very wide" Tennessee. As the frosts moved south so did the water birds. An increasingly ornithological Michaux added to his collection of bird skins those of marsh hens, white pelicans, Canada and blue geese, and kingfishers. Wild turkeys were so numerous he and his guide killed five from the canoe in passing.

Returning to Fort Massac on October 20th, he journeyed once again on horseback through woods and hills and across the prairies back to Kaskaskia. Occasional episodes of duck and goose hunting are interspersed in the journal among botanical observations, which include descriptions of the medicinal uses made by the Indians of certain plants, including species of spiraea, geranium, veronica, hackberry, smilax, and hercules club.

It seems that Michaux devoted considerable effort during those autumn days in Illinois to seeking out fur traders and trappers of the region to garner more information about the Missouri Country and the alluring lands beyond. On one occasion he was informed of an attempt made a few months earlier, by a Scotchman and a Welshman, with the support of a St. Louis Fur Trading Company, "to ascend the Missouri in a 4-oared Barge."

In mid-December the roving naturalist once more abandoned his horse for river transport, arranging with Pierre Richard of Kaskaskia to go by water via the Mississippi and Ohio and up the Tennessee River to the Cumberland region. On their second night out, they camped on the shores of the river where the Belle Rivière falls into the Mississippi. On the opposite shore the Spanish Governor of Natchez and upper Louisiana, Don Gayosa, had set up his camp. "He sent a boat to find out who we were," recorded Michaux, "and, learning that I was a passenger, he came to see me. He told me the news of the Peace between France and Spain. He offered me his services."[10] One hopes that a pleasant evening was passed between the official representative of Spain and the French naturalist so recently engaged in a plot to dispossess him.

After four days ascending the Ohio, they had passed Fort Massac, the mouth of the Tennessee, and entered the Cumberland a few miles farther upstream. Heavy rains, hail, snow, winter gales, and flooding made progress upstream so difficult they were from time to time forced to seek out a "hill high enough to relieve us from the fear of being flooded," and to remain camped there all day. On Christmas Day 1795 a day of continual rain and sleet, the party huddled in a makeshift shelter. New Years Day 1796 found them in the vicinity of Little River, where the soil of the riverbanks consisted of "a very rich mould mixed with clay." Here he lingered for several days observing the animals in the surrounding hillcountry, raccoons, opossums, bears, buffalo, and the water creatures, beavers, otters, and muskrats, as well as the birds, including large owls and the bright flashing parrakeets and brilliant western jays. Botanizing when possible, he added to his lists hornbeam, chokecherry, a new beech, and the tree he named *Nyssa montana*— "called by the French Creoles *Olivier sauvage* and by the Kentucky Americans black gum tree and by the Pennsylvania Americans tupelo." [11]

On the evening of the Twelfth Day, the last day of the Christmas season, winter struck in earnest. Snow began to fall and the weather turned very cold. After paddling all the way from north to south across Kentucky into Tennessee, at Clarksville Michaux bought a horse for one hundred dollars and continued on by horseback to Nashville, where he rested for three days before starting on again on the twenty-fifth, aiming back across Kentucky northeastwardly to Louisville through "Rain and Snow." Traveling was a severe ordeal for horse and rider: "The ground was covered with snow, the Roads rough and my horse fell lame. I was obliged to walk. I made 12 miles. I was unable to light a fire because the trees and wood were all frosted. I spent the night nearly frozen . . . being overcome by cold and weariness, having travelled afoot, having eaten nothing since the morning of the previous day and not having slept during the night. The toes of my right foot became inflamed." [12]

But relief was in sight. Overcome by cold, hunger, and inflamed feet, the exhausted naturalist found refuge and "every service hospitality could suggest," at the home of George Madison, where he was received "with all the civility that can be expected from a man who has had a higher education than the other inhabitants of the country." Michaux describes a pleasant and interesting evening with Madison and his wife, who gave him a pair of heavy woolen socks to wear over his shoes, a device he henceforth adopted for traveling in snow, as a source of great comfort.

Just before arriving at Louisville on February 2, Michaux "measured a *Liriodendron tulipifera* whose size was twenty-two feet in circumference, making more than seven feet in diameter."[13]

In Louisville, his last port of call before turning homeward for the long two months' journey back to Charleston, he conferred for the last time with General Clark, who was still trying to obtain recompense from the French government, as recalcitrant as his own government in settling accounts.[14] Then, gathering together his collections he had left in the care of a French acquaintance, he set out once more for Nashville. Among the interesting observations noted in his journal en route is that of February 10, describing the tea he had drunk for supper, made from the shrub he calls spicebush, or *Laurus benzoin* (*Lindera benzoin*), the Benjamin bush, which was said to restore strength. After arriving at Nashville, he spent several days at the home of Colonel Hays and arranged to purchase a horse to carry his baggage, plant and bird collections, packed his collections and otherwise prepared for the long journey home.[15]

That he still cherished hopes of exploring the West seems evident from the following entry in his journal for February 20: "Saw some French voyageurs, who spend all their lives in the Trade with the Savages, and asked the Terms on which I could obtain a guide to go up the Missouri River. One of them named————told me he would willingly engage for a year for the sum of 500 dollars in furs, that is to say 1000 dollars in money; another asked me 2000 dollars in money."[16]

His republican principles had lost none of their vitality, one concludes, from his relation of his experience on February 25, on his first night's stop after leaving Nashville, when his host, a Colonel Mansko, turned out to be a passionate monarchist "and a declared enemy of the French because he said they had killed their King. Although I had not dined I would not accept his supper, believing that a Republican should not be under obligations to a fanatical partisan of Royalty. I was greatly mortified that the night and the rain should compel me to remain in his house. But I slept on my Deerskin and paid for the maize he supplied me with to cross the Wilderness."[17]

Impeded by rain, snow, and bitter cold, which caused his horse's legs to swell, he pushed on, but by March 1 had reached only as far as Fort Blount on the Cumberland River, sixty miles from Nashville. There, undeterred by winter's blasts, he botanized over the countryside and was rewarded by the discovery of a new tree, the rare and beautiful yellowwood, *Cladrastis lutea*, which blossoms every other year in showy hanging panicles of pealike, fragrant white flowers. A young officer from the fort helped him to cut down some of them to collect their seeds and trunk wood and to dig in the snow-covered earth for roots to plant in the Carolina garden. Michaux, observing that the bark produces a yellow dye, foresaw the possibilities of the tree as a practical source for yellow coloring and wrote to Governor Blount to report his findings.[18]

At Knoxville he tarried for a week awaiting the coming of spring before venturing into the mountains. In his mid-March exploring along the Holston River, he noted those traditional and symbolic harbingers of spring, the exquisite trio of early blooming wildflowers, hepaticas, spring beauties, and bloodroot, as well as the much less common twinleaf, *Jeffersonia diphylla*. Michaux had discovered this plant in the mountains of Virginia on an earlier journey and had brought some shoots to William Bartram in Philadelphia, where Dr. Barton had described it, giving it the name *Jeffersonia* in honor of Thomas Jefferson. Only two species of twinleaf exist, the other in faraway China.

These lovely blossoms of early spring were his awaited signal, nature's all-clear for the homeward-bound naturalist to be on his way. Taking a different route across the mountains from the one by which he had gone west, he followed the trail along the narrow valley of the Nolichuckey by Bull's Gap and over Iron Mountain Pass, an arduous journey through dense forests of rhododendron, up to eighteen feet high, and across turbulent mountain torrents, a route to be eloquently described by the younger Michaux who traveled the same trail six years later.

It was late March when the naturalist arrived back once more at the hospitable haven of the Davenport home in the Carolina mountains—a kind of homecoming. For almost a week he roamed through their inexhaustible storehouse of green treasures, collecting in the high mountains near the Davenport house hundreds of plants, including *Rhododendron minus* and the flame azalea. There too he noted the *Corylus cornuta,* or beaked hazelwood, in flower, a plant found, he observed, "only in the highest mountains or in Canada."

On March 29 he set out on the last lap of his homeward journey, his pack horses laden with a rich harvest of fresh mountain plants for the garden of the Republic in Charleston. En route, on Sunday, April 3, about twelve miles from Lincolnton, he found along a little creek the magnolia he had discovered the previous June in the Cumberland Mountains, but here growing in company with *Kalmia latifolia, Viola lutea, Halesia,* and *Stewartia.* In his journal he recorded that he "remained all day to pull shoots of a new Magnolia with very large leaves, auriculate, oblong, glaucous, silky, especially the young leaves; the buds very silky; flowers white petals with a base of purple color. Stamens yellow, etc."—obviously the *Magnolia macrophylla,* which he had seen for the first time in the Cumberland Mountains the previous June.[19] The collection of this rare and beautiful plant seemed a fitting climax for his last journey into the region he loved. A last farewell it was indeed. After four months back at his plantation home near Charleston, a period for which we have no record in journal or letters, André Michaux left America forever. We are left with only speculations as to the reasons for his decision to return to France at this time, if indeed there was any other than the one we have long known, his precarious financial situation. Ever since the beginning of the French Revolution, he had received little or no financial support from his French employers, royal or republican, forcing him to rely on his personal resources to maintain the two American gardens, meet his expenses in the field, and cover the cost of packing and shipping his collections to France. As his son later testified, Michaux had all but exhausted his estate in supporting his country's enterprise. Only with renewed support from the French government could he hope to carry out his still cherished plan to expand his botanical research in America beyond the Mississippi to the Western Sea. A return to France seemed to offer the only possibility of collecting from the government any portion of the debt due him, and of placing his affairs on a sound financial basis for future research. It seems probable also that his son may have informed him of the devastation wrought by the years of the Revolution in the royal nurseries and gardens, where so many of his hard-won collections had been planted, and he may have hoped to retrieve some part of the surviving trees and shrubs.

Even as he made his preparations for departure from America during the last week of July and the first week of August, a letter was on its way to him from the minister of the interior in France, a letter dated July 12, 1796, commissioning him "to send seeds and plants to restock the National Nurseries, to spread on the soil of the Republic the useful trees of America, a service rendered more essential than ever by the almost total destruction of the National Nurseries." As Michaux had come to expect, there was in this letter no mention of reimbursement or even of salary, but in its place gratifying recognition, commissioning the naturalist "to contribute by your shipments to the honor and glory of the Republic, which is glorified by counting you in the number of its Savants, who compose the National Institute, who are destined to spread knowledge in all the Sciences."[20]

It seems unlikely that this letter could have reached Michaux before his departure, as six weeks was then the usual minimum for transatlantic passage. He embarked on August 13, 1796, from Charleston, on the *Ophir*. It was probably with mingled emotions of regret, anxiety, and hope that André Michaux, after eleven years of action-packed exile, watched the Carolina shoreline drop below the horizon.[21]

CHAPTER **14**

◈⑤ Return to France, 1796–1800

ON THE MORNING of October 9, after fifty-one days at sea, the *Ophir* drew near the coast of Holland. All that day the skies were fair and a favorable wind was blowing, giving little or no warning of the storm that broke upon them at five in the evening, becoming furious in less than two hours.[1]

All night the tempest raged, redoubling in violence, while the winds of gale strength forced the ship nearer and nearer to the shore. Though at dawn the vessel had still not struck, "the Captain, seeing that the sounding line no longer indicated sufficient depth, determined to run the ship aground, and, after four or five violent shocks, she stopped. Then the waves fell upon us with so much rage and violence everything on deck was carried away," reported Michaux. "The sails were ripped to shreds in less than one quarter of an hour." As the waves grew even more furious, everyone on board was repeatedly deluged and half drowned in water. Trunks from the cargo were hurled into the sea. Those that reached shore were rescued by the inhabitants of the little town of Egmond nearby, who thronged the shore in the hope of aiding those upon the doomed ship.

Battered by the waves for over three hours, Michaux, "awaiting an end to my suffering, and death," finally lost consciousness. Many hours later he came to himself, "in a room near a great fire, with new garments on and surrounded by forty to fifty inhabitants of the country." All aboard the wrecked vessel had survived and by evening had been "comforted and restored," aided by the inhabitants of the country, who "furnished us," says the botanist, "with all possible help, shirts, clothing, bread, meat, Eau de Vie, etc." Even his collections, for the most part, had been rescued, as he assured his friend André Thouin, to whom he wrote the news of his situation:

> *Almost all my collections are saved, that is to say all the plants and the herbarium, with the exception of two notebooks. . . . I have saved also a strong box of birds and quadrupeds, all the descriptions and the memoirs concerning the plants and animals. . . . I have to regret a box of birds which, too heavy, did not come ashore; a little trunk of papers, in which there are several additional memoirs for which I can make up the deficiency by memory. . . . I have lost all my clothes and personal effects, but that matters little to me. It is with the greatest difficulty I have saved my life for the ship was broken to pieces by the waves, and I was carried ashore, unconscious, with two other persons, the rest having saved themselves by swimming; nevertheless, I was sick for only two days.*

The letter continued with a request that Thouin kindly obtain from the minister of the interior an advance to Michaux for the expenses of the journey to Paris and for the reimbursement of the French consul in Amsterdam, who had supplied the most urgent needs of the destitute naturalist, including eighteen reams of gray paper necessary for drying the mass of plants in the soaked herbarium, as well as funds to purchase missing botany books. Observing to his seed-loving friend Thouin that a precious collection of seeds had been saved because it had been wrapped in linen coated with beeswax and that even three of the beautiful summer ducks had survived, Michaux ended this letter with messages to the colleagues and friends whom he hoped soon to see in Paris, Citizens Cels, Jussieu, and L'Héritier. "Say to them that in spite of my misfortunes and difficulties, they will be satisfied."[2] To L'Héritier, who had written to Michaux in Egmont to express his concern for his misfortunes, Michaux described the labor of restoring and repairing the damage to the contents of the eight chests and three trunks which had been entirely submerged in the sea: "I have been obliged to go over all the plants and change the paper several times. The first review has taken me sixteen days working from 4 o'clock in the morning until about 8 o'clock in the evening, and I have used seventeen reames of paper. . . . I find myself very happy that nothing will be lost with regard to the advantage to be derived from my travels and collections. I have not lost one single plant, only the colors are altered."[3]

On November 25, nearly eight weeks after his disaster at sea, the naturalist, his labors completed, set out at last for Paris. He embarked with his collections on a covered boat for the voyage from Amsterdam to Brussels, the first stage of their journey, after arranging with the admiralty office for the passage of his trunks and chests without customs inspection. En route to Paris, via Leyden, The Hague, Rotterdam, Brussels, and Ghent, he stopped in The Hague long enough to dine with the French minister and collect the 3,000 francs advanced by the French government in response to his request.[4]

His interest in birds had persisted. Even in the stressful days following the shipwreck he took pleasure in recalling that on the day of the fateful storm "there came on board ship two little birds, male and female, which I recognized as mountain finches," and, "the day after the tempest, an English gannet was found on the shore."[5] In Rotterdam he lingered to visit a famous bird collection,[6] and in Brussels he bought some Mississippi ducks to replace those lost in the shipwreck.

Two days before Christmas he arrived in the French capital, and on Christmas Eve hastened to the Jardin des Plantes for a joyful meeting with his former colleagues and friends. Received with the most gratifying acclaim by savants, government officials, and by the National Institute, of which he was an associate member, he entered upon a steady round of visits, dinners, conferences, and scientific meetings.[7] The group who now welcomed the naturalist within their circle included an impressive list of luminaries, among whom were André Thouin, Jean Baptiste Lamarck, Louis Lemonnier, Louis Daubenton, Claude Richard, René Désfontaines, as well as J. M. Cels, Antoine Laurent de Jussieu, Charles L'Héritier, and others, all scientists of renown.[8]

In his letter to André Thouin from Amsterdam, André Michaux had requested "I beg of you, inform my son of my arrival, for I do not know where he lives."[9] Communications in France had become so irregular and slow during the agonies of the Revolution that it seems probable the father had little up-to-date knowledge of the son he was about to meet again after nearly six years of separation, and only sketchy information of the youth's life during these crucial years of his maturing. Certainly when Michaux put his son on board ship in Charleston harbor, bound for his native land, he had no real comprehension of what was then happening in France, nor what those events presaged for the future. He believed that he was sending him back for greater financial security, superior educational opportunity, and better medical care.

François André had departed France as a boy of fifteen, raised on the fringe of the palace grounds, where, doubtless, as his father's companion, he had often visited the magnificent gardens of Versailles and witnessed the pomp and ceremony in the great courtyard of the palace and the comings and goings of the thousands of noblemen and their servants. Abruptly transported from the artificial elegance of this environment to the raw new republic across the sea, the youth had spent the next four or five years either in the rural South on the Charleston plantation, in the magnificent forests and mountains of the American wilderness, or the wild, semitropical regions of Florida, sharing with his father the labors, the dangers, and the triumphs of his demanding mission, and only occasionally exposed to the life of towns or cities.

When in late 1789 or early 1790 François André returned to the once familiar scenes of his childhood in France, he saw them through the eyes of a widely traveled youth of twenty, inevitably shaped by the variety and richness of his American experience.

Unfortunately, we have no contemporary documentary evidence of the young Michaux's activities during the ensuing crucial years nor of the effect upon him of the earth-shaking revolution taking place in the nation. We are reduced to reliance upon scraps of information garnered here and there from much later documents. From them we learn that he studied medicine at the old "Ecole de Santé" but we do not know when he pursued those studies nor even just when he was granted his Doctor of Medicine degree. We learn also that he received formal botanical instruction under the professors at the Jardin des Plantes (the Jardin du Roi of the Old Regime), but again we are not told when or for how long, or whether before, after, or concurrently with his medical studies. We do know that early in 1791 he took up residence in Paris at rue de la Harpe, number 133, an address very near the Collège du Médecin, and years later a friend of his, Elias Durand,[10] unequivocally reported in a biographical memoir prepared soon after Michaux's death[11] that he had studied medicine under the celebrated Corvisart and attended the clinical classes of Désault, chief surgeon of the Hotel Dieu, with a view of perhaps returning to America to practice.[12]

In view of the turmoil of French society during the last decade of the eighteenth century, it is not surprising that no documentary evidence of Michaux's educational years has survived. The blank pages of this period of his life do, however, invite speculation. It seems probable, for instance, that he followed the tradition established by Bernard de Jussieu of going to England to enrich his botanical studies, as his father had done during his apprentice years. Perhaps Michaux fils crossed the channel at some time during 1790 or 1791 when student exchanges between England and France were still possible. Evidence for such a visit, whenever it occurred, can be deduced from allusions in his *Travels* to what he had seen in England, as, for instance, in describing his travels in Kentucky, he wrote admiringly of the saddle and coach horses then being bred at Lexington, in contrast to the miserable-looking draught horses, which appeared to him still worse in Georgia and Carolina, remarking that "in short I must say that throughout the United States there is not a single draught-horse that can be compared to those I have seen in England." Similarly, he compared the poor oxen seen at work on the farms of upper Carolina unfavorably with those observed in England.[13]

Integral to any understanding of the significance of these years in the life and character of François André is some comprehension of the extraordinary events through which he lived in France during the first half of the last decade of the century. It is generally recognized that most of the reforms made by the revolutionary General Assembly up to the inauguration of the new constitutional monarchy in 1791 had been greatly needed. Many of those reforms survived the tumultuous years that followed and became part of the cultural heritage of modern France. The Assembly set up a sound framework for the constitutional monarchy, replete with checks and balances in the hope of ensuring a middle-of-the-road way for the future. It deserved success. However, before the close of 1791 events were conspiring to spell its doom.

In that spring came the death of Mirabeau, the most charismatic and influential leader to emerge between the beginning of the Revolution and the emergence of Napoleon. Although of noble birth, Honoré-Gabriel Mirabeau had become the beloved leader of the Third Estate, the representative of the common people in the Assembly. His death in April 1791 left a vacuum that could not be filled.

In June the attempted flight of the king and his family forfeited what lingering affection the people still had for the monarchy and a powerful traditional stabilizing influence was lost, cutting France loose from its moorings in the midst of a raging storm. Eroded morale and inept leadership fairly invited the next blow—the outbreak of war with both Austria and Prussia in the spring of 1792. By midsummer the army of France was disintegrating, her government in turmoil, and mobs were back on the streets of Paris. In mid-August a mob stormed the royal palace, overwhelmed its Swiss guards and forced the royal family to take refuge in the hall of the Assembly. Confronted by a threatening mob, a shaken National Assembly voted to depose the king and summon a National Convention. With the king in the custody of the people and foreign armies invading French soil, the moderate government fashioned by the revolutionary Assembly crumbled, leaving a leadership vacuum to be ineptly filled by a succession of fanatics, who would govern France by raw terror until the fall of Robespierre in 1794.

The elected Convention had no sooner taken over the reins of government than it found the country at war with most of the rest of Europe. Before the close of 1792, French armies were meeting with remarkable successes, in rapid succession conquering and annexing Savoy, the Rhineland, and the Netherlands. Spreading further terror abroad, the Convention ordered the execution of the king. Those incendiary acts were followed by a measure for a wholesale military draft that further fanned flames of dissent on the domestic front.

Out of the chaos in the summer of 1793 came those vehicles of terror: the Committee of Public Safety and the Committee of General Security, Robespierre, and the guillotine, which by the following summer had severed 20,000 French heads—events so revolting that a national revulsion began to surface. By the fall of 1795 even reactionary royalists dared to shout their dissent in the streets of Paris. To suppress the riots that ensued, a rising young general, Bonaparte, was sent to quell the disturbances and maintain order in the city. With his debut and the establishment of the Directory to take the government in hand, tensions relaxed. Although France's quarter century of trauma had yet a score of years to run its full course, after 1795 Frenchmen could once again feel secure in their homes, could sally forth and again speak their minds, albeit softly, without fear of prompt arrest and the guillotine.[14]

Rioting had continued intermittently through most of 1795. In April and May, responding to discontent following decontrol of food prices, mobs repeatedly marched on Convention Hall. But for the first time they were checked by firm action and no surrender to their demands. It is remarkable that through all those years of crisis and disorder the intellectual life of the capital continued to coexist in spite of the turmoil, as is demonstrated by the young Michaux's educational progress in that period. And even as the riots of April 1795 were in progress, we find him reporting to the new Committee of Public Instruction of the National Convention a message from his father in Charleston. He informed the Committee that his father had dispatched from the garden of Carolina quantities of seeds, the harvest of the previous summer spent in the Cherokee country, but the primary intent of his father's message was to express his concern for the two French gardens he had established in the United States. He asked the Committee to undertake the preparation of a report on them and "on the works to which Citizen Michaux has devoted himself."[15] It is probable that François André's status as a medical student served as a safeguard to exempt him from the menace of the revolutionary tribunals, but the process of keeping his balance and pursuing his career effectively amid the tensions of Paris during those years must inevitably have been a singularly maturing experience.

Unfortunately, neither Michaux, so far as we have been able to discover, has left any account of what must have been a dramatic and emotional reunion of father and son that December of 1796, in Paris, after six years of separation—six critical and sometimes perilous years for both. At the time of their parting so long ago in Charleston, Michaux père had said farewell to a raw adolescent youth of twenty, but the son who welcomed him home to Paris was an educated, competent, and socially poised man of twenty-six, already a promising initiate in the scientific circle of his father's colleagues. Whatever disappointments and frustrations André Michaux experienced on his return to France, and would experience in the next four years before he left Paris forever, he could have felt only joyful satisfaction in this son who now so perfectly fulfilled his hopes. One can be sure that during the next few weeks the two Michauxs "tired the sun with talking and sent him down the sky" as they filled in for each other all the separate and contrasting experiences of their eventful lives during the past six years in Paris and America.

There were American friends in Paris as well who provided the elder Michaux with links with his pro tempore home across the sea, most notably General Charles Cotesworth Pinckney, in whose Charleston home Michaux had often been a guest.[16] But he also visited, during these first exciting weeks in Paris, two men destined to play significant roles in the industrial development of the United States—Robert Fulton,[17] soon to astonish the world with his steamboat, and "Monsieur du Pont," a member of that talented and enterprising family whose name became synonymous with the industrial empire they established in America.[18]

The well-deserved honors and personal satisfactions of Michaux's homecoming were far from unalloyed. Cruel disappointment awaited him at Rambouillet. Of the more than 60,000 trees which he had sent back to France, only a fraction had survived. During the years of his royal patronage many of his shipments had been sent on by Marie

Antoinette to enrich royal gardens in her native Austria, while others were diverted to embellish the estates of court favorites. Of those that had managed to reach their destination in the royal nurseries and gardens of Paris and Rambouillet, where proper care awaited them, only a few had escaped the ravages of the Revolution. On the other hand, there still remained his herbarium and the large collection of seeds and plants from his last shipments and those that had accompanied him on his voyage home. With the resilience and resolution central to his character, Michaux prepared to retrieve his losses where possible and to begin his labors anew. In spite of the cataclysmic changes in the nation during his long absence, Michaux seems to have slipped back into his place in the scientific life of Paris with scarcely a ripple, responsive as always to the vital intellectual stimulation of the city. As for the political climate, one can imagine with what elation this longtime servant of the monarchy walked the streets of Paris for the first time as a free citizen of the republic.

At the end of January 1797 he ceased to keep his journal. The last entries concern the setting in order of the seeds he had brought back from the Illinois territories. He divided those seeds gathered on his last journey into hinterland America among Lemonnier, the Natural History Museum, and Cels, in whose gardens and nurseries so many of the plants he had collected were already thriving.[19]

He then requested the National Institute to appoint a commission to report on his American mission. Jussieu and Cels were entrusted with this assignment on the subjects of botany and agriculture, and Lacépède and Dolomieu on zoology and mineralogy. Receiving due recognition and merited honor for the achievements of his years of service in the United States, Michaux now applied to the government for a commission to return to that post to complete his researches. He submitted a report on the condition in which he had left the American nurseries, which he hoped to maintain, and stressed the advantage to science and to France to be derived from the expansion of his exploration of the American continent westward to the Pacific.

While awaiting the government's response to this petition, he sought the means necessary to meet his daily expenses. For seven years this celebrated naturalist had received no salary or other compensation from his government, and since his return to Europe, nothing beyond the mere pittance sent to Holland to relieve his destitution after his shipwreck. The Republic of France had repudiated all debts incurred by previous regimes, and the National Treasury was too depleted by the heavy expenses of war to meet its obligations on the domestic front or to reward its scientists, however deserving. Failing to receive the longed-for commission to return to America, Michaux, who had already exhausted his own fortune and his son's patrimony, again solicited the government for at least some portion of the debt due to him, only enough for subsistence and to enable him to publish the results of his research. The letters in which, at intervals over the next three years, this dignified and distinguished man was driven to petition his government for aid, make painful reading.

Living in Paris "with the same simplicity as if he had still been among the Indians," he struggled with two demanding tasks—preparing for publication his book *Histoire des Chênes de l'Amérique Septentrionale*, and his two-volume *Flora Boreali-Americana*. "My resources are exhausted," he wrote to the government in October of 1797, "and I can neither finish a work which is to be the fruit of twelve years of labor, fatigue, and perils, nor supply my subsistence." A memoir accompanied this petition, summarizing objectively and without exaggeration his remarkable career in the service of France and stating that his *Flora*, within six months of completion, "will settle the uncertainties and will give new knowledge and serve as a foundation for a complete natural history of North America."[20]

Hard-pressed as he was, he did not cease to be concerned, as well, for the fate of his American nurseries. Recalling with nostalgia especially the Charleston garden, where he had successfully cultivated so many rare and precious plants and trees collected on his journeys, he wrote (in duplicate) to Louis Bosc, who had at that time taken over the care of the Carolina establishment, and to the Himelys, his Charleston friends and patrons, also involved with the Charleston plantation, and remembered also to write to Saunier, now left on his own in charge of the New Jersey nursery.

It was about this time, too, that, searching anxiously for a way to regain financial independence by means of steady employment in his profession and inspired by his constant desire to use his knowledge and experience in the service of his country and of science, Michaux conceived a plan to establish a nursery of trees and foreign plants in the environs of Bayonne, below Bordeaux, on the low, sandy shore of the Bay of Biscay. To promote the project, he drew up a detailed prospectus setting forth the advantages of Bayonne for this purpose: its climate and soil, suitable to the greatest number of plants, its situation near the sea and the mountains, its nearness to such uncultivated lands as "Les Landes" whose empty and seemingly sterile acres, more than one hundred leagues in extent, could be reclaimed as forest lands by the planting of American pines, Weymouth pines (*Pinus strobus*), Canadian balsams, cedars of Lebanon; and the Pyrenees, almost denuded of trees, could be reforested by planting North American trees such as the tulip tree.[21] Bayonne had the further advantage of "easy correspondence" with the port of Bordeaux, accessible for importation of seeds and plants from all over the world. The process of reclamation would of necessity be gradual and require for its success the knowledge and experience of a professional cultivator.

After estimating the cost of such an undertaking to be "a sum of one hundred Louis a year for ten years" and outlining the specifications for the ideal cultivator to direct the project, qualifications which were patently his own, adding that he himself was on the point of beginning the establishment of such a nursery in the environs of Bayonne, he summed up the great benefits to be derived: "The first, to be able to remedy one day the scarcity of wood in the Pyrenees, the second, to procure the most suitable way to fertilize Les Landes. With the [financial] aids mentioned above, even though they may not be granted until after the war, one can unite to these benefits a great many others, such as to make known from the first years new excellent fruits, trees, and Plants useful to Medecine, to manufactures, etc."[22]

Nothing came of this practical and far-sighted proposal during Michaux's lifetime. In this as in many other ideas, based on sound botanical knowledge and comprehension of the principles of ecology, involving wise policies of soil conservation, reclamation, and reforestation, André Michaux was far ahead of his time. His Bayonne proposal was to bear fruit many years later in the successful restoration of the sterile lands of Les Landes and the reforestation of the Pyrenees.

The year 1799, marked in France by the rising star of Napoleon, brought to André Michaux, then concentrating all his energies on the completion of his book, a deep personal grief in the fatal illness of Louis Lemonnier, his friend and mentor, who had been like a father to him from his youth.[23] Michaux set aside everything else to be with and comfort his stricken friend, and, after the death of Lemonnier, he went to live at his home to give what aid he could to the widow and to take over the care of the cherished garden, where he had spent so many happy and instructive hours. Despite that distraction, by the end of this year he had completed the preparation of all the material for his folio volume, *Histoire des Chênes de l'Amérique Septentrionale*. The engravings were not yet finished, and work still remained to be done, as well, to put into final form for publication his *Flora Boreali-Americana*, when he received an offer to serve as naturalist on a voyage of exploration to the

Southern Seas, sponsored by the French government and commanded by Captain Nicolas Baudin.[24]

Baudin, born on the Île de Ré in Brittany, was a veteran of years of experience at sea, where he had served as captain of a ship of the line in the Austrian navy, and, in 1786 and 1789, had commanded two successful expeditions to the Indian and Pacific oceans to gather exotic plants for the royal gardens at Schönbrunn of the Emperor Joseph II, brother of Marie Antoinette. After the outbreak of war between Austria and his native France following the French Revolution, he had deposited his valuable scientific collections in Trinidad, from which he later retrieved them for the Museum of Natural History at the Jardin des Plantes in Paris. There he formed friendships and acquired patrons among the scientists, especially Lamarck, Cuvier, and Jussieu, whose influence with the National Institute, the Directory, and even with First Consul Bonaparte was instrumental in obtaining for him the coveted post as leader of the new *Voyage aux Terres Australes*.[25]

To André Michaux, for whom a return to America or to Persia now seemed impossible, the opportunity to accompany such an expedition in a professional capacity offered rich possibilities for botanical discoveries. Nevertheless, his state of mind during the last months before departure was very different from that of the eager young botanist of Louis XVI who, in 1785, had looked so eagerly forward to "the conquest of the New World." The mood in which he wrote his last urgent plea to the minister of the interior for even a small partial payment of the debt of 30,000 francs due him was one of disillusionment:

> *More than a month ago I had the honor to send you my accounts in the form prescribed. I described to you then my urgent need to receive some part of the funds owed to me. I entreat you to agree to consider my case.*
>
> *Here is a summary of my achievements: For nearly twenty years I devoted myself to serving my country. I have journeyed as a naturalist and as an agriculturist. I have visited Syria, Babylon, and Persia in all its length from the Indian Ocean to the Caspian Sea, etc. For eleven years, sent by the government, I traveled across North America from Hudson Bay to the tip of Florida. I have ascended many great rivers from the mouth to the source, the St. Lawrence River, the Ohio, the Savannah, etc. As a political agent I have gone among many savage nations on the Mississippi and the Missouri.*
>
> *I have brought back from the Orient monuments of the*

*highest antiquity, and plants, etc., and from America I have sent
more than 75 thousand tree plants, numerous collections of seeds,
plants, and herbarium, etc.*

*Your predecessors, Citizen Minister, have ordered me to
publish my works, and one sum of 12 thousand francs has been
decided upon by the minister, François de Neuf Chateau; I received at that time 12 hundred francs and, since more than sixteen months,* not an obole.

*The only resource of my fortune, which amounted at the be-
ginning of my work to 72 thousand francs, is reduced now to
what is due to me from your administration. My accounts have
been sent to your Bureau, since my return to France and, nevertheless, I have no prospect of receiving anything, either on my
present salary nor on the advances I have made from my own
funds.*

*Now I am on the point of leaving France and I have not
even the means to have my manuscripts copied in order to entrust
them to the printers. Through the prolonged delays up to the
present time, a part of my works and of my discoveries, instead of
bringing honor to France, are daily being published abroad in
foreign productions. In a few more decades the total loss will be
irreparable. It is my duty, Citizen Minister, to give you this last
information.*[26]

This chronicle of despairing need, borne with pride and dignity,
elicited, like its predecessors, no money but only regretful explanations
of the state of the Treasury, and extravagant eulogies of the destitute
naturalist. Saluting him as one "whose courage does not yield to any
obstacle and who goes again to brave the dangers of the sea and the
effects of diverse climates, for the purpose of enriching your country
with new discoveries," the minister assured Michaux, "botany will owe
to you its progress and France already counts you in the number of
those to whom she is indebted for foreign productions achieved
through continual hardships and brought in at the peril of their
lives."[27] These were prophetic words.

Michaux had requested the government, as conditions of his
participation in the expedition, not only a regular salary as research
naturalist, but also authorization to disembark and leave the expedition
wherever he deemed it beneficial to his mission. Frustrated in his hopes
of continuing his work either in Persia or in America, he looked now
toward the vast expanse of India with its wealth of exotic plants. As a

parting gift and a mark of esteem, the minister of the interior presented to him the twelve-volume folio work the *Hortus Indicus Malabarieus* to accompany him on his voyage, receiving, in turn, Michaux's grateful assurance: "My work on the oaks is on the point of appearing. My son, entrusted to oversee the printing, will have the honor of presenting to you a copy."[28]

Three weeks later Michaux made his last plea to the Ministry— "My departure is very near. I beg you, Citizen Minister, to give orders in your department to determine my salary."[29]

At last, a month before sailing date, Michaux was granted the same salary and expense allowance as formerly, as well as "a commission authorizing him to make in India and *wherever he shall disembark* all the researches relative to the progress of natural science."[30]

CHAPTER **15**

✑ Expedition to the South Seas, 1800–1802

EARLY IN THE MORNING of October 19, 1800, the expedition set sail from Le Havre amid an "impressive display" from the townspeople of good wishes and warm blessings for the success of the undertaking. The optimistic mood with which the voyage began was recalled with nostalgia, many years afterward, by one of the naturalists, Jacques Gérard Milbert, serving as geographer of the expedition:

> *I thought of the departure of that glorious expedition and of the moment when, as we passed the Tower of Francis I, we passed a band of musicians on the summit of that glorious edifice. As our ships entered the ocean, the fanfares were punctuated by repeated salvos from artillery in the forts and gunboats moored in the roadstead, the shore was covered with a gay crowd calling and waving good-byes, while a flotilla of little craft sailed along in our wake, despite the presence of the English fleet, which had suspended all hostilities. . . . [Though starting out to journey so far from my homeland] it would have been difficult to be sad amid*

the crowd of young sailors and distinguished naturalists all of whom were animated by the same zeal, the same enthusiasm for science.[1]

The purpose of the voyage was to examine in detail the southwest, west, northwest, and north coasts of New Holland (Australia) as well as the western coasts of New Guinea—regions as yet little explored which offered rich possibilities of research and discovery.[2]

The two corvettes, the *Géographe,* with Baudin in command, and the *Naturaliste,* under Lieutenant Commander Hamelin,[3] were especially outfitted for their scientific mission, with portions of the hold converted into a suitable repository for living plants and seedlings, grown from seeds collected on the voyage. In addition to officers and crew, the two ships carried a full complement of scientists, twenty-three in all, a category that included artists, engineers, gardeners, and naturalists, among whom was André Michaux, aboard the *Naturaliste.*

The conflict, always present on such an expedition, between "the demands of navigation and the demands of science," was to be exacerbated on this voyage by the character of Captain Baudin, a stern disciplinarian, who seems to have harbored from the beginning serious misgivings about the ability of his intellectual passengers—altogether too many for his liking—to comply with the rigid restrictions of life aboard his ships.[4] At a festive gathering at Le Havre, as they were about to set out on the long voyage, Baudin proposed, "We swear unity between officers and scholars. . . . Those who break this vow will be punished by the others' scorn."[5]—Words hardly calculated to reassure his independent-minded scholars.

However, the first weeks of sailing southward, with for the most part favorable winds and pleasant autumn weather, somewhat allayed Baudin's concern. His scientific passengers, he confided to his journal, seemed to be finding "this way of life most agreeable." As they approached the Canary Islands, flocks of larks, welcome harbingers of landfall, flew out to perch on the shipyards. As soon as the shores were sighted, "all the scientists and even some of the officers were so overjoyed they behaved like madmen." Confronted with the dramatic and beautiful spectacle of mountain peaks rising steeply from the sea, all hastened to supply themselves with sketchbooks and pencils and from one end of the ship to the other "there was not a soul to be seen who was not sketching."[6]

On November 2 the ships dropped anchor in the bay of Santa Cruz de Teneriffe, and in the afternoon officers and scientists alike went ashore to pay their respects to the Spanish governor as well as to the French consul, who had been in touch with Michaux before the arrival of the expedition. During their twelve days at Santa Cruz, delayed by myriad difficulties in obtaining supplies, an increasing friction became evident between Captain Baudin, intent on enforcing strict regulations on all aboard his vessels, and the scientists, to whom such rigid restrictions in port appeared not only meaningless and irksome but incompatible with the proper performance of their missions ashore. Finding the volcanic island a rich source of exotic flora and fauna, the naturalists understandably wished to go ashore as frequently as possible, to the annoyance of Baudin, who complained that "they came and went as freely as one does at a fair."[7] Michaux's biographer, who was his friend and colleague as well, tells us that, during his stay at Teneriffe, Michaux botanized freely on the mountains, "returning late every night and always laden with seeds and plants."[8]

The long voyage from Teneriffe to Île de France (now Mauritius), on the other side of Africa in the Indian Ocean, made even more exhausting by long windless periods when the ships remained motionless and becalmed day after day, and by intervals of terrific storms battering and driving the ships off course, did nothing to relieve the lack of harmony on board between Baudin and the scientists. Yet, from Baudin's daily journal entries, it is evident that there were many compensations and diversions. "The first arose from the sight of flying fish. The scientists, no doubt seeing them for the first time, were so amazed by them that each time the wash of the ship brought one out of the water the person who saw it became an object of respect for all the others."[9] There were also the capture of a large shark, new to many of the naturalists, and of a 200-pound porpoise, as well as the almost daily haul of exotic fish and molluscs from the deep, some more like beautiful flowers than like living creatures.[10]

By mid-December they had crossed the equator and in February 1801 were rounding the Cape of Good Hope, accompanied by Cape gannets, stormy petrels, and the seemingly legendary albatrosses, grey and white, some of which they shot, "one with a wing spread of 10 feet."[11] Day after day their sea hauls brought up from the depths singularly beautiful fish of curious shapes and colors. On March 3 Baudin recorded excitedly the discovery in their nets of a chambered nautilus "with its animal inside," a specimen he believed hitherto unknown.

At last, on the afternoon of March 14, after 122 days at sea since Teneriffe, the shout of "Land Ho" from the masthead hailed the welcome sight of Île de France on the horizon. Two days later the two ships anchored in the harbor of Port Louis, where they were to remain for nearly six weeks. There most of the naturalists left the ship to take lodgings in the town, eager to explore the island. On this island the French naturalist Pierre Poivre had established, half a century earlier, his famous botanical garden "Jardin des Pamplemousses," where he had collected beautiful plants and from which he had sent hundreds of rare species to France, including varieties of scented acacias, amaranths, iris and lilies. From this garden also his celebrated nephew, Pierre Sonnerat, had sent to the King's Garden in Paris specimens of his collection of those strange tropical trees, the palms.[12]

Michaux was entranced by the abundance and variety of the island's flora—exceeding in magnificence even that of Persia or of North America.[13] As was his custom when botanizing in new territory, he spent days at a time in the forest, accompanied only by a single black, living sparingly on bread and water and sleeping under the trees. Not only did he bring back rich collections from these forays but he planted, in turn, in the soil of the island, seeds and seedlings suitable for naturalization there. His need for a way station for his collection and a nursery in which to place his productions before sending them on to France was met by the hospitality of a resident of the island, Martin de Montcamp, who had traveled with Michaux in the deserts of Arabia years before. Montcamp not only invited the naturalist to reside on his plantation but provided him with land for his nursery and an assistant.[14]

As his exploration of the island's flora was still far from complete when Captain Baudin, in the last week of April, gave the order for the departure of the expedition, Michaux resolved to abandon the voyage, as his contract permitted him to do, in favor of continuing his botanical work in Île de France and of extending his research to the neighboring island of Madagascar, reputed to be an even richer botanical paradise. Concerned lest others associated with the expedition might follow his example, he kept his plan secret until the evening before the departure of the ships at which time he took formal leave of Captain Baudin, promising to send him a rich collection of plants. He also sent to the minister of the interior an explanation of his decision to remain at Île de France, and to the National Institute a detailed report on this French colony, as well as letters to his son, requesting supplies for his projected work on the island.[15]

Although the withdrawal of André Michaux from the expedition seems to have been professionally motivated and conducted with proper formality and discretion, there seems little doubt that wide-spread disaffection with Baudin as commander was largely responsible for the fact that a considerable number of scientists, as well as ship's officers, elected to remain on Île de France rather than to continue the voyage. Baudin noted that all but two of the ten scientists on the *Naturaliste* left the ship and, counting the desertions among the crew, more than forty persons in all remained behind.[16]

The rest of the voyage was plagued by ill-fortune, illness, and death, including that of many of the remaining scientists. Though Australia was reached and substantial collections eventually found their way back to France, the scientists in Paris were "horrified by the death toll." Baudin himself never returned to France, dying at Île de France on the return journey, of the tuberculosis from which he had suffered during much of the voyage. "Guillaumin, the historian, was to write, 'his pride, violent temper, scorn for the scientific work, and indifference to the sufferings and lives of others caused his death to be seen as a manifestation of immanent justice.'"[17]

The only comment we have from André Michaux on the expedition is a query in a letter to his son, dated from Île de France over five months after the departure of the ships for Australia.

> *Report to me exactly what is being thought in Paris of the disembarkment of officers, naturalists, artists, and part of the crew from the expedition, and especially how Thouin and Jussieu and the patrons of Baudin regard the matter.*
>
> *Monsieur Cels will probably share with you, my dear son, the letters I write to him; they will give you more details than I can tell you in this one. The only thing I am in need of in this country is some large, strong, gray paper, such as that in which I sent plants to Monsieur Ventenate.*

This letter, written to the son he was never to see again, has a special poignance as the last word we have in his hand. To pay for the purchases, he authorized his son to receive for him a portion of his salary "if the minister of the interior judges it suitable to give me, on account, 1,200 francs." Planning to go on soon to Madagascar and perhaps from there to India, Michaux, always a keen and thorough scholar in his field, asked his son to send him also "the continuation of the *Flora Indica,* of which I have three previous volumes, works in la Physiologie vegetale by Philibert, or anything else by this author. . . . In a word everything new on la Physiologie vegetale, everything which has appeared on the Botany of India." On a more practical level he asked for "12 pairs of silk stockings at 15 francs a pair, long and strong, and of a clear gray, 12 padlocks at 3 francs a piece." Remote from the world of Paris and out of touch with events there, he added, "If the war still continues, send me, of all that, only the gray paper, the 12 padlocks, and some work on la Physiologie vegetale."

Following the fond closing "I embrace you," he added postscripts: "If our friend Bosc is not in America, embrace him for me." One is especially touched by his eager concern for the progress of his botanical works, the fruits of his long labors, which he was never to see in book form. "My compliments to our friend Redouté.[18] At what stage is the printing of the two works: *Histoire des Chênes* and the *Flora Boriali-Americana*? If some information is needed, I can send it. How has Richard conducted himself on our behalf? I can send him some shells; I have not sent them because I wished to hear from him first."[19]

Michaux remained on Île de France for about nine more months after the writing of this letter. During that time his fellow naturalist Bory de St. Vincent,[20] who had sailed with him on the *Naturaliste* and had also remained on the island, left to go to the neighboring Isle de Bourbon (now Réunion Island) to study its natural history. From there he sent Michaux seeds and plants for his nursery at Île de France. With this friend and colleague Michaux had discussed his own plans for botanical research on the island of Madagascar, where he hoped to introduce the culture of European vegetables and fruits, to establish gardens in which to nurture native plants to be sent to the nurseries on Île de France, from which, in the proper season, they would be sent on to France—perhaps also to gather material for a flora of Madagascar, attempted before by French naturalists but never completed.

About the middle of June 1802 he sailed to Madagascar where he landed on the east coast near Tamatave. After exploring the area for a suitable site for a garden, he selected a place nearby where he set to work to establish his garden as a way station for the plants he planned to collect for eventual shipment to France.[21] Though he had been warned of the dangers of the climate in the low coastal regions of the east coast, Michaux, who had survived many hazards in a variety of climates, had great confidence in his own powers of resistance and proceeded to work with his customary zeal, putting in long hours under the tropical sun, preparing the soil for the garden, as usual setting an example for his hired laborers, who, as had often been the case, worked too slowly for his ardor.

As always he seemed to be working against time. For the first few months his health remained good. He intended, when the garden site was prepared and the plantings made of the plants collected in that area, to go up into the higher altitudes of the interior to settle in the cultural and governmental center of the island where the climate was said to be salubrious. But just as he was ready to leave the hot and humid coastal region, he was stricken by "the fever of the country," probably a tropical malaria, during the second attack of which he died, late in November 1802.[22]

It is probable that the news of Michaux's tragic death did not reach the French capital until the spring of 1803. The esteem and affection of his friends and fellow scientists at the Jardin des Plantes and their grief in his loss found moving expression in the *Memoires* written for the *Annales du Muséum d'Histoire Naturelle* by one of their number J. P. F. Deleuze, who knew and revered him. We are indebted to Deleuze for his comprehensive summary of Michaux's life and botanical travels and for his eloquent tribute to the character and achievements of his fellow naturalist.

Michaux would be mourned, Deleuze pointed out, not by fellow scientists alone, for "in every country he had visited he left friends from whom the news of his death will receive the tribute of tears, and his name will be the longer remembered because everywhere he employed himself in rendering services the evidence of which will ever exist and be ever renewed."[23]

No portrait of André Michaux has ever come to light. "Nor is there left to us a single tracing of the furrows or the smile wrinkles that may have been his."[24] The administration of the National Museum of Natural History at the Jardin des Plantes, in appreciation of his services to the science of natural history, and especially to that establishment, voted that his bust would be placed "on the facade of the temperate greenhouse, with those of Commerson, Dombey, and other travelers, by whom its collections have been enriched."[25] But this was never done. A more enduring monument remains in the achievements of his life.

Through the lens of his letters and journals we catch revealing glimpses of his character and personality. Unfortunately, few of those who knew him left a record of their impressions, but Deleuze has given us this description of his friend:

> *Michaux, though of a silent turn, was of a frank temper; he made few professions of friendship; but where he could do a service to any one he regarded no trouble. In his excursions in America having met with several Frenchmen in distress, he opened his purse to them, and procured them other assistance. Many proofs of this were found in the accounts of his expenses;*

but the names of those he had assisted were not mentioned. His extreme simplicity, and the love and habit of independence which had become familiar to him in his wandering and solitary life, gave a singularity to his manners and appearance; but in this a desire of making himself noticed had no share. His manners were not those of any particular country, but equally suitable to all: appearing neither like a Frenchman, Englishman, or Canadian, wherever he went he was found more to resemble the natives than any other foreigner.

In conversation he took little share, for he neither talked of nor listened to any thing that was not useful. When he passed through a town, he visited the markets, to inform himself of the various parts whence the productions came. In the fields he interrogated the inhabitants respecting the details of their mode of culture. In fine, to an activity which never permitted him to lose a single moment, he united a perseverance which was never discouraged.

His moral qualities were so well known, that when he was sent to America, after his salary was fixed, he received unlimited letters of credit on the towns through which he had to pass, to furnish him with such sums as might be necessary for the collections he thought proper to make, and for the expenses of his travelling. His bare receipt was every where a bill of exchange, which the government engaged to honour. Michaux only made use of this power for the precise object to which it was destined, never appropriating it to pay himself any part of the arrears of his salary. Under such circumstances he could leave his son but a very small part of paternal fortune. But this young man inherits a venerated name; knowledge acquired by his labours and travels in company with his father, and the strongest title to the countenance and protection of government.[26]

CHAPTER **16**

❧ The Legacies of
André Michaux

WHEREVER HE WENT in his green crusade, he introduced new vegeta-bles, fruits, plants, and trees—"and the traveler cannot penetrate into Persia, Africa, or the vast continent of North America without finding some family that will say, 'These are trees that we owe to André Mi-chaux.'" In France he introduced new plants, not only to the national gardens and nurseries, as well as to the private gardens of his friends, Cels, Malesherbes, Lemonnier, and others, but he also labored ef-fectively to spread throughout the country those foreign trees he con-sidered adaptable to the soil of the various regions of France—walnut, cypress, tupelo, varieties of oak, maple, and ash—thereby substantially enriching the national forests and French economy.[1]

Michaux's active life and extensive travels left little time for writ-ing. Yet he maintained, throughout the years of his botanical odyssey, careful records of his observations and discoveries which he looked forward to publishing in book form as the fruits of his labors for the advancement of science. As we have seen, he worked steadily toward this goal from the date of his return from America in 1796 until his departure with Baudin in October 1800. He had finished his book on the oaks, though the engravings were not yet completed, when he em-barked on his voyage, leaving to his son the responsibility of overseeing its publication, which took place the following year.[2] This magnificent volume, written in French, with an introductory essay, presents descrip-tions of twenty species and several varieties of American oaks, systemat-ically arranged according to the shape of the leaves and the fructifica-tion, annual or biennial, and including information on the regions of France where each species may be most successfully naturalized. Cop-iously and beautifully illustrated by P. J. and H. J. Redouté, the book begins with a preface by the author, written aboard the *Naturaliste*, enroute to the Southern Seas:

> *During the twenty years that I have spent in traveling in Asia as*
> *well as in America, I have not been able to find either the leisure*
> *or the means to make known the results of my observations. After*
> *my return to France I was devoting myself to this purpose when,*
> *named by the government to make part of the expedition of Cap-*

tain Baudin, I have again left my country, to go with this navigator and other scholars who are accompanying him, to sail the Southern Seas. Before my departure I have put the finishing touches to my Histoire des Chênes de l'Amérique *which I publish today,*[3] *and to my* Flora Boreali-Americana, *which will appear after that. I have left to my son the task of overseeing the printing of these two works.*

Particularly moving are the closing words in view of the brief time left to him:

There is another work which I would have wished very much to place before the public, the detailed history of my journeys; but the circumstances of which I have just spoken have not permitted me to undertake it; I do not know when I shall return, and I must content myself with presenting a summary of the itinerary of the countries I have traveled through, both in order to give an idea of what I have done to serve my country and to contribute to the progress of botany, and in order to be useful to travelers who will wish to visit the same countries, as well as, lastly, to make known the names of men of good will and friends of science who, outside of Europe, have contributed to my survival and to the success of my work.

The preface concludes with the statement that this summary of his travels will appear with his *Flora.*[4] It is followed by an introductory essay on the history of the oak, and a discussion of the nature and the uses of this family of trees, many of whose species Michaux had examined in all their variety during his American travels. Pointing out that this valuable tree grows naturally in all parts of the temperate zone, in Europe, in Asia, in America, and even in Africa, Michaux comments that its cultivation requires peculiar care as "transplanting, grafting, and other means of reproduction are not always favorable to it."

Nature has particularly formed this tree for large forests. There it reigns sovereign over the other vegetables and furnishes abundant nourishment for animals of different natures. In Europe, the deer, the squirrel, and the wild boar live during the whole winter on the acorns of our woods; in Asia, the pheasants and wild pigeons share them with the beasts; in North America, the bear, the squirrel, the pigeon and the wild turkey are also fed by

Quercus prinus, *rock chestnut oak. Illustration by P. J. Redouté, from André Michaux's* Histoire des Chênes de l'Amérique, *Paris, 1801. (Courtesy of the American Philosophical Society)*

the nuts of the oak. Several sorts of quadrupeds and birds on that continent, after having consumed the fruits of a territory, emigrate in innumerable flocks and droves to regions where these productions are more plentiful.[5]

Michaux considers the oak the tree, of all trees, whose wood is most widely and usefully employed, in the construction of houses, ships, and husbandry tools. It is useful also in medicine and indispensable to the tanner and dyer. "Indeed, it is the daily support of fire, so necessary to our existence." Michaux had observed the diversity among members of the oak family in many regions and over many years, and fully appreciated the difficulties in identifying the different species of oak. On that feature of the family he comments:

The oak family comprehends a great number of species which are not known; and the greater part of those which grow in America appear under such diversified forms when they are young, that we cannot be certain what they are until they have arrived at maturer age, or have got their full growth. It seems that nature has intended to multiply this tree, and render it of general utility, by causing to grow in the same latitudes various species which could accommodate themselves to the diversity of temperature and soil. For the oak does not always grow in the forests, nor elevate its top to a very great height. There are places which produce nothing but dwarf oaks, such as the Kermes *oak (Quercus coccifera), and some others, which are naturally small; while there are others which grow among the rocks, on the shores of the Mediterranean Sea, whose moderate height is owing merely to the degrees of the soil where they have taken root.*[6]

There follows a description of the effect produced on the growth of oaks by the custom practiced by the Indians and the pioneers of annually burning the meadows to renew the grass, attract the deer, and pasture the cattle, during which practice the conflagration spreads to the surrounding forests, destroying the great trees. "The horizontal roots of several species of oak, detached from the trunk, reproduce by themselves, and separately, shoots which produce fruit afterwards when not more than two or three feet high." To the casual observer these "dwarf trees" may seem to be a particular species.[7]

"The description of the oaks of North America has been hitherto obscure, for several reasons": only detached observation of the trees by botanists visiting this country, with too little attention to fructification, and the consequent combining of several species under the same denomination; and the failure to take into account, in the figures given of American oaks cultivated in Europe, the effects of a different temperature, and the like from that of their native land. Michaux's characteristically scientific method of clearing up his own doubts was to plant and cultivate during his residence in America "all the species which I have had opportunity to observe and collect; and after two years, I had the satisfaction to recognize all the varieties which had perplexed me so much when I traversed the woods."[8]

One regrets that space does not permit quotation in full from this introductory essay, for this alone would be sufficient to refute the oft repeated claim that André Michaux was exclusively a field botanist with no literary ability. This patently unjustified assumption, held by C. S. Sargent and other botanists, who willingly grant Michaux preeminence as discoverer and collector but are reluctant to allow him the authorship of his own works, is apparently based on the so-called crude and laconic style of the daily journal he kept of his American travels, although this cherished document was clearly intended to be only for the most part a convenient shorthand record of the day's observations, discoveries, and activities. Even so, though often hastily jotted down in the wilderness by campfire or moonlight, these entries at times contain passages of eloquent narration and description. The suggestion by Sargent that "some author of greater literary skill than Michaux possessed must have either written or recast and corrected the *Histoire des chênes de l'Amérique*" seems wholly gratuitous and ignores Michaux's statement in his preface to this work: "j'ai mis la dernière main"—"I have put the finishing touches."[9] In refutation of Sargent's suggestion, we fortunately have other evidence of Michaux's competence with his pen: not only the hundreds of letters he wrote, many of which, especially those to d'Angiviller and Lemonnier and Thouin, are models of epistolary skill, but also his comprehensive and lucid proposal for a garden in Bayonne for the naturalization of foreign plants, as well as the journal of his Persian travels, containing vivid descriptions of the East and stirring accounts of his adventures, as well as scientific data clearly presented.

It is even more surprising to find Michaux described as a man of little cultivation.[10] Not only was he an accomplished Latin scholar, familiar also with Greek and Persian, and several other languages, but a lifelong, dedicated student who carried with him on his journey to America a trunk full of books, and continued throughout his career to request shipments of the latest scientific publications to be sent out to him from France.

As an indication of the quality of his mind, one need only consider a list of his friends and associates, such as Lamarck, Lemonnier, Thouin, Cels, Bosc, and dozens of other savants, as well as his membership in the exalted company of the National Institute of France. It was for that distinguished society that Michaux prepared his memoir on the date palm tree, which he presented to the Institute on April 26, 1799.[11] This ten-page memoir is an excellent example of his ability to organize the botanical knowledge he had acquired through observation, study, and experience, and apply it effectively to a practical problem.

The first part of the memoir consisted of a convincing argument for the adaptation by France of enlightened programs of plant importation and naturalization in her American colonies where plants native to China, Africa, and India could readily be naturalized in regions situated in the same latitudes as the regions from which they came.[12] He pointed out the great economic advantages to the people of the colonies, as well as to France, of such a botanical and agricultural program, properly carried out. There followed a discussion of the best methods to be used in acclimatization to ensure the greatest success, with emphasis on the primary necessity of establishing a nursery or garden in which to plant seeds and cultivate plants.

As an example of foreign plants whose importation and naturalization would be particularly advantageous, Michaux cited the palm trees in their many useful varieties. "The trees of this class," he maintained, "occupy the first rank in the vegetable kingdom; they are to the vegetable kingdom what man is to the animals."[13] He selected for detailed discussion the date palms with whose cultivation and uses he had become thoroughly familiar in his travels in the East:

> The Arabs, to whom from time immemorial we have been indebted for the training of horses and camels and for the domestication of sheep, have always, as well, cultivated the date tree. The fruit of this tree has become, through their efforts, a food of basic subsistance and an abundant resource. I have traveled among different Arab nations, established on the shores of the Tigris, the Euphrates, and the Persian Gulf, who derive their chief nourishment from it. This is what I have observed: The Arabs cultivate three principal varieties of dates; the first is the most abundant, it takes the place of bread and is very wholesome; the second serves only to make brandy, it is dangerous to eat because it produces deadly indigestion; the third is eaten fresh soon after it ripens.[14]

The culture of the date demands very special care, and the Arabs have developed methods of cultivation that greatly increase the yield and improve the quality of this fruit. Two or three years before Michaux arrived in Basra in the Persian Gulf region in 1782, an incident occurred that illustrated the vital role of the date tree in the economy of these Arab countries where a man's wealth was estimated by the number of these trees he owned, and it was not unusual for an individual to own a forest of two or three thousand date palms.

The Persians, who at that time (1779–80) were besieging Basra, "ravaged the country between the city and the sea, which is very fertile and covered with immense forests of date trees. To carry out more easily their plan of devastation they cut down all the male palms only, so that the following year there would be no harvest."[15] But Michaux reported that some of the inhabitants, who had suffered in this way in previous wars, had preserved in glass vials some of the male flowers from the preceding year, which served to fertilize the female trees at the time of pollination and saved the harvest.

Michaux recalled that the dates cultivated on the seacoast of Persia were particularly delicious and were called royal dates, esteemed for the tables of governors and princes, "but the region, ravaged by wars for a hundred years, cannot furnish enough for export overseas. The caravans carry them into the interior of Persia, to Shiraz, Esfahan, and even as far as Rasht, on the Caspian Sea—as I have seen with my own eyes."[16]

The article concluded with a description of some of the other useful foreign plants that might be successfully naturalized in the French Colonies, including, among others, several species of palm trees in addition to the date palm, as well as the litchi of China, the pistachio nut, and the mango, especially the superior species of mango cultivated on the Persian Gulf, some seeds of which Michaux had brought back from Persia in 1785.[17]

The best known and most extensive of Michaux's works, the *Flora Boreali-Americana*, the first comprehensive flora of North America, was published in Paris in 1803, probably before March 19 and probably before word of the author's death had reached Paris.[18] The *Flora* was, indeed, as Michaux described it, the fruit of his labors, gleaned from the long and arduous years of botanical travels and covering in its scope the whole range of his journeys in the New World, from the Bahamas and Florida northward to the region of Hudson Bay and from the Atlantic westward to the Mississippi River and the Illinois territory. As we have seen, the final responsibility for the publication of the *Flora* had been delegated by Michaux to his son, who fully repaid his father's confidence, as he was in later years to fulfill his father's highest aspira-

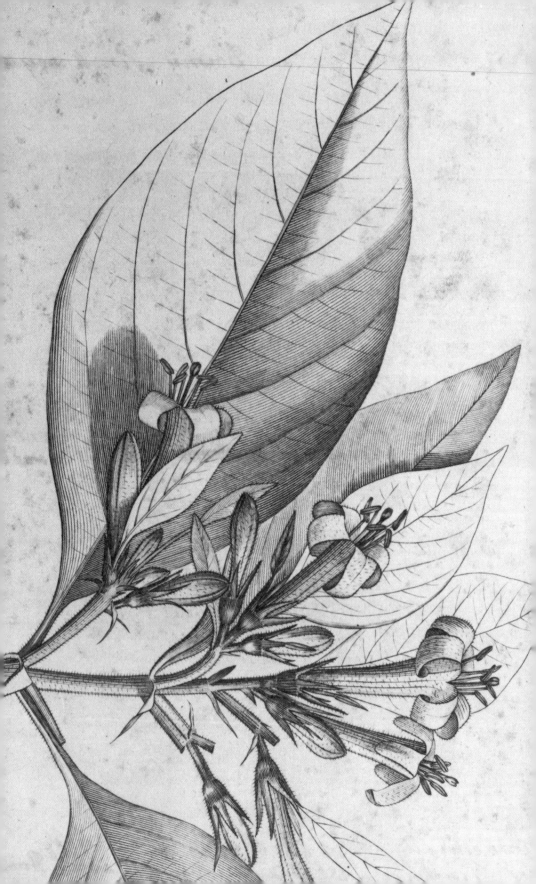

tions by his achievements in the field of science to which they both devoted their lives. In the preface, François André modestly described his task:

> *I now exhibit my father's Flora, gathered up from the author's*
> *unfinished manuscript (since he was unable to complete it him-*
> *self). . . . He had not yet put the final touches to the manuscript*
> *of the present work which indeed still consisted of loose sheets on*
> *which he had written out, one by one, tentative descriptions of the*
> *new genera and species. . . . Since my own training in botanical*
> *matters had not progressed far, I submitted these sheets to the*
> *scrutiny of some professional botanists in the hope that with their*
> *advice, I might better fulfill the editorial duty which had been en-*
> *trusted to me by my father when he set out on his expedition.*[19]

The well-known botanist Claude Richard is credited with the role of advisor and assistant to the young Michaux in his formidable assignment, as is indicated by the references to Richard in the postscript of André Michaux's letter to his son from Île de France.[20]

Since it seems likely that François André had worked closely with his father in the preparation of material for both the *Oaks* and the *Flora* during the four years they were together in Paris before Michaux père embarked with Baudin, he had already served a valuable apprenticeship and had, no doubt, already formed a close association with his father's colleagues and friends at the Jardin des Plantes, "the professional botanists" to whose advice he refers. Working with him also as friend and counsellor was the botanical artist P. J. Redouté, whose incomparable illustrations enhance the two volumes of the *Flora* as they did the magnificent *Oaks*.

The text of the *Flora,* including the preface by François André, is in Latin, and the classification of plants follows the Linnaean, or sexual, system. As François André assures us that no species is included except those the author had seen or gathered himself, each habitat notation has a special interest, evoking the presence of the indefatigable and dedicated naturalist wherever across the face of the American landscape— *in sylva Carolinae, in excelsis montibus, ad lettora Canadae*—he had observed or gathered the species.

Pinckneya pubens, *fever tree, described by André Michaux and named by him for Charles Cotesworth Pinckney. From P. J. Redouté's illustration for André Michaux's* Flora Boreali-Americana, *Paris, 1803. (Courtesy of the South Caroliniana Library of the University of South Carolina)*

The first review of the *Flora* to be published in this country seems to have been a two-page article in the *New York Medical Repository* for 1805, unsigned, but presumably written by the editor, Samuel Lathan Mitchill.[21] Describing the *Flora* as "a most desirable addition to the Natural History of our country," the review emphasized the importance of limiting the species to those seen or gathered by the author, assurance which "must give to this Flora great value, and render it peculiarly interesting to the lovers of Botany in the United States. Genuine descriptions recently made of the plants of the country by an actual observer, possessing remarkable skill and discernment in the practical as well as the theoretical parts of the Science, cannot fail to increase the facility of its requirement among our studious youth. To them, in particular, it will shorten the way to knowledge, and at the same time, render it much more easy and delightful."

One misses from the *Flora* any mention of the economic or medical uses of the various plants (an omission noted in the above review), which were aspects of botany of particular interest to Michaux and often discussed in his letters and journal. Had he lived, we might confidently have hoped to have other editions of the *Flora,* fuller and more complete, as well as, perhaps, that work referred to in the preface to the *Histoire des Chênes* as "another work which I would have wished to place before the public, the detailed history of my journeys."

"The reputation of Michaux, however, does not depend upon his literary achievements; he worked in the field and in the forest and not in the closet. Not one among the self-sacrificing explorers and collectors of the plants of this continent better deserves the gratitude and appreciation of the world of science. Not one of them has ever seen more clearly, or has endured more willingly and uncomplainingly, the perils and hardships of the frontier and the wilderness. His eye always detected the rarest and most interesting plants—the ambition and long the despair of plant hunters who have now for a century been following in his footsteps."[22]

In January 1901 the Bureau of Agriculture issued its report, reviewing the mission of André Michaux to America and its aims and achievements, with high praise for his work.[23]

"Three years ago," the report of the Bureau said, André Michaux returned to France, "after twelve years traveling in North America," to put in order "his manuscripts and herbarium and deposit them in this country. But his passion for dangerous voyages which can produce great results has prevented citizen Michaux from finishing his works. He has left it to his son to publish them, and has just set out with

Captain Baudin. He plans a journey twice as long as the expedition, itself."

Finally, in its retrospective observations, the report commented that the fruits of his American nurseries and his wide travels were shipments to France of "a very great quantity of seeds and plants," most of which were destroyed during the Revolution, owing to the "greed of the sellers and acquirers of those national assets"; although there yet remained some remnants of his work at Roule nursery, the Trianon, and the "great new nursery."

The report then expressed some tentative conclusions in respect to the two American nurseries: that probably the Carolina establishment should be sold, since the vegetation indigenous to that part of the United States would be adaptable only to southernmost France. As for the New Jersey garden, it had been proposed that it might be usefully retained for use as a depot where seedlings could be gathered or grown for shipment to France. Most importantly, it recited the belief entertained by Michaux fils that commercial nurserymen might more economically supply the needs of France in her quest for American seeds and plants to enhance the value of French farms and forests. It concluded with the recommendations that François André Michaux be sent to America on a two-year assignment, to sell the Carolina nursery, after sending its valuable stock of plants to France; that he should investigate the possible continued use of the Jersey garden; it would be useful as a temporary depot for seedlings destined for France, and adequate arrangements can be made for securing them through commercial channels, but if it would not be needed for use as such a depot, it, too, should be sold. By late spring we find that plans were already advanced to send the young Michaux back to America to carry his father's interrupted American mission to a satisfactory conclusion.

Before making his final decision to dispatch "Michaux fils, botanist" on the second Michaux botanical mission to the United States, the minister of the interior asked the Consultant Bureau of Agriculture for suggestions and advice in respect to the proposed expedition. In July he had its long report in hand.[24] It agreed that the Carolina establishment was not generally useful, reporting that Citizen Bosc had recently visited it and reported that Himely had kept it from going to ruin and that he should be promptly reimbursed to the extent of about 4,000 francs. He agreed that this garden was more valuable for the advancement of botany than for the advancement of forestry and agriculture, so the Consultant Bureau recommended, despite expected protests, that it should be disposed of after the plants of value there were removed and suggested that it be donated to the Society of Agriculture in Charleston, believing that that would make an "honorable bond for the French government" and might serve to get free returns in desirable seeds from there.

As for the nursery near New York, it recommended reimbursement of Saunier, but only for his disbursements for repairs, improvements, and taxes paid by him, "he having done nothing for the government . . . since the beginning of the Revolution." After observing that for thirty years Americans had been sending into France plants and seeds of trees of that area to France, it advised that Citizen Michaux be directed to renew and assure that correspondence and make contracts for the renewal of such services. Those measures, it was thought, might render the New York establishment useless. However, in view of the possible opposition to the sale of it, it was suggested that arrangements might be made for a tenant to have use of the place for his own benefit in return for annual shipments of seeds, as specified by Michaux, equivalent in value to its rental value, and that Saunier be given priority in the selection of such a tenant.

There were pages more in the report of the Consultant Bureau, given over mostly to procedural details on the means of accomplishing the recommended sales, the time of Michaux's departure, the shipments he was to make from America, how the seeds and plants were to be packed, the sorts most desired. Specimens of wood, a foot in length, of the branches of the trees of which seedlings or seeds were sent, were to accompany each species for comparison with those grown in France. It added the observation that André Michaux had made such a collection but that it had been left in America. It should be recovered, if possible, for it would be of much interest. While in America F. A. Michaux should also make further seed and plant collections in the mountains of North Carolina between August and November and promptly dispatch them to France, to arrive in time for spring planting. He should bring back with him the most valued seed when he returns. Before then he should find time also to make collections in the Allegheny and Cumberland mountains.

The report took occasion to bemoan the loss the country had suffered, in the course of the Revolution, of most of its nurseries, which left it with very limited facilities. It urged the Minister to move to recover these properties with the comment that the journey of Citizen Michaux fils will be almost useless if there was no place to receive what he would send back and what he would arrange to have sent in the future, adding a comment that the place designed to receive these

American treasures should be regarded as being for the rural economy, the forests and the art of botany, tantamount to what the government's holdings at Rambouillet were for the development of sheep productive of fine wool. Before appending its closing summary, the report provided a detailed financial statement of the estimated costs involved in the recommended expedition—16,000 francs (about $3,500.00). Of this sum it advised that 6,000 francs be advanced to Michaux before his departure.

By the middle of July 1801, the prolonged preliminaries were drawing to a conclusion. François André was summoned by the minister of the interior and provided with a letter of appreciation to Himely for his services in looking after the Charleston establishment since the elder Michaux's return to France, and given his formal commission. It included specific instructions to sell the Charleston garden after seeing to the removal and shipment to France of its useful plants and seeds. Finally, it directed "all agents of the Republic to assist, protect and defend Michaux, the younger, in the course of his mission, his researches and his travels."[25]

In July in the course of his preparations for departure Michaux somehow secured a quantity of the seed of that delightful, small aromatic evergreen, commonly known as bayberry, or wax myrtle, *Myrica pensylvanica,* which, by way of an expression of his gratitude to his fellow members of the Societé d'Agriculture du Seine-et-Oise, for their assistance in having him named to undertake his mission to America, he arranged to have Silvestre[26] distribute among them with instructions as to its culture.[27]

The timing of the appearance of *Histoire des Chênes* in late spring of 1801 was felicitous for the young Michaux, permitting him to carry with him when he sailed for America, a few months later, several copies of this magnificent volume, an appropriate introduction for him to scientific circles there, and, fittingly, in the field in which he, himself, would in later years garner fame.[28]

Part Two
❧ FRANÇOIS ANDRÉ MICHAUX

THE MICHAUXS, FATHER AND SON,
WERE AMONG THE FIRST OF THE
GREAT BOTANICAL EXPLORERS OF
NORTH AMERICA. . . . ONLY A SUPER-
FICIAL ACQUAINTANCE WITH THE
BOTANICAL LITERATURE OF NORTH
AMERICA IS REQUIRED TO COMPRE-
HEND THE VAST CONTRIBUTION OF
THESE TWO MEN IN HELPING TO SYS-
TEMIZE DESCRIPTIVELY THE PLANT
LIFE OF EASTERN UNITED STATES. RE-
COGNITION IS LONG PAST DUE TO
FRANÇOIS ANDRÉ MICHAUX FOR HIS
WELL-REASONED PRESENTATION OF
THE NEED OF FOREST CONSERVATION
AND FOREST MANAGEMENT.

ANDREW D. RODGERS III

CHAPTER 17

ᘏ Mission to America, Carolina,

1801–1802

ON AUGUST 12, 1801, François André Michaux was given a formal notification by the minister's office that a ship lying at Bordeaux intended to sail for Charleston on September 1. With great expectations and enthusiasm he was soon on the road to that ancient port which had long maintained close commercial relations with Carolina, partly owing to its remoteness from British waters and less likelihood of encountering interference from vessels of that persistent enemy of France.[1] His first letter from Charleston reported two interesting bits of fact in respect to his Atlantic crossing, which began on August 25 when the *John and Francis* weighed anchor and set sail down the wide estuary of the Garonne between its low-lying, sandy shores so reminiscent of those of her Carolina destination. By coincidence the vessel on which he was crossing the Atlantic again was under the command of the same captain with whom he had returned to France a decade before. A fortnight out on their six-week crossing they came in sight of the Azores—the Acorian Islands to Michaux—only to become becalmed in clear sight of the white stone houses perched on the declivities, each set apart by hedges, of the island of Graciosa to the north and São Jorge to the south, behind which, rising high in the sky was the spectacular pyramid of Pico set in the middle of the island that gives it its name.[2]

On October 9, 1801, the forty-fifth day after departing Bordeaux, the *John and Francis* arrived at the outside bar of Charleston harbor. The harbor mouth was then often difficult for ships to discover owing to the general similarity between it and most other inlets, without more clearly distinguishable features than the ever-changing soft seawalls of the low-lying barrier islands, which extend all up and down that coast, protecting the dense, dark green, wind-modeled forests beyond from the pounding waves ceaselessly rolling in toward them across wide white beaches and sandbars—white lace fringing nature's green velvet gown. But now there was the happy certainty among those aboard, fourteen of whom, including young Michaux, were passengers, that they had almost reached their destination—for through the clear October air across the harbor's wide expanse they could see the church spires of the town above its facade of imposing dwellings, and the Old

Exchange Building, then the custom house and commercial heart of the city, rising from the banks of the harbor at the foot of Broad Street, all close-packed on the southernmost part of the narrow, low, marsh-fringed peninsula between the Ashley River on the west and the Cooper on its east side as they flow together into Charleston harbor.

With the pilot came terrifying news. The city was in the grip of a devastating yellow fever epidemic that had already made dreadful ravages, carrying off a great number of the town's inhabitants, which they then counted as numbering 10,000 whites and 9,000 black slaves, all living crowded together on little more than a square mile of marsh-bordered soil, so loose and sandy that if one stepped from the brick sidewalks of its unpaved streets he would find himself ankle deep in sand.

No sooner had they dropped anchor off the wharves than friends of other passengers came aboard prepared to take them to refuge on Sullivans Island, lying on the north side of the harbor between the city and the ocean, a barren sandy island, almost devoid of trees, where many neighboring planters had built summer cottages to serve as refuges from the "intermittant fevers" endemic in summer on their lowcountry plantations until autumn. Being almost devoid of vegetation and open to the sea, Sullivans Island was swept by protective sea breezes that, experience had demonstrated, generally protected its residents from seasonal fevers and, on occasion, from the dreaded yellow fever epidemics. However, for François André the price of weeks of virtual imprisonment "in such a dull and meloncholy abode" was too great for him to join them, a decision that had nearly made him "the victim of my obstinacy, having been, a few days after, attacked with the first symptoms of this dreadful malady, under which I labored upward of a month."[3]

Although François André's comments respecting Charleston's economic and social life appear in the early pages of his *Travels*, published in Paris in 1804 under the title *Voyage a l'ouest des monts Alleghanys*,[4] they were obviously seasoned by further observations made before his return to France in the spring of 1803. The first contemporaneous account of his initial impressions are those recorded in a letter dated November 4, 1801, written from his father's botanical garden to which he had gone as soon as he was sufficiently recovered.

That letter, addressed to the minister of the interior, is largely a chronicle of the difficulties he had encountered since his arrival in

François André Michaux, from a portrait by Rembrandt Peale. (Courtesy of the American Philosophical Society)

Charleston.[5] First he reported his personal misfortune in having been stricken by the malady which continued to rage in the city where 160 Europeans were still ill with it, from which, although now recovering, he had not yet regained sufficient stamina to begin his planned autumn seed-collecting mission—a serious delay, the season already being far advanced. Even more distressing at the moment were the financial problems with which he was already confronted despite the 6,000 francs that had been advanced to him before his departure. Specifically, he had discovered that Himely was due 1,000 francs more than had been anticipated. As prices in Charleston "are three times as dear as in Europe," 3,600 of the 6,000 francs had already been expended, and he had yet to pay Himely the 4,200 francs due him. So he was forced to request that the remaining 10,000 francs approved for his expedition be forthwith sent to him through a Paris banking house so that it could be expeditiously dispatched to him. The only good news he had for the minister was that he had been offered 10,000 francs for the Charleston nursery property, for which his father had paid far less, and that, upon inspection of the plants left growing in the nursery, he had found a great many valuable specimens, although many were now too large for removal and shipment to France pursuant to his instructions. Three and a half months later the letter reached the minister and was immediately referred to the Bureau of Agriculture for advice. The Bureau recommended that another 6,000 francs of the balance appropriated for the mission be sent to Michaux.

Now seeing for the first time this southern cultural center with its slave-based, cash-crop plantation economy through the eyes of a mature, well-educated cosmopolitan European with the realistic and factual bent of a well-trained scientist, François André's observations and comments are notable. His particular interests were now directed toward, and would continue to focus on, the varieties of economic systems that in the early nineteenth century were emerging in the burgeoning new nation, and even more emphatically upon the American forests, their products and the unrealized potential he perceived for them.

In the latter category he observed at his landing "several ill constructed quays [that] project into the river, to facilitate trading vessels taking in their cargoes. These quays are formed with the trunks of palm trees fixed together, and laid out in squares, one above the other. Experience has shown that the trunks of these trees, although of a very spongy nature, lie buried in the water many years without decaying" and so are preferred above any other kind. Of greater economic interest was his early observation that "planks and building materials comprise [a] considerable article of importation," this despite the rich forest growths over almost the whole interior of Carolina, and the waste of those felled when lands were cleared for crops.

Reflecting the effects of the region's emphasis on a cash-crop plantation economy, he reported on the marked disproportionate prices for provisions. "For example, beef very seldom exceeds sixpence a pound, vegetables are dearer than meat. Independent of the articles of consumption that the country supplies, the port of Charleston is generally full of small vessels from Boston, Newport, New York and Philadelphia and from all the little intermediate ports, which are loaded with flour, salt provisions, potatoes, onions, carrots, beet-roots, apples, oats, Indian corn, and hay. . . . In the winter the markets of Charleston are well stocked with live sea fish, which are brought from the northern part of the United States in vessels so constructed as to keep them in a continual supply of water." The ships engaged in this kind of traffic load for their return trip "rice and cottons, the greater part of which is re-exported into Europe. . . . The cotton wool that they keep in the north for their own consumption is more than sufficient to supply the manufactures. . . . The surplus is disposed of in the country places, where the women fabricate coarse cottons for the use of their families."

Again, in the realm of his special interest, with obvious surprise at some facets of the strange economy that had evolved in its plantation-dominated society, he noted with particular interest that "wood is extravagantly dear at Charleston; it costs forty to fifty shillings a *cord*, notwithstanding forests, which are almost boundless in extent, begin at six miles and even less from town, and the conveyance of it is facilitated by the two rivers at the conflux of which it is situated; on which account a great number of the inhabitants burn coals that are brought from England."[6]

Meanwhile, back in Paris, in the offices of the minister and the Bureau of Agriculture there were continuing concerns respecting details of Michaux's American mission. Interoffice communications struggled with the problems incidental to the ways and means of getting funds to him during his travels, of proper instructions in respect to the sale of the Charleston garden, and the beginning of an ardent controversy in respect to the proposed "suppression" of the New Jersey garden, a controversy launched by a letter from Pierre Samuel du Pont, one of France's most notable leaders both before and during the Revolutionary period, which had reached the minister's

hands before any word had come from Michaux himself. In that
lengthy and detailed letter du Pont expressed his adamant opposition
to selling that property which he believed held great potential for
enhancement of the forests of France as a depot for seeds and seedlings
of a great variety of species, many superior to the French, and others far
more adaptable to poor sites than those existing in France.[7]

Having many connections with official Paris under both the Old
Regime and the Revolutionary government, perhaps du Pont had
learned, through friends, of the plans for François André's mission to
dispose of the two nurseries established by his father and had resolved
to launch an effort to save the one in New Jersey before Michaux
arrived on the scene. But it is more likely that, when Saunier received a
letter Michaux wrote him in mid-December telling him of a planned
visit to New York in the spring to carry out his instructions, the distressed gardener had immediately sought the intervention of the nearby du Ponts. Michaux's forewarning to Saunier was probably included
incidentally in a letter to him written in December, primarily to request
that he collect and ship to the minister of the interior, via Bordeaux, "3
or 4 boxes of shellbark hickory or mockernuts, *Juglans alba*" (now *Carya
tomentosa*).

New Year's Day 1802 found François André still in residence at
the Carolina nursery, quite recovered and busily preparing an inventory of its contents and selecting and labeling those items to be lifted
and packed for shipment to France. Flourishing there among the rows
of native trees he found many of the exotics, imported by his father to
enrich his host country, plants from faraway places: crape myrtles,
Lagerstroemia indica, from India to adorn the southern countryside
almost all summer long with showy red, pink or white flowers, and the
autumn, too, with brilliant foliage, while from China there were several
beautifully shaped trees bearing large shiny leaves and seeds in open
pods, known interchangeably as the varnish, or Chinese parasol, tree,
Sterculia (now *Firmiana platanifolia*), and thriving specimens of another,
the botanically ancient ginkgo, *Ginkgo biloba,* to be numbered in our day,
strangely enough, among the few trees sufficiently resistant to auto-
mobile exhaust fumes to thrive along the streets of our great cities; and
the now justly famous "mimosas" with widely spreading branches
adorned with fernlike leaves and in early summer with beautiful pink
or fawn-colored, powder-puff-shaped, powerfully fragrant flowers, *Albizzia julibrissin,* which had evoked high praise from Thomas Jefferson
when they blossomed in the garden at Monticello, where Jefferson

showed them off to guests as his "silk trees," the seeds of which had been brought from Persia to Europe by Michaux père.[8]

As he related in his next letter to the minister, there were also surviving in the garden a rich variety of choice native plants which had so prospered since being planted by his father that they were now bearing seed harvests. This is confirmed in a contemporary document, prepared by or under the direction of André Michaux's old friend and associate André Thouin, who had survived the great French trauma and was now administrator of the Museum of Natural History and Jardin des Plantes in Paris, charged with the culture and naturalization of foreign plants. That document is a "Catalogue of the rare seeds, sent during the year 10, from the botanical garden belonging to France, situated near Charleston in South Carolina for the Jardin des Plantes of Paris by F. A. Michaux fils commissioner of the Minister of the Interior for Agriculture in the United States."[9] It listed such rare plants as the *Pinckneya,* a rare monotypic genus found only in southeastern United States, and very rare there, and the *Gordonia lasianthus,* the hard-to-cultivate, steeple-shaped evergreen tree bearing magnificent shining foliage and beautiful, fragrant, snow-white flowers, one of the few and generally rare members of the tea family native to America. There were also long-leaf and slash pines, both highly productive of resin; two decorative members of the heath family that Michaux had called *Andromeda,* the beautiful sourwood, *Oxydendrum arboreum,* and a rare staggerbush he had found in Florida, *Lyonia ferruginea*; the pawpaw, *Asimina triloba,* sporting large handsome leaves and strange, triangular, deep red flowers, one of the very few temperate-zone species of the *Annona* family of tropical regions. Another "natural exotic" on that list of seeds was the sabal, or cabbage, palm, better known in Carolina as the palmetto, which, as François André had reported, was much used there in the construction of piers, bumper rails, and piling, its wood being soft and fibrous and not subject to destruction by sea worms. One more example from that list was a species of *Sarracenia,* the carnivorous genus including the pitcher plant—but the species sent was of one of the tall, showy species of trumpets, indigenous in the acid, wet pine flats of Carolina.

In his second letter to the minister dated New Year's Day 1802, François André reported the great variety of desirable native trees in the nursery's superb collection which "had survived almost total neglect" for several years.[10] He commented particularly on the wax myrtles, *Myrica,* the tupelos, *Nyssa biflora,* and the Ogeechee lime, *Nyssa ogeche,* which bears very acid drupes when only seven or eight feet tall, commenting that both of the latter would thrive in the standing waters of swamps. Those and some fifty others were on an appended list that he said he intended to remove and send back to France by way of Bordeaux.

He went on to mention writing to Saunier to request him to collect and ship the butternuts, but made no mention of the part of his letter that had evoked so much concern from du Pont, of his plans to go there in the spring to dispose of that establishment. However, he said he was resolved to sell the Charleston place but retain possession of it until his return to France, in accordance with his instructions; but the French agent in Charleston was opposing him in this and had told him that any sale should be made by the agent "without my participation." Nevertheless, he said he was eager to effect a sale and had already taken steps to accomplish it even though the price would be only as much as his father paid for it when he purchased it in 1786 because of the condition of the buildings, which were falling to ruin. In fact, "I have somewhat urged an interested planter to make this acquisition by pointing out to him that with this garden which contains some 400 species of trees and plants from all regions of America he will be in a position to procure for himself, from all the botanical gardens of Europe, all the trees susceptible to naturalization in Carolina, and further, that he would have made himself a correspondent for the Bureau of Agriculture."

He closed with another plea to the minister for funds, asking that he be sent the remaining 10,000 francs of the funds approved for his mission so that he could pay Himely the money due him.

Meanwhile, in France, a veritable barrage of letters from du Pont, or inspired by him, was descending on the centers of power, aiming to forestall any disposition of the American nurseries, particularly the New Jersey establishment, it being feared that it was already too late to do anything to save the one in Carolina, which du Pont himself thought lacked the potential he believed the more northern station offered for the forests and agriculture of France. His six-page, finely written epistle reached his colleagues of the National Institute,[11] the intellectual heart of the nation, soon after the opening salvo on the office of the minister of the interior had reached there in February. Regularly, throughout the winter and spring, the barrage descended on both that office and on the Bureau of Agriculture. Saunier added to his protest an appeal for his long-past-due salary and a new authorization for him to resume the usefulness of the New Jersey establishment.[12]

To the initial arguments the later appeals added citations of the great benefits already being realized by Germany, England, and Denmark from the great quantities of superior American trees they had been importing for years, making in those countries lands, comparable to those that in France produce nothing but brushwood, into areas of perpetually renewing wealth. The magic names of the "celebrated elder Michaux," of the minister Chaptal, and most particularly that of the illustrious Thouin of the Jardin des Plantes were cited in support of the stand against any alienation of those potential national treasures. Du Pont urged that the latter be consulted and his opinion secured before making any sale of facilities that were already available to give France a unique advantage over her European neighbors.

Despite these protests, even as they continued to mount, the minister of the interior, on April 3, addressed a letter to "Citizen Nekelman, merchant at Bordeaux" to be forwarded to François André Michaux, "agent of the government to divest the American nurseries of France." The letter to be forwarded was doubtless that of which a preliminary draft dated April 1 survives, acknowledging Michaux's letter of Nov. 4, 1801, telling of his yellow fever attack, and appealing for the remaining 10,000 francs appropriated for his expedition. Although the minister's letter told Michaux that 4,000 francs were being put at his disposal and urged strict economy on his part, it made no amendment to his instructions to dispose of both American gardens.[13]

The persuasive influence of du Pont evoked little effective support until the responding reports of the Institute, the Bureau of Agriculture, and the Société d'Agriculture at Versailles were received in his office.[14] Beginning in late April 1802, they soon inspired a burgeoning of favorable official responses. It was conceded that it was probably too late to save the Charleston garden, but the official word went out that the New Jersey garden should not be sold, but instead should be conceded to someone, preferably Saunier, on an annual basis, in return for regular shipments of forest trees and seeds to the Bureau of Agriculture equal to the rental value of the facility; that it should become a depot for other collections being gathered for shipments destined for France; that Michaux should instruct Saunier on the proper preparation and identification of Saunier's shipments; and that du Pont's offer of cooperation and a measure of supervision of the facility be accepted. Finally, in the matter of any payment to Saunier for back salary, the minister continued firmly opposed. He would only concede an obligation to reimburse him for the cost of repairs and taxes paid by him on the place.[15]

While these official stances were being formulated in the offices of

Paris, at the ports ships were arriving from the United States with increasing frequency, bringing the fruits of Michaux's mission. From New York came the boxes of butternuts from Saunier, and, in Bordeaux, Merchant Nekelman's warehouse on the waterfront was receiving a mounting stream of boxes and crates of seeds, seedlings, and cuttings from Michaux in Charleston. Lacking specific instructions as to their disposition, Nekelman had to hold them in storage there while he sought directions from the minister of the interior. As spring advanced the layered seeds began sprouting and sending rootlets into the packing moss, and the seedlings and cuttings burgeoned before their destinations were settled upon by the minister.

It was near the end of April before the earliest of those shipments reached Paris for opening and distribution for planting. Only then was a plan settled upon that all the shipments should be consigned to the directors of the nurseries of Versailles and Roule. The director of the Roule Nursery in Paris was first to open and inspect each shipment and send them on to Versailles for division between all the national nurseries, according to the climate considered most favorable, even though that required some (those needing southern climes, such as that of the Department of Landes) to be sent back by wagon to Bordeaux and beyond, almost to the Spanish border, before being given a spot in French soil. There is little wonder that their survival record was often very discouraging.

Meanwhile, back in Carolina, with the approach of spring, when François André was expected to be in New York, he was still in residence at the French Garden, proceeding apace with carrying out his instructions in respect to it. Most of the autumn after his recovery had been devoted to gathering seed for timely shipment to France for spring plantings and, after winter arrived, to several excursions into the interior of the Carolinas.[16] Now with the advent of spring he was free to direct his attention to effecting a disposition of the property, with possession reserved until his return to France. Apparently, the sale he had been eager to effect had not gotten beyond preliminary negotiations. The next firm fact we have in respect to the sale of the place is the public record, where we find a formal conveyance of the 111-acre place in Goose Creek Parish to John James Himely, for an expressed consideration of eighty pounds. Put on record at the same time is another instrument dated more than a month later, April 27, 1802, signed by both Himely and himself confirming the earlier conveyance, but with possession retained by Michaux until March 1, 1803.[17]

Those documents raise some unanswered questions. In terms of the values of the currencies of the day, the expressed sale price of eighty pounds was only about $200, an inadequate price for a property for which the elder Michaux had paid $500 a decade and a half earlier, and the minister of finance had thought might now bring 10,000 francs ($2,000). However, $200 (1,000 francs), together with the probably canceled debt due Himely of 4,200 francs (about $800) would put the value of the place, with its improvements, at about eight dollars an acre, a reasonable figure at the time, and the eighty pounds cash would have provided Michaux with much-needed funds for his planned travels to New York and thence into the transmontane West.

On the other hand, we are confronted with a conveyance soon afterward made by Himely transferring title to the "French Garden" to the Agricultural Society of South Carolina, without any cited consideration.[18] That document was executed two weeks before François André sailed for home in March 1803. It is, of course, quite possible that those two conveyances represent a change of mind by Minister Chaptal. It will be recalled that in July of 1801 the Consultant Bureau of Agriculture in its approval of the proposed expedition of Michaux fils had recommended such a disposition of the Charleston facility, but that proposal had been rejected by the minister of the interior. All in all, we are left with unresolved questions as to what actually transpired in respect to the transfer of the garden to the Agricultural Society.

With the disposition of the Charleston Garden settled, there was little more to be done in Carolina until the autumn seed season, when Michaux expected to return, to make more collections in the areas of Carolina and Georgia he had reconnoitered the previous winter, while there was now much urgently calling for his presence in the North to settle the increasingly parlous state of affairs involving Saunier, du Pont, and the New Jersey establishment. But there remained one other matter, a personal one for his father, which he had to attend to before leaving Carolina. Doubtless he had intended to travel to the Keowee River region, where he could have managed it himself. Now the urgency of his departure precluded that and forced him to seek the assistance of his father's old friend General Andrew Pickens, whom François, too, had met when he accompanied his father on one of his expeditions to the Carolina mountains.

As is confirmed by the public records in the Charleston County Courthouse, on January 7, 1788, three grant conveyances had been made to "Andrew Michaux" of tracts of land in the Ninety-Six District of South Carolina. Those deeds, signed by "Thomas Pinckney, Esquire, Governor and Commander in Chief in said State," had accompanying plats showing the lands embraced in those grants as 1,000 acres, 888 acres, and 1,000 acres, respectively, all located on Cane Creek, a tributary stream to the Keowee River.[19] Although the Charleston records reveal no subsequent transfer of those properties, there might have been deeds recorded in one of the new western county courthouses which had come into being after 1787 as the population of the Piedmont region rapidly increased in the post-Revolutionary years. Since doubtless the general had been privy to his father's acquisition of those properties by his friend and sometimes houseguest, François André sought his advice in the matter. In the ungrammatical English of that stage of his life he addressed a letter to the general:

Sir:

I take the liberty to recall myself to your remembrance and to return you kind thanks for the reception we meet with you about 14 years ago when we went in your contry after Botanicals researches.

I am arrived in Charleston about six months ago and I expect to set of for Philadelphia in few days and from there I will proceed to the Kentucky and come back to Charleston by North Carolina in November next.

Gen'al C. C. Pinckney, with whom you are well acquainted and I have seen often when he was at Paris two years ago has told to me that you will be so kind to give me some informations about three lots of land that my father have had surveyed in the month of June 1787 by Mr. Martin, Deputy Surveyor. Since 7 or 8 years the taxes have not been paid. I wish to know if this lots of land are of any value my intention being to sell them before to return to France.

You oblige me very much to let me know to who I must pay the taxes and the amount of them and in case this lots could not be sold what I must do to secure this property.

My father is returned to France since five years.

I am with respect

Your most obt. sert.
Francis Michaux[20]

He gave his Charleston address as care of "J. J. Himely, Broad Street, at Charleston," or to the care of "G'al. Pinckney."

We have been unable to discover what response he received from Pickens, and we have been equally unsuccessful in finding any record of a sale of those properties by Andrew Michaux, François Michaux, or by the sheriff for taxes past due. A convincing case can be made that François André learned that the market value of those grants was insufficient to justify the trouble involved in trying to sell them. We have discovered no further mention of them. A careful researcher who has made a detailed study of André Michaux's travels in that part of South Carolina is convinced that the lands involved in those conveyances were included in the 1849 purchase of nearly 18,000 acres of land in what is now Oconee County by the German Colonization Society of Charleston.[21]

CHAPTER **18**

✧ New York and Philadelphia, 1802

A FEW DAYS LATER François André was en route to New York, a passenger on one of the numerous packet boats then regularly coasting between Charleston and the cities of the North. "Trade is so brisk between the northern and southern states that there is generally an opportunity at Charleston to get to any of the ports of the northern states," he reported in his *Travels,* and "some of those vessels have rooms, tastefully arranged and commodiously fitted up, for the reception of passengers, who go every year in crowds to reside in the northern part of the United States, and return to Charleston in the month of November following." The price of a passage was about fifty dollars for the trip to New York, which usually required about ten days, except when "prolonged by violent gusts which casually spring up on doubling Cape Hatras." His passage was uneventful, consuming the usual ten days from port to port.[1]

The reception he met with in New York was highly pleasing, particularly the attention accorded him by the greatly esteemed Dr. David Hosack, prominent physician, serving at the time of Michaux's visit both as professor of botany and professor of materia medica at Columbia College.[2] Dr. Hosack obviously found the young botanical emissary a congenial guest, extending to him all the courtesies customarily reserved for eminent practicing professional colleagues in the medical arena. His young guest's medical training enhanced the interest he took in the tour of his hospital on which Dr. Hosack conducted him, and later another, to the prison to which Dr. Hosack was physician. The hospital drew mixed reactions; while the extensive buildings impressed him and the rooms were lofty and well aired, the beds left much to be desired. They were low, "edged with board about four inches wide and furnished with a mattress, or rather a pallias, filled with oat straw, not very thick, coarse brown linen sheets and a rug" for cover. On the other hand, he thought the prison "remarkable for the decorum, the arrangement, the cleanliness that reigns there, and more especially for the willingness with which the prisoners seem to work at the different employments alotted to them . . . each tasked according to his profession; some were making shoes, and others manufacturing cut nails, square and without any points," particularly useful for nailing wooden shingles on roofs as they do not rise up as if half drawn as other nails do.[3]

More to the liking of his guest was a visit to the professor's botanical garden which "he was at that time employed in establishing . . . where he intended giving a regular course of lectures. This garden is a few miles from town . . . on ground well adapted, especially for plants that require a peculiar aspect or situation." But most congenial of all for the visiting botanist was their botanical excursion into the forest bordering the Hudson in New Jersey, beyond the western Palisades, where the soil is shallow, hard, and flinty but nevertheless supported a wide variety of indigenous trees. Michaux's observations and comments on what they found in that forest clearly presage the path he was to follow in the years to come. Although up to now he had made no mention of undertaking the preparation of his work, *The North American Sylva*, that justly famous trail-blazing manual of American forest trees, the close observations and fine distinctions between species and varieties of oaks he made there, and the comparisons of them with those described in his father's *History of the Oaks*, leaves one convinced that, willy-nilly, he was already directed on course toward that aim. There in company with a variety of oaks—white oaks, water oaks, and black oaks—various species of hickories flourished. Among them he observed "mocker-nuts," *Juglans tomentosa* (now *Carya tomentosa*), "pig-nuts," *Juglans minima* (probably *Carya aquatica*), and "shell-barked" hickories, *Juglans hickory* (now *Carya laciniosa*) in the swampy spots. They evoked the comment that "the species and variety of nut trees natural to the United States are extremely numerous and might be the subject of a useful monography; but the work would never be precisely accurate . . . if those trees are not studied in the country itself." Next best would be to grow them oneself to observe them closely. To that end he said he took back home with him "some new nuts of six different species, which have come up exceedingly well, and which appear not to have been described."[4]

Those activities, however interesting and instructive to the insatiably inquiring young visitor, were, in truth, but interludes in and distractions from the duties of his mission that now weighed more heavily upon him than at any time since his arrival in Charleston. Much of the flood of letters, many altering his original instructions and not all consistent, and reams of advice, evoked in Paris by du Pont's campaign to save the New Jersey garden, must have greeted him on his arrival in New York, providing him with a full agenda to be cleared before he could succumb to the temptation to be off to the virgin forests of the transmontane country.[5] He had to consult with du Pont and with Saunier, reach an agreement as to the rental value of the garden property and buildings, convert that to an agreeable annualized valuation for the use of the property, and convert that value into the actual annual payments to be made by the tenant in a very different and varied sort of "coinage"—seeds of American trees, gathered, packed, and shipped to the minister of the interior in France, in quantities and varieties, strictly according to his instructions. Additionally, all those arrangements had to have the approval of the French consul and the agent for commercial affairs in Philadelphia.

Nevertheless, despite the numerous details involved, a general understanding had been reached during the weeks following his arrival in New York and the matter settled as to the disposition of the Jersey establishment—at least for the near future. Confirmation of that understanding is not embodied in any surviving formal contract. It rests mainly on a simple document, signed only by François André Michaux, which is actually little more than a list of seeds entitled "List of seeds which will be sent to the minister of the interior in the month of October, next, by Citizen Saulnier in execution of purchase agreement reached May 1802 by the subscriber, F. André Michaux." It listed fifty-six species, running the alphabet from *Acer* to *Ulmus* (maple to elm). Opposite each were the pounds of seed to be sent for a total of 119½ pounds weight for which Saunier would be paid 420 livres by the French consul in New York, a figure which Michaux himself converted to "eighty dollars or 360 francs," a helpful custom he would follow all the years to come in his correspondence with America.[6]

Now, with one of the dual objectives of his mission, the "suppression" of the Charleston and Jersey nurseries substantially arranged, Michaux could direct his attention to the second, but no less important, part of his assignment, that of seeking potential, strategically located suppliers of forest seeds and seedlings for an enhanced, continuing supply for propagation in the nurseries of France. Although neither "suppression" was yet quite complete, he had made an irrevocable commitment to surrender the Charleston facility to Himely the following spring, so, except for removal of such remaining plants as he might wish to ship during the coming fall and winter, there was nothing left to do there other than to evacuate the premises. The circumstances surrounding the deal with Himely invite an assumption that inherent in it was an understanding that the garden was to go to the Agricultural Society with an obligation on its part to serve as a supplier of the desirable seeds from the Carolina forests in return for reciprocal shipments of French farm and garden seeds. The arrangement made with Saunier now assured a supply of seed from the New York area under a modified "sharecropping" agreement whereby the New Jersey garden had been let to him in return for specified quantities of produce, its main difference from the conventional sharecrop agreement being that the produce to be paid by Saunier for use of the premises was not to be paid in produce from the place but rather nature's production in the neighboring forests.

If he hoped to meet the aim of the Bureau of Agriculture in promoting his expedition, it was desirable to secure additional suppliers to gather and ship seed regularly from diverse sections of the East. And by now his need of funds had become his most urgent problem. He believed favorable solutions to both these problems might be found in Philadelphia. During the previous year, following the succession of Thomas Jefferson to the presidency after a hotly contested election, the seat of the federal government had been moved to the new capital on the Potomac. Yet despite the trauma suffered by the city in the departure of the government, Philadelphia still retained its eminence as the nation's cultural capital where horticulture and botany, the gentle sciences, continued preeminent among the sciences that had found leadership there. Thus it was a hopeful young Michaux who set out southward on June 8 by stagecoach for Philadelphia.

He recorded in his *Travels* some of his observations from the coach window as well as mundane facts and figures, touching on the hundred-mile journey between the two cities.[7] Characteristically, everything was grist to the young Frenchman's intellectual mill. The charge for a coach ticket was five dollars per person. At the stops at the roadside taverns dinner could be had for a dollar, and half that amount for breakfasts and suppers, or beds for the night for those who wished to break the journey. After crossing the Jersey Marshes, the first place they passed through was Newark which impressed him as a pretty town, its attractiveness enhanced by its environs, mostly given over to apple orchards. "The cyder that is made there is accounted the best in the United States," but in his judgment it was far inferior to those made in France at St.-Lo or Bayeux. The only other town along the way he thought worthy of comment was Trenton. "Its situation upon the Delaware, the beautiful tract of country that surrounds it, must render it a most delightful place of abode." But what most surprised and impressed him was the extent to which the erstwhile forests of the region between New York and Philadelphia had been cleared away and replaced by farms that he described as being contiguous one to another all along the way.

Philadelphia was impressive. "Situated upon the Delaware, a hundred miles distant from the sea; at this period the most extensive, the handsomest, and most populous city of the United States. In my opinion," he wrote, "there is not one upon the old continent built upon so regular a plan." The market built on its widest street "is remarkable for its extent and extreme cleanliness . . . is in the centre of the town, and occupies nearly one-third of its length. The streets are paved with brick, and pumps, with a light above each, were placed along both sides about fifty yards apart." Several streets were "planted with Italian poplars of a most beautiful growth, which makes the houses appear elegantly rural." Its population, at the time computed to be 70,000, still held first place among the cities of the country. The few blacks there were free, and mostly in domestic service. Food was bountiful and less costly than in New York. But most remarkable, he saw no poverty. One never met there "a creature wearing an aspect of misery in his face; that distressing spectacle, so common in European cities, is unknown in America; love, industry, the want of sufficient hands, the scarcity of workmanship, an active commerce, property, are the direct causes that contend against the introduction of beggary."[8]

However pleasing the Philadelphia environment, even more pleasing to the ever-sociable visitor were the people he met with there. Many were friends who well remembered his magnetic father or were associated with him at the time of his proposed expedition to the Pacific in 1793. Among them was Dr. Nicholas Collin, minister of the Swedish church. He had served as chairman of the committee of the American Philosophical Society set up to raise the funds for that venture. Now Dr.

Collin was the regular presiding officer of the society since its president, Thomas Jefferson, had, the previous year, chosen to be inaugurated as president of the nation at the new, yet only partly ready, capital on the Potomac. Even more congenial were the Bartram brothers, John and William, the latter tardily becoming notable in his native country as the author of his now famous *Travels*, years after it had been published and widely acclaimed in England. Another fascinating new friend was the incredibly energetic Charles Willson Peale, who, in addition to being an accomplished artist and portrait painter, was the owner, curator, and chief showman at Peale's Museum, long a focal point of interest in Philadelphia, now on the verge of national fame since its recent removal, along with his numerous, talented family, into the Old State House (better known now as Independence Hall), topped by its handsome cupola in which hung the Liberty Bell. There he set up for display the centerpiece of its exhibited wonders, the world's first reassembled skeleton of a mammoth.[9] Michaux commented that those notable "gentlemen had formerly been particularly acquainted with my father, and I received from them every mark of attention and respect."

Yet another of the city's intellectual circle whose friendship would be far more significant to him was forty-six-year-old John Vaughan, a member of the American Philosophical Society for eighteen years, now its treasurer, and soon to become its librarian.[10] Vaughan was likewise well acquainted with the elder Michaux, for he had been the society's treasurer at the time its members were sponsoring his planned western expedition. Before François André departed the city on his own far more modest expedition to the West, he delivered to Vaughan a gift copy of his father's work on American oaks. It was probably an unbound copy and the ten dollars paid by Vaughan to "G.F.F.," for "Michaux's Oaks" more than a month later was to cover the charges for having it bound.[11]

Another botanical friend of his father's, whose home François André visited before his departure, was William Hamilton, who was away from home at the time but whose "magnificent garden" greatly impressed him. "His collection of exotics is immense, and remarkable for plants of New Holland: all the trees and shrubs of the United States, at least those that could stand the winter at Philadelphia. . . . It would be almost impossible to find a more agreeable situation than the residence of Mr. W. Hamilton."[12]

Doubtless he again visited the nearby farm of the Bartrams across the river, a far less showy place but of more enduring fame than

Woodlands. The Bartram garden continued to be a mecca for visiting botanists and horticulturalists, and it may well have been the Bartrams who suggested to François André one who might answer his need for a collector and export agent. This man, Mathias Kin, a native of Strasbourg who spoke only German, was well qualified for the role and readily enlisted by Michaux to collect in the fall a shipment of seed "six times greater" than that to be made by Saunier, for which he was to receive fifty dollars to be paid to him by the French commissioner in Philadelphia. Kin (often called Citizen King in the correspondence) made his first shipments to Minister of the Interior Chaptal in the ensuing fall, only to be discouraged by the long delay in receiving compensation, a common experience of those, including Michaux himself, in dealing with the French bureaucracy in the early days of the Bonaparte regime.[13]

With those arrangements made, the duties Michaux was to perform in the eastern states were substantially completed, and he was now free to turn his attention to the transmontane West. But he was still confronted with unresolved money problems. He had been led to believe that if he reached Philadelphia the chief commissioner of commercial affairs would provide the necessary funds to cover the expense of his contemplated travels in the interior. When he arrived there, however, he found that the commissioner had followed American officialdom in its move to the new Federal District, where he had found quarters in the village of Georgetown, leaving behind a subordinate whose only contribution to Michaux's immediate financial problems was a plan of procedure that would, itself, have to be approved in Paris before it could become effective. Faced with such an impractical proposal, a thoroughly frustrated Michaux dispatched an urgent appeal to the commissioner himself that brought only a brief note explaining that he was under the minister of marine and colonies and could provide no funds for anyone under the minister of the interior—but he would write to Paris about the problem.[14]

More than three months later all the correspondence evoked by Michaux's financial crisis and the bureaucratic snarl involved were summarized in a report prepared by Silvestre, chief of the Bureau of Agriculture in Paris, for submission to the minister of the interior for his consideration.[15] After reviewing Michaux's report of the arrangement made with Saunier in respect to the New Jersey garden, agreeable to du Pont's suggestions, for letting the place to Saunier in return for annual seed shipments, the report moved on to consider Michaux's financial plight, his immediate need for funds, and the commissioner's refusal to advance any financial assistance that forced him "with the aid of . . . friends" to contract a loan in order to proceed with his mission.

Finally, Silvestre's report addressed the crux of Michaux's concern, the ways and means of supplying him with funds for the continuation of his mission. It proposed a simple bureaucratic maneuver: the minister of the interior should propose to the minister of marine and colonies a transfer to him of the remaining 6,000 francs and send that sum to its commissioner in the United States for delivery to Michaux, the same plan suggested by the agent in Philadelphia when Michaux was there. Meanwhile, back in America, François André had by then completed his transmontane mission through the Ohio Valley and back across the southern Appalachians to the Piedmont town of Morganton, North Carolina, where he was resting, still in sight of the peaks of the Linville Mountains from which he had emerged the previous day.[16]

CHAPTER 19

❦ West to the Alleghenies and down the Ohio, 1802

IT WAS WELL INTO SUMMER, June 27, far later than he had hoped, in view of the nearly two thousand miles of difficult travel he had planned to accomplish before his return to Charleston, where he "was to be absolutely about the beginning of October," when François André climbed into the ponderous stagecoach and set out on the turnpike leading west from Philadelphia to Lancaster and thence to Shippensburg, 140 miles distant. At that time Shippensburg was as far as the stages went toward Pittsburgh. In explanation of his taking that inappropriate means of travel for an expedition for botanical observations, he said he "had not the least motive to proceed slowly through a much travelled region" to collect observations already confirmed by travelers who had written before me "on the vegetable productions and state of agriculture which were the chief object of my researches." It was his intent to avoid those parts most known and seek only in those less explored. Strong suggestions, those expressions seem to make, of an intent already in mind to publish an account of this expedition to the western parts of the United States and, beyond that, in the future, his great work on the American sylva—the work that was to be his driving objective during the next dozen years of his life.

So it was by stagecoach and turnpike as far as it would take him on his way to Pittsburgh at the head of the Ohio River. While disclaiming any real interest in those settled regions he was seeing from the stage-coach windows, he was ever an inveterately interested and thoughtful observer of the world around him, wherever he might be. It was characteristic of him to note and comment upon every contrast with prevailing customs in Europe. For instance, here the farmers' crops were all grown within the confines of fences to protect them from the livestock, which was left free to roam the surrounding woods and countryside; and the fences themselves in Pennsylvania contrasted markedly with those generally found in the South. Here they were the post-and-rail type, with split oak or walnut rails twelve feet long, fitted into mortise holes in the upright posts—a type requiring much labor but far less timber in a region where wood was already becoming "extremely dear," in the environs of the cities. He recalled, in sharp contrast, the fences most common in the South, called "Whitaker" fences, doubtless for some ingenious, long-forgotten homesteader, made solely of easily split durable rails of cedar, stacked alternately near their ends in zig-zag formation, a type wasteful of wood and more subject to destruction by the woods fires, but far less laborious to construct.

At Lancaster, a neat town of 5,000 inhabitants, situated in the heart of an extremely fertile farming region, so dominantly settled by Germans that only German speech was heard in the streets, Michaux stopped off to make the acquaintance of an amateur botanist of consid-erable note, Dr. Henry Muhlenburg, the local Lutheran pastor, but better known for his contributions to the botanical knowledge of that part of Pennsylvania.[1] There also, to his delight, he met William Hamilton, his father's friend whose place on the Schuylkill, Woodlands, had so favorably impressed him.

Michaux noted with particular interest the diverse housing they met with all along the way. "At Philadelphia the houses are built of brick. In other towns and country places that surround them, the half, and frequently the whole, is built of wood; but at places within seventy or eighty miles of the sea, in the central and southern states and again more particularly in those situated to the westward of the Allegheny Mountains, one third of the inhabitants reside in *log houses*."

Map accompanying F. A. Michaux's Voyage à l'ouest des monts Alleghanys, *Paris, 1804. (Courtesy of the American Philosophical Society)*

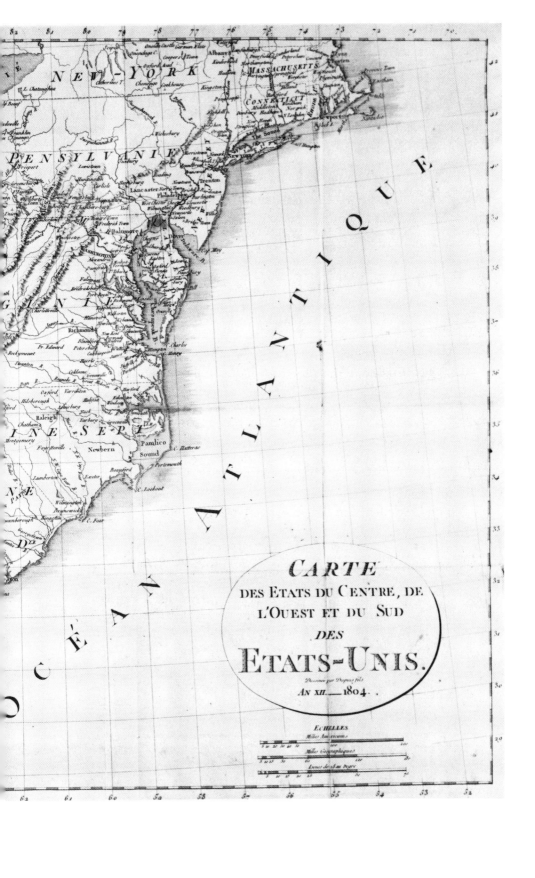

He followed the latter observation with a description of the manner of construction of those log houses that reflected throughout, from ridgepole to chestnut sill, their great dependence on the surrounding forest's resources.

> *These dwellings are made with the trunks of trees, from twenty to thirty feet in length, about five inches in diameter, placed one upon another, and kept up by notches cut in their extremities. The roof is formed by pieces of similar length . . . sloped on each side. Two doors, which often supply the place of windows, are made by sawing away part of the trunks that form the body of the house. The chimney, always placed at the extremities, is likewise made of the trunks of trees; . . . the back of the chimney is made of clay about six inches thick, which separates the fire from the wooden wall. . . . The space between these trunks of trees is filled up with clay, but so very carelessly that the light may be seen through at every part, in consequence of which these huts are exceedingly cold in winter, notwithstanding the amazing quantity of wood that is burnt. The doors move upon wooden hinges. . . . In the night time they only push them to or fasten them with a wooden peg. Four or five days are sufficient for two men to finish one of these houses, in which not a nail is used.*[2]

The amenities offered the traveler at the wayside inns were often only a little less crude. One "miserable inn" where they stopped inspired comments on the accommodations to expect in travels to the westward.

> *Inns are very numerous in the United States, and especially in the little towns; yet almost everywhere, except in the principal towns, they are very bad, notwithstanding rum, brandy and whiskey are in plenty. In fact, in houses of the above description all kinds of spirits are considered the most material, as they generally meet with great consumption. . . . At breakfast they make use of a very indifferent tea, and coffee still worse, with small slices of ham fried in the stove, to which they sometimes add eggs and a broiled chicken. At dinner they give a piece of salt beef and roasted fowls, and rum and water as a beverage. In the evening, coffee, tea and ham. There are always several beds in the rooms where you sleep; seldom do you meet with clean sheets. Fortunate is the traveller who arrives on the day they happen to be changed; although an American would be quite indifferent about it.*[3]

Beyond York, Michaux noted a significant change in the landscape as it became mostly barren and mountainous, but covered by a
deciduous forest of oaks, white, red and black, chestnuts and maples. So
it was surprising when they reached a place called Carlisle, which,
although located in a region that had little to offer, they found particularly interesting. The town with its two hundred modern dwellings,
presented a "respectable appearance," despite its "considerable number of shops and warehouses"; it was an emporium of barter, to which
the people living to the westward, all the way to the frontier, brought
the produce of their farms, to be traded there for "jewelry, mercury,
spices, etc." brought from the cities and ports of the East.[4]

At Shippensburg, although he would have wished for the sake of
economy to go on foot, Michaux was induced to join a fellow traveler,
an American officer, in purchasing a horse that they might ride alternately as far as Pittsburgh. Beyond Shippensburg the mountainous
terrain presents a series of steep ranges squarely athwart the road,
which in places deteriorated to "a steep and rocky path," and the
weather was torrid. "From the summit of one of these lofty ranges as far
as one could see, the view afforded nearly the same picture that the
troubled sea presents after a dreadful storm." Progress was painfully
slow through an overshadowing forest of little interest, being dominantly of white oak, relieved here and there by thickets of mountain
laurel, until they reached the river Juniata, a south-flowing tributary of
the Potomac. However, in its vicinity, when it was Michaux's turn to
walk, there were a few botanical rewards to be had: banks covered with
thickets of *Vaccinium,* shrubs of the blueberry sort; *Rhododendrum atlan-
ticum,* dwarf azalea, a rare deciduous species with fragrant white or
various colored flowers; and *Magnolia acuminata,* cucumber tree, whose
green fruits suggested its common name and were employed by the
backwoodsmen to infuse in their whiskey to give it a pleasant bitterness,
and "much esteemed as a preventive of intermittent fevers." That
information drew a degree of skepticism from the medically trained
traveler, who doubted "whether it would be generally used if it had the
same qualities when mixed with water."[5]

In the evening of the second day out from Shippensburg, when
the weary pair reached Bedford Court House and put up at an inn, they
found the village in a turmoil of rowdy rejoicing, as the populace
celebrated the arrival of news that the federal tax laid upon the whiskey
distillers had been repealed by Congress. That excise tax had led to the
disorders and civil disobedience known as the Whiskey Rebellion. Re-

peal of the tax, so obnoxious in the Pennsylvania hinterland, was one of the first financial measures of the new Jefferson administration. Michaux, with considerable distaste, reported the raucous evening:

> [The inn where we lodged] filled with the lower class of people, who made the most dreadful riot, and committed . . . horrible excesses. . . . The rooms, stairs and yard were strewed with drunken men, and those who still had the power of speech uttered nothing but accents of rage and fury. A passion for spiritous liquors is one of the features that characterize the country people belonging to the interior of the United States. This passion is so strong that they desert their homes every now and then to get drunk in public houses; in fact I do not conceive there are ten out of a hundred who have resolution enough to desist. . . . They care very little for cyder, which they find too weak. Their dislike to this pleasant and wholesome beverage is more distressing as they might easily procure it at a very trifling expense for apple trees of every kind grow to wonderful perfection in this country.[6]

Next day, after a brief stop for breakfast at a miller's roadside abode, they came on a man wrapped in a blanket and lying beside the road. According to spectators at the scene he had suffered a rattlesnake bite the previous evening. It was reported that his first symptoms had been violent vomiting, followed by a raging fever, which appeared about an hour after the bite. Michaux examined the desperately ill man and reported his leg and thigh "very much swelled, his respiration very laborious, and his countenance turgescent, and similar to that of a person attacked with hydrophobia whom [he had] had an opportunity of seeing at Charité."[7] When he attempted to question this patient he found that "he was so absorbed that it was impossible to get the least answer from him." However, he was told that "immediately after the bite, the juice of certain plants had been applied to the wound" before the arrival of a doctor who lived fifteen miles away. The plants they make use of for snake bite in those parts were numerous, he reported, almost all being succulents. Numerous too were rattlesnakes in "these mountainous parts of Pennsylvania; we found a great many of them killed upon the road." He failed to report the fate of this poor victim.[8]

Along the road they came upon a log house, very indifferently constructed, which served as a public house "tolerably well supplied with provisions for the country, as they served us up for dinner slices of ham and venison fried on the hearth, with a kind of muffins, which they baked before the fire upon a little board."

Michaux's companion, dissatisfied with their progress under the regime of alternate walking and riding, rented a second mount before crossing the next ridge, known as Laurel Ridge for the dominance there of the shrub they called the calico bush, *Kalmia latifolia,* more widely known as mountain laurel, the leaves of which the residents had discovered to be deadly poisonous to their sheep. Beyond Laurel Ridge lay the extremely fertile Ligonier Valley, where Michaux bade his companion farewell in order to make a botanical excursion suggested to him by William Hamilton to visit the place of Patrick Archibald, several miles off the Pittsburgh road, where there grew, according to reports, a shrub whose fruit was said to produce an excellent oil, presenting the possibility that in cultivation it might prove to be of great value.

Along the way to Archibald's he passed the place of an enterprising French settler who had established a furnace producing copper and brass pots and pans that were already being widely distributed across the newly settled parts. After missing his way several times "on account of the roads being indistinctly cut," he finally reached Archibald's, where he was kindly received. Patrick Archibald's establishment presented a commonly observed enigma of these still raw regions:

> *One would think that this man, who has a mill and other valuables of his own, might live in the greatest comfort; yet he resides in a miserable loghouse about twenty feet long, subject to the inclemency of the weather. Four large beds, two of which are very low, are placed underneath the others in the day time and drawn out of an evening into the middle of the room, receive the whole family, composed of ten persons, and at times strangers, who casually entreat to have a bed. By no means a sign of poverty [here where] there is not a single family but has milk, butter, salted or dried meat, and Indian corn generally in the house; the poorest man has always one or more horses . . . and rarely goes on foot to see his neighbor.*

The next day Michaux discovered the plant he sought and recognized as being a species found by his father in South Carolina fifteen years before. Although he did not identify it, he listed its salient features and commissioned Archibald to gather a bushel of its seed for Hamilton.[9]

Before departing Archibald's place he was asked by his host to see several of his relatives who were ill with measles, practicing doctors being so scarce in those parts that they often had to go twenty or thirty miles to fetch one. He found these patients imbibing their indigenous panacea, whiskey, "to excite perspiration," they explained. Dr. Michaux prescribed a switch to a concoction of the leaves of the viscous elm, vinegar, and maple sugar—all products of the area.

Soon after returning to the road to Pittsburgh, Michaux made the acquaintance of Samuel Craft, a gentleman from Vermont who was aiming for the Yazoo region of Mississippi, an area reputed to be incredibly fertile, where he hoped to locate sites for himself and some of his Vermont neighbors to settle, they being weary of the Vermont climate where the intense cold immobilizes the inhabitants for a third of the year. Upon reaching Pittsburgh they found lodgings for the two of them at a respectable hostelry operated by a fellow Frenchman. There they resided ten days before resuming their journey. For Michaux it was a profitable hiatus devoted to learning much about the town, the region, its vital and varied newborn economy, and of the great Ohio, formed there at the confluence of the Allegheny and Monongahela, down which they expected to travel together.

Having become accustomed to witnessing the laborious and wasteful process of clearing fields from the ubiquitous American forests, and burning the trees removed, he was surprised and interested to learn from Craft that in his part of New England the thrifty inhabitants commonly got their land cleared free of charge by persons seeking the valuable pearl ashes resulting from burning the logs removed, which they sold to glass and soap factories for their potassium carbonate content, a requisite of both processes.

The town of Pittsburgh, composed of some four hundred mostly brick residences, was beautifully situated overlooking the Monongahela and the Allegheny with a view far westward down the beautiful wide breast of the Ohio—the Belle Rivière of the many Frenchmen of generations past during their long but tenuous hold on the region. For near a half century this site had had historical importance, first as the site of Fort Duquesne, guardian sentinel of the French territorial claims to the Ohio and Mississippi valleys, later as the site of Fort Pitt, protecting the eastern settlements from Indian incursions. Those strongholds and the town's military importance had now become mere features of its historical past, the forts "entirely destroyed and nothing more seen than the vestiges of ditches that surrounded" them. But their site "affords the most pleasing view produced by the perspective of the rivers, overshadowed with forests, and especially the Ohio, which flows in a straight line, and, to appearance loses itself in space."

Michaux was intrigued by the variety and extent of the trade and industry Pittsburgh had succeeded in developing in the relatively brief period since it was only a military outpost, a period of less than thirty years. Much of his ten days spent there was given over to touring its enterprises. The most obvious of them, as they had observed on their way from Philadelphia, was its transport trade.

> *The conveyance of merchandise from Philadelphia to Pittsburgh is made in large covered waggons, drawn by four horses, two abreast. . . . They reckon it to be three hundred miles from Phila-delphia to Pittsburgh, and the carriers generally make it a jour-ney of from twenty to twenty-four days. The price of conveyance would not be so high as it really is, were it not that the waggons frequently return empty. Notwithstanding they sometimes bring back on the return to Philadelphia or Baltimore, fur skins that come from Illinois or Ginseng, which is very common in that part of Pennsylvania.*[10]

Generally at Pittsburgh, but sometimes at Redstone, then an important river port upstream on the Monongahela, much of the cargo brought by wagons was forwarded by riverboats to consignees along the Ohio and Mississippi as far down as Natchez, and some all the way down the sinuous waterway to New Orleans, where there was an active trade in the productions of the area. Corn, hams, and dried pork were the principal products mentioned by Michaux as being sent to New Orleans, and thence to the Caribbean ports; "they also export for consumption in Louisiana, bar-iron, coarse linen, bottles manufactured at Pittsburgh, whiskey and salt butter." Another major export borne by the river to New Orleans was the boats themselves that brought the cargoes. Boats and cargoes were sold or bartered away, the former to be broken up to retrieve the virgin timber boards of which they were built.

However, as interesting as were those complex, far-flung trading operations he described, the regional enterprises that held most inter-est for forester Michaux were those of the genre of the log cabins of the settlers, fashioned in the forest, of the forest, with no more tools than an ax and, perhaps, a hand saw, and put together without a nail. The shipyards that had sprung up along the Monongahela and Ohio dis-played much the same "making do" with what was at hand. He exam-ined in detail the operations of one located on the Monongahela a few hundred yards above the last houses of Pittsburgh and noted some of his observations in his *Travels*:

> *The timber they make use of is the white oak, or* Quercus Alba; *the red oak, or* Quercus rubra; *the black oak, or* Quercus

tinctoria [*now* Quercus velutina]; *a kind of nut tree,* Juglans minima [*probably pignut,* Carya cordiformis]; *the Virginia cherry tree,* Cerasus virginica [*probably chokecherry,* Padus virginiana]; *and a kind of pine which they use for masting, as well as for the sides of the vessels which require a slighter wood. The whole of this timber being near at hand, the expense of building it is not so great as in the ports of the Atlantic states. The cordage is manufactured at Redstone and Lexington, where there are two extensive rope-walks. . . . [In July 1802] there was a three-mast vessel of two hundred fifty tons, and a smaller one of ninety, which was on the point of being finished. These ships were to go in the Spring following to New Orleans.*[11]

In a footnote he added the information that after his return to France the next year he learned that the three-masted ship, christened the *Philadelphia,* had completed her voyage to the sea and was at anchor in the Delaware off Pennsylvania.

The boatyards Michaux observed along the Ohio waters, in addition to the expendable barges, also produced keelboats, more conventional river craft in shape and construction large enough to carry profitable cargoes but small enough and sufficiently light to be poled back upstream in two-way commerce.[12]

Much of that frenetic boat construction along the Ohio was the outgrowth of the opening of the Mississippi to duty-free shipment of American produce through New Orleans pursuant to the Treaty of San Lorenzo, better known as Pinckney's Treaty, for its negotiator, which had been concluded between Spain and the United States late in 1795, thanks to the patience and skill of Thomas Pinckney, younger brother of Charles Cotesworth Pinckney. Both were personal friends of the Michauxs.

Many settlers, aiming only for destinations along the Ohio in Kentucky or the Northwest Territory, would risk passage down the Ohio by means of lighter, less sturdily and more cheaply built barges. One afternoon during his stay at Pittsburgh, while walking alone along the banks of the Monongahela above the town, Michaux was intrigued by his first sight of a veritable flotilla of such craft.

I could not conceive what these great square boxes were which, left to the stream, presented alternately their ends, sides and even their angles. . . . However, on ascending the banks of the river, I perceived in these barges several families, carrying with them their horses, cows, poultry, waggons, ploughs, harness, beds, in-

*struments of agriculture, in fine, every thing necessary to culti-
vate the land, and also for domestic use. These people were
abandoning themselves to the mercy of the stream, without knowing the place where they should stop, to exercise their industry
and enjoy peaceably the fruit of their labour under one of the best
governments that exists in the world.*[13]

It was near the middle of July before Michaux and Craft set out
for Kentucky. To save time by avoiding the great detour the river makes
below Pittsburgh, they set out overland directly to Wheeling, a small
Virginia village on the river beyond its big bend. Taking the ferry across
the Monongahela, they landed at Coal-Hill, "a very lofty mountain
which borders the river" on its left bank. The first of the two nights
spent on what was virtually a wilderness road they put up "at an
indifferent inn at Charter Creek where there was but one bed destined
for travellers," so, when there were several, "the last that arrive sleep on
the floor, wrapped in the rug which they always carry with them when
they travel into the remote parts of the United States." Much of the way
to Wheeling was extremely hilly and steep, and the heat was intense;
but there were interesting observations to be made along the way: "The
line of demarktion between Pennsylvania and Virginia . . . marked by
rubbish piled up on lofty eminences"; extremely fertile soil that produced fifteen to twenty bushels of corn per acre if fully cleared, but only
twelve to fifteen if the stumps were left, this with but a single tillage;
"several beds of coal from five to six feet thick, growing horizontally,"
very common in this region where they were regarded as being "of no
account . . . as the country is nothing but one continued forest, and its
population scarce, but were they located in the East where coals are
imported from England, their value would be great"; but most impressive of all were the forests of the valleys where the trees grow "very close
together, and of large diameter, and their species more varied than in
any country I had seen before."[14]

Wheeling, where their shortcut met the river again, perched high
on the left bank of the river, had been settled some twelve years back,
but yet remained a single-street village of seventy houses, all of wood,
strung out along the lofty river bank, including a comfortable inn
named the Sign of the Waggon, where one might board at only two
dollars a week. Other prices there were likewise remarkably low: a
dozen fowl for a dollar, a hundred pounds of flour for a dollar and a
half.

There they purchased a dugout canoe "twenty-four feet long,

eighteen inches wide and about as many in depth." Too narrow to permit the use of oars, such craft had to be propelled by paddles or poles. They were all made of a single log, either pine or tulip tree, their softness facilitating the ax and chiselwork required in hollowing them out, and having the desired lightness. To protect themselves from the sun, the travelers covered its midsection by a cloth awning suspended between two large hoops fixed to the gunwales.

From the river travelers could get a view of the country behind Wheeling. "All that part of Virginia," Michaux recorded, "situated on the left bank of the Ohio is excessively mountainous, covered with forests, and almost uninhabited, where I have been told by those who live on the banks of the Ohio, they go every winter to hunt bears." Intermittently the banks diminish in elevation sufficiently to permit flooding of the forest floor during periods of high water. In places those "river-bottoms" between the mountains and the banks of the river extend back to a distance of five or six miles, areas of unsurpassed fertility and easy culture. "The soil is pure vegetable humus, produced by the thick bed of leaves with which the earth is loaded every year, and which is speedily converted into mould by the humidity that reigns in these forests. . . . I do not remember having seen [in North America] one to compare with the latter for the vegetative strength of its forests."

Twelve miles downstream they crossed to the right bank and made camp for the night. Being "exceedingly fatigued, not so much by continually paddling as by remaining constantly seated with our legs extended. Our canoe being very narrow at bottom, obliged us to keep that position; the least motion would have exposed us to being over-set."[15]

Three days later, about thirty-five miles above Marietta, they were afforded a dramatic illustration of the fertility of these river bottoms. They "had stopped at the hut of one of the inhabitants . . . who showed us about fifty yards from his door a palm [plane] tree, or *Platanus occidentalis,* the trunk of which was swelled to an amazing size; we measured it four feet beyond the surface of the soil, and found it forty-seven feet in circumference. It appeared to keep the same dimentions for the height of fifteen or twenty feet, it then divided into several branches of proportionate size. . . . Our host told us that if we would spend the day with him he would shew us others as large, in several parts of the wood, within two or three miles of the river." Michaux père had reported observing the same or a very similar sycamore and that twenty years earlier General Washington had measured this same tree and found it nearly the same dimensions. He had commented that "the largest tree in North America, after the palm [plane], is the poplar, or *Liriodendron tulipifera.* Its circumference is sometimes sixteen or even eighteen feet."[16]

On July 20 they reached Marietta, a beautifully situated town on the north bank, where the Muskingum flows in from the north. The place offered the travelers several sights and activities worthy of note. It was at Marietta that the idea of exporting the produce of the country directly to the West Indies had originated, and was first demonstrated when a ship built in the local shipyard was sent directly to Jamaica. The rewards that crowned that first venture continued to encourage expansion of their enterprise. Now in the boatyard on the Great Muskingum "they were building three brigs, one of which was of two hundred and twenty tons burthen."

Near the town they viewed the remains of several "Indian fortifications." When these were first discovered, "they were full of trees of the same nature as those of the neighboring forests, some of which were upwards of three feet in diameter. The trees have been hewn down, and the ground is now almost entirely cultivated with Indian corn."[17]

Resuming their navigation of the slow-flowing, island-studded river, they experienced an altogether too intimate association with a Kentucky boat destined for Cincinnati. They had joined this craft intending to spend a more comfortable night, less "sadly tormented by the fleas, with which the greater part of the houses where we had slept . . . had been infested." They fastened their canoe to it and climbed aboard the crude forty by fifteen foot craft "loaded with bar iron and brass pots. There was also an emigrant family in it consisting of the father, mother, and seven children, with all the furniture and implements of husbandry" and three boatmen to manage the craft. However, contrary to their hopes, they were even more tormented by fleas, and at two in the morning they ran aground. Under those circumstances they could not, as they were about to do, desert their hosts, "who had entertained us with their best, and who had made us partake of a wild turkey which they had shot . . . on the banks of the river." Getting out into the water with the boatmen, after two hours of painful effort, they got the vessel afloat again.[18]

Farther on their way delightful aesthetic compensations awaited them. Where the Kanawha flows in from the mountains of Virginia and Tennessee, for four or five miles the river maintains a width of a half mile and presents sublime scenes:

"Its borders sloping, and elevated from twenty-five to forty feet,

are, as in the whole of its windings, planted at their base with willows . . . the drooping branches and foliage of which form a pleasing contrast to the sugar maples, red maples and ash trees situated immediately above. The latter, in return [sic], are overlooked by palms [sycamores], poplars, beeches, magnolias of the highest elevation, the enormous branches of which . . . extend towards the borders, overshadowing the river, at the same time completely covering the trees situated under them. This natural display, which reigns upon the two banks, affords on each side a regular arch, the shadow of which, reflected by the crystal stream, embellishes, in an extraordinary degree, this magnificent coup d'oeil."[19]

In marked and painful contrast to the delight and inspiration of that sylvan scene was the nearby village of Gallipolis, an ill-fated French settlement on the same side of the river. When they beached their canoe and climbed the bank to the village, they found "it composed solely of about sixty log-houses, most of which being uninhabited, are falling to ruins; the rest are occupied by Frenchmen, who breathe out a miserable existence."[20]

Their visit to the Gallipolis settlements suggested to Michaux a botanical observation on the readiness with which some exotics escape and thrive to the extent of becoming menacing weeds. He noted that the spaces between every house there had been entirely claimed by *Datura stramonium*, the deadly poisonous Jimsonweed, or thorn apple, whose showy white flowers are its only redeeming feature. He noted that this weed would quickly claim for itself any land that had been cultivated, even years earlier. This weed is said to have been first introduced at Jamestown, Virginia, thereby acquiring its American common name. He noted, too, that mullein was another example of an Old World plant that had escaped and already spread abundantly all over the United States east of the mountains.[21]

It was August 1 when they reached the Kentucky village Maysville (then called Limestone for the first rock outcroppings of any sort in the humus-rich loam of the banks below Wheeling, three hundred miles upstream). During the ten days since their departure from Wheeling they had had to paddle steadily because of the slowness of stream, a labor intensified by heat and thirst, "for in summer the water of the Ohio acquires such a degree of heat that it is not fit to drink." With time growing short for him to accomplish his intended botanical expeditions into the interiors of Kentucky and Tennessee and a thousand more miles of travel ahead, Michaux decided to leave the river and begin there at Maysville his tour of Kentucky. Craft elected to continue by canoe down the Ohio and Mississippi and up the Yazoo to Natchez, where he hoped to find the fertile plantations he sought.[22]

At this point, before departing the river with which they had become so intimate, Michaux inserted in his *Travels* a potpourri of other observations he deemed worthy of note. He noted the fish and the shellfish the river offered. Of the latter it produced an abundance of mussels (more correctly, clams) five or six inches long, which, though the inhabitants did not eat them, served to supply excellent mother-of-pearl from which they made beautiful buttons. He collected some to take back to Bosc, who named the species *Unio ohiotensis*. Among the fish, with which the river abounded, the most striking and useful were the great "cat-fish, or *Silurus felis*" (probably the yellow cat, *Leptops oliveris*), weighing up to a hundred pounds or more, and easily taken by the inhabitants either by hook and line or spears.[23]

Of the human inhabitants residing along the river, he judged about half to have been "first inhabitants," those who first came there and stayed, and the other half to be replacements, who had purchased the sites of those who had moved on westward in search of "greener pastures." However, it appeared to him that all the men, first settlers and later arrivals alike, "employ the greatest part of their time in stag and bear hunting, for the sake of the skins, which they dispose of," leaving "scarcely any time to meliorate their new possessions, that usually consist of two or three hundred acres of which not more than eight or ten are cleared. . . . The houses that they inhabit are built upon the borders of the river, generally in a pleasant situation, whence they enjoy the most delightful prospects; still their mode of building does not correspond to the beauties of the spot, being nothing but miserable log houses without windows, and so small that two beds occupy the greatest part of them . . . [yet] they do not hesitate to receive travelers who claim their hospitality."

"The peach is the only fruit tree that they have yet cultivated, which thrives," superbly.

The price of the best land did not exceed three dollars per acre.

Finally, he described the attire and accouterments of a "first settler" they had met with on his way to get his wife and children, to take them to the new place he had selected on the banks of Missouri: "a westcoat with sleeves, a pair of pantaloons, and a large red and yellow worsted sash; carabine, a tomahawk, a little axe, which the Indians make use of to cut wood and to terminate the existence of their enemies;

two beaver snares, and a large knife suspended at his side, constituted his sporting dress. A rug comprised the whole of his luggage."

After discussion of the Ohio River's great commercial potential, he closed his comments with this opinion: "All those advantages, blended with the salubrity of the climate, and the beauty of the landscape . . . make me think that the banks of the Ohio, from Pittsburgh to Louisville inclusively, will, in the course of twenty years, be the most populous and commercial part of the United States, and where I should settle in preference to any other."

CHAPTER **20**

✑ Kentucky, 1802

MAYSVILLE, AT THE BOTTOM of a southward bend of the river, was relatively nearer the towns of inland Kentucky and was then one of the most popular landing places for immigrants aiming for the interior parts of the state. Confronted with "great difficulty in procuring horses on hire" and the undue advantage being taken by the inhabitants "in order to sell them at an enormous price," Michaux elected not to be among those taken advantage of, and, deciding to send his portmanteau by wagon, set out on foot for Lexington, reckoned to be sixty-five miles, a distance he covered in two and a half days.

For ten miles the Lexington road passed through a fertile region with several fine plantations "as well cultivated and the enclosures as well constructed as at Virginia and Pennsylvania." Beyond Licking River, however, it turned sandy and was littered with immense chalky stones and was so poor it was incapable of supporting anything but some scrubby white oaks and hickories. Near the river he tarried to inspect a salt mine in operation. Its source of salt was a shallow well the saline waters of which were evaporated in a row of twenty-five-gallon brass pans placed over a long pit in which a fire was kept burning. Michaux was appalled by the inefficiency of the operation, particularly the prodigious quantity of wood wastefully consumed. He suggested ways to improve the process, but his suggestions fell on deaf ears. Its gross inefficiency caused the price of its product to be very dear—up to five dollars a hundredweight—so dear, in fact, that many people were induced to busy themselves searching for salt springs, which were mostly found in places called licks "where the bisons, elks and stags that existed in Kentucky, before the arrival of the Europeans, went by hundreds to lick the saline particles with which the soil is impregnated." With disgust he added that there were "a set of quacks, who by means of a hazel wand pretend to discover springs of salt and fresh water," but they only did their divining where other circumstances indicated a favorable place.

Even in these remote frontier regions, thoroughly American in conduct and spirit, things French with surprising frequency were still encountered. At Millersburg, the first village on the road after entering Bourbon County on the way to Paris, its county seat (which he consistently calls the "manor-house" of the county), he was a guest at the home of Henry Savary, an enterprising Frenchman "very intimately acquainted with my father." That gentleman was said to be "one of the greatest proprietors in that part of the country," possessing "more than eighty thousand acres of land in Virginia, Tennessee and Kentucky" for which he was finding it difficult to secure purchasers. Observations made on crossing a small river nearby led Michaux to comment on a prevailing feature of rivers in those parts. That stream, "five or six fathoms broad, upon which two sawmills are erected, was so low I crossed it on stones comprising its bed, but in the winter it swells to such a degree that it can scarcely be passed by means of a bridge twenty-five feet" above the level at which it flows in summer, in striking contrast to the gentle, relatively even-flowing rivers of France. He added that those high-perched bridges of Kentucky were made of logs, laid side by side, from bank to bank, and quite without protecting railings.[1]

Lexington, "the manor-house for the county of Fayette," situated in a relatively flat region in the great bend of the Kentucky River, with a population of about three thousand, was the trading center of interior Kentucky. The highlights of his visit there of several days' duration were twofold; one being the striking demonstrations on every hand of the truth of Plato's aphorism that necessity is the mother of invention. The other was the opportunity it gave him to meet and enjoy the company of the man Michaux considered the leading scientific figure of the transmontane West, Dr. Samuel Brown.[2]

In many diverse ways the people of Lexington, utilizing what they had at hand, were improvising and inventing ways and means to meet the needs of a region far removed from established manufacturing centers. Those improvisations fascinated the cosmopolitan young Frenchman from the capital of civilization of the Western world. On a little river "near the town several tan yards are established to supply the wants of the inhabitants." He observed there "strong leathers of yellowish cast, tanned with black oak"—a surprise to him as he had not seen that species growing anywhere along the way from Maysville. He soon observed that its absence from view lay in the fact that his route was through land "either parched up or extremely fertile, and this tree grows in neither," its preference being gravelly, rather moist soils.

"The want of hands excites the industry of the inhabitants," he commented; "one of them has just obtained a patent for a nail machine, more complete and expeditious than the one made use of in the prisons of New York and Philadelphia, and another has a machine for grinding and cleaning the hemp and sawing wood and stone"—capable of breaking and cleaning eight thousand weight of hemp per day. There were also several potteries and gunpowder mills, the produce of the latter already being exported to the Carolinas and lower Louisiana. He attributed their gunpowder industry to the presence in the region of bountiful supplies of saltpeter, which is found on the floors of the numerous caverns in the area.[3] After inspecting some of those caves and observing that their nitrous deposits were well within its protecting walls, Michaux thought it reasonable to deduce that animal matter is not in fact necessary for the formation of nitrous veins—overlooking, as Jefferson had also done, that those caverns were commonly the shelters of roosting bats, whose droppings through the ages had contributed their nitrous substance.[4]

Necessity and isolation had forced other improvisations; one of the most obvious of which was the all-pervading barter system upon which Kentuckians' trade and commerce were almost totally dependent. The conservatism that dominated banking circles, the lack of safe transport and communication systems, and an inadequate supply of specie, confronting the frontier's great need for trade, had forced that reliance on barter, with all its attendant complexities.[5]

But most of all it was his meeting with Dr. Samuel Brown and the friendship that quickly developed between them that made François André's Lexington stay particularly memorable. He had brought with him letters of introduction to the doctor from three fellow members of the American Philosophical Society. Doctor Brown was best known for his introduction and wide use of smallpox inoculation, long before most doctors in the East. But he was also somewhat a scientific dilettante. At the time of Michaux's visit he was busying himself collecting fossils, analyzing the waters of mineral springs, and studying the niter deposits in caves. For several years he had held the chair of director of medical education at Lexington's Transylvania College. It was probably that wide range of interests and activities that so impressed Michaux, though they dissipated to a considerable degree the doctor's uncommon abilities.

One of the cardinal characteristics of the young visitor was his own omnivorous appetite for things new and different—among them the lively interest he frequently displayed in his American travels, in respect to things he thought uniquely American. In that category were the religious inclinations he observed among its inhabitants, particularly those such as the Kentuckians, who had elected to abandon the already substantially formalized societies of the old English colonies, in favor of new lives and new freedoms in the frontier settlements. In regions devoid of churches and established pastoral direction, they had shed the fetters of the monolithic, formalized church establishments of their forebears. That fascinated and mystified him, perhaps because formal religion appears never to have made any significant impression upon him or played any noticeable part in his development.

While at Lexington he was provided the opportunity to witness a display of a face of religion entirely new to him. He attended an immense gathering of people, most of whom professed Anabaptist or Methodist affiliations, who had generally, "independent of Sundays, which are scrupulously observed," little concerned themselves with religion, but for whom, in these newly settled parts, in recent years "the spirit of religion has acquired a fresh degree of strength" that commonly evoked in them ostentatiously emotional displays. These protracted summer meetings usually attracted two or three thousand persons who come from all parts of the country, within fifteen or twenty miles, took place in the woods, and continued for several days. Each brought his provisions and spent the night round the fire.

> *The clergymen are very vehement in their discourses. Often in the midst of the sermons the heads are lifted up, the imaginations exhalted, and the inspired fall backwards, "Glory! Glory!" This species of infatuation happens chiefly among the women, who are carried out of the crowd, and put under a tree, where they lie a long time extended, heaving the most lamentable sighs.*
>
> *There have been instances of two or three hundred of the congregation being thus affected during the performance of divine service; so that one-third of the hearers were engaged in recovering the rest. . . . [The better-informed people do not share the opinion of the multitude with regard to this state of ecstacy] and on this account they are branded with the appellation of* bad

folks. *Except during the continuance of this preaching, religion is very seldom the topic of conversation.*[6]

Another, more mundane interest of Kentuckians, particularly those around Lexington, was reported at some length by Michaux. Since time has proved this interest to be pervasive and durable, we shall let Michaux himself comment on the subject as he observed it at the beginning of the nineteenth century:

> *For some time past the inhabitants of Kentucky have taken to rearing and training horses and by this lucrative branch of trade they derive considerable profit. . . .*
>
> *Of all the states belonging to the Union, Virginia is said to have the finest coach and saddle horses, and those they have in this country proceed originally from them. . . . Almost all the inhabitants employ themselves in training and meliorating the breed of these animals; and so great a degree of importance is attained to the melioration that the owners of fine stallions charge from fifteen to twenty dollars for the covering of a mare. These stallions come from Virginia . . . and some . . . imported from England. The horses that proceed from them have slim legs, a well-proportioned head, and are elegantly formed.*[7]

However, the Kentuckians' equine interest did not extend to draft animals. They gave no attention to improving that breed "in consequence of which they are small, wretched in appearance, and similar to those made use of by the peasantry in France. They appeared to me still worse in Georgia and Upper Carolina." In fact, he was convinced that even throughout the entire United States there was "not a single draught-horse that can be in any wise compared with the poorest race of horses that I have seen in England."[8] That inconsistency in the Kentuckians' equine interest was compounded, in the view of Dr. Michaux, in respect to the state of its veterinary medicine. Although "many individuals profess to treat sick horses, none of them have any regular notions of the veterinary art which would be so necessary in a breeding country, and which has, within these few years, acquired so high a degree of perfection in England and France."

Finally, on the same subject, Michaux had sharp and interesting comments on the mustangs being ridden up from New Orleans and Natchez by the flat-boatmen returning to Kentucky. "Those wild horses," he reported, "which descend from those the Spaniards introduced" were caught on the plains of New Mexico by the "use of tame horses that run much swifter and with which they approach them near enough to halter them" and take them to New Orleans or Natchez "where they fetch about fifty dollars." The two he tried "were roan coloured, of middling size, the head large, and not proportionate with the neck, the limbs thick and the mane rather full and handsome." But they "have a very unpleasant gait, are capricious, difficult to govern, and even frequently throw the rider and take flight."[9]

Ever practical and down to earth, the younger Michaux often gives one the impression of having been really a businessman manqué. Almost invariably when he reported his observations of activities, whether of wilderness hunters, river boaters, or Kentucky farmers, he weighed the economic consequences involved and any commerce that might result. The Kentuckians' horse breeding activities were no exception:

> *The southern states, and in particular South Carolina, are the principal places destined for the sale of Kentucky horses. They are taken there in droves of fifteen, twenty and thirty at a time, in the early part of winter, an epoch when the most business is transacted at Carolina, and when the drivers are in no fear of the yellow fever, of which the inhabitants of the interior have the greatest apprehension. They usually take from eighteen to twenty days to go from Lexington to Charleston. This distance, which is about seven hundred miles, makes a difference of twenty-five or thirty per cent in the price of the horses. A fine saddle-horse in Kentucky costs about a hundred and thirty to a hundred and fifty dollars.* [10]

In Lexington, Michaux heard much talk of the association that had been organized there almost four years back to encourage the establishment of a vineyard under the direction of an experienced vinedresser who had newly come to Kentucky. The key man and inspirer of the enterprise, John James Dufour, a Swiss who had come to America in 1796 with the fixed dream of launching a wine industry in the United States, had devoted his first two years to a careful search for the most suitable region, site, and vines to be had. Once he had settled on those concerns, his family and many neighbors from the Vevey area north of Lake Geneva were to follow him and establish a community devoted to the enterprise. He believed he had found in the environs of Lexington a site that would duplicate, as nearly as possible, the latitude of Switzerland and the soil, terrain and climate that had made Vevey a successful wine center; but doubtless at the time he was also influenced by the frenetic enthusiasm for Kentucky then prevailing in the East. At any rate, he had arrived in Lexington in the summer of 1798 and quickly inspired there a sufficiently contagious enthusiasm for the enterprise to bring about the organization of the society and substantial subscriptions to promote its operations. But, as Michaux gathered from his informants, two very disappointing harvests and the current prospects at the vineyard had dispelled the local enthusiasm of all but the prime mover himself.

Having, along with many others, shared Dufour's interest in the possibility of viticulture in a country where no touring botanist could fail to note the numerous species of wild grapes flourishing wherever one went, Michaux determined to visit Dufour's establishment on his way to Nashville, although it required a substantial diversion from his route. When he reached the site of the enterprise near the Kentucky River, about twenty-five miles from Lexington, he judged its location excellent with "the vineyard planted on the declivity of a hill exposed to the south . . . about two hundred fathoms from the river." There about seventeen of the Dufour family and neighbors had joined him and given the venture the optimistic name of First Vineyard. Though they had devoted "unremitted labour" to a collection of some twenty-five species, occupying about six acres, all "fixed with props similar to those in the environs of Paris," success had not crowned their devoted efforts. Mildew destroyed the bunches on all but three or four species, and in previous seasons, as the fruit ripened, hoards of birds descended on the vineyard and consumed most of the rest.

Nevertheless, Dufour himself remained hopeful. He had found that two varieties—the Catawba from Carolina, probably, like the now popular southern scuppernong, a natural hybrid, and his Madeira vines—showed promise. So he persisted in his efforts at First Vineyard, even as most of his companions were deserting it to descend the Kentucky to the Ohio, where on the north side of the river other Swiss were settling in what is now Switzerland County, Indiana. There Second Vineyard and the town of Vevay were established the year following Michaux's 1802 visit. Later, before his *Travels* went to press, he learned that the plans for Second Vineyard had been successfully carried out. Doubtless, too, in later years he learned that Dufour himself had joined his fellow countrymen at Vevay, where he remained until his death in 1827, shortly after the publication of his pioneer work on grape culture in the United States, *The American Vine Dresser's Guide*.[11]

After two interesting days as Dufour's guest, on August 10 Michaux departed First Vineyard in the company of his host, who volunteered to show him a shorter route to the Nashville road. Although it was but four miles, the shortcut route through the forest required a ride of two hours "as we were obliged to alight either to climb up or descend the mountains, or to leap our horses over the trunks of old trees piled one upon another" in a forest chiefly of beech, hickories, and oaks, with sycamores in the bottoms. At Hickman's Ferry, where the road crossed the Kentucky, Michaux found the river so low that operation of the ferry was suspended, requiring travelers to ford the stream "which swells amazingly in the spring and autumn" when its waters rise from sixty to seventy feet above its present stage, filling it to its borders "of enormous chalky stones, remarkably peaked, about one hundred and fifty feet high . . . which bear, from bottom to top, evident traces of the action of the waters."

The trail to Nashville led across Muldrow's Hills, where the outlook provided a memorable sight:

From the summit of a kind of ampitheatre . . . the neighboring country presents the aspect of an immense valley, covered with forests of an imperceptible extent, whence, as far as the eye can reach, nothing but a gloomy verdant space is seen, formed by the tops of the close-connected trees, and through which not the vestige of a plantation can be discerned. The profound silence that reigns in these woods, uninhabited by wild beasts, and the security of the place, forms an ensemble rarely to be met with in other countries."[12]

After drinking deeply of the sublimity of the scene, he resumed his way along the lonely trail until late in the day when he sought shelter for the night at Skegg's Inn, a place that proved to be the worst he had met with in Kentucky—"a place destitute of every kind of provision," obliging him to sleep on the floor, wrapped in his rug, without the solace of even a bite of supper. Lacking any stable or even a fenced area, he could only loose his horse in the peach orchard with a bell on his neck to assist in finding him, should he stray in the night. But as luck would have it, "the peaches at the time were in full perfection" to be thoroughly enjoyed by his mount, as he perceived in the morning and noted the great quantity of kernels littering the ground under several trees the branches of which had been so loaded with fruit that they hung nearly to the ground.[13]

The next day he witnessed yet another instance of the abrupt and surprising contrasts Kentucky frequently offered, whether it be the contrasting soils he had observed or the feeble flow of the Kentucky

River at this season vis-à-vis the springtime torrents indicated by the water marks high on its bordering cliffs. Now, but a few miles from the sylvan beauty of the "close-connected" trees of Muldrow's Hills and the magnificent forest of beautiful, gray-bolled beech trees that bordered the Green River, he emerged with almost startling suddenness into the nearly treeless, gently rolling grass-covered hills known as the Barrens. It was a surprising and pleasing sight, despite the forewarnings that he "would have to cross over a naked space, sown here and there with a few plants" and "that at this season I should perish with heat and thirst, and that I should not find the least shade the whole way." For the last two or three miles the forest itself signaled his approach to this striking region as the woods became more and more open until they could no longer be called a forest, but only an area supporting a sparse scattering of post oaks, *Quercus oblusiloba* (now, *stellata*), black oaks, *Quercus velutina,* and hickories, with here and there shrublike willows and a few sumacs, all increasingly stunted even as they became more widely spaced. Nevertheless, it was a pleasant surprise when he emerged into "a beautiful meadow, where the grass was from two to three feet high," bespangled with the yellow blossoms of *Gerardia flava* (now *Aureolaria*), near the bordering post oaks upon the roots of which they are parasitic, and cone flowers, *Rudbeckia,* and the milk-colored umbels of the *Gnaphalium dioicum* (now *obtusifolium*), popularly known as rabbit tobacco, or everlasting, a plant widely resorted to in folk medicine as a panacea for almost every ailment of man.

This island of grassland in a sea of forests was an intriguing phenomenon worthy of careful scientific observations. It occupied an area about sixty miles in diameter, mostly in Kentucky, but spilling over into Tennessee above Nashville. At the time of Michaux's visit it was very sparsely settled despite the opportunity it afforded settlers to have fields ready for the plow, without the time-consuming and painful task of felling primeval forest giants and grubbing out their roots. Along the entire sixty or seventy miles of the road across the Barrens he saw but eighteen dwellings. He pondered that relative emptiness when the rest of Kentucky's good soil regions were so rapidly filling with settlers.

Through those gently rolling grasslands, unbroken except for an occasional red cedar or scrubby Virginia pine, Michaux rode for some thirteen miles before sighting on the horizon, near a place he called "Bears-wallow," an isolated settler's abode where he sought and was readily granted accommodations for the night. He proved to be a most welcome guest in that household, for theirs was a very lonely existence. The mistress of the house told him that she had resided in the Barrens upwards of three years, and that for eighteen months before his coming she had not seen anyone except her three children and her husband, and that he had been gone two of those months in quest of another spot to settle, as she was weary of living so isolated.

Next morning the main reason for the Barrens being so sparsely settled revealed itself. In response to his enquiry as to where he might water his horse, he was directed to their spring, about a quarter of a mile away. In seeking it out Michaux missed his path across the featureless terrain, a mischance that forced him to devote the entire morning to the quest for some other watering place. At length he was only barely successful, for when he found another spring it took him "upwards of an hour" to draw half a pail for the animal. The Barrens not only supports few springs, but streams, too, are almost nonexistent there. He discovered the cause of that when his curiosity led him to investigate several sinks—places where the surface earth had fallen into cavernous depths below, from which often came the sound of flowing water far out of reach below the surface.

Another deterrent to settlement in the Barrens was the great danger inherent in the wildfires that periodically swept the region with devastating effects, consuming everything in their paths as they raced across the open country, sometimes at speeds faster than a man might flee the fury of the flames. Before the arrival of the whites the Indians had regularly employed fire in those grasslands to corral the game they sought, or to drive the fleeing animals to within the range of their arrows. The settlers in turn continued to utilize fire each spring to remove the mat of the previous year's growth to permit their livestock to browse the new growth earlier than it would otherwise become available.[14]

Despite those handicaps Michaux was convinced that these extensive meadows were far from undesirable. He observed that of all the places he had seen in America, it was the Kentucky Barrens that he thought offered the greatest possibilities for the culture of wine grapes. Not only had he noted flourishing there delicious wild "summer grapes" (probably *Vitis aestivalis*), but the calcareous soils seemed very similar to those of the best vine regions of France. Moreover, he had observed that those grasslands belied their designation and, in fact, supported an immense variety of plants. "When I crossed these meadows," he wrote, "the flower season was over with three parts of the plants, but the time for most seeds to ripen was still at a great distance; nevertheless, I gathered about ninety different species of them which I took with me to France."[15]

Michaux concludes his discussion of Kentucky, with a series of observations and comments on the region, a number of which deserve attention, particularly those in respect to his special interests, agriculture and forestry.

Of the Kentuckians' livestock other than horses, "the number of horned cattle is very considerable. Those who deal in them purchase them lean and drive them" in herds of two or three hundred, to Virginia, along the River Potomac, where they sold them to the graziers who fattened them "for the Baltimore and Philadelphia markets." He reported the price of a good milk cow as being from ten to twelve dollars. "Milk in a great measure comprises the chief sustenance of the inhabitants. The butter that is not consumed . . . is put into barrels, and exported by the river to the Carribees." On the other hand, sheep were few "as their flesh is not much esteemed." But "of all domestic animals hogs are the most numerous." Some farmers fed 150 or 200. "They never leave the woods, where they always find a sufficiency of food, especially in autumn and winter," and hence become extremely wild herds. Every inhabitant recognizes those that belong to him by the particular manner in which their ears are cut."

Even by 1802 salt and dried provisions had become an important part of Kentucky's trade. In the first six months of that year 74,485 barrels of dried and salt pork had been sent down the river from Louisville alone. On the other hand, he was equally surprised to find so few inhabitants keeping any poultry despite their bountiful supplies of grain, a neglect he attributed to the surplus of their supply of pork and the ease with which it is prepared. Besides, many Kentuckians found the meat of poultry "insipid," and keeping birds confined and away from their fields presented problems, their fences being only sufficient to prevent cattle and pigs from damaging their crops. Protected from that devastation, "rye and oats come up extremely well. . . . The rye is nearly all made use of in the distilling of whiskey." [16]

The people of Kentucky, unlike European farmers, showed surprisingly little interest in the culture of fruit trees, despite a very favorable temperature and climate for that aspect of agriculture. "They have confined themselves to the planting of peach and apple trees. The former are very numerous, and come to greatest perfection. . . . The immense quantity of peaches which they gather are converted in brandy, of which there is great consumption in the country, and the rest is exported." Some have stills. "The others carry their peaches to them and bring back a quantity of brandy proportionate to the number of peaches that they carried. . . . Its prevailing market price: twenty-five cents a quart."[17]

Michaux thought the taxes imposed on Kentuckians very moderate. They pay, very tardily, he reported, forty cents for each white servant, fifteen for each black servant, six cents for each horse and fifty cents for each hundred acres of first-class land, whether in cultivation or not. More in his line, he found the Kentuckians remarkably adept at judging among the three classes used in assessing their properties or in their speculations by buying and selling land, even though its fertility had not been tested in cultivation. The more knowledgeable, at least, had discovered that they could make that judgment by noting the species of trees growing upon it. The only exceptions were those lands in Barrens, where there were insufficient trees to guide one's judgment. Forester Michaux was most impressed by that backwoods sagacity, and in his *Travels,* deals with it in considerable detail.

When Kentuckians announced the sale of lands, "they take care to specify the particular species of trees peculiar to its various parts, which is sufficient index for the purchaser." Lands of the first class would be indicated by the presence of chokecherry, *Padus virginiana*; white walnut, *Juglans cinerea*; yellow buckeye, *Aesculus octandra*; white ash, *Fraxinus americana*; and other species; hackberry, *Celtis laevigata*; slippery elm, *Ulmus rubra*; shingle oak, *Quercus imbricaria*; Kentucky coffee tree, *Gymnocladus dioica*; the honey locust, *Gleditsia triacanthos,* and the pawpaw, *Asimina triloba.* "These three latter species denote the richest lands." Where one found chestnuts, *Castanea dentata*; red oaks, *Quercus rubra*; black oaks, *Quercus velutina*; sassafras, *S. albidum*; persimmons, *Diospyros virginiana*; sweet-gums, *Liquidambar styraciflua*; and black gums, *Nyssa sylvatica,* one could conclude that the land on which they grew was of the second class. "Those of the third class, which commonly are dry and mountainous, produce very little except black and red oaks, chestnut oaks of the mountains, *Quercus prinus montana,* and a few Virginia cedars."

Michaux did not neglect to mention another widely accepted botanical index of fertile soils, one that is a grass rather than a tree, the American bamboo, or canes, whose generic name *Arundinaria* is attributed to Michaux père, the only bamboos native to a region other than the tropics. These immense grasses, attaining heights up to twenty feet, have a strange way of irregularly but simultaneously blossoming, seeding, and then dying, and only slowly coming back. His Kentucky visit must have followed one of those die-offs, for he remarked that in all the fertile parts the forests were then free of undergrowth although they formerly supplied "a species of the great articulated reed, called *Arundinaria macrosperma* (now *gigantea*) or cane, which is in the woods from three to four inches in diameter and seven or eight feet high."[18]

Finally, before concluding his "general observations" on Kentucky, Michaux returned to the subject of ginseng, which he had only briefly mentioned in discussing the wagon trade between Pittsburgh and Philadelphia. "Although it is not a plant peculiar to Kentucky . . . being found in America from Lower Canada" to Georgia, where it is common and widespread, he thought the people there could be in a position to rebuild a very lucrative trade in the roots of that perennial herb if they would only observe the proper manner of gathering and preparing them. In taking that view, he was reflecting and attempting to carry forward a conviction long entertained by his father who, a decade earlier in Charleston, had expressed similar views in an address to the Agricultural Society of South Carolina.

Like his father, Michaux fils was convinced that, seasonably gathered and properly prepared, the American *Panax ginseng* (now *Panax quinquefolium*) could again regain its erstwhile value of its weight in gold in Cathay. He pointed out that the principal fault of the American product resulted from the "Sang" diggers making their harvests in the spring and summer, whereas the prized ginseng of China, where it had long been under an imperial monopoly, was always harvested only in the autumn and winter. The Michauxs' belief in ginseng's commercial potential was later vindicated. In the decades after François André's advocacy, seventeen million pounds of ginseng were shipped to the Orient, until, in 1904, a fungus appeared and all but eradicated the plant from its American habitat.[19]

We rejoin Michaux at Nashville where he had arrived on August 25, the second day after departing the Kentucky Barrens, to his immense relief in forested country again.

CHAPTER 21

⸙ Tennessee and Return to Carolina, 1802–1803

ON MICHAUX'S DEPARTURE from Lexington, Dr. Samuel Brown had provided him with a letter of introduction to a gentleman of the law in Nashville, a recommendation that no doubt was partly responsible for his warm reception there, where he found the leading citizenry of the town "very engaging in their manners," albeit with little ceremony. He had scarcely arrived at the place before several who were at the inn invited him to their plantations.

Although Nashville was the "principal and oldest town" in that part of Tennessee, it was only fifteen years from its first settlement. It continued to suffer severe drawbacks inherent in its beautiful but challenging location on about thirty acres of almost bare rock upwards of sixty feet above the Cumberland River, an elevation that prevented its inhabitants from reaching the stream to secure water "without going a considerable distance or descending to it by a steep and dangerous path." Nevertheless, to the residents who occupied its modest houses, seven or eight of brick and one hundred and twenty of wood, those handicaps represented challenges, as did, too, the town's remoteness from any trading point, making prices very dear in the fifteen or twenty shops that supplied all their needs in the absence of any sort of manufacturing establishment.

Although Nashville was the first town to be met with to the northward on the newly opened road from Natchez that followed the old Natchez Trace, the path long used by boatmen on their way back to Pittsburgh, water transport still remained the only viable way for its inhabitants to secure their manufactured necessities, despite the great distances, mostly upstream, that they had to be transported: almost 1,250 miles up the Mississippi, Ohio, and Cumberland, or from Pittsburgh, after a 450-mile overland haul from Philadelphia and another 1,200 by riverboats.

Nevertheless, the town displayed a surprising vitality. One determined citizen was engaged in penetrating the hard limestone to the water level of the river below the cliff; another was publishing a weekly newspaper, and a group of forward-looking citizens were attempting to organize a college—an effort that came to fruition a few years later in

Cumberland College.[1] Among those prominent in that effort was Moses Fisk, a native of Massachusetts and a Harvard graduate, with whom Michaux soon developed a warm friendship. When he set out from Nashville, Fisk, who had business at Knoxville, traveled with him as far as the capital.

Before departing Nashville, Michaux busied himself collecting seed and plants in the environs. There he found, gathered, and shipped to New York twenty pounds of the wood of the beautiful yellowwood, *Cladastris lutea,* that his father had discovered years before in Tennessee and believed might prove valuable as a source of yellow dye. Ten pounds were to be delivered to Dr. Samuel Mitchill for experimentation and ten pounds to be sent on to the Board of Agriculture in Paris. His father, when he discovered this tree, had noted its resemblance to an oriental relative, the Japan pagoda tree, *Sophora japonica,* a source of dye there, and had then suggested that it might prove a valuable source of dye for America; but nothing had come of it. Michaux fils still believed its potential should be further pursued. At the same time he gathered some seed of the yellowwood which, he reported in his *Travels,* he took back to Paris where they had all come up and were growing well.[2]

On September 5 he resumed his circuitous route back to Charleston, now in company with Fisk. The road they took eastward to Knoxville followed Avery's Trace, the path of the pioneers of the early westward movement into Tennessee. However, its route from Nashville led back across the Cumberland and up its valley to Fort Blount, site of an early post on the south side of the river some sixty miles upstream. At every stop along the way they were guests at roadside plantations, the masters of which were all well known to Fisk. Except for the thread of the road, all those places were isolated from each other by a mile or two of splendid forests. Their fields of cotton and maize, now approaching harvest stage, appeared bountiful. The fertility of their soils confirmed Michaux's conviction that a rank understory of cane, *Arundinaria gigantea,* which abounded in the intervening forests was a reliable index of soil fertility. Although the comfortable homes on those plantations were still constructed of logs, there was ample promise of future prosperity.

Some planters had already attained that state, among them being several whose hospitality the travelers enjoyed as they somewhat leisurely made their way to Fort Blount. One of them was General Daniel Smith, a veteran of Indian wars and Kings Mountain and successor of Andrew Jackson in the United States Senate.[3] It was he who had laid out the town of Nashville at the direction of the Tennessee legislature. He had also prepared and published the best map of Tennessee up to that time. At his place, Rock Castle, to augment his income from his extensive farming operations, he had established a distillery which specialized in peach brandy that brought him a dollar and a quarter a gallon.

Their way eastward led them near Dixon's Spring, an astonishing phenomenon where quantities of water issued forth from the mouth of a cavern. A steady current of air also came from the orifice "strong enough to extinguish a light." Michaux was told that such large issues of groundwaters from deep in the earth were not uncommon in eastern Tennessee.[4] Their next recorded stop was at Cragfont, the plantation of General James Winchester, a distinguished veteran of the Revolution in the course of which he had served in battles from Staten Island to Yorktown and was twice a prisoner of the enemy.[5] He was now engaged in building a stone mansion for which task he had imported stonemasons from his native Maryland. Beyond Winchester's place the travelers crossed to the south side of the Cumberland, deep in a rock-walled chasm, to abandoned Fort Blount, built two decades past to protect the early settlers moving into Tennessee and Kentucky from harassment by the Cherokee.

Near the site of the fort the travelers were guests for several days at the splendid plantation of Captain William Sampson, a stop that gave Michaux the opportunity to ascend several miles up the Cumberland in a canoe. Along the banks of that lovely stream he enriched his collections "with the seeds of several trees and plants peculiar to the country, and divers other objects of natural history."[6]

Farther along the Knoxville trail they reached the homestead of one Blackborn, the last white settler before they entered the Cumberland Mountain territory of the Cherokee nation and passed through a region known as the Wilderness, which was still dreaded when André Michaux was there less than ten years back. It was then deemed reckless not to await the gathering of several well-armed companions before venturing its passage, much as he had awaited caravans to join in his travels in the Middle East. Even now it was still regarded as prudent not to cross the Wilderness alone. As Fisk had business at nearby Jackson Courthouse, Michaux chose to await his company while he profited by the delay to explore, in company with their host, a nearby noteworthy tributary of the Cumberland, Roaring River—an expedition he undertook despite an attack of fever and rash which he was treating with "a cooling regimen, and repeated bathings in the rivers Cumberland and

Roaring." Even under that handicap it proved a memorable and profitable expedition.

> *This river, from ten to fifteen fathoms broad, received its name from the confused noise that is heard a mile distant . . . occasioned by falls of water produced by the sudden lapse of its bed, formed by large flat stones contiguous to each other. These falls from six, eight to ten feet high, are so near together that several of them are to be seen within the space of fifty to a hundred fathoms. We observed in the middle of this river, great stones, from five to six feet in diameter, completely round . . . which nobody could form the least idea how they could have been conveyed there.*[7]

As he and his host followed the river upstream, they came on immense caverns leading into its precipitous banks. Michaux sampled an aluminous substance found within those caverns which was used by the inhabitants for dyeing fabrics, which was valued so highly that much of it was being exported to Kentucky for use there. The stream itself also evoked enthusiasm:

> *Large riverlets . . . terminate their windings at the steep banks of this river . . . and form magnificent cascades of several fathoms wide. The perpetual humidity that these cascades preserve in these places gives birth to a multitude of plants which grow in the midst of a thick moss, with which the rock is covered and which forms the most beautiful verdant carpet. All these circumstances give the borders of the Roaring River a cool and pleasing aspect which I had never witnessed before on the banks of other rivers.*

Along Roaring River he found "a charming variety of trees and shrubs not met with anywhere else. Among them was perhaps a unique concurrence of Magnolias, among them *Magnolia auriculata* (now *fraseri*), the ear-leaved cucumber tree; *macrophylla,* the large-leaved magnolia, or umbrella tree; *cordata,* the yellow-flowered magnolia; *acuminata,* the cucumber tree; and *tripetala,* also known as the umbrella tree. He reported that "the fruit of these trees, so remarkable for the beauty of their flowers and superb foliage, were in the highest perfection." He made a collection of seeds from them "to multiply them in France, and to add to the embellishment of our gardens," a remarkable collection from one place of all the native American magnolias except the *grandiflora* and sweet bay. He added that he was successful in his plantings of them on his return to France.[8]

Upon Fisk's return from Jackson Courthouse they resumed their way, although still without the added security of other company. To minimize the notorious hazards of the Wilderness Road, they made their passage as expeditiously as possible by staying in the saddle until midnight through extremely mountainous terrain, happily, without any event more notable than sights of "wild turkies; thirty or forty in a flight." When they finally stopped at a place by a small river where there was good grazing for their horses, they took the precaution of mounting watch by turns to guard their animals against straying or theft by stealth.

Next day they met a band of "eight or ten Indians who were searching for grapes, and chinquapins, a species of small chestnuts, superior in taste to those in Europe." A gift of the travelers' remaining provisions delighted these people, "for bread is a great treat for them, their usual food consisting of nothing but venison and wild fowl." By evening they reached West Point, comprised of a palisaded fort on a lofty site at the confluence of the Clinch and Holston rivers, and a "kind of warehouse where the Cherokees carry ginseng and furs, consisting chiefly of bear, stag and other skins," to be exchanged for "coarse stuffs, knives, hatchets" and other articles. Located nearby was Kingston, a village composed of thirty or forty log houses. There Michaux recorded reports given him at West Point on the present state of the Cherokee. He was told that they were now rapidly emulating the whites, cultivating possessions and making great progress, some having "good plantations and even Negro slaves." He described in some detail those they had encountered in the region.

More to the point are Michaux's observations in respect to the American forests, the focus of his expedition. Along the road across the Wilderness he noted that the forest was composed of an immense variety of species; in fact, it impressed him as perhaps including all the species of the mountainous regions of America. The better sites were dominated by oaks, maples, and nut trees, with pines abounding on the poorer. It was mystifying to him that for miles along the way all the pines had died recently enough to still retain their needles. He was told that this die-out occurred every fifteen or twenty years, but he was unable to get any plausible explanation of such widespread mortality.[9]

An equally striking phenomenon was noted between Kingston and Knoxville. In an extensive region of grass-covered, flinty soil the trees were uncommonly widely spaced, sixty to ninety feet between them. It was his conjecture that he was observing an area that had been a grassy prairie or barren but was now in the process of being reclaimed by the forest. Beyond Knoxville on the east side of the Holston River he came on a related phenomenon. For several miles the road led through a coppice, with the bunched, saplinglike hardwood stems not above twenty feet in height, the like of which he had never before seen in America, which so aroused his curiosity that he sought from some of the local residents an explanation. He was told that the area had been formerly "part of a barren or meadow, which had naturally clothed itself again with trees," but then had been swept by a prairie fire that had killed the young trees to the ground. Their roots had survived to produce suckers that had grown into a coppice. This confirmed his conjecture that the spacious meadows of the southern states "owe their birth to some great conflagration that had consumed the forests, and that they are kept as meadows by the custom that is still practiced of annually setting them on fire."[10]

From West Point they followed the valley of the Holston up to Knoxville, Fisk's destination, which, although founded fifteen years since, was then the seat of government of Tennessee. Seated on the Holston, there a hundred and fifty fathoms wide, it was now a village of some two hundred houses with several shops, but no industry. Its center of community activity was an inn, The Sign of George Washington, where a traveler and his mount could be accommodated at a dollar and a quarter a day.

After departing Knoxville on September 17, Michaux continued up the valley road for five more days to Jonesborough, one of the earliest settlements beyond the Appalachians. Founded well before the outbreak of the Revolution by fiercely independent pioneers, mostly from the back country of the Carolinas who had settled the fertile region between the Nolichuckey and the Watauga, it became the domi-nant settlement of folk who soon afterward became known as the Backwater men. They had become famous in the Revolution, when, in response to the "grapevine telegraph" telling of the dire straits of the patriot cause in the early fall of 1780, they had banded together and crossed the mountains to become the nucleus of the gathering partisans who gained fame when they met the tories under Patrick Ferguson at Kings Mountain. Soon afterward they again gained national attention when they staged a small revolution of their own, declared their inde-pendence from North Carolina and established the short-lived trans-montane state of Franklin. A few years later a people of a far gentler sort, Quakers from Pennsylvania, had joined them there. It was with one of those families that Michaux had spent his first night after leaving Knoxville. At their clearing he had been much impressed by the size of their apple trees and the excellent fruit they produced, particularly in view of their being grown from pips. Nevertheless, his host, like most

Tennessee settlers, was partial to his bountiful peach trees, producing as they did the raw material for brandy.

The omnivorous intellectual appetite of the young traveler found much else in the fare offered him on his way from Knoxville to Jonesborough of sufficient interest to be noted in his *Travels*. Near Knoxville the rather scrubby pines indicated the poor quality of the flinty soil which also supported the dwarf chinquapin oak he called *Quercus prinus* (probably now *Q. prinoides*) so laden with acorns the branches bent to the ground. He had last seen them growing on the edge of the Barrens in Kentucky. This same area supported numerous sourwood, or sorrel, trees which he called *Andromeda arborea* (now *Oxydendrum arboreum*) which, with their racemes of pearllike, fragrant flowers, he not only thought "would be one of the most splendid ornaments of our gardens," but whose acid leaves, which in fall became brilliantly scarlet, he believed would be a better source of red dye than the sumacs commonly used to produce it.

As we have noted, minerals, metals, and chemicals were of great interest to him. About thirty miles from Knoxville he visited an ironworks to secure a sample of the ore used. A few miles farther, beside the road "in a reddish kind of soil," there were quantities of rock crystals, each about two or three inches long, beautifully transparent, with perfectly matching prisms on each end; in less than ten minutes he found forty of them. When he reached the Nolichuckey he found quantities of the beautiful yellow flowering horse chestnuts, a species new to him, *Aesculus octandra*. Among their companions in that area of particularly fertile soil there were tulip trees "five or six feet in diameter, perfectly straight, and free from branches for thirty or forty feet." There he found quantities of honey locusts, *Gleditsia triacanthos*, prized by the Indians both for the honey in their giant bean pods but also for their wood, the material from which they made their bows.[11]

Lacking sufficient forewarning of the state of alternate roads across the mountains to Morganton, he chose the Iron Mountain trail, believing it the more expeditious route. But a few miles beyond the fork, he began to discover that he had chosen both the slower and the more difficult way, as the road deteriorated to a scarcely discernible path "encumbered by forests of rhododendron, shrubs from eighteen to twenty feet in height, the branches of which, twisting and interwoven with each other, impede the traveller every moment, insomuch that he is obliged to use an axe" to permit the passage of even a mounted horseman. "The torrents" his little caravan of two horses "had continually to cross added to the difficulty and danger of the journey, the horses being exposed to falls on account of the loose round flints . . . with which the bottom of those torrents are filled." But his greatest concern was the constant fear of losing the path completely in what had turned out to be a region all but devoid of human habitation. For twenty-three miles there was no sign of man except a few blazed trees at the crossing of the boundary line between Tennessee and North Carolina and several rude signs euphemistically proclaiming "the road." But even those aids were lacking where most needed beyond the divide on his descent of the rugged eastern slope, where, in the midst of a forest of rhododendron, it led to a tumultuous stream "called Rocky Creek, whose winding course cut the path in twelve or fifteen directions" requiring him to alight each time to lead his animals down the creek bottom of slippery rocks while searching out the continuation of the path, which was rarely opposite the one he had left and frequently concealed by the all-pervading foliage "since whole months elapse without its being passed by travellers."

Despite the difficulties of the trail he eventually found his way to "a charming plantation upon the Doe [Toe] River" of "one Davenport," who, he had learned from a neighbor the evening before, had been the host and guide of his father when he visited this region to discover its productions and with whom he had climbed to the summit of Grandfather Mountain and there sung the *Marseillaise*. Despite his haste to get back to Charleston, he stayed the final week of September 1802 at Davenport's place exploring that beautiful region, so bountiful in botanical offerings. By the time he had turned his travel notes into his *Travels*, he had learned of the death of his father, and inserted in the text of this work, in recounting his visit at Davenport's, "I was at that time very far from thinking that at the same time when this worthy man was entertaining me about his old travelling companion, I lost a beloved father, who died a victim of his zeal for the progress of natural history upon the coast of the island of Madagascar."[12]

His three-day journey from Davenport's led him over both the Blue Ridge and Linville mountains, before he reached Morganton, well into the North Carolina Piedmont. As he usually did, following his departure from a significant region, he inserted in his *Travels* his "general observations" on the area he had left, often intermingled with specific observations and incidental events. An example is his discussion of the huge flat-headed salamander, commonly known as hellbender, *Cryptobranchus alleganiensis*. Davenport had caught one in the Toe River for him, just as he had done for the elder Michaux when he was his guest. That earlier specimen had provided the description of that grotesque creature in the *New Dictionary of Natural History*. Of a very different genre, then of great importance, not only for the value of their hides in commerce but for the settlers' subsistence was the black bear, common in those mountains. Michaux detailed their diet of roots, acorns, and chestnuts, how they were taken, the superiority of their meat and oil, and their importance to the inhabitants in the winter.

Also among his general observations were cogent reflections on the region; among them his expressed conviction that the Southern Appalachians are the most lofty part of the entire range. He was further convinced that the same region supported an unmatched richness of temperate-zone plant life. He recalled seeing in his father's notes "that he had observed trees and shrubs upon the Yellow and Grandfather Mountains that he did not meet with again till he reached Low Canada." The fertility of those mountains was well indicated by the "vegetable strength" of the red and black oaks, sugar maples and the chestnuts that grow there to a "prodigious height."

At Morganton he was surprised to find that its only trading station was a Charleston establishment, despite the three-hundred-mile wagon haul of all the goods brought there to be sold, and a return haul of the bear and deer skins, dried hams, butter, and ginseng received in exchange. That haulage required a month's time for a large wagon drawn by four horses and two drivers, traveling about twenty miles a day. The season being now more advanced than he had anticipated, he chose the most direct route to Charleston which, even so, required two weeks more of tiresome travel. It led through Lincolnton, a town of about forty houses, two or three large shops, and a semiweekly newspaper that generally received its two-dollar subscription price in commodities. It was near there that he encountered one of the few exceptions to the generally drab and poverty-stricken aspect of the countryside all the way to the environs of Charleston. In an area of good soil on the South Fork Catawba a colony of Pennsylvania Germans had settled and, here also, in the tradition of their former homes, "their plantations are kept in the greatest order, and their lands well cultivated." On the eighty-hundred-acre plantation where he stopped "one hundred and fifty are cultivated in cotton, Indian corn, wheat and oats, and dunged annually" to present an aspect of "a great degree of perfection" for this part of the country. Additionally, his host had erected on a nearby stream a sawmill, a cotton gin, a tannery, a forge, and a distillery to make peach brandy.

The first town met with in South Carolina was Chester, which, although it had but thirty houses, supported two inns and two "respectable shops." Farther along the way was Winnsboro, one of the oldest towns of the interior of the state, with about one hundred and fifty houses, some being the summer houses of lowcountry planters. More impressive was Columbia, the new capital of South Carolina which, although established only a dozen years back, already had about two hundred houses, "almost all of them built of wood and painted grey and yellow; and although there are very few of them more than two stories high, they have a very respectable appearance." He was told that the legislature, "the union of the delegates of . . . the counties that send them in a number proportionate to their population, meet there annually on the first of December, and all their business is transacted in the same month; it then dissolves, and except at that time the town derives no particular advantage from being the seat of government."

From Orangeburg, composed of twenty houses, all the way to Charleston "the road crosses an even country, sandy and dry during the summer; whilst in autumn and winter it is so covered with water, that in several places, for the space of eight or ten miles the horses are up to their middles." Across that region "every two or three miles we meet with a miserable log-house . . . surrounded by little fields of Indian corn . . . that do not yield more than five bushels per acre." In that flat country disease was obvious in most inhabitants, adding its toll to the miseries of their stark diet.

Those roadside huts and their patches of poor corn were even worse than those he had seen along his route between Morganton and Columbia, through hilly regions clothed with forests of pine, oak, hickory and maple, growing in soils mostly "extremely bad." There, "straggling five or six miles from each other," were small clearings, and on each a rude log cabin, many already abandoned owing to the surrounding fields having lost such fertility as they had after a few years of careless cultivation, forcing their tenants to move farther west where much better land could be had at less cost than in those parts of Carolina. None of those clearings supported any fruit trees, except peaches, and not more than one in twenty had even a cabbage patch to vary the prevailing diet of corn.

Almost the only redeeming feature in Michaux's somber picture of the rural regions of Carolina across which he traveled in the early fall of 1802 was the forests of the lowcountry. For those who recall *Uncle Remus,* it may be said that in those forests Michaux was again in his own special brier patch. Except for occasional small areas cleared for the cabins and corn patches and the more fertile areas bordering the rivers, the entire region still remained a virgin forest dominated by towering, straight, longleaf pines, with a scattering of scrub oaks, sometimes forming an understory. "These trees, frequently twenty feet distant from each other, are not damaged by the fire that they make here annually at the commencement of spring." Bearing few branches below their crowns, they can be evenly split for lumber and fence rails. The small oaks beneath were used only for fuel.

Mostly, however, it was the rich and varied broadleaf silva of the lowcountry swamps that enthralled Michaux. Those swamps that every few miles interrupted the parklike expanses of the pine barrens supported a great variety of trees and shrubs and were, he observed, of two varieties, each with its own associated flora. The broad, more fertile swamps were dominated by the swamp chestnut oak, *Quercus michauxii*; *Magnolia grandiflora*; and the small but great-leafed umbrella magnolia, *M. tripetala.* Deeper in its confines, where water generally stood, bald cypress was the towering giant, with water locust, which he called *Gleditsia monosperma* (now *G. aquatica*), as its neighbors along with the rare nutmeg hickory, *Carya myristicaeformis,* with a range restricted to the area he was crossing, a species first described by him.

Characteristic of the smaller, more narrow swamps were the sweetgum, *Liquidambar*; and bays, the fragrant sweetbay, *Magnolia virginiana,* red bay, which he called *Laurus caroliniensis* (now *Persea borbonia*), along with black gum (*Nyssa*), perfectly at home in standing water. And, of course, somberly adorning them all with its long gray beards was that floral hallmark of the southern lowcountry, and as Michaux noted, "peculiar" to it, Spanish beard, *Tillandsia usneoides.*[13]

With those observations François André concluded his account of his 1802 expedition of "nearly eighteen hundred miles." However, he appended a few more comments on the agriculture of the Carolina and Georgia lowcountry to augment those he had made the previous year. Among them were some of significance on the subject of what was to become euphemistically referred to as "the South's peculiar institution."

Incidental to reporting the increasing emphasis on growing cotton and a rapidly diminishing rice culture, he observed that all the plantations also cultivate Indian corn, although on the best land their yields are but fifteen to twenty bushels to the acre and that "the chief part of what they grow is destined to support the negroes nine months in the year; their allowance is about two pounds per day, which they boil in water after having pounded it a little; the other three months they are fed on yams. They never give them meat. In other parts of the United States they are better treated, and live nearly upon the same as their masters, without having any set allowance." He continued:

Through the whole of the low country the agricultural la-bours are performed by negro slaves, and the major part of the planters employ them to drag the plow; they conceive the land is better cultivated, and calculate besides that in the course of a year a horse, for food and looking after, costs ten times more than a negro, the annual expense of which does not exceed fifteen dol-lars.

I shall refrain from any reflexion concerning this, as the opinion of many people is fixed.[14]

Considering the hardships of travel in the American hinterland in 1802, François André's expedition beyond the mountains undoubtedly had been strenuous, even for a travel-seasoned thirty-two-year-old of well-demonstrated hardihood. Equally certain is that his return to the Charleston Garden offered no opportunity for the luxury of a well-earned period of rest and recoupment. Instead he was confronted by most urgent and immediate demands upon his time and energy: the seed harvesting he had promised for this year. Gathering seeds in the forest demanded more travel and countless hours in a variety of forest types. The garden itself could supply some seed, but mostly its contri-bution was to be an immense number of seedlings, products of the plantings he had made before he sailed for New York. Those seedlings, each of which had to be lifted and carefully packed for shipment in time to reach Paris before spring, likewise represented an immense task. When one takes note of the surviving bills of lading and the correspon-dence dealing with shipments made from Charleston in the fall and early winter of 1802–3, the industry, efficiency, and conscientiousness of the man are impressive indeed. Michaux himself sheds little light on the assistance available to him to accomplish those labors. Presumably the two "aged negroes," so often mentioned in connection with the Charleston facility, were still there, but it is unlikely that they could have supplied the labor force required. Be that as it may, he accomplished his mission in a manner pleasing to the minister of the interior and his Bureau of Agriculture associates.[15]

Even more to his credit is the fact that he had accomplished all that without the assistance of the financial resources that he had counted upon receiving for more than a year. Soon after his return to the garden, he had gone into town with full expectation of finding there the long-awaited 6,000 francs, but there was nothing awaiting him. By coincidence, as the official record reveals, the same day Michaux arrived back at the garden, action on his pleas for payment of his stipulated funding had, in the interval of more than a year, advanced only far enough for the minister of the interior to write a suggestion to the minister of marine and colonies that he accept a transfer of 6,000 francs from him and have that sum remitted through the commissioner in the United States to Michaux. That is the last word we find on the subject until he was back in Paris.[16] By necessity we are left with only a reasonable assumption that his Charleston friends, most notably Himely and Charles Cotesworth Pinckney, came to his rescue with interim financing for his preparations for departure and his return passage.

The previous season the source of most of the seeds and plants shipped to France had been the Charleston garden itself. But this season, for greater variety and a much greater quantity of seed of forest trees, Michaux found,it necessary to extend his seed harvests farther afield. His western tour had greatly enhanced his interest in forest trees, particularly those that might prove useful and adaptable to conditions in France. To intelligently select the most promising species, he needed to see the mature tree of each species in its native habitat to judge its potential contribution to European forests, and observe the soils and conditions best suited to each. Moreover, a wider variety of Carolina seed was needed to round out the collections he had arranged to have made by Matthias Kin in Philadelphia and Paul Saunier in the New York area.

There are dozens of surviving documents—bills of lading, announcements of arrivals and forwarding arrangements from the ports of arrival, some by wagon, some by canal or riverboats—and dozens more of correspondence with the collectors, the shippers, the harbormasters at the ports of arrival, and at least as many between the minister of the interior and the Bureau of Agriculture and the government nurserymen, dealing with the ultimate destination, division, and planting of each shipment, and, alas, all too frequently, with the utter ruin of some, owing to delays in their transport. It would be difficult, if not impossible, and of doubtful worth, to correlate all those documents and the shipments to which each relates. For our purposes it is sufficient to know that Kin and Saunier each made at least one shipment comprising several barrels in early 1802, and Michaux made at least three, one of which accompanied him when he sailed from Charleston about March 1, 1803, for Bordeaux, once again on the *John and Francis.*[17]

The "List of seeds of trees, shrubs and plants of North America addressed to the minister of the interior, and observations upon the soil where they should be preferably cultivated," which accompanied a large shipment he put aboard the *Dragon* in Charleston harbor, is an interesting and revealing document.[18] It contains more than 160 species of seeds and plants, of which about 100 are packets of seeds, 50 of plants in various quantities, and a dozen are of seeds "stratified," packed spread out on layers of moss. The numbers of individual plants varied from single specimens of the palmetto, *Sabal palmetto,* and coral honeysuckle, *Lonicera sempervirens,* to 25 bayberry, *Myrica pensylvanica*; 50 each of red bay, *Persea borbonia,* and *Magnolia grandiflora*; to as many as 75 *Gordonia* seedlings. Anyone with even the slightest experience in collecting the seed of wild plants, particularly those of tall trees whose fruits are appealing to birds and squirrels, such as the magnolias and mulberries, or with digging and packing seedlings, cannot fail to be greatly impressed at the all but incredible performance that single shipment represented. Obviously, like his father, the younger Michaux was a man of rare energy and patience, unstintingly dedicated to the performance of his mission.

The list has other facets of more than passing interest. Sixteen of the listed species are marked by horizontal lines to indicate that they should be started under the protection of the Orangerie.[19] Among those there were two species, whose seeds had been first brought to America by Michaux père, the mimosa (now *Albizzia julibrissin*) and the Japanese varnish tree, *Sterculia platanifolia.* Those reexports to France indicate, perhaps, that efforts there to acclimatize them had failed and these seeds represented a renewal of effort to succeed there.

There are yet other interesting observations to be derived from the list. The seeds and plants of the staggerbush, *Lyonia mariana*; the *Kalmia hirsuta*; the star anise, *Illicium parviflorum*; and those of the rare and unique monotype *Pinckneya pubens* almost certainly came from plants established by his father in the French Garden, for the natural occurrence of all those species is far from Charleston. Others such as the seed of the ginseng, *Panax quinquefolium,* natives of the mountain areas of the Carolinas and Tennessee, had been collected by François André along roads he had traveled the previous fall.

There is yet one more feature of that list deserving comment. Although it contained the names of dozens of forest trees, all of which Michaux regarded as deserving the time and effort of gathering their seed in the hope that they might augment the very limited variety offered by the forests of France, there were two that he singled out as particularly desirable, the bald cypress and the sweet-gum, *Liquidambar,* for both their rare beauty and their utility. To them he devoted a full page of comments in which he pointed out that cypress thrives in swamps, even in those deep swamps that in France commonly produce little of value. Its very fine light-weight wood is easily worked and is extremely durable, making it especially valuable for shingles for rooftops. He pointed out that the wide range of the beautiful and useful sweet-gum in America, indicating its rare environmental tolerance of climate, soil, and terrain, its rapid growth, and the beautifully colored, easily worked wood it produces, especially useful in cabinetmaking, combine to make it a most promising addition to French forests.

Of the shipment of seed and botanical specimens that a few days later was put aboard the *John and Francis* to accompany him on his return voyage to Bordeaux, we have no such detailed inventory as that of the *Dragon* shipment. We do have, however, a partial list in his handwriting, headed simply "List of seeds—1803," with the names of fifty-two species, almost all American forest trees—five species of maple and five of hickories and walnuts, and four of oaks. Set opposite each is the weight of its packet, figures that totaled 137 pounds. Almost none of the names on that list appear on that sent with the *Dragon* shipment. Missing from both lists are several species whose seeds Michaux, in his *Travels,* reported gathering and taking with him when he returned to France. Among those was the yellowwood, *Cladastris lutea,* which in recent years has become a popular ornamental, whose seeds he had collected in quantity at Nashville, and the five species of magnolia, whose ripe fruit he had collected on Tennessee's Roaring River and had carefully packed to preserve their delicate viability. Nor does he mention the ninety species of seed he gathered in the meadows of the Kentucky Barrens except for the species of wild grapes he found there, the fruit of which he had sampled and declared of "good quality." They must be counted as having been part of the collections accompanying him when he sailed for Bordeaux.[20]

Much more obviously sociable than his father, François André, after finishing the deployment of his collections aboard the *John and Francis,* spent his final days in Charleston in warm farewells, not only to the circle of friends he had inherited from his father, such as brothers Thomas and Charles Cotesworth Pinckney, the ever-helpful Himely, and Jacques Renaud, who had come to America with his father and now shared with Himely their Tradd Street address, but many others whose friendship he had made since his return to Charleston. There were those at the Charleston Library Society and a newer generation of members of the Agricultural Society of which both he and his father became members, and his fellow physicians at the South Carolina Medical Society, especially his friend Dr. Ramsay, many of whom had interests common to both the Michauxs—all of whom had extended him hospitality for which he was deeply grateful, as he would repeatedly demonstrate in years to come.[21]

When on March 26, after a relatively short and uneventful crossing, he set foot again on French soil, it became apparent that the familiar, turbulent France of his youth had become as strikingly transformed during the two years of his absence, as he had found the United States of his youth after a decade's absence. One momentous event during his absence was the Concordat of 1801 between France and the Catholic Church, which through the ages had played such an important role in the shaping of France. This ended a decade of militant state antagonism against the church symbolized by the secularized Revolutionary Calendar designed, as it was, to eliminate the memorials of Christian names and holy days that had been built into the Julian-Gregorian Calendar during a millennium of church dominance.

When François André sailed for America, France was at war, as she had been during all his recollection, except for the five years of his youth following the War of American Independence. Now there was peace, albeit a brief and fragile peace soon to be shattered by the outbreak of the Napoleonic Wars, destined to last without interruption for twelve long years. A few days after his return, France suffered an immense loss, a forfeit to preparations for the impending war, when Napoleon sacrificed Louisiana, the last of her once great New World forest resources.

However, overshadowing those momentous changes in his homeland was the accelerating rise of the magnetic Corsican to imperial status, culminating eighteen months later in his placing on his head the imperial crown and rapidly assuming all the power and trappings of a Roman emperor.[22]

For François André Michaux, the most momentous event that had occurred in his absence was that which had befallen him in his personal life, the death of his beloved and admired father, "a victim of his zeal for the progress of natural history." Just when he learned of his loss we do not know; however, there had been sufficient time since his death in late November 1802 for word of it to have reached France by the time he reached Paris. It could only have been devastating news for the young returnee, left without a surviving member of his immediate family and without the person with whom he had grown to feel the closest personal relationship of his life. The four years between his father's return from America and his departure with the Baudin expedition had been a busy and happy period of mutual dependence, affection for, and pride in each other, and a rare intellectual rapprochement as they worked together with the Redoutés and Richard to prepare the *Histoire des chênes de l'Amérique* and *Flora Boreali-Americana* for the printers. Those labors of love and close association in a common aim had become the firm bonding agent of their lives, fixing them in place together so closely that they appear almost as one. The poignancy of his loss must surely have been sharpened when the two volumes of his father's *Flora*, published not long before his return, were handed him by Richard. They represented the crowning achievement of a beloved father and congenial companion in enterprise, who now would never see them.[23]

CHAPTER **22**

~§ Paris, 1803–1804

To ASSUAGE THE POSITIVE HURT and negative stark emptiness caused by word of his father's death, François André plunged with inspired intensity into a diversity of activities. The most urgent among them was the preparation of a report to the minister of the interior, covering his American mission. As soon as he could make a final inspection of the seed collection that had accompanied him on the *John and Francis* and been wagoned to Paris, he set out for a visit to the family home at Satory. By mid-May, however, we find him in quarters at Place de l'Estrapade, No. 16, near the Panthéon, carefully copying a compact narrative report of his eighteen-month American mission.[1]

He followed that report with another to the Bureau of Agriculture, devoted mostly to the practical recommendations he believed essential to forward their aim to improve the quality and variety of French forests through the establishment of superior American species.[2] An important purpose of his mission had been to discover practical ways and means to assure that an ample flow of seeds from diverse regions of the United States could be obtained through commercial channels for naturalization in French forests. He pointed out that, generally speaking, the same plant species extended from Canada southward into Virginia and that a distinctly different flora prevailed in the more southern regions. Except for the pines and the cypress of the South, he continued, there were few tall species there that did not also occur to the northward. Nevertheless, to obtain these desired southern species, he again recommended Jacques Renaud, who for several years "cared for the botanical garden established in Carolina," for he knew the trees and shrubs of the region and how to pack them and would render those services at moderate cost. For the New York area such services could be gotten from commercial nurserymen, but he strongly suggested instead that Paul Saunier, also trained by his father, who could be depended upon to supply the seeds and plants of that region in abundance. Moreover, Saunier's shipments would have the special attention of Samuel du Pont and his son Victor, who had a commercial house in New York, both of whom had taken a great interest in the Bergen Woods establishment.

To collect for the Bureau in the middle states, he also suggested the Bartram brothers, John and William, although they would not, he believed, add to the varieties that Saunier could supply, and the Bartrams' services would be more costly. Also recommended for that area was the zealous Matthias Kin, who, he believed, would be the best person to enlist to make shipments, but he too would be drawing his shipments from the same general area as Saunier.

To secure the seeds and plants of the transmontane regions, he mentioned in his report to Chaptal only a Frenchman, M. Robert, described as "well known to M. Barbi-Marbois." Robert, who had been introduced to him by Dr. Samuel Brown of Lexington, lived in that region and had volunteered to enter into an arrangement to supply seeds of Kentucky in exchange for those of French vegetables, farm crops, and vineyards.[3]

Probably at the behest of the minister, in the hope that it might assist in concluding his continuing disagreement with du Pont and Saunier, a third report was prepared by Michaux and presented to the Bureau of Agriculture, this one devoted entirely to the New Jersey nursery. In it he reviewed the history of the establishment and discussed its future utility, the claims of Saunier for back compensation, expense reimbursements, the value of his promised but unused passage back to France, and the arrangements he had made with him permitting him to continue in possession of the garden property in return for annual seed shipments. Although this report did not settle these differences, it appears to have persuaded Chaptal to stand firm in his opposition to most of Saunier's claims.[4] It was not until September 1803, when the elder du Pont was back in Paris, that a settlement was reached and a draft accepted in the amount of 979.25 francs in satisfaction of all of Saunier's now very stale claims.[5]

Meanwhile, Michaux's own unpaid reimbursement for his mission to the United States continued to demand his attention well into the summer. A communication between two officials in the Bureau of Agriculture indicated that in July there were still unpaid sums due him and concluded that Michaux fils performed his mission to America, devoting twenty months to it, and that his request for payment should be granted.[6]

To those financial matters another should be added—the handling of his father's affairs. We have found little or nothing indicating what property, if any, his father possessed at the time of his death other than what remained at the time of his departure for the Indian Ocean—unpaid reimbursements still due him from the government. Whether there remained any hope of collecting those obligations or any other substantial assets, there were duties to be attended to in connection with his father's affairs, including the responsibility to promote the sale of his posthumous *Flora Boreali-Americana,* newly published in both Paris and Strasbourg.[7]

To all those demands upon his time and attention there were yet others to be added. In May and June came a veritable deluge of shipments of seeds and plants from America—the shipments dispatched the previous winter pursuant to the arrangements he had made with others in the United States and those collections he himself had made. Many had suffered long delays in their passage owing to the difficult international scene—others were unaccountably delayed in France after timely arrivals. Although they were all addressed to the minister of the interior and were distributed under his direction, Michaux was involved as consultant as to how they should be introduced to French soil.

Moreover, for Michaux himself it was most important that he put his American notes and diary entries in order before they had grown cold. That those upon which his *Travels to the West of the Alleghany Mountains* was to be based must have had his dedicated attention, throughout the months following his return to Paris, can be assumed from the short lapse of time before its publication, which, according to its title page date, An XII—1804, could not have been later than September 23, 1804.[8] At the same time, the descriptive notes he had made on every species of American tree he had observed on his mission must also have clamored for attention, for already it was apparent he had visions of his magnificent trailblazing work on American trees.

As the raison d'être of François André's 1801–3 mission to the United States had been to collect the fruits of the French nurseries established there, and to arrange for future collections and shipments of American plants and seeds deemed desirable for the improvement of French gardens, fields, and forests, it is appropriate to consider the tangible fruits of his mission. There are numerous surviving documents dealing with not only the shipments sent by him but also with those he had arranged to be collected and sent by Saunier from New York and Kin from Philadelphia. Although it is extremely difficult to correlate them positively with one or another of those shipments, we can follow as a sample one of those he himself made from Charleston through their disposition after their arrival in Paris.

Although the *Dragon* had departed Charleston more than two weeks before Michaux sailed for Bordeaux, she was three months at sea before she reached Ostend with François André's nine boxes and barrels of seeds and plants addressed to the minister.[9] In a formal communication dated May 20, 1803, a commercial agent in Brugge addressed the minister in a style reflecting Napoleon's 1801 Concordat with the Catholic Church: "With the protection of God and the direction of the wagoner, Thomas Canberi, . . . after a delay of fifteen days" nine boxes of seeds and plants had been dispatched to the minister from Ostend.[10] Only seven boxes got the care one might have expected from the announcement. Two years later official correspondence was still going on concerning the two missing boxes, which had been found at Rouen.[11]

When the other seven reached Paris, it appears that most of their contents, like Michaux's other shipments, were sent out to the nursery at Versailles. The shipments that had preceded this collection there had already aroused sharp competition for the privilege of sharing in their division. The stimulus of some seeking that privilege was a commendable desire to serve science and the institution each represented. Such was the nature of the request addressed to the minister by André Thouin on behalf of the Museum of Natural History and his professional colleagues there: "Citizen Michaux has just advised us that he has brought from the United States a collection of seeds and living plants for the government. We wish that it should be well understood that the museum will share in those objects and that Citizen Bosc be authorized to deliver them to us. That measure will enrich the garden of the establishment with many plants it now lacks." The professor's request was promptly granted. But so were those of many others with justifications not now discernible. For example, Citizen Vilmorin, in a formal petition reciting his membership on the Council of State, said he greatly desired "l'exotiques" and got without difficulty an authorization directed to Director Goulard at Versailles to grant his request. Several other petitioners were similarly accommodated throughout May and June, leading one to wonder, considering the long duration of their encasement in transit, the tardiness of their introduction to alien soils, and the erosion of the collections in response to these petitions, whether any substantial number of François André's so arduously gathered bountiful collections remained to augment the gardens and forests of France.[12]

By mid-1804 he had completed his manuscript and taken it to Levrault, Schoell et Compagnie, the successor firm to Levrault frères, who had published his father's *Flora*, for an estimate of the costs involved in getting it published. From his correspondence with Levrault we learn that François André had changed his residence from Place de l'Estrapede, near the Museum of Natural History and the Jardin des Plantes, to a superior location on the Left Bank at Place St. Michel, overlooking the beautiful, quietly flowing waters of the Seine where they divide to surround the Île de la Cité, the historic, water-protected site of ancient Paris, and the Cathedral of Notre-Dame. There he was destined to reside for the next twenty years or more, first at No. 12 and then, a short time later, moving only two doors down to No. 8.

The luster that had been earned for the Michaux name in scientific circles, dramatized by the sad news of André's death, a martyr to botany in faraway Madagascar, and soon further enhanced by the publication of François André's *Voyage a l'ouest des Monts Alleghanys*, inspired wide recognition from associates, colleagues, correspondents, and others of the natural history circles of both France and the United States. For François André, even before the publication of his *Voyage*, as revealed on its title page, this recognition took the form of election to membership in the Society of Natural History of Paris and appointment as correspondent of the Society of Agriculture of the Department of the Seine-et-Oise. In the case of his father, also honored by membership in distinguished scientific societies, the most appropriate recognition lay in the fact that *Michaux* had already become the specific name of hundreds of plant species—intangible but durable monuments to his devotion and dedication to the "gentle science" of botany.[13]

At this period in France much was being heard in natural history circles of the garden that Madame Bonaparte was developing on her estate, Château de Malmaison, some ten miles down the Seine from Paris. This three-hundred-acre estate with its splendid château had been purchased by the magnetic and glamorous West Indian Creole in late 1799 while Napoleon was in faraway Asia Minor futilely besieging Acre, the ancient Phoenician city on the coast of Palestine, which soon turned out to be the checkpoint of his disastrous Egyptian adventure. Now, three years later, she was matching her dynamic husband in his strides toward imperial majesty. The château had been transformed into a fitting palace where she could appropriately display the finery of her jewels and gowns.[14] To advance her ambitious plans for its gardens, she had recently appointed the brilliant young botanist Charles-François Mirbel[15] director of its grounds, thereby focusing upon her Malmaison garden the attention of his colleagues, among them François André Michaux and Jean Chaptal, fellow botanist, doctor, and minister of the interior, under whom Michaux's American mission had been undertaken.[16] It was probably from Mirbel or from Chaptal, or more likely from both, that Michaux learned that Madame Bonaparte greatly desired to secure for Malmaison specimens of the American *Magnolia macrophylla*. It is not surprising that Josephine, already familiar with the beautiful *Magnolia grandiflora*, with its magnificent, polished, evergreen foliage and great cream-white flowers, redolent with seductive fragrance, should also desire in her garden specimens of its relative, the large-leafed magnolia, the superlative characteristics of which had been described to her. This extraordinary tree, with its extravagant foliage and flowers—leaves up to thirty-two inches long and a foot wide, and giant blossoms measuring up to a foot and a half in diameter—both exceeding those of any other plant native to the United States—is rarely seen, even in its native South, where Michaux père had discovered it growing in the Carolina mountains.[17]

Although we cannot be certain as to when and how Michaux learned of Josephine's desire to have some of these rare magnolias in her garden, nor can we be certain from whence and from whom they came, we do definitely know that in March 1804, a few weeks before she became empress, a shipment of two barrels of plants and seeds addressed to Minister of the Interior Chaptal and sent from America at the behest of Michaux arrived from Bordeaux containing six *Magnolia macrophylla* plants and collections of the seed of *M. grandiflora*, and of the dwarf chestnut, as well, called by Michaux *Fagus pumila* but known as chinquapins (now *Castanea pumila*) to the Indians, who particularly prized them for their small but superior nuts.[18] The cost of the shipment was 228 francs, the equivalent in today's money of more than sixty dollars for each tree in the shipment, a price that indicates they must have been quite large. Almost certainly they came from Carolina where all three species are found, and probably the *macrophylla* were the half-grown seedlings from the French garden, planted there by André Michaux and left behind by François André because of their size. Beyond that we can conjecture that he had written to Himely of his wish to have them sent to the minister despite their size, and that he, with the assistance of the experienced Jacques Renaud, had arranged with the Agricultural Society for the permission to remove them for shipment. For good measure, or perhaps also at François André's suggestion, they had added the *grandiflora* and chinquapin seeds, plentiful in the old garden in the autumn. In any case, when the barrels arrived in Paris there was much ado. In the end the national nursery at the Jardin des Plantes and that at Roule were each given one of the six *macrophylla* and the remaining four were sent to Malmaison for Madame Bonaparte. "Citizen Michaux, Naturalist" received from the minister a formal note of thanks for his good offices in the matter.[19]

Meanwhile, great changes were rapidly taking place in the upper levels of government as Revolutionary France became Imperial France. Reflecting this transformation, the forms of address "Citizen" or "Citizeness," universally applied during the Revolutionary years, were now abandoned for the traditional forms. A letter sent to Saunier by the minister (acknowledging receipt of three boxes of walnuts and acorns, sent to "Monsieur" Michaux, through "Monsieur du Pont," which had arrived in good condition) was addressed to "Monsieur Saunier, gardener at the nursery at New York" while the minister once more assumed the title "Monseigneur" when he instructed Saunier that all future shipments be sent directly to the minister himself. In justification for the change he explained that he proposed to make a distribution of them to "Her Majesty the Empress."[20]

CHAPTER 23

∾§ Dr. F. A. Michaux, Author and Scientist, 1804–1806

THE PUBLICATION OF HIS FIRST WORK, the *Travels*, in 1804, was a momentous event in the life of F. A. Michaux, M.D., as he was identified on the title page.[1] Looking back over the period of his life since his embarkation for America in the summer of 1801, he could scarcely have avoided a considerable measure of satisfaction in his steady rise in professional status in his chosen field of natural history. Now, still young at thirty-four and emerging from the reflected light of his brilliant and ardent father, he was well on his way to securing distinction on his own in that field by the publication of his first work and the wide and favorable international recognition it soon would achieve, in spite of the distractions and tensions of the crucial events of the times.

The rare year of peace that had followed the Treaty of Amiens in March 1802 had been shattered in the spring of the following year when the long-anticipated war with England had become a reality with the formal declaration of war on May 16, 1803. Anticipation of the great financial strains of this war precipitated the sale by France to the United States of Louisiana, in that same spring of 1803, a loss to France of critically needed natural resources.

The raison d'être of both the Old Regime and the Revolutionary authorities when they had launched the American expeditions of both Michauxs, father and son, had been the continuing concern caused by the depleted state of the nation's forest resources which continued to threaten France's security and to inflict domestic privation on her people. Her inability to depend upon overseas forest resources had been thrice demonstrated in a span of two-score years; first, with the loss of the forest resources of Canada upon which she had long been accustomed to rely for the quality timber essential to naval needs, and then second, with the loss of those of Louisiana, first to Spain and then, after a brief period of repossession, by sale to the United States. Clearly, France would have to depend on her own forests more than ever before.

Already suffering from the strains of war, France was shaken in the late summer of 1803 by the exposure of a Bourbon conspiracy designed to effect a coup and place upon the French throne a Bourbon heir. By spring of 1804 the hopeful candidate for the throne and most of his fellow conspirators had been executed, paying the price for their failure to recognize that the vacant throne had already been spoken for, emphatically if not overtly, by a most uncommon commoner who was not even a Frenchman. On May 2, 1804, the legislative bodies had resolved that Bonaparte should be emperor of the French Republic and that his imperial power should be hereditary in his family. A plebicite three weeks later, by a vote of 3,572,329 to 2,569, the people ratified the nation's giant step backward, not to the autocracy of Louis XIV, but all the way back to the "glory" of Imperial Rome. But in 1804 the confirmation of the vicar of Rome was still needed to place the formal stamp of approval on the coronation and complete the rapid metamorphosis that fate and Napoleon had wrought.

The ceremonial finale was set for December 2.[2] That great day dawned cold and gray, with a threat of snow in the wind—in no way diminishing the effect of the great spectacle that, in accordance with meticulously drawn plans, began at nine in the morning, as the initial processions departed their appointed places for the Cathedral of Notre-Dame. Fortune had provided François André Michaux with a rare vantage point from which to witness the great procession of notables, his own residence. Place St. Michel, opening onto Quay St. Michel, along which all the left bank traffic would pass on its way to the cathedral, provides a clear view of the towering bulk of the great structure, less than three hundred meters distant. Whether he chose to watch the processions proceeding up both sides of the river from the palaces and public buildings below to converge on Place de Parvis upon which the cathedral's great doors open, or whether his recent rise in degree had enabled him to be among the thousands with access to the cathedral and the ceremony itself, we do not know. In any event, he was almost certainly an observer, at least in part, of the most momentous and dramatic spectacle of his lifetime, freighted as it was with stirring years of excitement, tragedy, and disasters of immense proportions for his beloved France.

After the ceremony, for six hours the crowds continued to pour out of the great cathedral into the early gloom of the December evening and, in falling snow, to reform their processions for the return march down the river. They had seen the deed done with pomp and ceremony, outdoing the magnificence of the Old Regime—but with one significant difference. They had seen, not the Pope, but Napoleon himself place the crown upon his own head and, afterwards, a small jeweled crown on the head of his empress, Josephine. The pope, accepting a role far less important than was customary for the head of the church, merely sang the Mass and blessed the new-crowned heads.[3]

The momentous historical events of 1804 inevitably pushed the happenings in the lives of most individual Frenchmen into relative obscurity. Thus far, from what we know of Michaux's life during that year, his was no exception, although, in fact, 1804 was one of the most significant years of his life.

No sooner had he delivered to the Levrault house the completed manuscript of his account of his 1801–3 American mission than he turned his attention to another, even more absorbing project he had been harboring in his mind—one of much more significance in the history of forestry in both France and the United States and of even greater relative importance in the development of his own career. The idea had been germinating in his mind even as he was preparing his proposal for his 1801 mission, but it was only during that mission that he had the opportunity to view as a trained scientist the forests of America, their immense diversity and prolific production of bountiful yields of quality timber, that those ideas had come into focus.

As he moved from the poor sandy soil around Charleston which, nevertheless, supported superb stands of lofty, arrow-straight longleaf pine, interrupted here and there by water oaks, sweet gums, and great sprawling live oaks, to New York and the rich diversity of hardwood forests on the New Jersey side of the Hudson where he botanized with Dr. Hosack, and thence through the fertile regions of Pennsylvania and the rugged mountain forests of its western parts and over the mountains to the lime-rich Ohio Valley with its unsurpassed boreal hardwood stands, so impressed had he been by the marked superiority of each of those forest types to those supported on counterpart areas in France that he had become possessed by the conviction that his fellow countrymen should be authoritatively apprised of their country's relative deficiency in that respect, to challenge them to undertake great forward-looking measures to remedy that deficiency for future generations. It would be an immense undertaking, but one, he was convinced, demonstrably practical and freighted with enormous potential.

His was by no means a new idea. Others had concerned themselves with it and some had done something about it. One of those was André Thouin his father's dear friend and François André's mentor when he was a student of botany at the Jardin des Plantes. For forty years Thouin had been experimenting with the acclimatizing of exotic species of plants, most importantly forest trees he secured from Britain's North American colonies. Dedicated to his studies for the common good rather than his own aggrandizement, he freely shared with his young friend his careful inventory studies of French forests. Michaux, himself, in the course of his American tour, had gathered many data for comparison of the forests of France with those he had seen in the United States. Almost as helpful were the careful records Thouin had kept during his four decades at the Jardin des Plantes of his experiments in acclimatization of many American trees vis-à-vis comparable native species. They presented challenging contrasts.[4]

There were other gardens, not far distant, that had even more numerous and varied plantings of American trees than the Jardin des Plantes. One in Montrouge (now in suburban Paris), was owned by his father's friend, the well-known Jacques Martin Cels. François André had visited it before his departure for America in 1801, and found it deserving of its reputation of being the most beautiful in France. Cels had close ties with Baron Silvestre and others at the Bureau of Agriculture. Through those ties Cels had been a frequent sharer of the seeds and plants sent back by Michaux fils in 1802 and 1803. Another helpful garden, one exhibiting even more ancient plantings of American trees, was at Malesherbes, near Fontainebleau, some thirty miles south of Paris. For planting there, the elder Michaux had sent exotic seeds and plants from both Persia and America.

Throughout the summer and fall of 1804, François André made expeditions to all those gardens, taking note of and recording the factual data on their successful naturalizations. To the information secured from them he added data learned from his own plantings. He had been making experimental plantings of seeds he had reserved to himself from his collections in the United States. Where he made those plantings and how extensive they were have not come to light, but the reports he made of his successful plantings and the seeds allotted to him from later shipments following his return strongly indicate that they were more extensive than a tiny parcel of land behind his Paris residence could have supported.

Before the winter of 1804–5 he was at work on an admirable dissertation entitled *Mémoire sur la Naturalization des Arbres Forestiers de l'Amérique Septentrionelle.* In the style of the day, the title, in translation, continues: *In which is indicated what the old Government had done to reach that aim; including a systematic Table of the trees of that country with those produced in France.*[5]

With his well-prepared paper in hand on a winter evening in

1805, François André appeared before his fellow members of the Société du department de la Seine-et-Oise to present his impressive thesis designed to shed new light upon a familiar subject through an array of heretofore unassembled, overwhelmingly persuasive facts. His opening sentence gave due credit to two pioneers who, decades earlier, had launched the idea of introducing into France superior American trees to enhance the quality and production of her forests and had undertaken to demonstrate in their own gardens the practicality of that idea. Their efforts in that direction were so well known to members of the society that no other identification than their surnames was necessary. It was well known that "the happy success that resulted from the attempts of Malesherbes and Duhamel-Dumonseau[6] to naturalize in France divers species of North American forest trees has inspired many to follow their example, but it was not until after the War of American Independence that such culture, previously voluntary enterprises, began to be regarded as a useful reality" by the government. The Old Regime had become aware of their work and the importance of their results to French civil and maritime construction and, in 1784, laid plans to sponsor a major effort to secure and introduce into the royal park at Rambouillet a great number of seeds and plants of American forest trees, with the idea that they and their progeny would later be introduced into the forests of France.[7]

It was François André's firm conviction that the success of American forest trees in France could be no longer questioned. All one needed to do to see the truth of that conviction, he said, was to visit the ancient domain of Noaialles at St. Germain, the plantings made at Malesherbes and the gardens at the Trianon or Rambouillet, where one could observe thriving young American trees of the most desirable species with heights already of as much as twenty-five feet. At the nurseries of the Trianon and Malmaison and that of Cels at Montrouge one could find an abundance of American oaks, walnuts, hickories, and maples, fruits of his father's mission to the United States, progressing "with the same vigor as in their native country." That was as it should be, for all the middle regions of the United States, where most of the more desirable species of forest trees thrive, endure both far colder and much warmer weather than does the Paris area. Even the Carolinas, where *Magnolia grandiflora* are native, experience colder weather than Paris suffers. Pertinent to that observation, he cited a specimen of that beautiful tree thriving at Nantes for twenty-five years, having then a height of thirty feet. In fact, he remarked that in his experience the only valuable American forest trees he had failed to adapt to the Paris area were the live oak, *Quercus virginiana,* and the longleaf pine, *Pinus palustris.*[8]

To serve as a convenient guide to accompany his *Mémoire,* Michaux had prepared a large folding table listing 90 species of American trees attaining heights of from 40 to 120 feet believed desirable for naturalization in France, with columns briefly detailing their principal characteristics: heights, habitats, soils suitable, the quality of their wood, and the regions of France believed appropriate for their culture. He expected that compilation to assist in selection of specific priorities, after determining the priority of aims. As to the latter he was convinced that top priorities should be given to the importation of species capable of producing the highest-quality timber and those that could produce timber of value in swampy areas and those adaptable to sterile sandy soils, these being areas that were producing nothing more than worthless, scrubby growths. While he believed that the quality of the wood produced should generally control the selection of species, it was of even greater importance to get those wastelands into advantageous production. Many desirable American species can grow in all manner of soils. Among the twenty oaks and thirteen nut-bearing species listed in the table, several are endowed with that adaptability. Rapidity of growth was to be another consideration in the selection of species for introduction. While he had not provided a column to indicate that attribute, he presented several impressive examples of the growth performance in France of some of the listed species. Citing studies made by Fénille[9] of American trees growing at Malesherbes, he mentioned a sycamore, *Platanus occidentalis,* only twenty-five years old with a girth three feet above the ground of five feet and a straight trunk forty-five feet high, a Carolina poplar the same age measuring more than six feet in circumference; and, at Moret, a twelve-year-old Virginia poplar almost five feet in girth, with a limb spread of more than twenty-five feet—the most extraordinary growth Fénille had ever observed.[10]

Although his table included a column that listed the qualities of the wood of each species, he said he had based them largely on what he had been told by Americans familiar with them. To verify or correct those judgments, so important in the selection of the better species for importation, he suggested that a collection be made of samples of the wood of each species of sufficient size to submit to the Society of Agriculture for tests of its desirability. Parenthetically, he mentioned that such a collection numbering about a hundred samples had been made by his father but had been left in Charleston in the expectation that he would be returning to America to complete his mission. However, when François André returned to Charleston in 1801, he found it in confused disarray, its labels mostly separated from the specimens, nullifying its utility.

Everything thus far presented in the *Mémoire* had been merely introductory to its central purpose: to propose, in light of his American experience, what he believed to be the most advisable ways and means of securing a regular and bountiful supply of seeds necessary to accomplish the improvement of the quantity and quality of the French forests. In his view this was of vital importance to the nation. When he had been sent to America in 1801, both he and the ministry had thought that the nurseries in New Jersey and at Charleston were no longer practical or economical establishments essential to getting adequate supplies of seeds of the desired trees of the country and that established commercial nurseries could be used more effectively and economically to supply those needs. But after his return to the United States he was disabused in that conviction. Americans, in their pioneer state of development, were mainly interested in removing forests, not in planting them, so there was little incentive for anyone to engage in gathering seeds except, in some instances, small quantities of the seeds of trees of the neighborhood, and France now required not pounds, but hundreds of pounds of many species, many to be gotten only at places far from any established nursery. Moreover, he had found that the few established nurseries there dealt only in fruit trees and could not be interested in any enterprise that required traveling far afield to seek the desired species.

Consequently, he had become convinced that in order to effect the desired purpose, it would be necessary to have in the United States one person charged exclusively with making large collections and sending them to France. That person would have to speak English, be knowledgeable of the various species desired, the timing of their seed maturities, the means of gathering, drying, packing, and shipping them, even to the placement of the boxes on the vessels, which for maximum protection should usually be between decks, and he should be willing to devote four or five years of dedicated work to the project— very demanding specifications, very difficult to come by, and the arrangements to be made with him, very complex. Obviously, it would require another mission to America, an extensive and extended one, involving an expenditure of an estimated 8,000 francs. In his view, it should be "for the Forestry Administration to decide whether this slight sacrifice, continued for four or five years, would not be compensated by the benefits which must result for the French Empire from so worthy an undertaking to be counted among the useful public enterprises that honor the reign of Napoleon."[11]

Aiming to reinforce that challenge, Michaux proceeded to present, with more directed focus, selected facts from the table, a series of analyses to demonstrate the immense potential benefits he foresaw flowing from large-scale introductions of American forest trees into French forests.[12]

First he separated all the ninety species appearing in his table into two groups, one listing the thirty-four species peculiar to the northern states of the United States, extending from New Hampshire and Vermont south to upper Virginia and westward into Ohio, Kentucky, and Tennessee, and the other containing those on that list also to be found in the Carolinas and Georgia. It numbered forty-two species, leaving but fourteen of the ninety that could only be collected from some southern place, such as Charleston, while most of the rest would be readily available in the more northern states.

Next he divided his list of desirable American trees into groups according to the types of soil they require. The largest of the four groups, containing forty species, was of those that can thrive in mediocre, rocky, or mountainous regions, not suitable to most farm crops; twenty-four of these could do well in swampy land, and eight in poor sandy places. Of all ninety, only eighteen would need fertile soil. Another series of groupings revealed that fifty of the ninety provide excellent wood for carpentry and civil and marine construction. The wood of thirty-nine was less so, being more or less light. Forty-one of the listed species, when mature, produced logs generally free of branches for thirty-five or forty feet.

His last set of groupings of the ninety species was Michaux's judgment of their relative desirability. He put thirty-six in his group of the more desirable. Surprisingly, but understandably in those pre-plywood times, we find two of today's most merchantable species relegated to the lower classes: the tulip tree, *Liriodendrum tulipifera,* to his third class, and sweet gum, *Liquidambar,* to his fourth and lowest class.

With those analyses he concluded his *Mémoire,* as he had begun it, by drawing upon facts and figures gleaned from past researches conducted by his beloved and widely admired former mentor, André Thouin. According to a paper Thouin had inserted among those of the Royal Society of Agriculture in the winter of 1786, there existed in all of France only thirty-seven species of forest trees that reach heights of thirty feet, whereas in North America there are ninety species that attain heights of more than forty feet. Moreover, among the thirty-seven French species only eighteen make up the bulk of her forests, as opposed to ninety in America.[13]

Of the eighteen species usually found in French forests, sixteen would grow in all sections of the country and two only in southern France, whereas in the United States Michaux could count seventy-six that grow in both its north and south, all of which can bear cold as low as that reached in northern Germany, and even those forty species that he had himself seen growing only in the southern and maritime parts of the United States can withstand very well the temperatures of the middle parts of France.

Of the eighteen species usually found in French forests, thirteen will grow in mediocre, sandy, rocky, or mountainous lands, but in the United States there are forty species that thrive in such soils. While in France the remaining five will grow in wetlands, in America the comparable figure is twenty-four. Finally, of the eighteen prevailing French forest trees, strictly speaking, only seven are suitable for carpentry while in America fifty-one species are appropriate for construction purposes.

François André's fact-filled presentation was enthusiastically received—so much so that a prestigious committee was named to study it in detail and report back to the society their conclusions as to what action, if any, it should take in response to the challenge so forcefully presented. To that committee Messrs. Perthuis,[14] Correa de Serra,[15] and Cels were named.

At a meeting of the society on the ensuing March 14, 1805, those learned gentlemen presented their report "upon the project of M. Michaux, relating to the naturalization of North American forest trees." Their five-page report was read to the society and the recommendations made in it approved. An excerpt from the minutes of the meeting, over the signature of its secretary, Silvestre, stated that "the society, in its meeting 22 Ventose, has adopted the attached report and decided that it be sent, with the *Mémoire* of M. Michaux, to His Excellency, Monseigneur, the minister of finances."[16]

As their report would reveal to the minister, Michaux's proposal had elicited a considerably higher degree of endorsement than the simple approval stated in Silvestre's excerpt from the minutes: "The *Mémoire* of M. Michaux is so rich in facts, and those facts are so bound together and so simply presented that it is impossible to present an extract of what its author has seen and observed in his long stay and the benefit of voyages in to the United States of America devoted solely to the object of which he speaks."

Consequently, the committee left the scientific and botanical part of Michaux's presentation to speak for itself and addressed itself to the utility of his proposal, the appropriateness of the means he would employ to attain them, and the reasonableness of the costs of putting those means into effect in relation to the benefits to be derived through it. After repeating several of the more striking comparisons exposing the extreme poverty of the French forests in quality, number, variety, and size of its species in comparison to those of eastern America, the committee stressed the great need in France for an infusion of more species capable of growing in unproductive areas:

The marshy places in France can produce only wood of little value; the United State has in similar areas the bald cypresses, junipers, willow oaks, and red maples, all productive of useful and esteemed wood. The arid sands and sterile, chalky places produce [in France] nothing but a species of inferior pine, [but in the United States] the most arid sands and most sterile places produce the live oak, from which is gotten the wood that is most durable and useful in naval construction. We could multiply such examples for the Mémoire *furnishes many.*

"The means that Michaux proposes are very simple; it being only to send to the United States someone to arrange for the employment of a sender of plants and seeds," and the committee was convinced that he was perfectly suited in experience, botanical learning, and knowledge of the country to perform that mission.

The requisite expenditures are limited to eight thousand francs for a few years. It would be an abuse of your patience to establish the relation between that amount and the benefits sure to result from the execution of the plan, through the increase in revenue from existing forests or through the establishment of new forests in places now abandoned.

We conclude then that the project, presented by M. Michaux, combines appropriate methods with useful objectives, incalculable profits which would result.

Soon after the meeting at which the report of Perthuis, Cels, and Correa de Serra was read and acted upon by the society, the *Mémoire,* the tableau, and the report were published together in pamphlet form.[17]

For final approval of Michaux's proposal it was still necessary to obtain confirmation from the minister of finances, to whom the *Mémoire* and its accompanying report from the committee of the Agricultural Society had been sent. Added to the strain of waiting for word from the minister of finances was Michaux's distress in the resignation of his friend Chaptal in late July 1804 as minister of the interior, in order to become a member of the Senate. Over the years of their association a high mutual esteem had developed between the minister and the young naturalist, and now it seemed as though the fate of his proposed mission, upon which he had set his heart, might be in the hands of a minister with whom, probably, he had no acquaintance; thus it was with much uneasiness that he awaited a response from Chaptal's successor, Jean-Baptiste Champagney.[18]

Spring ripened into summer and still there was no word on his proposal from the Finance Ministry. But this time François André's anxiety and suspense must surely have been ameliorated by word reaching him on every hand of the warm reception his *Travels* was being accorded, both at home and abroad. In the course of the year 1805 three English translations of the work were published in London and a German translation at Weimar.[19]

While we are following small events of a quiet and peaceful nature, albeit significant in their contributions to the partnership of man and nature for the betterment of mankind, Europe was enthralled by the earth-shaking adventures of the Little Corporal, now the emperor Napoleon, that in 1805 reached the first of their several crises. He had not wished the events of that year to come to pass as they did. On the contrary, he had opened the new year with a personal letter to George III in which he urged that France and England settle their differences without further resort to arms. The British monarch's reply was a new continental military alliance against him; this one with Russia, continuing England's time-honored "balance of power" diplomacy. In June, when Austria joined the Alliance, the gauntlet was hurled. In mid-October, Napoleon's army trapped and defeated the Austrians at Ulm, and six weeks later annihilated the Allied armies at Austerlitz, a victory that effectively secured his dominance of all of Europe save yet unconquered Russia and sea-girt Britain, which had been saved from invasion by Nelson's victory at Trafalgar the week after Ulm. After Austerlitz only Britain stood in the way of his redrawing the map of Europe to suit his taste. Nevertheless, during the weeks following Austerlitz he had begun such a redrawing with the Germanic states.[20]

It was in the all-pervading atmosphere of tension and excitement, marching armies and immense battles, each with fast-moving political and fiscal consequences, that the peaceful proposal of François André

Michaux for yet another botanical mission to the United States had to compete for official attention and the requisite funds to support it. In the hope that he might forestall his proposal's withering on the vine through neglect, he ventured another—a brief note—to the minister. "I had the honor," he wrote, "to read to the Society of Agriculture of the Department of the Seine a *Mémoire* in which I directed attention to the importance of introducing into our forests great numbers of the lofty species of trees of North America. The society, appreciating the views set forth in it, and the means proposed for promptly attaining that goal, approved having it printed and sent to the minister of finances. Those conclusions honor me, and induce me, Monseigneur, to ask you to accept a few copies as testimony of my respect for your person and of my entire devotion to the general welfare.[21]

That note and the *Mémoire* that accompanied it appear to have had the effect of freeing the key log in a logjammed river, setting off chain reactions releasing, into the surging flow, the accumulated forest harvest to resume its way to its destination. Action was almost immediate. Two days later a note of thanks went to Michaux from the minister and copies of the *Mémoire* dispatched to the professors of the Museum of Natural History, to Lizermes, director of the nursery at Roule, and his counterpart at the Luxembourg Gardens, with notes requesting their advice.[22]

At that point there is a gap in the pertinent surviving records extending to mid-January of the next year, 1806. They resume as final arrangements were underway for Michaux's departure on his second American mission. Just how his proposal which, ten months earlier, had been sent to the minister of finances, had ripened into an approved and funded project under the sponsorship of the General Administration of Waters and Forests (a division of the Ministry of the Interior), we do not know. We become privy to the action again only as final details were being arranged before his embarkation from Bordeaux, once more destined for Charleston.

There had been much to be attended to before his departure in January, a sailing time that would enable him to set out on his American travels with the coming of spring. There were letters of introduction to be secured to persons residing in New England and other parts of the United States he had not visited before, farewell gatherings at the homes of friends, and reading matter to be obtained for the long voyage. Among the latter, the accounts of travelers in other lands especially interested him. As he planned his new American venture, he was increasingly concerned as to just how his collections of seeds and those of Saunier would be coordinated, a problem that he thought should be resolved as far as possible while he was still in Paris. With that intent he addressed a letter to the minister of the interior proposing that during his stay in America Saunier's collections should be made under his direction and Saunier's annual allowance for seed collections should be channeled through him.[23]

Although that letter had gone to Champagny, the new minister of the interior, on January 17, he had received no response to it when word reached him that the ship he was to take from Bordeaux had arrived at Lorient, its final port of call before Bordeaux and departure for Charleston—news that led Michaux to depart Paris for Bordeaux in great haste. We next hear of him through a letter dated Feb. 21 from his Bordeaux merchant friend, Neckelman, to the minister, informing him that it had been almost a month since Michaux had sailed for Charleston; but that he would forward the packet of letters the minister had sent for him at his first opportunity to Charleston or New York.[24]

The packet Neckelman had reference to contained two long letters, one to Michaux, the other, in his care, to Saunier. Those letters advised Saunier and Michaux of the minister's decision that during Michaux's stay in the United States, Saunier should receive half his annual allowance and his seed collections should be made under Michaux's direction and be reduced in quantity to reflect his reduced allowance.[25]

CHAPTER **24**

✧ Second Mission to America,

1806–1808

CONSTRUCTING A NARRATIVE ACCOUNT of F. A. Michaux's second American expedition presents very different problems from those encountered in that of 1801–3. For the latter there were quantities of surviving contemporary documents, as well as his own account of his voyage into the interior of the United States. Unfortunately, the corresponding documents needed to shed light on his expedition under the sponsorship of the Administration of Waters and Forests (generally referred to as the Forestry Administration) were not similarly preserved, and his subsequent writings, mostly embodied in his *North American Sylva,* were far from cohesive and contemporary. Nevertheless, a few long letters and reports provide a fair basis for reconstruction of this mission.

We return to François André at sea on an American merchant-man, walking the deck of the vessel exulting in its westward course and the freedom it promised from strife-torn Europe and war-oriented France and the prospect before him of visiting again, and more exten-sively, the vast American forests that so enthralled him. But that was not to be as soon as he had hoped. Three days out of Bordeaux on course to Charleston, where he expected to find early spring in progress and the season right for the first of the five planned expeditions westward into the interior, a vessel, soon observed to be a British man-of-war, was sighted bearing down upon Captain Baur's little merchantman. Mi-chaux reported the incident in a letter to his friend Charles Cotesworth Pinckney: "You have doubtless learned in due course of the unfortu-nate encounter which the ship of Captain Baur, on which I had taken my passage to go to Charleston, experienced. Personally," he con-tinued, "this circumstance was not at all disagreeable for me, for in addition to the fact that I was treated with all possible regard by Messieur, the Captain Whitely, and Messieurs, the officers of the *Scan-dia*(?), I had the pleasure of seeing the Bermuda Isles and a little corner of Nova Scotia."[1]

Once satisfied that Michaux was a genuine naturalist, Captain Whitely seized the opportunity to drop him off at his next port of call, St. George, on the most northern island of the Bermudas. There on those beautiful, ever-flowering islands the courteous treatment ac-corded him on Whitely's ship continued in the long European tradition that the natural sciences, especially botany, were without nationality, even in times of war. He was given the freedom of the archipelago, permitting him to make the most of the rare opportunity presented by those unique islands, the world's only temperate zone coral islands, thanks to the warm Gulf Stream waters that wash their shores. For most, that freedom would have spelled an alluring opportunity to bask in the spring sun on one of its beautiful, pink-tinted beaches protected from the chill breezes of the season by towering, rugged, coral cliffs, while watching the myriads of shorebirds above and incredible displays of fascinating sea creatures, visible to great depths through the crystal clear waters of the sapphire Gulf Stream. Instead of succumbing to their magic, François André, appreciative but industrious as always, in

the Michaux tradition, was soon busily studying the geological, biolog-
ical, and botanical features of the islands and gathering his observations
in a paper, *Notice sur les îles Bermudes et particulièrment sur l'île Saint
Georges*.[2] When that paper was published in Paris later in the same year,
François André had, in effect, contributed one more illustration of the
European tradition of that day, of the internationality of science, for
almost certainly, without British cooperation his manuscript could not
have so expeditiously reached Paris.

Although Michaux's letter to Pinckney was not a long one and was
mostly devoted to enlisting the general's assistance in collecting a substantial loan made during the Revolutionary War to the state of South
Carolina by a close friend and associate of Michaux père, it sheds some
light on François André's activities following his release from his Bermuda internment. When the British military authorities became satisfied that keeping him interned was serving no good purpose, they
arranged passage for him on a vessel destined for New York via Halifax,
Nova Scotia, such an indirect route that it was mid-June, more than
four months after his departure from Bordeaux, when he finally
stepped ashore at New York. There is reason to believe that he stayed in
that area at least long enough to visit shipyards and building-con-
struction projects to note the timber species employed for specific uses
in that region, the first of a series of such investigations he planned to
make at all the principal Atlantic ports. The only other report of his
activities at this time that has come to light is two entries in *Jefferson's
Garden Book,* the first dated July 8, 1806, which recorded that John
Vaughan had sent from Philadelphia to the president in Washington
for the newly arrived "F. A. Michaux his *Voyage* [*Travels*] and a pamphlet relative to American Trees." The other, four days later, recorded
that Jefferson had sent his thanks to Michaux for those publications
and told him he had his father's *Flora Boreali-Americana* and had seen
his work on the American oaks, "both of which are valuable additions to
our Botanical libraries." Unquestionably the pamphlet was his 1805
Mémoire on American forest trees. Also, doubtless he had seen the copy
of his father's work on American oaks that Michaux fils had delivered to
the Philosophical Society on his 1801 visit to the United States.[3]

With those things done, he set out on the expedition he had
planned to make from New York in the late summer—skipping for the
present those into the southern interior originally planned for the
spring and early summer. Of that expedition we have little specific
information beyond what he recounted in his letter to the general.
"Since I arrived in the United States three months ago," he wrote, "I

have carried out a very interesting journey, crossing all the country between North River [the Hudson] and Lake Erie. All those regions are peopling with extraordinary rapidity, and the vegetation is everywhere admirable by reason of the extreme fertility of the soil." That voyage would have taken him into parts of western New York and Pennsylvania and northeastern Ohio.

While in New York he had also visited the Bergen establishment and arranged with Saunier that, owing to the delay in his arrival, he would not take any part of the gardener's annual stipend for seed gathering in 1806 and at the same time informed him of the dissatisfaction with his recent seed shipments, the tardiness of their dispatch, the lack of variety, and the reduced quantities; complaints that were apparently sufficient to effect great change in Saunier's next shipment.[4] In January 1807 ten boxes containing a wide variety of seeds reached France, not at Neckelman's wharf at Bordeaux, as directed, but in Nantes, where they remained for weeks immobile owing to the consternation and fear provoked by the fact that the letter of advice accompanying the shipment was in English, the use of which in commerce had been strictly banned as part of the boycott ordered by Napoleon forbidding the entry of any goods from England, designed as a countermeasure to the British blockade of Napoleonic Europe.[5] With this shipment, however, that ban did little more than evoke expressions of concern and delay its eventual delivery in Paris and the distribution of the contents of the boxes.[6]

Between Michaux's letter to Pinckney from New York in late October 1806 and the spring of 1807 we have little definitive knowledge of his activities. A letter he wrote the minister of the interior from Philadelphia on January 10, 1807, puts him back there in early January. In it he told the minister that he had just learned, to his mortification, that Mathias Kin, with whom he had arranged in 1802 for a collection of a quantity of forest seeds from the Philadelphia area, had never received payment for it. Obviously upset by the failure of a commitment he had made, he urged the minister to have the records searched to determine to whom that payment had been entrusted, if indeed it was ever made. He had the impression that it had been made through Victor du Pont.[7]

It is a reasonable conjecture that Michaux had stayed on in the New York area during the remainder of the fall season, probably much of the time with Saunier, as he was accustomed to doing, putting in order his notes and collections made on his expedition to the Lakes Ontario and Erie, particularly his collections of the wood samples he was now assiduously accumulating. Each specimen had to be prepared in such a way that it would display smoothed and polished lateral and cross section but leave a sufficient length of its bark intact for identification purposes. When he moved down to Philadelphia in January, there was even more to keep him busy—friends, especially John Vaughan at the Philosophical Society, and fellow botanists to visit with and collections from the forests of the area to be made and prepared.

In late spring he was in Boston investigating the shipyard there and collecting in its environs before setting out to visit John Vaughan's eldest brother, Benjamin, and another brother, Charles, both of whom resided on the family estate of their mother, Sarah Hallowell (which he never stopped spelling Hollowell) on the Kennebec River a few miles below Augusta, Maine, then a district of Massachusetts. The Vaughans were remarkable people—most especially Benjamin, then fifty-six years old, who had left England some ten years before to establish his home in the relative isolation of rural Maine.[8] There in his study, amid the accumulating volumes of his library, which at his death was judged as exceeding in number any other in New England, except that at Harvard, he usually devoted much of his days to the maintenance of an immense correspondence, mostly with persons of consequence on two continents, including, eventually, all the first six presidents of the United States. After his visit François André would be added to that distinguished company.

At Hallowell, Michaux spent several weeks in the congenial home of the elder Vaughan, but visiting frequently the nearby home of brother Charles Vaughan, formerly a leading developer of urban Boston, in partnership with his wife's brother-in-law, Charles Bulfinch. When the weather was fine he made expeditions in the area, among them to Winslow, Norridgewock, and Farmington, collecting the seed of such early fruiting trees as elms, maples, and birches and specimens of the wood of many others of the region.[9]

Meanwhile, back in Paris, Augustin Bosc of the Bureau of Agriculture was writing to the minister of the interior complaining again of the bad condition and lack of variety of Paul Saunier's last shipment and suggesting that a letter be directed to him with copies to the consul at New York and to Michaux, directing them to see that those deficiencies be remedied. Bosc went on to say that "Michaux has made a shipment of seeds to the minister this year containing a box of red maple, the one from which they extract sugar, and a box of yellow elm that we do not have in the nurseries . . . new proof of the zeal and industry of Michaux," deserving a letter of commendation. He added that the ship-

ment was "purely the result of his love of sylviculture and his desire to
please you, for he has received no funds from the ministry and his
advances have not been reimbursed.[10]

The advent of August found François André back in Boston,
where he was swept up in a social whirl that he reported with obvious
relish in a letter to his recent host, Benjamin Vaughan. Obviously a
social attraction himself, it is remarkable as well that most of those he
mentioned in his opening paragraph are names now remembered as
historical personages.[11]

> *The desire to see the new turnpike from Newburyport to Boston,*
> *which I had heard so much about, determined me not to go back*
> *by Salem. I really admired this new road, the most beautiful of*
> *any I have seen in the United States. On my arrival I visited im-*
> *mediately Messieurs the Doctors Warren, junior,[12] and*
> *Gorham,[13] and Mr. Gardiner.[14] The latter has presented me to*
> *Doctor Dexter[15] and Monsieur the Judge Davis,[16] an informed*
> *lover of botany. In a word, Monsieur, since my return I have*
> *found myself so surrounded by marks of attention and kindness of*
> *the part of these gentlemen and a great many other persons that I*
> *have not remained one hour at home. The 29th I had the honor*
> *of being invited by Messieurs the* Selectmen[17] *to a brilliant*
> *party on Deer Island, at which there were more than 80 people.*
> *Mr. Thomas Pinckney[18] was among the number. This event*
> *brought me new acquaintances, among others, Mr. the Rev.*
> *Mackeen, amateur botanist. I count on spending part of this eve-*
> *ning at the home of Mr. Bulfinch[19] and tomorrow at 4 o'clock in*
> *the morning I set out for Burlington [Vt.].*

From Philadelphia, two months later, writing again to Benjamin
Vaughan at Hallowell, Michaux recounted in considerable detail an
expedition he had made to Lake Champlain, setting out from Boston
before dawn on August 2, 1807. The stage route took him diagonally
northwest across New Hampshire and Vermont to Burlington, on the
Vermont side of the lake.[20] The poor shallow soil that characterized the
country along the route in Massachusetts and New Hampshire as far as
the village of Amherst was distressingly reflected in the poverty of the
harvests being made on the little farms they passed. After Amherst,
however, both terrain and soil exhibited marked changes, increasingly
displaying scenes "much resembling the District of Maine, being generally mountainous and clothed in forests of much the same trees, such as
hemlock, spruce and even Norway pine."

The second day after leaving Boston he had fallen ill and been forced to surrender to his misery at Windsor, New Hampshire, and take refuge there for eight days before taking to the road again. Despite the circumstances, he judged it "an agreeable enough village," where the quality of the soil began to improve, sometimes even becoming excellent along their way past Lake Sunapee and beyond the Connecticut River and through Randolph and Montpelier; although the land grew increasingly hilly, sometimes excessively so, nevertheless the little farms they saw exhibited excellent pastures. For Montpelier itself he had nothing good to say. "Montpelier, 40 miles distant from Lake Champlain," he wrote, "composed of 40 or 60 houses, is a place to die of boredom, being shut in by high mountains, which limit one's view to six hundred yards; and its surroundings offer nothing to justify the allusion in its name [to its famous French namesake], it being the ugliest village I have seen in the United States." Moreover, he found the region between it and Burlington on the lake "frightful country, covered with enormous boulders" resting in stony soil so that one cannot hope to encounter a single field except along the Winooski River, which the road rarely approached. However, a few miles before Burlington came some relief from such sour observations by the tree-loving traveler when they entered a forest of "very considerable extent of white pine of the greatest beauty" despite the soil which became so sandy as they neared Burlington that "one cannot walk without getting into sand over the tops of one's shoes."

Only when the stage left them at Burlington did Michaux indicate that he was traveling in company of a fellow countryman he later identified as a friend, a French officer, M. Parmentier, a native of Lorient.[21] At Burlington they chartered a sailboat for a three-day, ninety-mile sail southward up Lake Champlain, the shores of which, they were surprised to find, were already "well inhabited, especially on the Vermont side where the soil is good and cheap, 3 or 4 dollars an acre." As they neared the end of their sail they went ashore on the New York side to visit the old forts at Crown Point and Ticonderoga, concluding after their inspections that the latter, built by the French a half century since, was infinitely more superior. There still remained its caverns capable of lodging three thousand men. Beyond Ticonderoga the lake became almost too narrow for sailing, appearing to be "no larger than the Kennebec at Hallowell," and its waters, which had been crystal clear, now became opaque and its borders choked with weeds, changes that doubtless accounted for the fact that, according to the inhabitants, the salmon ascended no farther up its waters.

There were other landings to observe the logging operations in progress and interview the loggers, who told them that the logs of white pine and oak they were felling would be floated the length of the lake and down the Richelieu River to the St. Lawrence and Quebec, where they would be put aboard ships for England. Those cut farther up the lake were floated to a nearby place (where the travelers left their boat) then known as Skeensborough (now Whitehall), where they were cut into planks that in winter would be sledded down to Albany, where they would fetch eight dollars per thousand board feet.

Departing the lake at Whitehall, east of the lake at its southern terminus, they took the road to Albany via Saratoga. Although along the shores of the lake the forests of white pine had seemed inexhaustible, along the way to Albany they were already exhausted. Carefully noting the terrain they crossed and his observation of the forests of Champlain, Michaux made a prescient comment: "What wealth for the city of New York if a canal should be opened between the lake and the Hudson river by way of Wood Creek! The expense would be moderate." That suggestion would become a reality a mere two decades later when the Champlain Barge Canal was constructed.

At Albany the travelers became fortuitous participants in an event now familiar to every schoolchild. We have an account of it recorded many years later by Michaux himself, in 1848,[22] and an interesting sequel reported by Elias Durand, a close friend of Michaux's, in a memorial to Michaux shortly after his death.[23] Here is Michaux's account of the event:

> *[Between Albany and New York, one hundred and sixty miles down the Hudson] at that time decked sailing vessels arrived and departed every day with twenty-five or thirty passengers. The passage generally took thirty-six or forty-eight hours, according as the wind or tide were more or less favorable.*
>
> *We had been three days in Albany, when the arrival from New York of a vessel propelled by steam was announced. This boat, which was decked, was about 25 metres [82 feet] long, and was commanded by the inventor, Mr. Robert Fulton. Many of the inhabitants of the city and strangers who were there at the time went to visit it; everyone made his remarks upon the advantages consequent upon this new means of navigation, but also upon the serious accidents which might result from the explosion of the boiler.*
>
> *The vessel was lying alongside the wharf; a placard announced its return to New York for the next day but one, the 20th*

*of August, and that it would take passengers at the same price as
the sailing vessels—three dollars.*

*So great was the fear of the explosion of the boiler, that no
one except my companion and myself dared to take the passage in
it to New York. We quitted Albany . . . in the presence of a great
number of spectators.*

*Chancellor Livingston, whom we supposed to be one of the
promoters of this new way of navigating rivers, was the only
stranger with us; he quitted the boat in the afternoon to go to his
country residence, which was upon the left bank of the river.*[24]

*After Chancellor Livingston had quitted us, Mr. Fulton ex-
pressed his surprise that, notwithstanding the number of passengers who were going to New York, only two Frenchmen had
had the courage to embark with him.*

Before they disembarked a little after noon the next day, a cordial
friendship had developed between the inventor and the naturalist.
Michaux told him the purpose of his travels, "to examine the forests of
this part of North America," to study the trees in respect to their uses in
the arts and publish a work on the subject. Fulton approved of the
project, predicting it would bring him both honor and profit. He
showed them the mechanism of the engine and dwelt enthusiastically
upon "the incalculable advantage of this means for ascending the great
rivers of the interior, particularly the Mississippi." Michaux in turn told
Fulton of the seams of coal which he had observed along the Ohio,
which might greatly alleviate the need for more efficient fueling of the
vessel, information Fulton declared "the most agreeable facts I could
hear." Before they parted Michaux had agreed that on his return to
Paris he would call upon the minister of war in the hope that he might
be interested in taking advantage of Fulton's invention.

The friendship between Michaux and Fulton persisted through
the years. Durand reported that years later, after Fulton's death in
1815, "Michaux having found in Paris a model in clay of a bust of his
friend by Houdon, bought it and caused it to be put in marble by the
best artist he could find at a cost of 1000 francs. He obtained permission
afterwards from the government to have it placed in the Marine Department of the Louvre, near that of Papin, who had done so much for
steam."[25]

From that digression let us return to François André's letter to
Benjamin Vaughan. He went on to say that when he arrived in New
York he found letters from France awaiting him, one of which said that

as soon as he returned to Paris they planned to send him to botanize in Chile, with an allowance of 25,000 francs per year. "But," he commented, "I will never consent to such a mission. I am content with the honor which can result from my *North American Sylva,* for which I am giving myself so many hardships."

To assist him in that aim and his current mission, he had requests to make of the Hallowell Vaughans; from Benjamin, specimens two or three inches in diameter, of the woods of hemlock, spruce, and white cedar, while from younger brother Charles he desired two quarts of white birch seeds, saying the tree near the block-maker's place was loaded with them, and also a quart of those of the yellow birch. In return he was delivering to John Vaughan a supply of seeds of some vegetable species newly popular in France.

While in New York he fell ill again, delaying him there another fifteen days. The delays caused by his two illnesses frustrated his plan to travel to Charleston via Kentucky and Tennessee, where it was already too late for the seed season; and taking that circuitous route would also make him too late for collecting seeds in Carolina. So he determined to set out forthwith for Charleston.

It had been an exceedingly busy summer for the "voyageur for the Forestry Administration in North America." Although we have only related what we know of his expeditions, records of the Bureau of Agriculture confirm continuing shipments by both Saunier and Michaux himself to the minister of the interior. The great bulk of his seed shipments throughout his 1805–8 mission went to the Administration of Waters and Forests. Despite the mounting ferocity of the Napoleonic Wars, the seeds were, surprisingly enough, being received in quantities that would earn great admiration for him when his peers later evaluated and reported on his mission.[26]

For anything more than the merest outline of Michaux's activities during the ensuing eleven months following his October 1807 letter to Benjamin Vaughan, the surviving records once again fall silent. To account for that period we have but a three-sentence summary in another letter to Benjamin Vaughan, written from Philadelphia in the late summer of 1808: "Since I left the District of Maine I have continued to lead a very active life, having traversed all the Atlantic States. I have visited more particularly South Carolina and Georgia. A little after my return to the North, I set out again to see again the other side of the Allegheny Mountains, whence I have been returned for many weeks."[27]

He went on to express his satisfaction with this, his final American mission. "At last," he wrote, "I have the extreme satisfaction of seeing that I have completed my researches on the utility of the forests of the United States, at least as far as one person could, aided more by ardent zeal than by great financial resources. Now, when I see the mass of information that I have obtained, I myself am surprised to have done so much in so little time. A similar task in any other country would have been deemed government business, or at least that of some native of that country." He was inspired to resolve that "on my arrival in Paris I will busy myself without let up with the publication of my work."

He added an acknowledgment of the receipt of a "pretty drawing of the moose which Mademoiselle" (Vaughan's young daughter) had "very kindly made" for him, "and I send her my most sincere thanks and all my gratitude." He concluded his letter with an announcement of his imminent return to France, events "having interrupted all communication with Europe, so that I can no longer fulfill the obligations I contracted with the Forestry Administration."[28] He had resolved to embark for home from Philadelphia within two weeks. "My grateful heart will never forget the honorable and friendly welcome that I have received from you, Monsieur, and your respected family."

It appears that it was during the course of this visit to Philadelphia that Michaux became well acquainted with the striving ornithologist Alexander Wilson, to whom thereafter he often affectionately alluded. It is also likely that he met there Thomas Nuttall, recently arrived from England, who in later years would expand Michaux's *North American Sylva* to include the trees of the trans-Mississippi West, for both had associations at that time with Professor Benjamin Barton and the Bartrams.[29]

Late November found François André back in Paris, at first giving his address as Quay Pellitier, No. 30, the home on the Seine of his friend Fortin. It was merchant Fortin who handled the Paris business end of many of his seed shipments. Early in the month Michaux had arrived on the American vessel the *Union*, at the Brittany port of Lorient, 360 miles from Paris. There he had been delayed for eight days by another attack of the recurring illness that had several times interrupted his American travels, preventing him from boarding the stage for Paris. When he finally reached Paris, the imminence of the departure of "*l'Union*" on her return voyage to Philadelphia prompted both him and his friend of long standing and erstwhile fellow student at the "ancienne" Ecole de Santé, Raffeneau-Delile,[30] to seize the opportunity to dispatch letters to Philadelphia—among them one from each to Dr. Caspar Wistar.[31] Raffeneau-Delile wrote that he had just had the pleasure of a visit with his friend Monsieur Michaux, who had opportunely arrived in Paris only four days since.[32]

Obviously there were a multitude of claimants shouldering one another for the time and attention of the newly returned voyager, including his Michaux and Claye relatives. Only secondary to his family were his many friends and associates avid to receive firsthand accounts of the three years of his absence. There was catching up to be done on the scientific developments while he was away, and attending to the missions he had agreed to undertake in Paris for Wistar, Barton, and others. There were reports to be made to the Forestry Administration, the minister of finances, and the minister of the interior recording his accomplishments in America and petitions for reimbursement for his expenses and the anticipated honorariums for fulfilling his missions during which, in effect, he had had two masters—a situation that added complexity to such formalities and proceedings. Finally, but doubtless the most important in François André's mind, there were his notes, collections, and recollections to be put in order for use in the work to which he was now deeply dedicated, his *North American Sylva.*

At the moment the most pressing demand was to get his finances in order after three years abroad, much of the time in expensive travels. Although he had departed on his mission in 1806 under the sponsorship of the Forestry Administration, the reward he should get for his services was unspecified. This is indicated in a letter to the minister of the interior in which he wrote that "before leaving France, I was invited by your predecessor to make shipments to" him. There was only his own estimate of the cost of his undertaking, 8,000 francs, contained in the 1805 Report that had inspired the expedition. Early in December there was correspondence between the various agencies involved and the minister of finances, seeking a resolution of that aspect of the American mission of "this botanist of the woods." His services to the minister of the interior being relatively minor, there was little difficulty there. Before the end of the month he had submitted to him his expense account, accompanying it with a packet containing forty horse chestnuts, the Ohio buckeye, *Aesculus glabra,* "still unknown in Europe," which would certainly "add infinitely to the embellishment of our public gardens." Early in January 1809 reimbursement of his expenses and an honorarium of 2,000 francs were approved and a recommendation made that he be given the important post of inspector of nurseries.[33]

Just what was settled upon as his compensation from the Forestry Administration is not so clear. Early in January in an interdepartment communication there is a statement that the emperor "has proposed that M. Michaux be compensated proportional to the payment that would have been allowed . . . for someone paid by the Forestry Administration for the services rendered by Michaux." The same memo estimated the value of those services for the "encouragement of the sciences and arts . . . [at] 60 or 70,000 francs could be easily supported by receipts." No surviving documents reveal what was finally accorded him but, judging from the enthusiasm generated by the results of his mission, it is most probable that he was well rewarded. An example of this enthusiasm survives in an internal communication requesting that the question be "put before the eyes of His Majesty" to settle on the compensation of M. Michaux "for the distinguished services he has rendered the Administration of Forests during the North American mission entrusted to him . . . recognizing his zeal and the fruits which the Forest Administration has derived from the useful discoveries." The memo continued with the suggestion that he be accorded "the position of inspector of nurseries belonging to that administration which he is qualified to fill, this in recognition of the signal services which his father and he have rendered to France."[34]

As we are without any original official documents to shed light on the details of the services Michaux rendered the Forestry Administration in return for its sponsoring his 1806–8 American mission, it is fortunate that the Agricultural Society, which had played a major role in getting the mission approved, had maintained a continuing interest in it. Almost immediately after his return to Paris the mission was again on its agenda. To subject it to a thorough review, a committee composed of its leading botanists and arboriculturists was named to survey and report to the society their opinion of the achievements of the mission. Named to that committee were Allaire, Bosc, Petit-Thouars, and Correa de Serra. At the society's meeting on Feb. 1, 1809, Correa de Serra was ready with the report, which, like François André's 1805 proposal, was soon published in pamphlet form.[35]

That we may have a better idea of the very significant role of the younger Michaux in the advancement of French forestry in the early nineteenth century and the seeding of American forestry, we quote comments from that report:

"Mr. Michaux, by his long sojourn in the United States, and by his knowledge of botany and cultivation, was highly qualified to carry out with success a project so useful to the Empire as the naturalizing of foreign trees." After outlining his extensive American travels from

Maine to Georgia and five separate voyages westward into the interior regions, the report continued:

> *His abundant and repeated shipments to the Forestry Administration prove the zeal with which he fulfilled his commission and earned the gratitude of the country. . . .*
>
> *The nature of the wood [of each species] of the American forests and their economic uses have been usually neglected by botanists who have traveled in that country. Such knowledge is found in the possession of artisans who utilize the various woods, and, although we know that the arts and sciences should communicate with each other, and can assist each other, most often they follow their own gods, each without knowledge of the other.*

To avoid that failing, everywhere he went in his travels he visited the shipyards, cabinetmakers, house builders, tanneries, and even the basketmakers, gathering from them a mass of information respecting the qualities of the various woods of America "as the Academy of Sciences has done in respect to all the Arts. . . . He has particularly observed the trees whose woods, because of their nature and usages, are objects of commerce" between the various parts of the country and England. To forestall the confusion often caused by the use of common names, often applied to quite differing species and not infrequently varying in different parts of the country, he had attached to each specimen the common name or names associated with it. To supplement his observations on the one hundred and thirty species described, of which two-thirds are used in the arts in the United States, he had collected samples of their wood "large enough for one to judge their qualities. They comprise chiefly the pieces of the numerous species of maples, elms, birches, pines, walnuts and oaks."

After discussing such beautiful woods as the maples produce, especially those displaying the "bird's-eye" patterns, those of the hickories and most particularly of the black walnut, "most esteemed for government construction," he reported on the great variety of oaks, distinguished by whether they bear acorns every year or in alternate years, the wood of the former being far superior. The pines of America, running the gamut from the heavy, highly resinous longleaf pine of the coastal plains of the Carolinas, Georgia, and Florida, a species which he thought could be grown with profit in the sands near Bordeaux, to the magnificent white pine of the north with its easily worked wood, and the red spruce, *Picea rubens,* also of the northward forests, which produces the resilient wood deemed best for sail spars, were especially desirable and useful.

Finally, Michaux had observed in detail the appearance and disappearance of the various species, reflecting the latitude, altitude, qualities of soils and moisture, studies that had intrigued his father, who had hoped to prepare a work on the "botanical topography" of the United States. Michaux called this new field of study "botanical geography." The committee thought such studies, "perhaps the least advanced part of science," valuable to "direct the cultivator." Although he realized that there was much more to be done and that additional importations of seeds and plants would be necessary, his own shipments during his mission had been bountiful. From them 250,000 seedlings were already thriving in the nurseries.

Correa de Serra concluded the committee's report with the conclusion that "it is not necessary to emphasize the usefulness of such a journey and such a work, its very obviousness makes us dispense with relating minutely the reasons which convince us that M. Michaux has the greatest claims to the gratitude of every good Frenchman, and particularly to that of the Society of Agriculture."

CHAPTER 25

❧ Paris: 1809–1814, Franco-American Scientific Intermediary

BEFORE MIDSPRING 1809, the final duties of his second mission completed, François André Michaux, now in his fortieth year, settled into a pattern of life he chose to follow for years to come. It was a pleasant, stimulating, intellectual, and social way of life, remarkably unvarying, even as crisis after crisis shook his beloved city and nation and the lives of the people around him. Nevertheless, they were productive years during which he maintained a steady course toward his goal: the creation of his work on the great forest across the sea that for so long had enthralled him.

The principal distraction from his task developed soon after his return to France in 1808, when he fell naturally, almost inevitably, into the role of liaison agent between the scientific circles of the vital young republic across the western waters and those of the ancient scientific center of the Continent, a role for which he was particularly qualified by his Franco-American background, his sociable nature, and unflagging interest in people, coupled with his fascination with a wide variety of scientific interests.

In May 1809 we find him writing to Dr. Wistar to thank him for the news of their mutual friends in Philadelphia and to inform him of the latest medical publications to be found in Paris; he said that he had lately sent the doctor two medical works and that Raffeneau-Delile had sent him a third.[1] He added that by the next boat he would send another written by a young doctor who, through extensive experiments, had concluded that the center of life lies not in the brain but rather in the spinal column. His work was so convincing, he said, that the Imperial School of Medicine had ordered his experiments duplicated. He further reported that there had been no new works on comparative anatomy, but Wistar would find much of interest on the subject, especially among the observations of Cuvier, in the *Annals of the Museum of Natural History* of which he had sent fifteen numbers to the Philosophical Society along with volumes of the *Memoirs of the National Institute*. "As for myself," he reported, "I am always occupied with putting my notes in order for publication of my work and I hope to be sending you the end of this year the first five numbers. The success or nonsuccess it meets with in the United States will determine whether I am to go on with it."

In his next letter to Dr. Wistar, this one in late November, Michaux gave us the earliest of many instances of another Franco-American role he was naturally falling into—that of the informal Parisian host and mentor to an almost endless stream of his American friends, and their friends, who despite the perils of the sea and hazards of visiting in war-torn Europe persisted in their pilgrimages to its great capital.[2] He acknowledged the "double pleasure" of a letter from the doctor with its news and its introduction to him of Dr. Patterson, who had delivered Wistar's letter some five weeks back.[3] Patterson, he reported, "appears already accustomed to our great city (and is accustoming himself to French ways)."

Michaux then reported, as he would continue to do with only variations on the theme for years to come, on his long and arduous process of preparing his *Histoire des arbres forestiers de l'Amérique septentrionale*. "I hope," he wrote, "you will receive before spring the

beginning of my work and that you will find it useful in the United States. I recommend myself to the influence of your friends, and yours personally."

He then thanked the doctor for the part he had played in Michaux's election to membership in the American Philosophical Society, "a pleasure and honor I by no means expected."[4] He closed with a final paragraph of the sort of comment on the state of affairs in Europe that would become almost as characteristic of François André's letters to his Philadelphia friends as the hallmark of a silversmith on the pieces he fashions. "Magnificent and pompous fetes are being prepared in which the emperor will appear with all the Asiatic pomp and surrounded by the kings of his own making."

To complete the adumbration of Michaux's life during the several ensuing years from the few surviving 1809 letters from him to America, we have one to John Vaughan, written the same day as that to Wistar, sent with Wistar's by Captain Frost's *Madison*, destined for Baltimore, responding to two Vaughan had written him in the summer requesting his assistance in securing for the society's library several scientific works unavailable in the United States.[5] Most notable and most costly among them was the then not quite completed ten-volume fifth edition of Linnaeus' *Species plantarum*, much revised and edited by Karl L. Willdenow.[6] Vaughan had also asked for other volumes not obtainable in America on physics and mineralogy, and the recent numbers of several scientific and literary journals. Michaux replied that he had shipped via Dieppe nine volumes of the Willdenow and the other requested books; also two numbers each of the *Annals of the Museum*, the *Annals of Chemistry*, three of *Journal of Literature*, one of *Journal of Philosophy*, and two of the *Journal of Physics*, one of which he had gotten from their mutual friend David Warden.[7]

In the same box he had put another book for Dr. Wistar, a package containing the portraits of Dr. Barton and Mr. Patterson, the engravings that Dr. Barton had asked him to get Professor Claude Richard to prepare for Barton to use in illustrating the different types of leaves in his new edition of his *Elements of Botany*, and others Alexander Wilson had requested for his *American Ornithology*. In a letter to Michaux the hard-pressed Wilson confided to the sympathetic naturalist: "I have sacrificed everything to print my *Ornithology*."[8]

After renewing his offer and desire to render any service for the

John Vaughan (1756–1841), librarian of the Amerian Philosophical Society and longtime correspondent of F. A. Michaux. From the portrait by Thomas Sully. (Courtesy of the American Philosophical Society)

Society and "your and my friends," he furnished Vaughan with a detailed itemized statement of the cost of the books (all unbound, as was customary in the international book trade in those days), and the cost of the packing and haulage to the port, a total of 196 francs, which he converted to $37.40.

Before closing, Michaux acknowledged receipt of his membership diploma from the American Philosophical Society, which Patterson had brought him, and promised to write the society to express his gratitude for its recognition of the work for which he was then deeply occupied with the drawings and engravings. After the customary formal closing he added a postscript saying he was sending Vaughan "a separate number of Humboldt in which he questions your friend, Ferer."[9]

For François André Michaux the year 1809 had been a time of momentous transition. Gone forever were wilderness travels far from home. It marked the beginning of his writings and drawings that were to flower into his *North American Sylva,* with its important new emphasis on facets of practical forest culture that clearly presaged modern forestry. At the same time 1809 definitely marked the inauguration of his unofficial and informal position as liaison between American scientists and the European realm of science in all its contemporary aspects. In addition, it had seen his reputation as an outstanding scientific figure confirmed by his election to the Philosophical Society and the entrenchment of his day-to-day association with many of the most notable men of science in the international scientific circles of the most sophisticated city of the age.

Almost as if that transition had been a studied, conscious step into a new way of life, François André's surviving correspondence opened the next year with a letter in English—the first we have found since his painfully worded 1801 note to General Pickens about his father's Keowee land claims. He wrote William Bartram at some length in easy English, albeit with a continuing confusion of gender and tenses:

> I am sincerely obliged to our common friend, Mr. [Alexander] Wilson, to have give me in his last letter, news of you and family. The marks of friendship that you have invariably bestow on my father and me will be constantly present to my memory. . . . The seeds came in hand in good order. The only thing I cannot but observe is that you really put too much of each kind for the small sum of money that I have sent; consequently I am under a double obligation toward your brother John, and your nephews.
>
> By this same occasion, I send somme Literary Journals for the

Philosophical Society. In the same packet, I include a small par-
cel of seeds of two sorts of Pine, Pinus maritima, *et* P. laricio.
This last is a very interesting species, growing in the mountains
of Corsica. As it grow very well at Paris, I suppose he will sup-
port well your climate. You claim those seeds of Mr. J. Vaughan.

    Since my return not a day is passing away without working
steady to my American Sylva. *Drawers, engravers, type and*
copper printers, are busy about it; and the French edition, or at
least the first number, is to appear the first of May; and by the
same time, I shall send over the engravings to be added to the
American edition, in case Mr. S. Bradford will be disposed to re-
publish. I am very anxious to know how he will meet in America;
and in particular, your opinion respecting it. Also of Mr.
Hamilton and Dr. Muhlenberg.[10]

By mid-March 1810 Michaux had learned, probably through
Warden, that the English had captured the *Madison,* doubtless for
violation of Britain's blockade of all the ports of Napoleonic Europe.[11]
Extremely disturbed for fear that the shipment that had been put
aboard it at Dieppe, almost three and a half months before, had been
lost, he nevertheless delayed for two weeks writing to Vaughan to
inform him of the disturbing outlook for the books and journals for the
Philosophical Society, the portraits of Barton and Patterson, and the
engravings for Barton and Wilson, doubtless in the hope of news that
this harmless part of the ship's cargo had been released and had
reached America. Meanwhile he had accumulated many more journals
to be sent to Vaughan, as he had now subscribed to most of them for the
society, and now felt compelled to write him of their impending shipment, despite his reluctance to distress his friends with the disappointing news that he had "learned with much chagrin of the capture of the
Madison" whose captain had been entrusted with the box sent in late
November. "I still have some hope that you will recover that shipment. . . . This time I hope we will be more fortunate" with the shipment being now sent, mostly of scientific journals in a box clearly
marked "Literary and Scientific Journals for the Philosophical Society
of Philadelphia." "My volume 3 moves forward and already I am
working toward finishing the plates to accompany the American edition. In two months I will send you the French edition."[12]

    His expressed hope that the box that went by the *Madison* might
eventually be received was not merely a wishful expression, in view of
the long tradition in both England and France that seed and plant

shipments enjoyed a status superior to blockade and embargo decrees. Scientific materials had much the same status.[13] However, in this case his hope was not rewarded. As the contents of later shipments would reveal, he sent replacement volumes for the set of Willdenow's *Species plantarum*, and would allude again to the lost engravings for Professor Barton and Alexander Wilson.

As François André Michaux settled into the scientific and scholarly life to which he had dedicated himself, one needs to bear in mind the historical context in which he was living and working. In the fall of 1808 Napoleon had determined to launch a bold and, as it turned out, reckless strike aimed at the hated rival, England, in the only way within reach of his land-bound prowess, by seizing control of the Iberian Peninsula to force compliance with his Continental blockade against British exports, most flagrantly defied in the harbors of Portugal. It was a costly move, unpopular at home, and seriously damaging to the morale of the army. The winter campaign on the peninsula imposed greater hardship and suffering on the army than even in its 1800 march across the Alps. Moreover, he was forced in January to leave it uncompleted in order to counter moves by Austria in the Danube regions.[14]

After a winter devoted to preparations, in spring the emperor led an army of 310,000 including 100,000 new conscripts, eastward to subjugate Austria again. In yet another costly campaign, which lasted through the summer of 1809, culminating in the two-day-long battle at Wagram, in the heart of Austria, one of the bloodiest battles in history, her subjugation had been completed. However, other attractions in the region delayed his return to Paris until October, at which time Michaux was occupied in gathering and packing the shipment destined for the ill-fated *Madison*. By the time it had been dispatched, the peace Napoleon had wrung from the Austrian monarch had been concluded and sweetened by the promise of a princess of the royal house to be substituted for the fruitless (for him) Empress Josephine.[15]

Two months later in a letter to William Bartram in March 1810, Michaux wrote that "our great Emperor is about to marry. The only good that will do, at present, is to prevent a great effusion of blood, by preserving the life of many thousand; considering that event will afford a continental peace for some time."[16] A week later to John Vaughan he was more specific in his comments: "Some great celebrations are being prepared for the marriage of the emperor. This event holds out to us at least two years of the Continental peace—it is always something"—a comment prescient indeed! It was almost precisely two years later when

Napoleon launched his next great adventure, his disastrous invasion of
Russia.[17]

It was with no small measure of ambivalence that Michaux observed these historic events unfolding. While as a patriotic Frenchman
he could not but take pride in the prowess of his fellow countrymen in
their imperial adventures, he consistently had nothing good to say for
the imperial dictatorship—a far cry from the laissez faire government
he admired in America where people "enjoy peaceably the fruit of their
labour under one of the best governments that exist in the world."[18]
More and more his government was displaying distressing defects.
Recent experiences had demonstrated the necessity of having his inno-
cent shipments to America await the company of a trusted friend, and
he was soon charging the police with seizing private mail, conditions
that forced him to have his letters hand-carried by a trusted traveler.

Even having a protector accompanying a shipment did not assure
its safe arrival. John Vaughan had written him in February 1810 of the
loss of a shipment sent the year before in the care of a traveler. Nevertheless, in August he ventured another, this one in the care of his
friend Rembrandt Peale, who had come to Paris shortly before Michaux himself had returned from Philadelphia in 1808.[19] Rembrandt,
the most successful of the several artist sons of Charles Willson Peale,
had become a trusted friend. It was a particularly precious shipment
that he was entrusting to his care, for it included thirty-three copies of
the first part of his *Histoire des arbres forestiers de l'Amérique septentrionale*,
the part devoted to the pines and spruces of America. Two letters from
Michaux to Vaughan accompanied the shipment.[20] One, in French,
appointed Vaughan his American agent: "Being always confident in
your friendship and knowing how much you aim to favor useful things,
I hope, despite your many duties, you will be willing to be charged with
my affairs in relation to the editions French and English of my work on
the forest trees of North America." The other, a long one in English,
spelled out in detail the disposition of the shipment: "Of these 33 copys
3 will be taken out, it is to say, one is for you, that I pray you to accept as a
mark of my gratitude, one for the Philosophical Society that I desire
you present to her in my name, one for the Agricultural Society of
Hollowell, wishing that copy to be send to your brother B. Vaughan,
who I hope will likewise present to her in my name."

Assuming that Vaughan would accept his nomination to serve as
his American agent, he proceeded to instruct him as to the disposition
of the remaining 30 copies. They were "to be disposed of at the price 6

dollars each copy, who is the same price they are sold by me in France."
Sixteen should be offered for sale in Philadelphia, first to those on a list
he suggested, which included the Agricultural Society, Linnaean Society, Drs. Barton and Wistar, Irénée du Pont, Mr. Fulton, Mr. W.
Hamilton, Mr. Muhlenburg, Mr. Bartram, and Mr. J. Barlow.[21] "However, it is well understood that I do not consider those persons under
the least obligation to take that work if it don't please them or find it of
too dear price. It is only that they might have the preference." As for the
remaining 14, he desired "Mr. Bradford to send 4 to Charleston, 2 to
Baltimore, 2 to New York, and 6 to Boston."[22] Of those for Charleston
he noted particularly that he wanted Henry Middleton of the Library
Society of that city to "get it" for the Society and that others, C. C.
Pinckney, Thomas Pinckney, and Mr. Middleton, himself, be offered
copies. He called attention to the table on page 15 listing the 144 species
represented in the work and noted that the price was to be 40 cents each
"American money" and that the bookseller could retain a 25 percent
commission. Finally, he expressed his need to get the proceeds as they
were received, and his great concern as to the fate of his entire project.
If 50 copies could not be sold, and no English edition was made in
America, "the French edition itself could not go on further" obliging
him "to suspend the publication . . . because the number of my subscriptions in France is not sufficient to pay my expenses."

During the month following that shipment to Vaughan of the first
part of his *Histoire des arbres*, obviously with mounting concern that he
might be forced to suspend publication of his pioneering work, Michaux relieved his gnawing fear with five more letters to Vaughan and
Wistar, all aiming to stimulate promotion of his work by them and the
Philosophical Society. One of these communications was a long, unad-
dressed statement signed and dated by him, headed "American Edition: To be communicated to any person who would undertake an
American edition." That document, dated September 10, 1810, written
in English and designed to encourage any interested publisher to
undertake the project, is significant. It contains, in fact, a summary of
what he deemed to be the design, intent, and importance of the work to
which he had dedicated himself.[23] Now in a position much like that of
Alexander Wilson, with the first volume of his *Ornithology* in his saddle
bag, setting out to secure new subscribers to defray the cost of the next
volume, Michaux had in the first part of his work a handsome sample to
serve as bait for any possible publisher who might be persuaded to
gamble on the project. And, as with Wilson, his early responses were
discouraging.[24]

But, as would soon become obvious, times were far from propitious for launching of any such undertaking during the parlous 1810–12 period. The constantly changing embargoes and unilateral international decrees were making communications and business dealings between the United States and Europe extremely hazardous and shipments of tangible materials even more of a gamble. Those were only the more obvious difficulties. Far more significant were those presented by the sad state of the American economy. The depradations inflicted on American shipping by the European combatants and the complex politics of Jefferson's Embargo had combined to throw the country into a steadily deepening economic depression that greatly diminished the likelihood of securing a publisher willing to undertake such an expensive and speculative undertaking. Communications were becoming increasingly difficult. Six months passed after Michaux had sent his formal proposal before it reached Vaughan, during which time conditions had steadily worsened. And they continued to worsen as war involving the United States loomed larger until, with its formal declaration on June 19, 1812, the country was plunged into a costly and fruitless shooting war without rhyme or reason, since over the years leading up to it American shipping had suffered greater losses to Napoleon than to Britain, and its nominal cause, the impressment of American sailors, which had been the American special grievance against England, found no place at all in the treaty that ended the conflict.[25]

Despite the hazards of the times, Michaux continued to make shipments of parts of his work as fast as they came to him from the printer; and continued assiduously to perform the duties he had assumed of keeping nineteenth-century American science abreast of contemporary developments abroad. To minimize the risks inherent in transatlantic communications, he made special precautions part of his routine procedure. All important letters were dispatched in duplicate, each by a different route, and not by the mail that went aboard in bags, for "the police take them," he explained, but in the personal care of trusted friends. Likewise, it became a regular requirement that each shipment should be put in the care of a traveler boarding the vessel for America. It is impressive that he managed to find so many American vessels still making the transit despite the blockade rules of France that forbade them to enter Continental ports.

In mid-January, for example, he wrote Vaughan that he was taking an opportunity accorded him by "Mr. Russell to send you by the frigate now at Lorient the collection of scientific journals for the society; also other books, which I have obtained for my work, which you and Mr. Bradford can sell for me . . . two copies of the *Statistique de la Nouvelle Espagne* containing two volumes and an atlas, although the price is enormous—57 dollars."[26] That still left him with ten more copies of that monumental work of Humboldt he needed to sell.[27] He concluded with other implications of the sad state of international affairs; a plea that any money sent him be sent by bill of exchange or in gold, and the precaution that letters to him should always be hand carried. There were bright spots, however—the significant news that at last he had secured sufficient subscribers for him to continue with the publication of the French edition and there had been good news from Vaughan, after fifteen months without a word. "I learn with pleasure," Michaux replied, "that there is in the making an American edition of my work. I am surprised that Mr. Bradford has not written me a word."[28]

It appears that Vaughan, in conveying the welcome news of an American edition of his work, had also expressed some doubt as to the reliability of Bradford's commitment. Nevertheless Michaux clung to the hope that in fact an American edition of *Histoire des arbres*[29] was under way at Bradford's, for six months later he still held that belief.

Meanwhile in a shipment made early in December 1811 by the American ship the *Constitution*, he sent copies of the remaining six parts of the work for the society and the others receiving gift copies, and advised Vaughan that the 300 copies of the illustrations requested for Bradford would be finished in fifteen days and sent him by the first opportunity. Included in that shipment was a great atlas for Mr. Randolph "who resides at Monticello," Jefferson's son-in-law, a "superb" but very expensive work, the *Galerie de Florence*, sent by Warden to Nicholas Biddle, then in the process of preparing his classic history of the Lewis and Clark expedition, many journals for the society, and a variety of learned works for both the society and "divers persons."[30] By the same vessel in a letter to Wistar he thanked the doctor for sending him a copy of Pike's expedition and said he gave it to his printer, who was so impressed by it that he made a translation of it which would appear in fifteen days.[31]

In reporting the contents of François André's letters, perhaps we dwell inordinately upon the two subjects that generally dominate them—his activities as book and journal supplier to the learned circles in the United States and the long and arduous progress of his work on the trees of North America, and perhaps risk giving the reader a picture of a narrowly focused man, who, on the contrary, was one always avidly interested in a wide spectrum of life and the contemporary scene, and always socially inclined and interested in making and keeping congenial friends. In fact, much of his December letter to Wistar was given over to introducing a greatly admired friend, the Portuguese savant Correa de Serra, who, after residing several years in Paris, had concluded that the time had come to abandon that war-dominated capital for the more peaceful air of Philadelphia. Describing Correa de Serra as former forester of the Royal Academy of Science of Portugal, a member of the leading learned societies of Europe, and a man greatly interested in the progress of the sciences and arts in the United States, Michaux assured Wistar that he would be well rewarded by making his acquaintance. To Vaughan he wrote a letter entirely devoted to introducing Correa de Serra to him and to "our philosophical society." There was in his December correspondence even a rare bit of evidence of susceptibility to the feminine beyond domestic scenes such as he had observed with warmth at the Benjamin Vaughan household. To John Vaughan he wrote "at the solicitation of a most amiable lady who is a great lover of plants of the tropics," asking Vaughan to solicit the aid of his brother, living in Jamaica, in securing for her the seeds of a list of plants, including among others those of the mango, breadfruit, avocado, colonial apricot, Mexican vanilla, and "other species of wild trees and shrubs."

While such peaceful interests occupied those devotees of science, on the wider scene all Europe and peripherally the United States as well were in a state of mounting ferment. The Peace of Tilsit, in 1807, had served to restrain the Russian bear while Napoleon concentrated on problems nearer home. Although his marriage to Marie Louise had given promise of two years of uneasy truce, during that interim Czar Alexander was becoming increasingly restive under the limitations that Tilsit had imposed on Russia's mutually beneficial trade with Britain. When it became obvious that Napoleon's armies were fully occupied with the stubborn resistance they were encountering on the Iberian Peninsula, the czar became ever more tolerant of violations of the Continental Blockade Napoleon had raised to choke off England's trade with the Continent. With the intent of forcing the czar to comply with the Tilsit accords, the emperor had abandoned the peninsular campaign to his generals, to devote his energies to building a massive military force, sufficiently powerful to fight a major war on the peninsula and another beyond his eastern borders.

In June 1812 a war-weary Europe watched as the emperor led his massive force of a half-million men across central Europe on its long and tragic march to Moscow. Eight months later, in January 1813, through the bitter cold of an exceptionally severe winter, Europe witnessed the return of the shattered, half-frozen, and half-starved remnant of the Grand Army, numbering less than one in ten of those who had set out in June, suffering its weary way across the German states without their magnetic leader, who had long since abandoned his dispirited troops to rush back to Paris to restore order after word reached him of a nearly successful coup designed to overthrow the empire.[32]

Meanwhile, mid mounting woes France had received a small measure of encouragement when news arrived from America that the United States had declared war on Great Britain, proclaimed June 20, 1812, by President Madison.[33]

After assembling three more cases of books and journals for the American Philosophical Society and its members, preparing the requisite declarations for duty, and entrusting them to the hazards of wartime commerce, Michaux wrote an interesting letter to Wistar, from which we excerpt these paragraphs:

> You can have no doubt as to how agreeable a surprise it has been for me to have met again our mutual friend and former travel companion Mr. J. Biddle.[34] I am now under obligation to him for the pleasure and opportunity for a better acquaintance with the curiosities of Paris, which I have little visited in a long time. We have climbed to the tops of the tallest buildings of this great capital, and we have penetrated the depths of the earth upon which it stands, the immense caverns from which was extracted the stones which were used to construct its buildings. A great part of those caverns comprise the Catacombs where are gathered the bones of fourteen cemeteries, estimated to contain about two million people—the population of Paris is some 600,000 souls. Among the millions of skulls that I saw, all of which are arranged in a most orderly way, I noticed that one in twenty have the coronal suture with meshing junctions so profound that they make together a single unit of bone. In short, it provided a good course in osteology.

> The famous school of Rouen where they made models in beeswax of the parts of the anatomy has failed and no longer makes them. However, a pupil of Lemonnier, director of an establishment, which is attached to the school of medicine, is reported to make the models you desire, but twice the size, being five feet long, requiring three hundred pounds of beeswax and ten months

to make. They ask five hundred dollars for it—an enormous price I think you should reject.[35]

Delays in the diplomatic affairs that had brought Biddle to Paris as courier caused his departure to be several times deferred, allowing Michaux time to secure from Germany some surgical instruments and medical treatises for Wistar and other books specifically for Dr. Barton, Dr. Wistar, Nathaniel Biddle, and Rev. Muhlenburg.[36] These, with a last minute inclusion of 300 copies of the eleventh and twelfth parts of Michaux's *Sylva* for Bradford, Lt. Biddle had consented to have placed on the *Hornet*, the ship that was to take him back to the States. In his letter to Vaughan apprising him of the shipment, Michaux mentioned that he had written Alexander Wilson for three copies of his *Ornithology* and a copy of the latest edition of Jedidiah Morse's *Geography,* while warning him that the American minister, Joel Barlow, had advised him that for security he should address those books to him and send them on a government ship.[37] In a postscript he thanked Wistar again for sending the report of Pike's expedition, which he arranged to have published in Paris, and promised him a copy. Doubtless with a like intent he asked that Wistar send him that of the Lewis and Clark expedition.[38]

Alas, nearly four months later, in mid-May, Michaux wrote Vaughan that "in spite of all good intentions of my good friend Capt. Biddle, he did not get the shipment aboard the *Hornet*. It is most distressing." Barlow had agreed to write again to Cherbourg to urge Capt. Jones to put them aboard his man-of-war, the *Wasp*. But the society would have to claim them at any port that he put into. Yet he was now doubtful that Capt. Jones would take them, as he had refused to take for him a small parcel weighing no more than a pound. In fact, Barlow had advised that the only way to have the society's shipments sent by naval vessels would be for the society to obtain from the president of the United States a permit for the captains to receive periodical scientific works, if addressed to the Philosophical Society.[39]

France in 1812 required all but superhuman patience of its citizenry. Of a shipment made at this time he commented that "God knows when it will depart and when it will arrive." Those doubts were by no means the last word on its difficulties. Six weeks later in a despairing note to Vaughan he wrote: "What chagrin for me! Now for six months, nothing for the society. Many journals but no means to send them." Still hopeful, he had arranged for his friend John Morton, who was going to Baltimore, to carry the seventeenth, eighteenth, nineteenth and twentieth parts, of his work, which would be entirely completed on February 1, 1813. His letter added these doleful comments: "Commercial affairs here go from bad to worse. The news from Spain is bad. The Grand Army has evacuated Moscow after having burned the last tenth of the city which remained. In Paris a month ago we almost fell into a terrible revolution through a conspiracy which nearly succeeded. Had it succeeded civil war would be raging in all its madness and Paris would be like Moscow."[40]

On the wider European scene Napoleon's disastrous Russian adventure had sorely tarnished the shining image of the emperor as an invincible leader, seriously weakening the bonds of force and fear that had kept many of his satellite states in subservience. Several were soon emboldened to cast their lots with the growing alliances fostered by England and the czar. Although it had been a chastened Napoleon who had arrived back in Paris in November, he soon recovered his irrepressible belief in his own invincibility. After energetically putting together yet another army of new, ever-younger and more reluctant conscripts, by March 1813 he was again beyond the Rhine on the fields of Mars, beating the German states back into submission.

During the latter half of 1813 and the first quarter of 1814, Napoleon, in the field with his troops, from time to time displayed again his military genius; but more often he appeared a wounded bear at bay, striking out in desperation at one or another of his surrounding tormentors, sometimes breaking free of encirclement, only to be forced to stand and fight again. Eventually, the hopeless outlook resulted in Napoleon's surrender and abdication on April 13, 1814, and his banishment to Elba.[41]

An uncommonly calm and businesslike letter from Michaux that reached Vaughan four months later reported that the three valuable boxes that had been at Cherbourg for more than a year had been returned to him. He would send selected items from them by Ferdinand Hassler, the head of the United States Coast Survey, who had been trapped abroad by the War of 1812.[42] In that letter his customary closing comment on European current events, which so long had contained only bad news, was replaced by a happier comment: "The season has been magnificent and everyone looks forward to a bountiful harvest."[43] However, conditions in France continued chaotic and communication with the United States had been very nearly severed. A letter written in September 1813 which managed to reach Vaughan reported that "I have been without letters from you since June 16, 1812. The police open and burn all letters indiscriminately. . . . Never has business been worse. The war begins again. God knows when it will end."[44]

That was the last letter we find either to or from Vaughan for another ten months. Nevertheless, conscientious as always, Michaux continued his efforts to discover and utilize ways to send the society's accumulations of journals and the books he continued to find and purchase. During that lapse in the Michaux-Vaughan correspondence Vaughan had received a letter from Obadiah Rich of Boston that would have been of immense interest and encouragement to Michaux. During the previous year on Rich's visit to Philadelphia, Vaughan had shown him a collection of the plates intended for use in an American edition of Michaux's work on American trees. If Bradford and Inskeep did not intend to go on with the project, Rich wished to purchase them with the intention of translating the French edition and publishing the work "to advance that delightful science among my countrymen."[45]

It was not until late in June 1814 that Michaux's correspondence with his American friends resumed with a letter to Dr. Wistar.[46] Napoleon had by then been on Elba for nearly two months. The First Treaty of Paris, which reduced France back to her 1792 boundaries, was in the final stages of negotiation and would soon be signed. Louis XVIII, brother of Louis XVI, the Monsieur, brother of the king, who had been the principal sponsor of André Michaux's Persian mission, had been put upon the vacated throne of France. Michaux commented to Wistar on some aspects of those events:

> *I have entertained the hope that the reduction of France (resulting from the coalition of 11 nations aiding this transition) would bring universal peace, but English liberality does not extend all the way to the American nation.*
>
> *The American and English negotiators are about to reconcile their differences at Ghent. I hope the outcome will be a happy one but I fear English pretenses, of which one has reason to be apprehensive because of the declaration of the Allied powers not to interfere in her differences with America.*

A few days later in a detailed letter to John Vaughan he had more in the same vein. "We have after so many victories succumbed to peace and are smaller than in 25 years. We have peace, trade is dead, the army very discontented, crying continually. *'Vive l'Empereur!'* "[47]

Through friends at the American Legation, particularly Jackson, secretary of the Legation, arrangements had finally been made for Michaux to send by the American vessel *John Adams,* in the care of

William H. Crawford,[48] the retiring American minister to France, all the large accumulation of journals and books for the society, including those that were to have been taken by Captain Biddle more than two years before, and the 300 copies of the plates for the final numbers of his *Histoire des arbres*, which had been completed for more than a year. For the use of Vaughan, his agent in the matter, he appended a page-long summary of the work headed "Edition française," indicating his continuing expectation of an American edition, concluding it with this summary of the price to be charged for it: "The price of each number is at 1 doll. 50¢; the 1st vol. 4 numbers 6 doll.—2nd vol. 8 numbers 12 doll. and the 3rd vol. 12 numbers 18 doll. In all—36 doll."

Three weeks later, still taking advantage of the safe conduct provided by returning minister Crawford, before the *John Adams* sailed, he sent another note to Vaughan to go by him. It told him that after his long letter in which he had mentioned Jackson's help, he had made the acquaintance of the gentleman and was delighted to find him a most agreeable man, very interested in natural history.[49] Along with the works being sent Vaughan for the Philosophical Society and those for Dr. Wistar, Dr. Warren of Boston, and Speir Smith, "son of the General," of Baltimore, all going by the *John Adams*, was also a collection of works "for my account," probably works received in exchange for his *Histoire*, which he wished Vaughan to sell for him. The list is interesting: six four-page maps of the French Empire, six maps of Europe, three octavo Bibles, six large Bibles with Bible atlases accompanying each, a costly illustrated edition of the *Fables of Fontaine*, a copy of his father's *Flora*, a three-volume illustrated *Travels in the Ottoman Empire*, and a French-Spanish dictionary.[50] That John Vaughan was to go to the trouble to dispose of that miscellaneous inventory for Michaux's benefit is indicative of the warm friendship that had developed between the men, reminiscent of the decades of mutual benefit correspondence between John Bartram and Peter Collinson.[51] Further indicating Michaux's friendship and esteem for his American friend is a note and a bound set of *l'Histoire des arbres* sent in December to John Vaughan— the first bound set he had sent to America: "I pray Monsieur J. Vaughan accept this copy in exchange for that which he has, it being most probably not bound, [from] his much obligated servant, F. André Michaux."[52]

CHAPTER 26

~§ Paris, 1814–1819,
The North American Sylva

WITH THE SIGNING of the Treaty of Ghent on Christmas Eve 1814, ending the War of 1812, most of the hazards of Franco-American communication and commerce were removed. The brief interval of peace that ensued provided three months of unprecedented activity in the scientific and cultural commerce between Michaux and his American friends. Writing a month later, Michaux acknowledged Vaughan's letter of November 21 reporting the safe arrival of the *John Adams* with all those things sent under the protection of Crawford. He told Vaughan that another large box of journals and books was on its way and that he was busy preparing yet another. That letter and several that followed in rapid succession acknowledged remittances of funds to support their reviving cultural commerce. Among the items on the way to Vaughan were the long completed later numbers of his *l'Histoire des arbres* to round out the gift copies for the Philosophical Society, Benjamin Vaughan, for the Hallowell Agricultural Society, Thomas Jefferson, and Bradford. In April he wrote of yet another shipment composed mostly of medical books for Dr. Wistar and Dr. Warren of Boston, and other scientific works for Zack Collins, Speir Smith of Baltimore, and for McMahon.[1]

Although the peace that followed Napoleon's abdication had continued to hold throughout those busy months, it became immediately precarious on March 1, 1815, the day Bonaparte again set foot on the shore of Provence. Soon after his abdication the heads and ministers of the victorious Allies had convened in Vienna to divide the spoils of victory and to plan measures to put more distance between France and the erstwhile emperor. On March 7 a courier arrived in Vienna with the electrifying news that Napoleon had escaped Elba after less than nine months of exile, during which many of his former leaders had gathered around him again. By the time news of his escape reached the assembled Congress of Vienna, he and his coterie had landed at Cap d'Antibes. Undaunted by the cool reception accorded them in Provence, Napoleon and some 1,600 followers departed the Mediterranean shore aiming for Grenoble and the more friendly regions of the interior Alpine foothills, and thence to Lyons where the gates were thrown wide for an enthusiastic reception of his steadily growing train of followers. He reached Paris March 20 and proceeded directly to the Tuileries Palace from which, but two days before, Louis XVIII had fled. Thus began the amazing but infamous Hundred Days and its renewal of the fruitless slaughter that had marked France for a full quarter century.[2]

Writing to John Vaughan in early May, Michaux reported the reaction to these events by the now unusually united European family of nations: "We are in attendance at great events. Seven to eight hundred thousand men are on the point of entering France."[3]

A few days later in a letter to Samuel Bradford he was more expansive:

> We are verging on the moment when the most terrible war is going to burst over France as all the powers of Europe which are already united on our frontiers—5 or 600 thousand men all set to destroy the French army. If courage and talent could make up for numbers I believe that victory would be granted us.
>
> All these misfortunes are the result of the follies of the Bourbons, an impious race who by their inept measures alienated the masses of the merchants and people of means of whose numbers have risen to 12 million out of the 25 million that compose the population.
>
> Napoleon leaves Paris in a few days to put himself at the head of the army.[4]

Seven weeks later, before dawn on June 18, 1815, an Allied army of 213,000 men drawn from those combined forces, met Napoleon's hastily reconstructed army of 126,000 on a rain-sodden Belgian field near the village of Waterloo. Following a fierce, daylong battle, it became clear to Napoleon as night approached that he had lost his great gamble. Leaving behind 25,000 dead and wounded and 8,000 prisoners, he and his vanquished force, closely followed by the victors, retreated to Paris where on June 22 he appeared on center stage for the last time as he went through the ceremony of his Second Abdication. Two weeks later, with the Allies in possession of the city, Louis XVIII was restored to the throne of France. By July 15 Napoleon was on his way to St. Helena.[5]

Although Michaux was harboring great concern for the fate of France, he was, nevertheless, able to keep his attention unswervingly on the pursuits to which he had dedicated himself, despite the ordeals and trials being imposed on the country both by her own leaders and her enemies. The primary purpose of the letter he had written to Bradford in early May, even as he was predicting the terrible times ahead, had been to encourage him, now that the war with England had ended, to "resume" the publication of the American edition of his work. "I think you already have the certainty of success of this enterprise from the reception the public has accorded the first part. It is something I greatly desire to know, inasmuch as, if you have renounced the publication, I will busy myself with producing an abridged edition with black illustrations."

He was thinking of new enterprises. "I presume," he continued, "you have seen the beautiful map of Mexico published by M. Humboldt. As a special favor I have obtained twenty copies . . . although it is not regularly sold without the work" (*Statistique de Mexique*). He announced his "intention to have it reengraved in Paris, with the addition of lower and upper Louisiana, making use of the map of Lafond and the travels of Lewis and Pike," and published "on a grand scale" on two sheets. "If you think, Monsieur, that I would be able to place 150 copies of this map at $4.00 each I will immediately occupy myself with getting it engraved."

Apparently it was from the ever-faithful Vaughan that he learned the bad news of Bradford's failure, for in a letter in late August (his first after Waterloo), he wrote: "I am very distressed that Bradford has failed. If no other bookseller wishes to undertake the translation of my work, rather than lose the 500 copies of the illustrations I would carry out a project which I am discussing with M. Correa and he will explain to you."[6]

He continued with a report on their cultural commerce. Among the items he had gotten the requested artist materials for Mr. Sully and the works of Humboldt for the Charleston Library Society and thirteen copies of a new map of South America to be sold for his account.[7] His customary Franco-American social function came in for attention, too. He reported to Vaughan that he had, as requested, shown "Mr. (Charles) Hare of Philadelphia" the sights of Paris. Framery had been named by the restored Louis XVIII to be the consul general to the United States, and he would be residing in Philadelphia, as would also the brother of their mutual friend Beaujour, who would be the new consul there.[8] There were questions about several long-delayed book shipments and then, his business concluded, he unburdened himself of the bitterness he felt at the treatment being imposed upon the French people after their "rescue from the Corsican dictator."[9]

On the same day in the same vein he also wrote in English to the well-known Philadelphia nurseryman and horticulturalist Bernard McMahon, telling him he had sent the requested six copies of his father's *Flora*, along with some literary publications for John Vaughan in the same box. He added these three paragraphs:

The great events which have happened in france since the return of the ex-Emperor have throw the country into a critical situation. The Allies who term themselves the friends of the french people, show really that the are their greatest enemy. enormous contributions are lay on the people; & Commerce and arts are dead and no prospect soon to flourish.

It is said that the armys of the sovereigns and princes who have united for to deliver france of the tyranny of Bonaparte, are of 800 thousand they are all present in france, living on the inhabitants of the country or of the towns. It appear that they will remain perhaps 2 or 3 years it will not go way before they all partys will be reconcility with the King.

Certainly I dont see no better places at present than America, and every day I hear of people having the project to go to the United States.[10]

The remaining four months of 1815 were marked by a more active commerce between Michaux and his American correspondents than ever before. With the cessation of the fighting that activity was possible despite complaints of the sad state of the economy, the ineptitude and unpopularity of the king, and the burdens imposed by the Allied occupation. More pertinent to our study are the renewed efforts by Michaux to give a new start to the aborted American edition of his work.[11]

Two letters to Vaughan in December typify his concerns as 1815 drew to a close. The earlier one introduced to Vaughan Dr. Edmind Valli of Florence, "who is offering himself to the United States to conduct research and experiments dealing with yellow fever. He is among the savants of Europe and has written upon those maladies. He has had the courage to expose himself to them in Constantinople and by that means has proved that medical treatment reduces its mortality although it does not prevent the disease."[12] His letter went on to report that France was "in a most deplorable situation" and that "in the spring there will be a great migration to all parts of America." In the second letter he wrote:

I desire much to know if anyone wishes to make a translation of my work in the United States. If not I will have the trans-

lation done in Paris for publication with black and white illustrations which will permit sale at a quarter the price.

It is said that more than twenty thousand passports have been applied for to leave France. A great division of political opinion continues and most certainly the king can hold on (at least by what is said) only by 25 thousand English troops in Paris and 150 thousand Allies who occupy our strongholds. For myself, I never involve myself in political affairs.[13]

After the disruption of normal life caused by the momentous events of 1815, the life of François André Michaux again became that of a popular, scholarly Parisian bachelor enjoying an active social life within the scientific and intellectual circles of the city. From his comfortable, conveniently located quarters at Place St. Michel No. 8, close by the Seine and near the center of the artistic and scientific heart of the city, he was now able to resume, with fewer interruptions, the useful functions to which he had dedicated himself—the enhancement of the knowledge, appreciation, and improvement of the forests of both France and the United States, the two countries dear to his heart, while at the same time serving the relatively isolated American scientific circles, in which he had friends to whom he was devoted, from Maine to South Carolina, as their liaison with the center of nineteenth-century science. While that cultural commerce produced for him a modest pecuniary profit, judging from his correspondence, one cannot but be convinced that he found much more rewarding returns in the relations and friendships developed with many of the more notable men of science in both France and America, as well as in the free access to a steady flow of the relatively costly scientific works of Europe, enabling him to gain from them a rich fare for his own insatiable appetite for scientific information.

Apart from those objectives to which he dedicated most of his adult life, François André, the man, comes through to us as an interested, intelligent, even fascinated observer at the focal point of action, during a singularly dramatic period in the history of Western civilization. With the exception of the time given to his two American missions, he had been in Paris witnessing events from the early days of the Revolution, through the Reign of Terror and the Empire, and many years thereafter.

In marked contrast to the eventful first half of his life, after the climax year of 1815 the life of the younger Michaux generally appears to have been one of conscientiously maintaining his scientific liaisons

Black Walnut.

Juglans nigra.

with his American friends and completing and distributing his *North American Sylva,* while cultivating the informal social life he obviously relished that provided him with associations with the great and near great figures of the Parisian scientific community. Those associations had increasingly involved him in active participation in a growing list of scientific and cultural societies. Obviously, to attempt to report in any detail those repetitious years would be neither fruitful nor interesting. Only minimal recounting of them is needed to provide a framework on which to hang the more interesting aspects of Michaux's life during the years of his maturity and the insights they provide of the cosmopolitan scientific circles in which he moved.

In 1816, for example, a year typical of the dozen or more to follow, there were some six or eight shipments of his selections of books and journals to Vaughan, many for the society but others for distribution to Michaux's American friends, medical works for Dr. Wistar and Dr. Warren of Boston, geographical and travel works for the Pinckneys and the Library Society of Charleston, botanical works for Dr. Barton, agricultural works for Jefferson, and miscellaneous works for Speir Smith of Baltimore, Benjamin Vaughan of Maine, and Philadelphia friend Zack Collins. From time to time new recipients were added: mathematician Ferdinand Hassler, newly appointed director of the United States Coastal Survey; Dr. Daniel Drake of Ohio, finishing his medical studies in Philadelphia; and Mrs. Gabriel Manigault of Charleston, who desired whole sets of a variety of cultural works, such as four volumes of Voltaire, sixteen volumes of critic and playwright François de la Harpe, a protégé of Voltaire, a two-volume French dictionary and a five-volume ancient history, and many others, all to grace the splendid Manigault mansion which was nearing completion when Michaux was there.[14] In addition, with almost every shipment went some works Michaux had received in exchange for his work, some to be consigned to booksellers Bradford or Dobson to be disposed of on a 20 percent basis for his own account. Each collection entailed the exercise of considerable discernment, knowledge of a wide variety of cultural resources, and mature judgment of the tastes and desires of each of his American recipients.[15]

At the same time there were often other duties of a sort that many of his American friends had become accustomed to expect from him. Current examples were his services as mentor and guide for Dr. Bar-

Juglans nigra, *black walnut. From P. J. Redouté's illustration for* The North American Sylva *by F. A. Michaux, Paris, 1817. (Courtesy of the Rare Book Room of the University of South Carolina Library)*

ton's son, Edward, when he arrived in Paris for study abroad, finding suitable quarters for him, taking him on a tour of the sights of the city and introducing him to congenial potential friends. A little later, there were two more young men from Boston, Edward Everett[16] and George Ticknor,[17] both destined for brilliant careers, now aiming for Göttingen for study at the university there, demonstrating further Michaux's continuing interest in Franco-American intellectual relations, as does also the interest he was taking in Albert Gallatin's[18] appointment and anticipated arrival in Paris to serve as the new minister to France.[18] Space permits no more than samplings from his 1816 letters to the United States.

In a letter to John Vaughan he sent to mathematician Frederick Hassler "a thousand compliments and wishes for him to enjoy more tranquility of body and spirit than he could have had in Europe." On the despairing temper then prevailing in France he commented that "there will be a great migration to the United States in spring, for in political opinion, there is far from any accord."[19]

In a letter to Vaughan carried by Petry, newly appointed French consul for New Orleans, he cited the experience of young Edward Barton to illustrate the truth of the report "that all letters and journals are seized just as in the reign of Bonaparte," with the information that "Ed Barton has been three months in Paris without receiving any letter from the U.S."[20] On the French economy he reported that "commercial affairs languish." He added that he had written their friend Correa de Serra to congratulate him on his having been named Portuguese minister to the United States.

To John Vaughan, after discussing the routine matters and finances relating to his book shipments, he turned to the subject uppermost in his mind: "I am busy making the English translation of my work and it is going so well that before four months I shall be able to send you the first part. . . . It can be sold at 30 percent less than the French."

After telling Vaughan that a 20 percent mark up should be charged on the books sold for his account, he devoted the remainder of his letter to the most disturbing news of the day:

> *A great conspiracy, intending probably the overthrow of the Royal Government, was on the point of exploding last week. But the attempt has failed and we are assured that several hundred persons have been imprisoned.*
>
> *There is also near Grenoble a revolutionary movement in which more than twelve hundred men tried to seize possession of the city, but they have been suppressed by the Royal troops, and*

two hundred persons have been captured. You see, Monsieur and friends, that our situation is not very pretty.[21]

On June 14 he wrote that with his next book shipment he would send Vaughan seven copies of the "Great French, Latin and Chinese *Dictionnaire Chinois*," a 1,400-page work prepared by Guignes under the sponsorship of Napoleon, one copy as a gift to the society and the others for sale for his account.[22]

In another instance of the function he had assumed as promoter of Franco-American cultural advancement he introduced "Mr. Gallaudet," who would be "bringing you this letter.[23] He has been appointed by the State of Connecticut to instruct and advise on the teaching of the deaf and mute. He comes from the School of M. l'Abbé Siscard, priest for the deaf and mute. This young man has been professor at the Institute and has a rare intelligence and a high degree of instruction."

In a letter to Caspar Wistar he extended his thanks to the doctor for books brought him by Dubac.[24] In return he was sending the doctor a newly published pharmacy book. One of the copies of Wistar's own newly published *System of Anatomy* (the first American book on the subject) sent him for presentation to Dr. Bayer, he had delivered to Raffeneau-Delile, "who knows Dr. Bayer," to make the formal presentation. As another intended recipient of Wistar's work, "M. Garard, has died, the copy sent for him has been given to the Bibliothèque d'Ecole du Medicin, a large library used by all the students."

> *The most interesting news from France is the return of good weather after 3 months of rain, which, if it had lasted 15 more days, would have brought famine and 2,000,000 deaths.*
>
> *For the rest, my dear Doctor, we have in Paris much tranquility. More than 10,000 spies for the provost courts to judge each act of speaking with lack of respect for the King and his august family, and still we have (in France) 150,000 foreign soldiers*, being all the price for their bringing us the sacred principle of legitimacy. *We continue to pay each. . . . you see, we are in times of compensation.*

On September 18 writing to Vaughan again after a largely repetitive letter in early July, Michaux acknowledged receipt of two remittances aggregating 4,800 francs, adding the comment that "those funds will be useful and agreeable for me to begin my English edition."[25] The maps, also sent by Vaughan, had also very opportunely reached him, for "the editor of the new map of Louisiana had suspended his work until their arrival."

The letter continued with a request that any copies of his work that Vaughan still had on hand be exchanged for copies of Jedediah Morse's *Geography* or his *American Gazateer,* for "when the first part of my English edition is published no one will wish the French any longer." He went on to confirm that he was sending another shipment of books for sale for his account, among them was a great work, *The Anatomy of the Elephant,* and many others, and several copies of the *Dictionnaire Chinois,* which he received from the minister of the interior in part payment for money still due him from his last American expedition. The *Dictionnaire* is a work Bonaparte had had done at great expense. One of them was a gift for Vaughan and another for the Society. For Thomas Jefferson there was *Les Mémoires de la Société d'agriculture.* He closed with the latest news of their mutual friend Edward Barton. He had "left 8 days ago for Edinburgh"; and then this final comment: "We have in Paris 40 thousand English and the same in the rest of France."

The record of the year 1816 closes with a letter to Vaughan in mid-December to accompany a supply of copies of a prospectus for his *North American Sylva* which he requested Vaughan to distribute to the libraries in Philadelphia, New York, Charleston, and other cities and to friends in both North and South. For these added burdens imposed on his distant friend to whom he realized he was "already much indebted . . . this will be drawing anew on your kindness in selling all of my English edition." Nevertheless, confident as always of Vaughan's assistance, he launched into details to guide his booksellers. They should be allowed $1.25 of the sale price of $4.00 for each half volume. The edition would number 600 copies in all, of which 100 would be uncolored. He planned to retain 150 in color and 40 uncolored for sale in Europe.

He concluded with news of their friends: Dr. Price, who brought with him Vaughan's last two letters, had reached Paris two weeks back and been introduced to Senator Grégoire, who greeted him warmly.[26] Bonpland had left France for Rio-janvier to explore again in South America, this time alone and "at his own expense, his affairs being in disorder."[27]

Michaux closed, as usual, with his customary comment on affairs in France. "Decidedly, the Royalists-constitutionalists at the head of which is the king and his ministers—have the upper hand over the Ultra-Royalists, which means that you will not keep for long our *illustrious* ambassador," Beaujour.

The pattern of Michaux's life during the next few years continued remarkably little altered from that for 1816. He remained a very busy man. His book shipments and the progress made toward completion of the English version of his work even appears to have accelerated but without any apparent neglect of his participation in the enjoyment of his services to Americans, most of whom, but not all, were men of scientific interests, newly arrived in France, or to fellow countrymen going to the United States. Both the frequency and size of his shipments of cultural works reached their peak as the difficulties of overseas communications diminished, and more Americans desiring European works joined the established group centered in Philadelphia and the Philosophical Society. Shipments became as frequent as one a month. In New England, Bowdoin College, in Boston, Jacob Bigelow, and booksellers Root in Boston and Louis Belair in New York as well as James Eastborn, also in New York, began tapping the Michaux supply line for European science and culture.[28] In Baltimore the amateur botanist Victor LeRoy joined Speir Smith in using his services, and in Charleston the South Carolina Medical Society and banker-botanist Stephen Elliott[29] added their patronage to that long established with the Pinckneys and the Library Society, while in Philadelphia a more active bookseller, Mathew Carey, emulated Dobson in taking advantage of the discriminating advice and conscientious services Michaux had long rendered the Dobson establishment.

On the state of affairs in France, Michaux continued to record his comments. In February 1817 he reported that "the feared famine has waned and the government has consolidated itself, and the ultra-royalists are now in complete disarray." However, there is again the prospect of a very good harvest although prices continue inconceivably high. Among the Allied occupation troops "the Prussians we have act badly and are so detested that the presence of Count Rupin (the king of Prussia) is not agreeable to Parisians."[30]

His 1817 letters continued to mention a remarkable number of notable American visitors and Europeans setting out for America with his blessing. In February there was young William Keating, armed with a letter of introduction from a member of the Philosophical Society, to pursue postgraduate study in mineralogical chemistry.[31] In May he reported the arrival of their mutual friend lawyer-banker John Sergeant, who had come on a diplomatic mission to Paris.[32] In August it was "young Dobson," son of the Philadelphia bookseller, who "has agreed that I be his correspondent. I have bought many scientific books for him and subscribed to sixteen scientific and literary journals to send regularly to him." Also "young Vanusin has arrived in France and I have introduced him to many persons. He has been admitted to the Ecole des Mines," while "Dr. Price is well and Paris pleases him."[33] Also we find a long letter in English written in September to Dr. Bigelow of Boston, giving him the advice he requested in respect to his *Florula Bostoniensis*.[34]

More pertinent to our subject is the progress made by Michaux in 1817 toward the completion of his *North American Sylva*. In January he had shipped to Vaughan 260 copies in color and 32 in black of the first half volume of the English version, which he had, himself, undertaken to translate from the French edition. Of them some were gift copies for Vaughan to distribute: one in color and one in black for "our society; for you, my dear friend, one in color and one in black; for B. Vaughan, one in color; for T. Jefferson, one in color; for Correa de Serra, one in color; for the Society of Agriculture [of Philadelphia?], one in color; for William Barton, one in color; and one in color for Mr. Bigelow of Boston." Each of the 600 copies printed will be numbered.[35]

However, now there were new worries. After all the work to bring his project to this point, he was coming to realize that even when finished his work would need a supplemental volume to complete its coverage of all the American forest trees, and it now was apparent that his eyesight had become too feeble for him to make another trip to America to prepare it. That being the prospect, he would grant the bookseller the right to print four or five hundred more copies to go with an anticipated supplemental volume.[36] By spring more grave doubts were haunting him. "I harbor a certain presentment of its failure of success. What chagrins me is the embarrassment and trouble I have caused you." Those fears persisted into the summer. In July, when he sent only 360 copies of the second half volume, he explained that he had not made a larger shipment "because of my doubt of success, despite the encouragement of Americans here. Meanwhile the translation continues, but not the printing of the plates, which is very expensive. I must have in the United States 350 sales to continue." Perhaps, also, the preparation of the plates was becoming too burdensome and difficult in view of his failing sight and the retouching of the color plates was taking all his time.[37]

In December he concluded a letter he wrote to Dr. Wistar with a plea to his old friend: "I count, dear Doctor, upon your friendship to help me procure 175 buyers, the number necessary to publish the last three parts." However, it was too late for the doctor to assist his friend.[38] He died in January 1818 before that letter could have reached him. We do not know when word of the doctor's death reached Paris, but when it did it was for Michaux a stunning blow. Without doubt Wistar had been the most congenial of his many American friends. For a full decade the volume of his correspondence with him had been exceeded only by that with Vaughan, much of which was merely routine business in nature. His letters to Wistar reveal a warm and sympathetic mutual relationship and a wide range of common interests, among which medical science was clearly dominant. In a letter written in June he told Vaughan that he had inserted a memorial eulogy to Dr. Wistar in the *Moniteur*, a journal that, during the Napoleon regime, had become the official organ of the French government.[39]

At this time Michaux was becoming increasingly concerned by the mounting impositions he was inflicting on his friend Vaughan. As 1817 receded into history he gave thought and words to the great and accumulating debt he owed to his steady, dependable, and helpful friend for all his assistance and support—help that had been essential to the financing and production of his magnum opus: "As we approach the end of the year, I take this occasion to renew the expression of my respect and attachment and constant devotion; and also the wish I have for your good health."[40]

In February 1818 Michaux launched another effort to relieve Vaughan of this latest burden by making another serious attempt to interest a Philadelphia bookseller, this time Mathew Carey and Sons, in an agreement to purchase, as they appeared, 350 or even the entire 450 uncommitted sets of the *Sylva* at the incredibly low figure of $2.86 for each of its seven parts, or $20 a set for those with colored plates and $1.50 for the uncolored. He told Vaughan, in a letter accompanying a draft of the proposal, that he had reason to believe that the Careys would accept, and in anticipation he, himself, had signed the draft in order to advance the conclusion of the transaction. However, before submitting it to Carey he requested Vaughan to be certain that Dobson, whom he still preferred, would not be willing to undertake the same commitment.[41] In an addendum to this letter Michaux corrected downward by twenty-five the 450 figure he had mentioned as available for purchase by Carey. He had forgotten the twenty sets engaged to the minister of the interior for the public libraries and five he was "forced to give to the police."

Nevertheless, despite the Careys' lack of interest, Michaux "stuck to his last." In mid-June 1818 he wrote that "this English edition of my work has caused me great torment; I much wish that Mathew Carey had accepted the proposal I made him." A week later he wrote that "it is with great pleasure that I inform you that my work will be entirely finished

on the first of next January. Never has a work cost so much pain, trouble, fatigue and expense!"[42]

Characteristically, Michaux was as overoptimistic in respect to the progress of production as he was overpessimistic in respect to its reception. It was not early in January but mid-July 1819 before the final part came from the printer. Doubtless part of that delay may be accounted for by the necessity of reprinting the text of the first part. It will be recalled that when he started on his English version of his *Histoire des arbres* he had told Vaughan that he was making the English translation himself. After the first part of his English version had been published and distributed, he came to realize that his command of the English language was inadequate and so, before declaring the work completed, he had decided to have the translator of the subsequent parts supply an improved text to be substituted for his version. That done, finally, on July 19, 1819, he was able to write to Vaughan (in English, incidentally) that the work was complete:

> It is with great pleasure that I inform you of the expedition (by the **Stephane** which is to sail the 1st of August) of a box which contains the 6th and 7th numbers of my work, which is thus wholly completed—also the reimpression of the 1st number that has been considered a benefit to the work. That number is to be delivered gratis to the subscribers as to those who will purchase the work.
>
> The box contains 180 copies of each of those numbers. . . . I will be very glad if you will have sent to Messrs. Kirk, Root & Son, Booksellers at Boston. It is a very respectable house and solid.[43]

In his next letter, a routine one, he sealed its conclusion with a renewed confession of his obligation to Vaughan. "I bear always the burden of the pain and embarrassment that this work has caused you. How happy I would be if you were able to witness my gratitude. It will be eternal."[44]

While Michaux was announcing to Vaughan the completion of his English-language edition, even as he was continuing to express his doubts that the work would be accorded the recognition he had hoped for, there were signs that those fears were unwarranted. As early as November of 1817 Hezikiah Howe, a bookseller at New Haven, had written Vaughan that in view of the mounting interest in botany he

Gordonia lasianthus, *loblolly bay. From P. J. Redouté's illustration for* The North American Sylva *by F. A. Michaux, Paris, 1817. (Courtesy of the Rare Book Room of the University of South Carolina)*

wished to subscribe for six sets of the *Sylva*. His letter was soon followed by one from Lewis D. Belair, a New York bookseller, asking for four copies of those parts of the *Sylva* then available. Six weeks later Belair had written for ten more sets.[45]

It was also in the latter part of 1817 that Michaux was delighted to renew a long-standing family friendship that had begun thirty years back when his father settled in Charleston. Beginning in the dark days of the 1790s the name J. J. Himely appears and reappears in the Michaux record. Himely's mercantile establishment on Broad Street had been used as Michaux's mailing address in his absences, and the Himely home on Tradd Street was the later address of Jacques Renaud, who had accompanied the Michauxs to Charleston in 1786. Now the son, H. H. Himely, had arrived in Paris to serve as agent of commerce for Courvoisier and Rovoisy. Within a month he had sent "upward of 100,000 francs of dry goods" to the United States. François André frequently seized the opportunity to utilize Himely's almost daily shipments to America to include his book shipments, and Himely's trips to the United States to carry letters and escort his boxes for Vaughan.[46]

There are surviving letters dispatched in the summer of 1818 to Philadelphia to advance scientific exchanges between France and his American correspondents. In one of them he reported having delivered copies of the *Transactions of the American Philosophical Society* to the Institute of Mathematics and Physics (later the Academy of Science), in the hope of arranging a regular exchange of journals.[47] In another he wrote to Robert Carr,[48] nephew of William Bartram, now in charge of the Bartram garden, seeking to obtain for friends the seeds of such outstanding American plants as the *Magnolia tripetala, M. acuminata* and chinquapin, and the tubers of the American lotus, *Nelumbo lutea*. A third, to John Vaughan,[49] reported that he had delivered his letter to William Maclure[50] and secured books their mathematical friend Hassler had requested. A fourth introduced Victor Leroy, a native Frenchman and "a great amateur botanist" who had emigrated to Baltimore.[51]

Michaux's letter introducing Leroy was more than the routine courtesy frequently extended acquaintances with kindred scientific interests setting out for America's scientific center. Leroy had volunteered to pick up from Vaughan ten copies of his *Sylva* and take the responsibility for placing them in Baltimore and Virginia. Almost forty years later, another long-standing friend, Elias Durand, writing a memorial on Michaux after his death, recalled the mutual desire of both Leroy and himself to serve their admired friend.[52] He recalled Leroy, who "having been earnestly solicited by his friend [Michaux] to send him all the seeds and young trees which he could procure in the vicinity of Baltimore" had enlisted Durand (then also residing in Baltimore) "as a fellow botanist to assist him in this undertaking." Consequently, they

went to work together in earnest, during the autumn of 1819 rambling in the woods with a negro boy, climbing and beating Oaks, maples and Hickory trees, uprooting the shrubs and young trees that fell in our way, and collecting seeds of every sort. The result of our campaign filled up several large boxes which were forwarded to Michaux, in the early part of the winter.

When I visited Europe in 1824, Mr. Leroy favored me with an introduction to his friend, recommending me as his co-laborer in the collections which had been forwarded to him from Baltimore, some years previous. This letter did not fail insuring me a hearty welcome at the hands of Mr. Michaux. I saw him frequently, and breakfasted with him at his winter quarters in Paris, on the place St. Michael, which was then a market for garden vegetables and fruits. We seldom sat at the breakfast table, without having previously taken an inspection round through the stalls where fruits and vegetables were sold, and he was pleased to point out to me the rarest and most beautiful with a passing notice of their origin.

Mr. Michaux was extremely desirous to show me, in detail, his fine nurseries, especially those which contained his Maryland trees, to "contemplate" the result of the troubles and fatigues they had cost me, but the weather was so unfavorable, during the whole season, that I could visit but one of them, which I found wholly planted with Maryland Oaks, and covering an extensive plot of ground. Though the young trees, then devoid of their foliage, had suffered much, the second year from the depredations of a herd of swine that had trespassed upon these grounds, they still appeared vigorous and promising, and are, I suspect, the very same trees that are now (as I see by the Paris papers) adorning the Quai des Tuilleries, and some of the new Boulevards of the French metropolis, under the denomination of American Oaks thirty-six years old.

In acknowledgment of the service I had thus rendered him, Mr. Michaux presented me with a copy of the French edition of his magnificent work, beautifully bound in three volumes, and containing a double set of plates, the plain and colored.

Mr. Michaux's person was tall, strongly built, but not corpulent. His complexion was fair; he was slightly pock-marked,

*and possessed prominent features. His light blue eyes had a pecu-
liar expression that startled me at first. His countenance was
stern and cold on first approach; but it smoothed off and bright-
ened gradually, as he spoke and became more familiar; his utter-
ance, in the beginning somewhat slow and cautious, became
rapid, and impressive, and his conversation gay and even hu-
morous. All his manners were quite simple and unaffected, frank
and lively—they were altogether those of an open-hearted country gentleman, in whose presence, young as I was at the time, I
could feel neither embarrassment nor shyness.*

From this excursion into the future with Elias Durand we return
to Michaux in Paris in 1819. Among the highlights in his life that year
were his own changing sentiments in respect to conditions in France
and its government to which in the past he had generally accorded little
respect. The previous year he had indicated a measure of acceptance
when he reported "we have an abundance of grain and an abundance
of excellent wine. Affairs are generally well and all is calm." In 1819 his
conversion to approval of the regime appears complete: "France is
enjoying great tranquillity and its people are happy. The harvest of
wine and wheat again this year has been most abundant. Commerce is
little active but there is enough for the people to live. Money is abundant. The health of the king is good. Pray God he will be long preserved.[53]

In these expressions Michaux was reflecting sentiments that had
come to prevail in France in respect to the reign of Louis XVIII.
Actually, on the whole, France during that period of the Bourbon
restoration was so "well governed, prosperous and contented" that it
has been regarded as "one of the happiest periods in [French] history."[54]

At the same time there were particularly pleasing developments
in the realm of Michaux's own special interests—scientific and cultural
exchanges between France and the United States. Late in 1819 he
received a formal notification from the Académie Royale that it had
resolved that it would reciprocate in an exchange of its publications
with those of the American Philosophical Society.[55]

CHAPTER **27**

⇜ Vauréal, 1820–1834

ALMOST AS THOUGH ONE DOOR were being closed and another opened and entered, the advent of the third decade marked a major transition in the focus of the life of François André Michaux. The familiar pattern that had been repeating itself year after year during the second decade was all but gone by the end of 1821. He had entered upon his fiftieth year, a time of life that often induces introspective examination and invites questioning whether the course one has been following deserves the dedication of one's downhill years. In Michaux's case an additional question was involved in his problem. Would his failing eyesight soon prevent him from scanning the new scientific works for selection of those to be sent his now numerous American clients and prevent him from continuing the activities and correspondence incidental to those duties that for so long filled his days? By 1820 the frequency of his letters to Vaughan was already lessening, even as the letters themselves continued to exhibit his accustomed interests. He was still inspired to comment on governmental affairs: the "exasperation of the parties of the ultra-liberals, the ultra-monarchists and the ministerial," "the revolution in Spain" that "has caused almost universal joy," and the state of affairs in the countryside "where the winter has been very bad for the grain crops." And he still exhibited a continuing interest in the "news of our friends": "Keating is in Germany, Mr. Maclure is at Montpellier. His health is better." Mr. Vanusin was returning to Philadelphia and would carry his letter to Vaughan. "The young Vanusin, since he came to Paris, has worked to acquire knowledge with uncommon zeal and tenacity," a zeal that "will procure for him a reputation justly acquired." The magnificent new map of Mexico and Louisiana that he had first proposed preparing in 1815 was finally completed and he was sending Vaughan a copy. He told him that he had arranged to send two hundred copies to A. Girard to place in New York for distribution.[1]

Beginning in 1820 his book shipments dropped sharply, but he continued to collect and send the journals for the society, although at far less frequent intervals, while his activities in experimental forestry, seed importation, and correspondence with colleagues increased sharply. Those changes of emphasis are reflected in a renewal, after a long lapse, of seed orders from Bartram's Garden and in letters to superintendents of national domains involved in forestry experiments and culture, one discussing a special kind of planting soil and another to assist the superintendent in obtaining more seed of exotic trees.[2] He was now much involved in the forestry experiments being conducted by his father's old friend André Thouin at the Jardin du Roi, to whom he addressed a letter from Le Havre, where he had gone to assess the damage suffered by an extremely large shipment comprising eighteen large cases of American forest seeds and plants intended for the Do-maines du Roi. The packing cases had been invaded by rats and mice, and seemed in hopeless condition, exuding an awful stench of dead rodents. However, after opening the cases and sorting their contents and repacking them for forwarding to Paris, he was delighted to find the bulk of the shipment still viable.[3]

Although for some eighteen months it had become increasingly apparent that Michaux had determined to change the focus of his life, it was not until November 1821, in a letter to Vaughan, that he revealed one of his reasons for making the change and the major step he was now planning. "Monsieur," he wrote in his customary formal yet affec-tionate letter to his dear friend:

The Himely family returns to the United States and I am profiting by this good occasion to send you the rest of the journals of the Society.

The friendship you have for me will make you learn with pain that for two years my sight has failed considerably and that since that time I can occupy myself only momentarily in reading or writing and always less than a quarter of an hour each time.

This circumstance, very distressing for me, has made me de-cide to live for two thirds of the year in the country, but as the place which I have chosen is a little village (Vauréal), near Pon-toise, 7 leagues from Paris, I can count on coming here [Paris] once each week so that my affairs as well as those of my friends and of the societies in the United States will not be neglected.

I am informing you by this means that by arrangements made with Henry Himely I have sold to him at thirteen dollars a copy all those [copies of my Sylva] *that remain in your hands and are not yet sold. I request you therefore to have them turned over to him.*

I am equally on the verge of negotiating with a bookseller in London for the copies remaining to me here in Paris.

I shall have, Monsieur and friend, eternal gratitude for all

*the interest you have taken in my enterprise in which you have
shown me the greatest mark of friendship and esteem.*[4]

Despite his assurances to the contrary, the customary letters and
international exchanges were neglected during the next thirteen
months. Obviously his failing sight only partly accounted for this neglect. His acquisition, early in 1822, of a site on the Oise for his
prospective home and gardens in Vauréal and the planning and supervision of the construction of the substantial, three-story masonry main
building and an adjacent gardener's pavilion proved too distracting and
time consuming to permit any other activities that could be deferred.
Also, there was much more to the project than the buildings going up
on the crest of a hill near a highway leading south from the village
toward the Seine, where there was a clear view down to the exquisite
Oise. To secure the privacy he sought, he built a high masonry wall
along the highway and an orchard, a vineyard, a garden, and a nursery
area for his beloved exotic forest seedlings to be prepared for the next
season—activities enough to explain his complete diversion from his
accustomed activities.[5] Not until February 1823 did he give them attention again, and even then his correspondence was little more than a
catalog of the journals accumulated since his last shipment. Only a
postscript has anything else: "France is in a most disastrous situation,"
he wrote, "and no one can foresee when there will be an end of the
misfortunes about to overwhelm her through the war with Spain,
opposed by general opinion."[6]

The source of this distress was not only the war but the equally
disturbing bitter rivalry between the "ultras," the extreme right-wing
party, and the liberal factions, in which the ultras became dominant and
entrenched for the remainder of the decade, and to Michaux's despair
succeeded in purging the Sorbonne faculty of its liberal professors and
turning its administration over to a reactionary priest.[7]

There were but two more brief notes, both within the limitations
imposed by his failing sight, written to Vaughan in 1823, one in the
spring and the other in the summer, merely notifying Vaughan of two
more shipments of journals for the Philosophical Society and the Library Society of Charleston. Only the latter had any other content. A
sentence in it reveals an additional cause for the sparsity and brevity
that now and henceforth would characterize his correspondence. "I
have been sick for a long time," he wrote, "and am not yet fully
recovered." He reassured Vaughan that although recently he had not

Home of F. A. Michaux. Vauréal, Val d'Oise, France. (Photograph by Anne de Brunhoff)

been sending the journals regularly, "henceforth I will certainly do so every month." However, there was also in that business note an indication that he was then still securing seeds and plants from America, in a reference to the payment of a draft from William Bartram's nephew Robert Carr.[8]

After those two notes, except for a single letter written the following January, we find no surviving Michaux correspondence for the next three and a half years, when it resumes without explanation of the long interval of silence. The January letter is a significant one:

> *During the nearly eleven years that my father almost every year visited some part of the Union, he never failed to experience in the course of those travels the most marked good will on the part of the inhabitants of the places he stayed. The pleasure that he experienced can be attributed to the goodness of his character and his strict morality. Nowhere did people fail to admire his ardent zeal to add to the progress of the natural sciences, most particularly botany.*
>
> *He camped almost always in the woods where at night by the light of the fire my father recorded the observations he had made during the day.*
>
> *If the journals that I offer to the Philosophical Society of Philadelphia (to which I have the honor to belong) include nothing that may be useful to American botanists of the future, at least they can be sure of having under their eyes the notes written by the hand of one who had dedicated most of his existence to the progress of Botany, the life that he lost (if I can so express it),* with his weapons in his hands *in laborious researches, on the coast of the Isle of Madagascar.*
>
> F. André Michaux
>
> *Paris, January 15, 1824.*
>
> *P.S. The two notebooks from 1785 (September) to 1787 were lost in his shipwreck on the coast of Holland.*[9]

Robert M. Patterson, corresponding secretary of the society, wrote on a blank page of Michaux's presentation document a copy of the society's acknowledgment:

> 21 May, 1824
>
> *The Am. Philos. Socy'ty having received from you, our associate, the Valuable Donations of the Botanical Journals of your respected father, André Michaux, kept during 11 years (1787– 1796) whilst exploring the Botanical riches of this country; we*

accept them with a due sense of your kindness and of their impor-
tance. To us they are peculiarly interesting. We lament his un-
timely end by which Science [was] deprived of one of its most
useful and intelligent Votaries. I am directed by the Society to
transmit this thanks for yr. assistance in thus advancing the de-
sign of this Institution.

After the gift of those treasured journals there is a three and a half
year hiatus in the correspondence between Michaux and his American
friends before it resumed in the summer of 1827 with at least a partial
explanation of its interruption. Michaux's long illness and failing eyesight, in combination with his expenditure of time and energy at his
new home at Vauréal, had forced him to enlist a friend, Arthur Bertrand, a Paris bookseller, to take over the time-consuming shipments of
the journals and other requested publications for the Philosophical
Society. Bertrand was already serving as the Dobsons' Paris agent making similar shipments to them. When he undertook to collect and ship
those for the society, he simply included them in the boxes being sent to
the Dobsons. Less conscientiously meticulous than Michaux, Bertrand
had not notified Vaughan at the time he made each shipment. This, and
the confusion of the shipments destined for the society with those for
Dobson, can account for Vaughan's belief that Michaux was failing to
perform the services the society had so long depended upon.

When their correspondence resumed in 1827, a somewhat miffed
Michaux acknowledged a letter of Vaughan reporting his disappointment, and defended himself and Bertrand, placing the blame on the
Dobsons for the society's "disappointment in not receiving the journals
regularly." Henceforth, each month, when he went to the city he would
personally collect the new journals, deliver them to Bertrand, and send
Vaughan a notification of the contents and the date of each shipment.
That letter carried for the first time the address of his place of residence
when in Paris—Quai aux Fleurs No. 19, a location very near his longtime abode at Place St. Michel, but on the Île de la Cité, in the Seine,
almost in the shadow of Notre-Dame.[10]

With that new procedure in effect, the Michaux-Vaughan correspondence revived and continued with only two year-long lapses, for
the ensuing seven years. Most of it continued to be routine, brief
business notes. However, now and then, here and there, are comments
on other subjects, names mentioned, letters of introduction going both
ways, furnishing ample evidence that Michaux, despite the remoteness
of his usual abode, continued immensely interested in their mutual

friends and in scientific advancement, especially in botany and medicine.[11] Great productions too evoked his enthusiasm. Among those "the great lavishly illustrated" twenty-four-volume work on Egypt, begun at the time of Napoleon's invasion of that country thirty years before, and paid for by the government, was the sensation of the day— but a costly one, originally priced at $600 later reduced to $180, which Michaux hesitated to buy for the society without specific authorization.[12] In scientific exchange there was great interest in a work from America, Thomas Say's *American Entomology*, replete with handcolored plates, "the most beautiful publication of its kind ever issued from an American press."[13] Among the friends and scientists whom he saw during these years, many of whom were members of the Philosophical Society, were Stephen Elliott of Charleston and Dr. Samuel Brown, who had recently arrived in Paris bearing the society's response to Michaux for his gift of his father's journals. There was scientist Ternaux, setting out for America; and Philadelphians Dr. Caspar W. Pinnock, namesake of his erstwhile friend Caspar Wistar, and George Ord, patron of Alexander Wilson and fellow member of the Society, arriving in Paris; mathematician Hassler, again visiting Europe; educator and patron of the arts William Maclure, returning to the United States after years spent in France; and his dying friend Warden, staying on in France to the end; and Auduin of the Jardin des Plantes, who, on his return to Paris, had become a courier from Vaughan to Michaux; and there was correspondent Baron Cuvier, then the most distinguished scientist of France. Books were still being sent for friends in the United States: the three-volume folio edition of *Suidas' Lexicon of Greek and Latin* to Stephen Elliott along with other works for the Charleston Medical Society.[14]

In January 1830 a disturbed Michaux wrote Vaughan a reiteration of his desire to continue to see that the society's journals went forward regularly, "I do not consider myself discharged," he says. "I always see that the subscriptions are paid." To straighten out Vaughan's complaints of missing numbers, he asked that "an exact list" of any missing numbers be sent him. He was also surprised and disturbed to "have seen in American publications that M. Maclure is about to publish a new edition of my *Sylva*. Please inform me if this is true."[15]

By March his worries had grown. George Ord—vain, verbose, but able, businesslike, and conscientious—in Paris for an extended stay, had barged in to systemize the chain of supply of the society's European materials, this despite the fact that Vaughan had positively refused to authorize him to make any move to supplant Michaux in that function. Nevertheless, Ord wrote to Vaughan from Paris that "had you placed the agency of the Journals into my hands, you would have had no reason to complain of delay in receiving them. As it is you must fit in with M's way of transmitting them." When Ord proposed to relieve him of the burden, Michaux replied that it was an advantage for him to be the agent as it gave him the opportunity of reading the journals.[16]

However ungracious and irritating his letters make him appear, Ord had useful advice for Michaux and in his next letter reported having instructed him on the means whereby he could avoid payment of any duty on the shipments to the society by packing them separately and marking them as sent by its order.[17]

By late fall 1830, when Michaux next wrote Vaughan, France had suffered yet another revolution. The "ultra rightist" Charles X had been deposed and replaced by Louis-Phillipe of the duc d'Orleans line of the Bourbon family. Michaux commented on the change. With his recollections of past national convulsions—the Reign of Terror and its parlous, briefly sustained successor regimes, the rise and fall and ultimate tragedy of the empire, and the uninspiring restoration—Michaux, as well he might, had grown skeptical of the ability of France to fix upon a stable and satisfying government, and fearful of the international consequences of each convulsion. To Vaughan he confesses his fears:

> In respect to our political affairs, we are having a bad time. It is likely that all of Europe will be on fire by spring. It will be a war of extermination. At least for the present we are tranquil in Paris and even in all of France; 15 thousand workers will begin and continue all winter building guns.
>
> The National Guard of Paris is already perfectly equipped. It numbers 70 thousand men. Our new king and his family are cherished by the whole nation. This affection rests upon his morality and his love of doing everything as well as he can.[18]

It was not until 1832, after another two-year interval, that we find the next tracing of Michaux's life. At that time, at the age of sixty-two, from all appearances he was living a comfortable and enjoyable life on his handsome estate on the Oise, with a housekeeper, a gardener, and doubtless other domestics. In addition he maintained quarters in a choice section of Paris for his use during the winter months and whenever he made his periodic visits to the city. Such amenities imply at least a moderate degree of wealth, yet, insofar as the record shows, other than possibly during his youthful years in minor positions at one of the hospitals or at the Jardin des Plantes, he had never had any regular remunerated employment. Moreover, it seems improbable that either his periodic services as consultant in his fields of expertise or his activities as European book agent for his American correspondents, many of which were free services for friends or organizations with which he was affiliated, or rewards for past hospitalities, might have produced sufficient income to support his way of life at this period. It is only through a few lines he wrote some twenty years later, shortly before his death, that we are given the facts as to the sources of his modest wealth.

Written in the course of the preparation of his final will, these lines told of the loss of his father's patrimony in the Revolution and the ensuing economic chaos while his father was still in America, and of a long-standing rift between himself and his Claye relatives that probably foreclosed the possibility of any inheritance from his mother's family, and then, in a direct statement, says that what he possessed was the fruit of his own efforts—the compensation he received from the government for his American expeditions and from the works he had published.

That information of Michaux's financial success during the early decades of the century lays the foundation for a related revelation in his next letter to Vaughan, written in the summer of 1832.[19] As usual, he began with the business of the books and journals for the society, and then, also as usual, he reported on the illness of a mutual friend, and followed that with his customary report on French current events, this time given over to the terrible scourge of a cholera epidemic in Paris that had "cruelly afflicted" the city. "In Paris alone, since the first of April, the mortality has been 25 thousand people," and the malady was still destroying at least a hundred a day. Finally, he turned to his own affairs.

> *Confidentially, I tell you that in my will I have bequeathed to our Philosophical Society the sum of ten thousand francs, the said sum to be invested, with the income annually to be awarded to those who devote themselves most usefully to economic forestry in the United States. My will is deposited with M. Nollival, Notary, Rue des Bons-Enfants in Paris. The president of the society shall be the only person other than you to know of this disposition.*

Six weeks later Vaughan penned a warm response:

> *Your welcome letter of 27 July has reached me strongly marked with your never changing attachment to our Society & this country. I have shown it to DuPonceau who feels as you and I on this subject. Would we could make more feel as you do. Being indis-*

*posed I defer to next packet a Comm'n from D.P. and myself.
Meantime accept our cordial thanks with an acceptance of our
sincere wishes that your useful life may long be spared. Societies
live ages; to them 20 or 30 yrs are nothing and assistance is always in time acceptable.*[20]

Vaughan's letter continued with thanks for Michaux's good offices
in the matter of the great work on Egypt and for consulting an authority on that region as to its worth to the society. He authorized him to
proceed with its purchase and shipment. For Michaux's information he
said that he was sending eight copies of the society's *Transactions*, six for
exchange with French cultural organizations and one each for Warden
and Michaux.

CHAPTER **28**

≈§ Harcourt, 1834–1855

FROM 1834 ON, for the twenty-one remaining years of the life of François André Michaux, primary records of his activities are scarce indeed,
sometimes mystifyingly so. For example, when in 1834 his very active
correspondence with Vaughan and the American Philosopical Society
all but ceased, he had been five years engaged in the first recorded
regular employment of his life, but never, as far as we have discovered,
made any mention of it to friend Vaughan. It is from other sources that
we learn that about 1828 he had accepted the position of administrator
of Harcourt, an important and historically famous domain in the Norman department of Eure, about 120 kilometers west of Paris and a
hundred from his Vauréal home.[1]

Similarly, we find no mention of another important event in his
life during the same period, the "late autumn of his life" marriage to a
cousin, Marguerite Guierdet, a woman thirty-one years his junior, who
had been for some time his housekeeper. Although in later years, after
her husband's death, she married again, her second marriage was not a
successful one, and when she died her remains were interred next to
Michaux's grave and inscribed without reference to her second matri-
monial venture.[2]

It is unfortunate that we have so little of Michaux's writings dealing with his Harcourt years and continuing, perhaps, to the time of his death two decades later. Although we believe that the work he did at Harcourt represents the culmination of Michaux's trailblazing work in practical, economic forestry, we have little contemporaneous documentary proof to support that conviction. The almost total lack of documentation of his work there during those harvest years of his life can be accounted for by the strange and mystifying mandate he refers to in his will, in which he wrote that, as "for my writings on agriculture and other subjects, I have expressed most formally to my wife my wish that they not be communicated to anyone, but that they shall by her be burned." Nevertheless, two of his letters that shed some light upon his activities at the Harcourt Domain, being in the hands of others, escaped that documentary holocaust and have survived the hazards of the intervening years.[3] What could be gleaned from a visit to Harcourt and the evidence visible in its forest exotics and arboretum, together with bits of information from other sources, all appear to support our conviction.

The Harcourt Domain lies about fifty kilometers southwest of Rouen in the heart of the forest domains of Eure, the most forested department of Normandy. The public domain of Harcourt comprises about three hundred acres, mostly in a variety of forests except in the immediate environs of its centerpiece, the ancient château, with a history going back ten centuries and intimately linked with Norman history, which accounts for its having once served as the seat of English government on the Continent. The massive castle itself, replete with open cour d'armes and flanked by moat and battlements, is a composite structure, erected at intervals throughout the millennium of its existence, but mostly during the thirteenth and fourteenth centuries and is now being restored. A. Jardillier, whose historical background paper is distributed to visitors to the château, concludes with this paragraph: "Thus in the course of years the château of Harcourt, which was for two centuries like the Sleeping Beauty of the Forest, finds again its former splendor. High above the ground, Harcourt offers to its visitors, in a magnificent setting of rare trees, the jewel of its long-ignored site, crowned with the golden halo of history."

How intimately Michaux was associated with the château, or whether, when in residence there, he resided in one of its apartments or in a nearby outbuilding, we do not know. Be that as it may, it dominated the scene throughout the two decades of his association with the domain.[4]

Early in the nineteenth century the château and the surrounding

Château d'Harcourt, Eure, France. (Courtesy of l'Académie d'Agriculture de France; photograph by Anne de Brunhoff)

forest had been purchased by L. G. Delamarre from the family through whom it had descended. During the quarter century of his tenure he became so engrossed in his Harcourt forests and those nearby, and disturbed by the long-standing critical national problem presented by the paucity of French forest resources, that he devised the property to the Académié d'Agriculture de France for use as pilot demonstration forest, to research and demonstrate ways and means of alleviating that continuing national problem—a particularly fortuitous development for French forestry, enhanced by Harcourt's location in the heart of the forests of Eure.

The selection of Michaux, with his long-sustained international study of practical forestry and his experimentation with the introduction of superior exotic species to enhance the potential of French forests, was a most felicitous choice to launch and direct this "pilot" forest toward its destined role in guiding foresters and forest owners to practical forest development. He conceived and put into effect a long-term management plan that essentially embraced the principles of forest management now routinely accepted by foresters as basic to good management. It was based on a plan of rotation designed to gradually improve both the quantity and quality of the forest's annual growth accretion through a systematic process of regular harvesting, clearing, and replanting every area of the forest with its optimum species. Consistently followed, the procedure would ensure regular annual harvests of steadily improving quantity and quality while ultimately transmuting the forest to optimum production.

In designing and putting into effect his plan for the management of the Harcourt forest, Michaux had the benefit of the advice and assistance of two outstanding fellow members of the Académié, one, Pépin, was then the chief gardener of the Jardin des Plantes at the Museum of Natural History. To Pépin goes the credit for the introduction of the Douglas fir and its companion forest giants from the American Northwest into the Harcourt area. The other colleague was Adolphe-Théodore Brongniart, a famous paleobotanist and professor at the museum, who would himself later become director of the Harcourt forest and arboretum.[5]

To implement their plan, extensive regular plantings were made in the Harcourt forest between 1833 and 1848. To systematize the planned transmutation of the forest, its entire area was divided into nine management areas of about twenty-five acres each, separated by access roads, the Allées d'Harcourt, one of which now bears the name of Michaux and two others the names of his colleagues. The forest stand on each of those areas was carefully inventoried and the goals of each defined upon the basis of the established aim to secure, on that particular soil and terrain, its optimum growth and quality. It was judged that a ninety-year rotation would make that aim possible. To that end one of the nine areas was selected each year for harvest operations. The volume of each of these harvests was determined by a calculation of the growth on the area during the previous nine years. A sufficient area to produce that volume was clear-cut and the clear-cut areas from which the annual harvests were taken were then prepared and planted in species deemed superior for qualitative or quantitative production on that particular soil and terrain. Thus, over a period of ninety years of such step-by-step improvement, with harvests a tenth less than the annual accretion, the forest as a whole should be supporting a large, nearly optimum stand of vigorously growing, superior timber. Obviously, in practice, along the way, trial and error operations would have to be recognized and the plan modified to accord with the lessons learned.

After at least another fifteen years of Michaux's association with the Académie's Harcourt demonstration forest, we are provided with our only contemporary insight into what he was doing there during those years. Through that small window we have a glimpse of the work that he had been inaugurating and carrying forward there. We find him still hungry for more facts, and for more experimentation to reveal more facts, to provide judgments and the means of applying them to improve forestry economics. In a letter that incidentally provides a striking revelation of the continuing timber starvation still prevailing in France in the mid-nineteenth century, Michaux wrote to his young colleague, Brongniart, at the Jardin des Plantes.[6] Writing from Harcourt in November 1845, the optimum season for setting out seedlings, he reported that he had been busy with supervising the seasonal transplanting of seedlings into the forest. Responding to a request from Brongniart for a supply of quantities of a variety of species of forest seedlings, he told him he had lifted, packed, and shipped him 2,000 two- and three-year-old beech trees, a supply of a small relative, *Alnus cordata,* suitable for coppice wood production in swampy areas, and 200 chestnut seedlings—along with advice on the planting and pruning of them. An unsolicited addition to the shipment was a heavy box weighing twelve kilos containing five beautiful oaks with especially good roots, having twice been transplanted. He went on to describe "our affairs" at Harcourt, indicating Brongniart's close association with the research in progress there. After five years of effort, he said he had at last succeeded in making the nearby lime burners use pine fagots with the result that they so preferred Harcourt's pine prunings that "all our production of our pines are reserved in advance," thanks to a similar conversion of the bakers in nearby Brionne. He thought that those conversions carried a great point, for "the bundles of pine fagots are now so in demand that we foresee that forty thousand will be sold forthwith." That observation inspired a touching remark: "No, my dear colleague, not any of our colleagues of the society, other than you, begins to glimpse or in anywise appreciate the importance of our Harcourt property; but what troubles I have experienced in bringing it to this state of prosperity."

It was in a paragraph reporting on routine matters at Harcourt that the continuing critical shortage of forest resources is exemplified. Speaking of two of the more recent additions to the Harcourt staff, he said he continued "content with Turgis: he perfectly fills our need, but he has not the energy necessary to stop the intrusions of the hundreds of women from the [adjacent] communes who rush into our woods, impelled as they are by poverty. Thanks to Mr. Aubert they no longer dare enter our forests. They tremble at his visage. It is to his firmness that the suppression of their raking up the pine needles will be due. Those women formerly came with their carts to carry away a great quantity. Generally the owners of pine woods have not been able to prevent the poor from collecting the straw," a practice that results in denuding the forest floor of its litter, the source of much of the essential nutrients for forest growth, which Michaux, even in that early stage of forest science and management, recognized as being a very damaging practice.

Before concluding his letter, he solicited the professor's cooperation in a study he then had in progress: "I am busy with a work which I believe will be interesting. It is to establish for the report: a comparison in the money value of the prunings from my twelve-year-old oaks and those of our sylvestre pines [Scotch pines] on an area of the same size after 45 years. To cite other examples, will you let me know (1) the period you made your prunings, and (2) what is the mean price you get per hectare?"

In a pesonal postscript he told his colleague that "we" (presumably he and his wife) would be in residence at Harcourt for another month, and that "for the spring we are preparing to have a peacock."

Although we have little more than those samples of Michaux's activities during his Harcourt years on which to hang some two decades of his productive life, it becomes apparent that he was much involved in many time-consuming research projects. In fact, earlier in the same year of his letter to Brongniart he had published an illustrated report on a new, improved system of supporting vinyard vines;[7] and a few years later, a long paper on the causes of yellow fever.[8]

It is certain that Michaux's engagement with the Harcourt project lasted at least through his eighty-third year, for it was in 1853 that he made his greatest single contribution to the advancement of forestry in his native France—the establishment and planting of the now famous Harcourt Arboretum, which today displays to some 15,000 visitors a year an immense variety, about 155 species, of temperate-zone forest trees collected from all the continents of the world except Australia.[9] This original, the first such arboretum in France, may be appropriately regarded as being the rich, ripe harvest of a unique life overwhelmingly dedicated to the advancement of forestry. More specifically, the arboretum was the natural, even inevitable, outgrowth of Michaux's Harcourt forest plan. When his sylvicultural plan was devised, an essential to its progress was a ready supply of a variety of forest tree-seedlings for the annual plantings on the areas harvested. Obviously, from the beginning the establishment of a nursery was a necessary adjunct of the operation. Only from such a facility could Michaux have sent Brongniart the thousands of beech trees he shipped to him. The Harcourt forest plan itself inevitably convinced its administrator that only a kindred but different sort of garden could possibly round out the demonstration of arboriculture to which it was dedicated. If the forest stand was to be steadily improved by introducing a variety of superior species, many species would have to be planted and seen through their juvenile years to guide the selection process. But most of all, such an arboretum-nursery would provide for the interested the opportunity to see at close hand, within the confines of a convenient, readily accessible small area, the wide variety of forest tree possibilities for the forests of their region.

So it came to pass that it was to François André Michaux, rich in years, rich in forest knowledge and sylviculture, yet still innovative, that the opportunity came to lead the way in the establishment of such a garden at Harcourt.

It was also at about the same time that he was laying out and preparing areas in the arboretum to receive its first specimens that Michaux was making his final arrangements to provide an even more consequential stimulus to American forestry. It had been more than twenty years since he had written to John Vaughan telling him that he had made a provision in his will for a bequest of 10,000 francs to the American Philosophical Society to enable it to make annual awards to persons who practice economic forestry. At the same time he and Vaughan were still corresponding regularly and rendering each other valuable mutual assistance. He was also involved in lively correspondence and frequent social associations with several other members of the society; but by 1852 John Vaughan had been dead for eleven years. Also long gone were Dr. Barton, his two Bartram friends, John and William, his beloved and congenial Dr. Wistar, and the greatly admired Jefferson, as well as botanical friends Muhlenberg and William Hamilton.

Some thirty years of rural residence on his own lovely acres on the banks of the Oise, years of intimate involvement in village affairs as mayor of Vauréal, and two decades of absorbing involvement in experimental forestry at Harcourt had filled that interval with a variety of activities, leaving little time to foster and cultivate a continuation of his association with a society far across the Atlantic, now composed of a new generation of members. When he first named the society as a beneficiary in his will, Michaux was still a citydwelling bachelor with strong nostalgic bonds to the great American forests. Meanwhile, he had forged new ties to his own green world, one quite within his purview. So the strength of those early devotions and the steadfast intention of the man speak loudly and clearly in the letter he addressed to a president of the society with whom he thought he was unacquainted, as he harked far back to the years of his father's prime and his youth and their associations with the forests beyond those distant shores that yet remained the object of his continuing devotion and concern.[10]

To this impersonal "Monsieur the President of the American Philosophical Society of Philadelphia," he deemed it necessary to furnish a bit of background to explain the raison d'être behind his continuing interest in America and the society, almost as though he were a stranger introducing himself. Harking back "to the voyages taken by my father and by me, together and separately in the States of the Union during 1786 to 1808," to study their botanical offerings, having for his father mainly the advancement of botany, which had resulted in his *Flora Boreali-Americana,* while his own intent, although "less scientific, but perhaps more generally profitable" to the people owning, farming or using "wood in many different ways." To those ends he had prepared his *North American Sylva* which, to his great satisfaction, had been honored by an American edition. He hastened to add, however, that he did "not consider that work as complete as it should be," lacking many trees growing in the Floridas, and, because of the season when he observed them, some species do not include their seeds or flowers in their accompanying illustrations. "If, Monsieur the President," he continued, "circumstances had permitted me, I would have returned to the United States and in a new edition I would have remedied some errors and omissions. I would then have been able to offer the American nation a work more worthy of it. But have arrived at a very advanced age (approaching my eighty-third year) I have in this respect only regret to express and the hope that some American arboriculturalist may complete my researches" and publish a supplement which "would be useful and would bring honor without end to one who undertakes it."[11]

He then moved on to discuss the arboricultural justification for his Harcourt work—the complete absence of forest production on many areas of Europe where often "its sandy shores are entirely deprived of vegetation," and many other areas likewise remaining "equally uncultivated from beginning of time," producing only heather (*bruyère*), "a small shrub not found in all the United States. Up to the latest times all those lands were considered completely useless. To alter

Forest Tree Arboretum, established by François André Michaux, Do-
maine d'Harcourt, Eure, France. (Courtesy of l'Académie d'Agriculture
de France; photograph by Anne de Brunhoff)

the fixed opinion that those vast areas were worthless had been a substantial part of the justification of his Harcourt years: "For almost twenty years I have been busy with that kind of cultivation and with the most complete success on an extensive property administered by the National and Central Society of Agriculture of France, of which I am a member and consequently a co-proprietor."

After expressing his opinion based on his experimentation there that *Pinus sylvestris,* the Scotch pine, "of all the resinous species of trees, be it in Europe or North America that I have cultivated and compared its vegetation, I have recommended that in the Northern and Middle states, one should give it preference . . . [and plant it] in parallel rows, prune modestly, and thin out every four or five years. On that property over which my colleagues have given me the direction, I have devoted myself also to the culture of leafy trees. I made notable improvement in the prevailing manner of coppice harvesting (which presently in Europe furnishes 90 percent of the fuel wood), it being the most sensible mode of culture and most favorable to tree culture and that most easily exploited."

The aged forester had as yet not surrendered to the infirmities of age and still displayed his old optimism: "In a work as concise as possible which I will publish next, I shall assemble everyting taught me on the subject by practical experience. The aim of that publication will be to inform the owners and cultivators of lands in the northern and central states of the United States of the most expedient means to procure on their lands quality wood for construction and thereby remedy the rapid destruction of the forests in the northern part of North America."

He saved for last his long-harbored intent to provide his greatest contribution to that aim and the motives that inspired it:

> *I close this letter, Mr. President, by informing my honorable col-*
> *leagues of the society of my wish to demonstrate my gratitude to*
> *the great and glorious American nation for all the assistance and*
> *hospitality that my father and I received in our long and often la-*
> *borious voyages into the interior, then little inhabited. I have*
> *made for the Society a testamentary disposition to provide it with*
> *the means of promoting the development of the science of sylvicul-*
> *ture in the United States.*

This letter and a sealed packet containing a duplicate of his will were entrusted for safe delivery to Isaac Lea,[12] a leading American publisher and widely recognized amateur naturalist and a member of the society, whose acquaintance Michaux had "been so happy to make while he was in Paris." Lea, not without expressed trepidation and concern, nevertheless, mailed the letter and packet, as he had already arranged to visit Italy before returning to Philadelphia.

Lea's covering letter is pertinent.[13] Addressed to Dr. R. M. Patterson, president of the society, with whom Michaux was actually well acquainted, Lea spoke with admiration of their "venerable fellow member" as one "whose whole heart seems to be devoted to the promotion & improvement of the arts connected with the studies of his long, laborious and useful life. The expressions of his feelings towards our country & more particularly to Philadelphia must gratify us all, as he declared to me that he preferred our city to any place he had ever resided in. In speaking of our excellent late President, Dr. Wistar, he was affected quite to tears."

Although he still had several more years to live, his letter and the will contained in its accompanying packet are virtually Michaux's swan song.

Almost three years later to the day, on October 23, 1855, Michaux died at his home in Vauréal.[14] There also he was buried, not in the village cemetery, but in a plot he had prepared on his estate between the house and the river, in the midst of a grove of exotic trees, mostly American. Whether that breach of custom was the outgrowth of a traditionally reported schism between him and his parish priest, and whether that rift was merely part of a community schism (also traditionally reported) involving the management of a nearby village communal property, or whether it indicated a reported quarrelsome nature, we can only comment that we have come across no other evidence or confirming report of the latter. On the contrary, over the years his correspondence and writings, and those of others in speaking of him, indicate only an uncommonly friendly and sociable nature.[15]

It was almost a year later before word of his demise reached Philadelphia, and it came then, not from France, but from his friend Professor Asa Gray at Harvard.[16] Michaux had told Gray of his intended legacy to the Philosophical Society, probably on the professor's latest visit to France in 1851, so when word of Michaux's death reached Gray through a friend, he assumed that the society had received official notice of the event. As it turned out, unknown to him at the time, Gray himself was also a legatee and had not, himself, been officially notified. When he learned, several months later, that the society had received no notice of Michaux's death, he wrote its secretary, imparting to him the pertinent part of a letter written to Mrs. Gray the previous autumn by

Mrs. Vilmorin, the wife of a close associate and friend of both Gray and Michaux:

> *I have to speak to you of the death of our good friend M. Mi-chaux. He was carried off with frightful suddenness by a stroke of apoplexy in November last.*[17] *He had occupied himself the whole day, planting American trees, he himself directing his journey-men. He withdrew from his work in good health, dined moder-ately, but with good appetite. He went to bed as usual and fell asleep. About one o'clock in the morning, his wife heard him moving about and calling. She instantly rose from her bed and ran to his apartment. He was still struggling on the floor when she entered his room, but on reaching him she found that he had breathed his last. Physicians were called in immediately, but all in vain, life was totally extinct.*

So it was that it was almost a year after Michaux's demise before word of the event reached the society, permitting the opening of the sealed packet. When the contents were disclosed it became the society's turn to notify Asa Gray that he was among Michaux's beneficiaries for a modest legacy of two hundred dollars.

Like the letter addressed to the president of the American Philo-sophical Society, which had accompanied the sealed packet, inscribed in French, "Testamentary dispositions of F. André Michaux in favor of the American Philosophical Society of Philadelphia," both the contents of the packet and its succeeding amendatory documents, are pregnant with valuable biographical data on Michaux and his family.

Inasmuch as the packet itself contained only extracts from his will of May 30 and October 11 of that year, 1852, and they were confined to the legacies he intended to provide the Philosophical Society and the Massachusetts Society for Promoting Agriculture, most of his testa-mentary revelations did not come to light until long after his death when all those documents were revealed. Because of its potential histor-ical importance, it seems appropriate to report now Michaux's intent inherent in those legacies when he prepared his 1852 will. As spelled out in those excerpts, the bequests to those societies were strictly and precisely limited by his directions as to their use. Those bequests, totalling $22,000, "equivalent to 111,860 francs, $14,000 to the Philo-sophical Society and $8,000 to the Massachusetts Society for Promoting Agriculture" (which Michaux persisted in calling the Society of Agricul-ture and the Arts of Boston) were to have similar objectives, "to encour-age arboriculture, principally in the states of Pennsylvania and Massachusetts, and secondarily in New Jersey, New York, Connecticut, New Hampshire and Maine." More specifically, four-fifths of each legacy (in purchasing power in that day, very substantial funds) were to be expended for the purchase of a farm producing cereals or livestock, which was to be rented out and the funds received used to award "each year honorary premiums to those arboriculturalists or horticulturalists who shall have cultivated or improved indigenous or exotic trees or vegetables that are useful or remarkable for their beauty"—but only such as can thrive without protection.

The remaining fifth of each legacy was to be similarly divided and four-fifths expended to "purchase, on the seashores, one or more lots of sandy and sterile ground, and also some lots in the mountainous regions of the most stony soils or quagmires . . . that have been heretofore regarded as unproductive and never been cultivated—lands which I shall shew may very well be brought into very profitable culture of resinous trees." The remaining fifth was to be used by the societies "for sowing and planting those grounds, as I shall point out in a series of instructions wherein I will make known the modes which have best succeeded with me in France on such areas which for ages had remained uncultivated and branded as completely sterile."

Such specific directions for the establishment and conduct of a diversity of experimental research projects on geographically and geologically diverse areas, and the provisions for rewarding contributions of others to the progress of arboriculture, indicate a clear vision a century into the future when forest experiment stations, the Soil Conservation Service, and the United States Forest Service, together with a multitude of volunteer organizations, would be bending their efforts to stimulate the transformation into productive forests not only of such areas as he described but millions of acres of other once fertile lands, so manhandled that they, too, had become virtual wastelands.

Octogenarian Michaux, in the three remaining years of his life, never sent the follow-up directions he promised to send to the societies. We can only suspect that when he undertook their preparation he came to realize that precise directions for the transformation of diverse wasteland areas, by him unseen, into productive forests could only be visionary. Surely it must have dawned on him in that interim that attempts to fetter future generations by specific directions to guide them in an unforeseeable future were wanting in both philosophical and legal wisdom. Perhaps futile attempts to prepare such directions were the focus of the strongly mandated instructions to his wife relegating his unpublished writings to the flames. Even more likely, it was perhaps his inadequate attempts to provide such instructions that prompted his decision to scrap all his previous testamentary documents—that of 1832 and those of May and October 1852 and supplant them with an entirely new will—that of September 4, reread and again signed on October 5, 1855, less than three weeks before his death.

From that last will we glean other previously unrevealed biographical facts. Its opening paragraph, in which testators customarily identify themselves, contains Michaux's summary of the honors accorded him by his peers in recognition of his fruitful and significant life: "member of the Imperial and Central Society of Agriculture, correspondent of the Institute for the Academy of Sciences, presently president of the Society of Agriculture and Horticulture of the Arrondissment of Pontoise, member of the American Philosophical Society, Philadelphia, and that of the State of Massachusetts (Boston), now mayor of Vauréal."

Then, to lay the foundations for his testamentary dispositions, he largely eschewed familial obligations. "I have no children," he wrote, and "I have never had brothers or sisters; I have only cousins, children of first cousins." Then he provided information on the sources of his modest wealth: "My father's patrimony was entirely lost in the course of the revolution, and the depreciation of the currency that followed in 1793; and during his long stay in America (eleven years), and by other causes. That which I possess I owe to myself, the works I have published, and gratuities granted me by the first Imperial government at the recommendation of Count Chaptal, then Minister of the Interior."

After mentioning that he had already conveyed to his wife a life ownership in his real property, he then alluded to his long-sustained gratitude to America "for the warm welcome and cordial hospitality that my father and I, together or separately, have received in our long and perilous travels all over the United States," and again named the American Philosophical Society and the Massachusetts Society for Promoting Agriculture to receive the two major bequests among the several made in the will. In this final draft of his will he made two changes in those bequests. He reduced the amount to the Philosophical Society from fourteen to twelve thousand dollars. A far more significant and consequential change was his omission of any specific restrictions upon the use of the funds, leaving only the expression of his intent in making them—the hope that they might contribute to the progress of agriculture and sylviculture in the United States. The funding of those bequests was to be derived from certain French government bonds, from which his wife was to draw the income for the remainder of her life.

Bequests of 4,000 francs to the Society of Agriculture of the department of the Seine-and-Oise, seated at Versailles, and 2,500 francs to the city of Pontoise manifest a sustained loyalty to his birthplace and his home community. Family loyalty, on the one hand, and a family schism, on the other, are inherent in other bequests: those made to two of his surviving paternal relatives, no closer related than second cousins, were 5,000 francs to André Michaux of Versailles, son of his first cousin André Michaux, farmer and past mayor of the commune of Bois-d'Arcy, and 3,000 francs to cousin Charlemagne Blet, lawyer. The single reference to a Claye relative was deferred to almost the final paragraph of the document. The only other personal bequest was that of 1,050 francs to "Asa Gray, professor of botany at the University of Cambridge (Boston)," the only monetary bequest to one not a relative.

He directed that his personal copy, in color, of his *North American Sylva,* a precious copy by reason of its being autographed by the president of the United States, Thomas Jefferson, be sent to the president of the Museum of Natural History in Paris, there to be placed in the library of that establishment. He leaves our curiosity unsatisfied as to how Jefferson's signature had been secured.[18]

The rest and residue of his estate he devised to his wife, but not until he had made a final specific legacy, "to my cousins, children of L. R. Claye, the sum of 120 francs, payable on my decease, for the price of a gun which their father sold me on that condition twenty years ago." He then added a directive that "all other claims on their part should be rejected; I owe them nothing"—words that clearly indicate a family schism still charged with emotion.

His will contained his last words to a world he had eagerly enjoyed for eight decades, and for most of that long tenancy had striven to advance in the wide fields of his special competence and in which he had planted viable seed to grow to bear fruit for future generations.

Although Michaux, through his last testament, had planted viable seed, between the bedding of the seed and their first harvest lay a long hiatus, in the course of which there were near losses of viability before, eventually, a long-sustained period of careful nurturing ultimately produced rewarding harvests of immense significance in the history of American sylviculture. The terms of the bequests to the two societies that deferred their use until after the death of his wife were patently the main cause of the long hiatus but, in the case of the bequest to the Philosophical Society, it was exacerbated by lackadaisical and uncoordinated steps by various members of the society, and two long periods, one of more than three years and another of more than four years, of complete failure of any communication with the notary charged with the administration of Michaux's estate, to effect the society's legal status as holder of a future interest in its legacy, subject only to Madame Michaux's right to receive the income from it during her lifetime. Another complicating factor was that she did not long remain Madame Michaux; having, not long after the tardy arrival in Philadelphia of news of Michaux's death, married one Adolphe Bezier, an aggressive, litigious figure with a special animosity toward the notary handling the estate and seemingly with an eye on his own self-interest. Finally, in February 1862 the Beziers commenced legal proceedings alleging abandonment of its legacy by the Philosophical Society, it having failed, for a period of four years since the requisite papers to effect its claim had been sent it, to execute and return them to the notary. Eventually, as its case continued to worsen, the society was forced to abandon its efforts to handle the matter through the uncoordinated efforts of volunteer laymen and to employ legal counsel. At length, the society's claim was firmly established and a settlement reached, but not until after the intervention of the diastrous Franco-Prussian War had so sharply reduced the value of French currency that the funds received had scarcely half the value the testator had intended.[19]

The whole mishandled, discordant, and costly affair had consumed some fifteen years—at least a decade of which, in retrospect, was clearly unnecessary. Before the close of 1858, the society's counterpart legatee, the Massachusetts Society for Promoting Agriculture, despite the problem of the variance between its name and that used by Michaux in his will, already had in hand the government bonds bequeathed it, subject only to the interest on them being payable to Michaux's widow as long as she lived. Ironically, the Massachusetts Society had no knowledge of the legacy until informed of it by the Philosophical Society, and then had proceeded exactly as it was advised by the Philosophical Society in getting delivery of its legacy. The society's failure to follow its own advice had, as it turned out, cost it a dozen years of effort and a reduction of its legacy to approximately equal that received by the Massachusetts organization.

Nevertheless, when it came to the application of the two legacies, pursuant to Michaux's expressed intent, the laurels were, and still remain, with the Philosophical Society. Surviving records of the Massachusetts society show little beneficial use of its fund before the adoption of a resolution on June 10, 1874, that "the amount received ($7,807.67)" under Michaux's will be added to the society's general fund.[20] Thereafter its use became unidentifiable. In marked contrast, the application of the funds received by the Philosophical Society followed the intent of the testator with such effectiveness that it has earned a significant chapter in the history of American forest conservation.

CONCLUSION

⨪ The Michauxs and Forestry in America

WHEN THE EARLY AMERICAN SETTLERS landed on the Atlantic shore of what was to become Britain's North American colonies, they set foot on the margin of a vast region almost totally covered by primeval forests. The common view of that pervading forest soon became equivocal, for although it provided, readily at hand, bountiful supplies of wood for fuel and shelter, as well as not insignificant measures of food, no cultivation of the land and little pastoral use of it was possible beneath the forest canopy. When the colonists set themselves to wrest from the forest the fields and pastures they desired, the forest became emphatically their stubborn enemy, exacting long and painful struggles to loose its tenacious hold upon these areas essential to their survival. That onerous process tended to overshadow the forest's bounties. That and a conviction that soon became prevalent—that the New World forests were inexhaustible—easily fixed in the minds of many an image of the great American forest as a formidable and stubborn antagonist standing in the way of progress and civilization. Conquest of the forest soon became regarded as a heroic struggle, often romanticized. The cleared patch in the woods, a crude log cabin amid a clutter of stumps, and a double-edge ax somewhere in the picture became virtually the hallmark of a vital, all-conquering, heroic and expanding young America.

That deeply engrained ambivalence persisted into the heyday of the westward march of the transmontane settlements of Kentucky, Tennessee, and the Old Northwest when the Michauxs arrived with their credentials as ambassadors to the great American forest, by then, in their view, already sorely mutilated. It was to become their lot, at first unintended, to set in motion a significant chain of causation that during the remainder of the nineteenth century was to lead to the now prevailing concept of the essentiality of a productive coexistence of man and nature, of forests and people. Joseph Wood Krutch, a leading spokesman of the modern ecological movement, in his introduction to Rutherford Platt's *Great American Forest* singles out the Michauxs as the early nineteenth-century harbingers of a then barely incipient realization of the imperious necessity that Americans save their forests from the continuing ruthless and wasteful process of conquering by destroying.[1]

Among the settled population and visitors alike, while the more prescient were becoming alarmed by the rapid destruction of their forests, observable on every hand, others continued to embrace the long-held traditional belief that America's forest resources were inexhaustible. Meanwhile, another myth had become the fixed contrary opinion of many: that the forests, once destroyed, could not be regenerated. It fell to men of a later day to demonstrate the falsity of both those beliefs and show that, on the contrary, forests not only could be regenerated but also be made far more productive than the forest primeval itself. Preeminent among those were the Michauxs, father and son— especially the latter.

Not only were they the first trained botanists to travel extensively in America and carefully study its forests, but the focus of their expeditions, the very raison d'être of their American travels, was tree and forest oriented. Both published notable pioneer works on American trees. The younger Michaux made his influence felt during his lifetime through his books, particularly his *Sylva,* the earliest manual of American trees, a forestry-oriented work replete with observations on the quality and uses of the wood each species produced and its value as a forest tree. Through his will Michaux fils posthumously projected and enhanced his influence during a critical period of maturation of American society, particularly during the half century following his death, the period of the rise of American forest consciousness and the birth and growth of professional forestry in the New World.[2] A clear and unbroken chain of events leading to that end can be discerned running from Michaux père to Michaux fils and his *North American Sylva,* the examples of his forest researches, the nursery and arboretum at Harcourt, and on through his bequest to the Philosophical Society for the promotion of sylviculture and forestry in the United States, to the rise of forestry in America during that period.[3]

Others, too, have perceived the great debt owed the Michauxs.

One, a leading authority on the history of forestry in America, Andrew D. Rodgers, recognized it.

The Michauxs, father and son, were among the first of the great botanical explorers of North America. . . . Only a superficial acquaintance with the botanical literature of North America is required to comprehend the vast contribution of these two men in helping to systemize descriptively the plant life of eastern United States. Recognition is long past due to François André Michaux for his well reasoned presentation of the need in America of forest conservation and forest management. [4]

A half century before any movement to set up publicly owned forest preserves, the younger Michaux had "observed that unlike Europe, neither the federal nor state governments were reserving forest lands to safeguard the nation's economy." [5]

Another student of the early development of forest conservation in the United States, Gilbert Chinard, likewise recognized the Michauxs' contributions: "Above all their contemporaries they stand, by themselves, both as specialists and men of vision. Both of them . . . substantially contributed to the cause of forest conservation in America as well as in their native country." [6]

He goes on to point out that François André Michaux's introduction to his *Sylva* "remains one of the most important landmarks in the history of forest conservation in America." Early in the nineteenth century it was the publication of his *North American Sylva* that sparked the torch of enlightenment for the American forest-conservation movement. By 1877 the torch Michaux lighted had been passed to a magnetic thirty-four-year-old professor of botany at the University of Pennsylvania, Joseph T. Rothrock. [7] The dynamic and versatile Rothrock, physician and amateur forester, in that year began an annual series of lectures on forestry and related subjects under the sponsorship of the Philosophical Society's Michaux Fund. Those lectures were destined to become famous in the history of the rise of American forestry.

Before continuing the important subject of Rothrock's Michaux lectures, we need to observe another Michaux-related event. In the spring of 1870, as preparations were being made for the Centennial Exposition in 1876 and its site, the present three-thousand-acre Fairmount Park, was being laid out for the great occasion, the park commissioners adopted a resolution addressed to the Philosophical Society:

[François André Michaux] who travelled long in this country,

*and described our Oaks and forest trees in a work of great merit
and splendor, should have his name and that of his father (who
had by like travel and study, rendered service to science), honored
in Fairmount Park in a manner to be a memorial to their devotions, and to promote the objects which had occupied their
lives . . . there shall be a grove of Oaks, in the Fairmount Park
forever to bear the name of the "Michaux Grove," in which, if
practicable, shall grow two oaks of every kind that will endure
the climate . . . [and] that any surplus . . . from the Michaux
Fund . . . shall be devoted to the cultivation of Oaks of every variety capable of cultivation in our climate in the park nursery,
which oaks, to the extent of two of each kind cultivated, be distributed to other Public Parks in the United States.*

The Michaux Fund for several years continued supporting the
project, which also included a park nursery that by 1876 contained
80,000 trees and shrubs, 100 species of which had been imported from
Europe.[8]

Now let us return to Rothrock's first series of lectures presented in
Horticultural Hall, which had been erected mid the thriving young
oaks of the Michaux Grove. They marked the beginning of a substantial
joint effort of Rothrock and the Michaux Fund which continued from
1877 to 1894. At first audiences were small, but they increased as
interest in the subject mounted. It is significant that this span of years
coincided with the period in which forest conservation in the United
States matured from dreams of a few ardent promoters to an established governmental function—reflecting the changing temper of the
times, to which the Rothrock lectures substantially contributed. There
is unanimity among historians that the historic Michaux lectures had a
profound effect in the building of popular sentiment for forest conservation.[9] Building that sentiment to the point necessary to bring about
government action required twenty-five years of "arduous pounding"
to prepare the public for such ideas. Most effective of those pounders
was Joseph Rothrock. His influence at home, in Philadelphia and
Pennsylvania, was especially effective, enabling him to found, in 1886,
the Pennsylvania Forestry Association, the oldest state forestry association with an unbroken history.[10]

By 1894, when Rothrock presented his fifteenth and final course
of Michaux lectures, it had already become obvious that the Michaux
legacy and Rothrock's persuasive skill and ardor had developed a wide
favorable public sentiment. In 1893, even before the lecture courses

were concluded, the Pennsylvania legislature established the Pennsylvania Forestry Commission, and Rothrock was appointed to lead it. The new commissioner forthwith turned again to the Philosophical Society's Michaux legacy committee for assistance. In a letter to the committee he stated that, despite the prevailing interest in forestry, "there is an utter absence of the data required for the proper presentation of the important questions involved," and that he knew of no use that could be made of the money more in accord with the wishes of the testator. The requisite funds were forthcoming and two years later the commission's report, a 348-page work, almost all from the pen of Rothrock, "refreshingly factual and scientific, and free of sentimentality," was published and presented to the legislature. That report became "a landmark in the emergence of effective forestry in America," emphasizing the crying need of "protection and sound management."[11]

The impact of the report was electric, in view of the state's sad decline in its timber industry, from first in the nation in 1860 to dependence on imports of timber, less than four decades later. Action was prompt and forward looking. In 1897 the legislature authorized acquisition by the state of unseated lands for forest reservations, specifying only that the lands be on the headwaters of the rivers of the commonwealth. Purchases began the next year. Those acquisitions prompted the establishment of the Department of Forestry and the naming of Rothrock to head it.[12]

The new department promptly set itself to perform its responsibilities. Among its acquisitions in 1901 were tracts of cutover lands between Chambersburg and Gettysburg in a region of streams tributary to the Potomac, Susquehanna, and Delaware rivers, aggregating some 32,000 acres. With later additions, increasing the area to 77,000 acres lying along both sides of U.S. Highway 30, a short distance south of the Pennsylvania Turnpike, those purchases became the first of nineteen Pennsylvania State Forests and, appropriately, it was named Michaux State Forest for the Michauxs, father and son. To help protect the new forest, a fire lookout tower, the first in the country, was erected in 1905 utilizing the timber at hand for its construction. Even before that tower was erected, a forest tree nursery was established there to produce the seedlings with which to plant the burnt-over areas—again, the first in the country. White pine seedlings from it, which were set out in an abandoned field, marked the first ever of such silviculture in the United States. These "firsts" were followed by yet another, the State Forest Academy, which was started there in 1903.

Those were all developments that would surely have gratified the Michauxs. So, too, would the Michaux State Forest's other services—protecting the area's many impoundments to provide the water supplies of cities in the area. Now its timber harvests infuse their substantial value into the commonwealth's economy. Finally, from the Michaux State Forest flow widespread benefits probably unanticipated by its founders, the public recreation resources it provides. What with the establishment of two state parks within its bounds, and its lengthwise transection by the Appalachian Trail, Michaux State Park has become an immensely popular recreation area. During the decade of the seventies the number of its visitors grew from ninety thousand to more than a million per year.[13] Beyond that, the manifold and diverse uses of Michaux State Forest have made it a classic example of sustained yield, multiple-use forestry, the modern evolution of the Michaux's eighteenth- and nineteenth-century concepts of forest conservation and use.

At this writing, almost 130 years after the death of the younger Michaux, the Philosophical Society's fund that he dedicated to the promotion of silviculture in the United States continues to contribute significantly to its intent, long after the utility of his *North American Sylva* as a manual of North American trees has dwindled to the status of an admirable document in the history of American forestry. Continuing the contributions of the Michaux Fund to the advancement of American forestry is a long-term experimental research project under way at the Morris Arboretum at Philadelphia. It involves basic research in the genetics of the most important genus of temperate-zone hardwoods, the oaks, a cooperative project of the Morris Arboretum, University of Pennsylvania, Northeastern Experiment Station of the United States Forest Service, and the Philosophical Society's Michaux Fund. Its aim is to fathom the complex genetics of oaks, a genus particularly prone to producing natural hybrids.

Active work on the carefully conceived project began in 1953 with the gathering by the Forest Service of 150 separate acorn collections from twenty-three states, representing thirty-seven different species. That harvest was planted in specially designed rodent-proof beds. Now, thirty years later, the work continues. Periodical reports on the results regularly appear. The work and its results suggest the possibility that "super oaks" of more valuable varieties, like the "super pines" now being routinely planted in the South, may one day be gracing the hills and valleys of many small, unproductive woodland holdings not adaptable to pine culture, transforming them into areas productive of quality timber far more valuable to their owners and society.[14]

All in all, it is surprising that two Frenchmen, father and son, whose joint lives spanned more than half of both the eighteenth and nineteenth centuries, men without wealth, prestige of birth, militancy of conduct, outstanding artistic talents, or high goverment office could, nevertheless, as advocates of the beneficial use of nature's productions for the advantage of human existence, have contributed so much to that aim, not only in their native land, but in America as well. Theirs was a dedication intimately bound up with the spirit of the Enlightenment—a fascination with the utilization of scientific knowledge acquired through both observation and experimental research. In the realm of botanical advancement, its focus was first on exploration and discovery and the international exchange of botanical productions, the area in which Michaux père was notable, for to cultivate potentially useful plants and trees they first had to be found and their properties observed before their utility could be studied and tested through experimental culture, the area in which Michaux fils led the way. Together, their contributions were of significant and lasting value.[15] America's great debt to these two devoted Frenchmen has been and remains beyond question.

ABBREVIATIONS ❧ NOTES
BIBLIOGRAPHY ❧ INDEX

✎§ Abbreviations

AHS	American Historical Society
AM	André Michaux
AN	Archives nationales. All citations so noted are from microfilms at APS of Michaux-related documents in the Archives nationales or Bibliothèque nationale.
APS	American Philosophical Society
AT	André Thouin
BM	Bibliothèque du muséum national d'histoire naturelle
Bur. of Ag.	Bureau de l'Agriculture
BV Papers	Benjamin Vaughan Papers, APS
Bot. FA	*Les Botanistes Français en Amérique du Nord*
Com. Com. Af.	Commissioner for Commercial Affairs
CWL	Caspar Wistar letters, APS
FAM	François André Michaux
JAM	*Journal of André Michaux* ("Journal de mon Voyage," ed. C. S. Sargent)
JD	AM, Journal de Dépense
JV	John Vaughan
MacPhail	Ian Macphail, *André & François André Michaux* (bibliography)
Mem. ab.	AM, "Mémoire abrégé"
Mich. col.	Michaux collections in Archives nationales and Bibliothèque nationale and Bibliothèque du muséum National d'histoire naturelle
Mich. Papers	Michaux Papers, APS
Min. of Ag.	Ministre de l'Agriculture
Min. of Fin.	Ministre de Finance
Min. of Int.	Ministre de l'Intérieur
Mus. of Nat. Hist.	Muséum national d'histoire naturelle
Nat. Inst.	Institut national de France
Perse J.	"Journal de Mon Voyage en Perse"
Proc. APS	*Proceedings of the American Philosophical Society*

SCHM	*South Carolina Historical and Genealogical Magazine*
Sylva	FAM, *The North American Sylva*
Thwaites	*Early Western Travels,* vol. 3, ed. Rueben Gold Thwaites
Trans. APS	*Transactions of the American Philosophical Society*
Tr. FAM	FAM, *Travels to the West of the Alleghany Mountains,* in Thwaites

◆§ Notes

Chapter 1 ₴❧ Youth and Apprenticeship, 1746–1782

1. AM to unidentified friend, L'Orient, Sept. 8, 1785, Mich. Papers. L'Orient, now Lorient, was established in the seventeenth century as a port for ships of La Compagnie des Indes for trade with India and China.

2. No complete authoritative list of plants introduced by AM is possible. We have included here only those for which we have documentation among the following sources: K. W. Hunt, "Charleston Woody Flora," pp. 671–72; W. C. Coker, "Garden of André Michaux," pp. 62–72; Donald Culross Peattie, *Almanac for Moderns*, p. 383; M. D. Hodgins, "Pride of India Tree," pp. 22–25; Evelyn McD. Frazier, *The State* (Columbia, S.C.), Feb. 24, 1967, p. 2B; see also ibid., June 4, 1961; U. P. Hedrick, *A History of Horticulture in America to 1860*, pp. 191–94; and the unpublished diaries of Dr. Charles Drayton, Drayton Family Papers, Historic Charleston Foundation, Charleston, S.C.; microfilm, South Carolina Department of Archives and History.

We have not been able to determine which or how many of the "Chinese azaleas" AM introduced into this country from Europe, where oriental azaleas had been grown at least as early as the late seventeenth century. "In southwestern China is found one of nature's great caprices—the Rhododendron storehouse of the world. Here, within the briefest distances, species occur by the hundreds in the most amazing wealth of shape, size and color" (John C. Wister, ed., *Garden Book*, pp. 448–56).

3. Louis Guillaume Lemonnier (1717–1799), son and brother of noted astronomers, became a physician in 1728. His special interest and ability in botany first brought him into favor with Louis XV and appointment both as physician to His Majesty and as professor of botany at the Jardin du Roi in Paris.

4. Pierre Poivre (1719–1786), French naturalist and botanical collector principally on Mauritius, where with his nephew Pierre Sonnerat he developed a botanical garden, Le Jardin des Pamplemousses. See Marguerite Duval, *The King's Garden*, ch. 8.

5. Louis XVI (1754–1793) succeeded his grandfather as king of France in 1774.

6. D'Angiviller was a member of L'Académie des Sciences and an enthusiastic friend of Buffon and Rousseau.

7. James Bruce (1730–1794), Scottish explorer who in 1773 arrived in France en route from Africa to be welcomed there by Buffon and other savants. His *Travels to Discover the Source of the Nile* was published in 1790.

8. There were five members of the Jussieu family who were distinguished botanists associated with the Jardin du Roi: Antoine (1686–1779); his brothers, Bernard (1699–1777) and Joseph (1704–1779); Antoine Laurent (1748–1836), nephew of the preceding; and Adrian (1797–1853), son of Antoine Laurent. Bernard had been in charge of the classification of the plants in the

botanical garden created by Louis XV at the Trianon; Joseph distinguished himself as plant collector in South America; Antoine Laurent was the creator of the "natural" classification of plants (M. Alfred Lacroix, *Notice Historique sur les Cinq de Jussieu*).

9. Carolus Linnaeus, or Carl von Linné (1707–1778), Swedish naturalist.

10. Georges Louis Le Clerc, comte de Buffon (1707–1788).

11. Known as the Jardin des Plantes since the birth of the Republic.

12. André Thouin (1742–1824). Though he acquired a long list of honors, the focus of AT's life remained the garden where, in modest lodgings, he became a revered figure who welcomed there plant lovers from many lands, among them Thomas Jefferson.

13. Joseph Banks (1743–1820) became president of the Royal Society.

14. Hans Sloane (1660–1753), naturalist whose extensive scientific collections became the nucleus of the British Museum.

15. Kew Gardens: Peter Collinson in London writing on Aug. 21, 1776, exclaimed, "The Stuartia flowered for the first time in the Princess of Wales' Garden at Kew, which is the paradise of our world, where all plants are found that money or interest can procure" (William Darlington, ed., *Memorials of John Bartram*, p. 282).

16. *Nouvelle Biographie Universelle* (puis *Générale*).

17. Lamarck (1774–1829), botanist to the king, a title AM would also have, had completed by 1785 his massive *Dictionnaire de Botanique* and *Illustrations de Genre*. In 1788 he became associate botanist at the Jardin du Roi.

18. J. P. F. Deleuze, "Notice Historique sur André Michaux," translated by Charles Konig and John Sims as "Memoirs of the Life and Botanical Travels of André Michaux," pp. 325–26.

Deleuze (1753–1835), French naturalist, friend and colleague of AM, served as both assistant naturalist and editor of the *Annales* at the Mus. of Nat. Hist. at the Jardin des Plantes.

19. Jean François Xavier Rousseau (1738–1808), cousin of the philosopher Rousseau, rendered important diplomatic services to France through his familiarity with Persia and the languages of Asia Minor.

20. E.-T. Hamy, "Voyage d'André Michaux en Syrie et en Perse," pp. 351–88 (all quotations from Hamy are the authors' translations).

21. "Monsieur," brother of Louis XVI, was them comte de Provence. He became king of France, 1814–15 and 1815–24, as Louis XVIII.

22. AM, Perse J., p. 1 (all quotations from AM's Persian journal are the authors' translations).

Chapter 2 ☙ Persian Expedition, 1782–1783

1. Hamy, "Voyage," p. 355; AM, Perse J., pp. 4–5.

2. AM throughout his travels invariably took pains to establish relations at each port or city with some professional or amateur in his field, an important aid in plant collection and exchange.

3. Payas, tribesman from Paya, a district north of Alexandretta.

4. Hamy, "Voyage," pp. 356–67; AM, Perse J., pp. 7–8.

5. Hamy, "Voyage," p. 357; AM, Perse J., p. 9.

6. AM to AT, Aleppo, July 30, 1782, Deleuze, "Memoirs," pp. 326–27.

7. The Kurds, then and now, pastoral and warlike tribes of Kurdistan but ranging also into Turkey, Iraq, and Iran.

8. Beylan, a village near the ancient gates of Syria. Some months before, the bishop of Beylan, making the same journey, was forced to pay more than 1,000 piastres in bribes (AM to his father-in-law, Claye, Aleppo, Sept. 30, 1782, Hamy, "Voyage," p. 359).

9. Hamy, "Voyage," p. 359; AM, Perse J., pp. 11–12.

10. AM to AT, Aleppo, July 30, 1782, Deleuze, "Memoirs," p. 327.

11. Hamy, "Voyage," p. 361.

12. AM to AT, Aleppo, July 30, 1782, Deleuze "Memoirs," p. 327.

13. Chretien-Guillaume de Lamoignon de Malesherbes (1721–1794), minister under Louis XVI, labored to effect reforms in France to increase civil liberties of Protestants, to secure freedom of the press, to abolish lettres de cachet, and other abuses. He was noted also in literary circles, and was an amateur botanist of note whose garden was visited by Thomas Jefferson in 1785. Because he returned to France to volunteer his services as counsel for the king at his trial, he and his whole family were sent to the guillotine during the Terror.

14. AM to AT, Aleppo, July 30, 1782, Deleuze, "Memoirs," p. 327.

15. Lemonnier to AM, Hamy, "Voyage," p. 365.

16. AM, Perse J., p. 27; Hamy, "Voyage," p. 365.

17. AM to Claye, Sept. 30, 1782, Hamy, "Voyage," p. 365.

18. Ibid.

19. Although both Rousseau and his wife had been born in Esfahan, AM considered them Europeans because of their ancestry and his official status as French consul (Hamy, "Voyage," p. 366; AM, Perse J., p. 27).

20. AM to Monsieur, Brother of the King, Baghdad, Jan. 14, 1783, Hamy, "Voyage," pp. 372–73 (authors' trans.).

21. AM, Perse J., pp. 48–51.

22. AM to Monsieur, Brother of the King, Baghdad, Jan. 14, 1783, Hamy, "Voyage," pp. 372–73.

23. Hella, now Hillah, is on the lower Euphrates, near where the ruins of Ancient Babylon would later be found. Hamy, "Voyage," p. 374.

24. Hamy, "Voyage," pp. 374–75; AM, Perse J., pp. 52–53.

25. The marshes AM is describing cover about 6,000 square miles and are the home of the "People of the Reeds," or Marsh Arabs (Wilfred Thesinger, *The Marsh Arabs*).

26. AM to FAM, Bassora (Basra), May 15, 1783, AN (authors' trans.).

27. Hamy, "Voyage," p. 377; AM, Perse J., pp. 58–62.

Chapter 3 ୧✒ Persia, 1783–1785

1. Hamy, "Voyage," p. 380.

2. AM to FAM, "Monsieur Michaux, Le Jeune," Shiraz, Mar. 21, 1784, Mich. Papers (authors' trans.).

3. Sir John Chardin, *Journal du Voyage . . . en Perse et aux Indes Orientales*.

4. Hamy, "Voyage," pp. 382–83; AM, Perse J., p. 7.

5. *Diospyros* is the principal genus of the ebony family (*Ebenaceae*) that includes the American persimmon, *D. virginiana*.

6. *Gleditsia*, a genus of the *Fabaceae* family that includes the American honey locust, *G. triacanthos*.

7. AM to Monsieur, Brother of the King, Hamy, "Voyage," p. 384.

8. Deleuze, "Memoirs," p. 328.

9. Ctesiphon, ancient city of Babylon, on the Tigris 45 miles below Babylon.

10. Deleuze, "Memoirs," p. 329. This monument was described in Millin's *Monumens Antiques*, vol. 1, p. 58.

11. Hamy, "Voyage," p. 385. This stone, known as Caillou Michaux, preserved in the Nat. Lib. in Paris, is celebrated in the history of Oriental archaeology.

12. Ibid., pp. 385–86.

Chapter 4 ⬧ King's Botanist, Mission to America, 1785

1. Three years later the two ships of the expedition vanished without trace somewhere in the South Seas.

2. AN doc. serie 012113A, Divers no. 3 (authors' trans.).

3. Ibid.

4. Gilbert Chinard, "André and François André Michaux and Their Predecessors," p. 350.

5. Born Michel Guillaume Jean de Crèvecoeur (1735–1813); author of the influential *Letters from an American Farmer*, he has been given credit for bringing AM to the U.S. (William J. Robbins, "French Botanists and the Flora of the Northeastern United States," p. 363).

6. Note, for example, Darlington, ed., *Memorials*.

7. Brooke Hindle, *The Pursuit of Science in Revolutionary America*, pp. 11–76 passim.

8. Bernard Faÿ, *Franklin, the Apostle of Modern Times*, pp. 499–500.

9. Howard C. Rice, *Thomas Jefferson's Paris*, p. 51.

10. Thomas Jefferson, *Notes on the State of Virginia*, p. 55.

11. In later years, speaking of the Jardin, Jefferson rememberd it as being "in the country situated on the eastern edge of the city" (Howard C. Rice, Jr., *Thomas Jefferson's Paris*, p. 121). Jefferson to Martha (Jefferson) Randolph, Oct. 18, 1808, Edwin Morris Betts, ed., *Jefferson's Garden Book*, p. 378.

12. The turkey, already long domesticated in France, was the Mexican species, smaller and less handsome than the North American *Meleagris gallopavo*, here referred to.

13. "Instruction aux Sieur André Michaux, Botaniste du Roi," AN (authors' trans.).

14. Ibid.

15. About $1,000 American money of the day.

16. Although some documents give Saunier's age at that time as 17, it appears certain that 34 is correct. His name is spelled *Saulnier, Sumer, Saumier, Saunier*. Paul himself wrote it *Saunier* and so it appears in the official documents of his assignment and in AM's correspondence (William J. Robbins and Mary Christine Howson, "André Michaux's New Jersey Garden and Pierre Paul Saunier," pp. 351–70).

17. The wide influence of the Jardin du Roi is indicated by AT's complaint to D'Angiviller of the impressment of his apprentice gardeners, five demands in four months for gardeners to accompany expeditions to far-flung regions (AT to D'Angiviller, Paris, Aug. 5, 1785, AN doc.).

18. Among the volumes provided for the gardener were Philip Miller's *Botanical Dictionary* in French, a treatise on theoretical and practical culture, and a catalogue of all trees then cultivated in France.

19. AM to Cuvillier, L'Orient, undated, AN doc. (authors' trans.).

20. AM to D'Angiviller, L'Orient, Sept. 2, 1785, AN doc. (authors' trans.).

21. AM to Anon. (probably AT), L'Orient, Sept. 8, 1785, AN doc. (authors' trans.).

22. AM to D'Angiviller, L'Orient, Sept. 27, 1785, AN doc. (authors' trans.).

23. Louis-Guillaume Otto, comte de Mosloy (1754–1817), French diplomat, came to U.S. with La Luzerne and served 13 years as chargé d'affaires. Member of APS. Returned to France for a brilliant career, negotiating the Peace of Amiens and the marriage of Napoleon to Marie-Louise of Austria.

24. Otto to D'Angiviller, New York, Oct. 27, 1785, AN doc. (authors' trans.).

Peter (Pehr) Kalm (1716–1779), Swedish naturalist trained by Linnaeus, spent three years in the middle states and Canada, collecting natural history specimens and material for his well-known *Travels into North America*, published in 1770.

Capt. Jonathan Carver (1710–1780), American explorer and adventurer, author of widely popular *Travels through the Interior Parts of North America* (London, 1778).

Mark Catesby (1683–1749), English naturalist whose magnificent *Natural History of Carolina, Florida and the Bahama Island* (London, 1754) was probably the most valuable contribution to natural history of colonial America.

25. Otto to D'Angiviller, New York, Nov. 25, 1785, AN doc. (authors' trans.).

26. "Memo" to all "Captains of Packet Boats" of the King en route to the Port of New York, Versailles, Aug. 21, 1785. AN doc. (authors' trans.).

Chapter 5 ᙖ➤ *New York, Entrée and Establishment,* *1785–1786*

1. For example, "Between December 1st and 15th, having purchased winter clothing for himself at a cost of $14.75, he went with laborers, twice to

Elizabethtown, and also to New Ark (Newark) New Jersey, a trip which necessitated the crossing of three rivers to Harlem . . . and Snake Hill in New Jersey" (Robbins and Howson, "André Michaux's New Jersey Garden," pp. 353–54).

2. AM to d'Angiviller, New York, Dec. 1785, probably early in the month, AN doc. (authors' trans.).

3. The château of Rambouillet, former home of Catherine de Médicis and Henry IV, set in the royal hunting grounds, was a favorite residence of Louis XVI, a passionate huntsman.

4. AM to D'Angiviller, New York, Dec. 8, 1785, AN doc. (authors' trans.).

5. Abbé Nolin to D'Angiviller, Paris, Feb. 6, 1786, AN doc. (authors' trans.).

6. C. Berger to D'Angiviller, Nantes, Feb. 4, 1786, AN doc. (authors' trans.).

7. AM to Lemonnier, New York, Dec. 9, 1785, BM doc., AT Collection, in *Bot. FA,* pp. 241–43 (authors' trans.).

8. AM to D'Angiviller, New York, Dec. 1785, AN doc. (authors' trans.).

9. AM to Dutartre, New York, Dec. 9, 1785, AN doc. (authors' trans.).

10. AM to Lemonnier, New York, Dec. 9, 1785, BM doc., AT Col., in *Bot. FA,* pp. 241–43 (authors' trans.).

11. JD, Dec. 15, 1785. (All quotations from JD are authors' trans.).

12. AM to D'Angiviller, New York, Dec. 1785, AN doc.

13. Otto to D'Angiviller, Nov. 25, 1785, AN doc.

14. AM to D'Angiviller, Jan. 18, 1786, AN doc.

15. AM to D'Angiviller, New York, Jan. 18, 1786, AN doc.

16. AM to Lemonnier, New York, Jan. 26, 1786, BM doc., AT Col., in *Bot. FA,* p. 245.

17. AM to D'Angiviller, New York, Jan. 18, 1786, AN doc.

18. William Livingston (1723–1790), lawyer and soldier, commander of N.J. militia in Am. Revolution, mem. APS, first governor of N.J., holding that office until his death. His niece was Consul Otto's first wife.

19. "An act to enable André Michaux to purchase lands in the State of New Jersey under certain restrictions," Mar. 3, 1786, New Jersey House of Assembly, Mich. Papers.

20. Otto to D'Angiviller, New York, Mar. 11., 1786, Mich. Papers. This letter contained a copy of the N.J. Act.

21. Conveyance of the Bergen nursery site was from Nicholas Fish to André Michaux. The price, according to AM's estimate of the exchange rate, was $750 (AM to D'Angiviller, New York, Jan. 18, 1786, Mich. Papers).

Nicholas Fish (1758–1823) soldier and government official, was Lt. Col. in Am. Revolution, Adj. Gen. of N.Y. in 1786, and later a leading Federalist politician.

22. Robert Morris (1734–1806) merchant, banker, and financier in the Am. Revolution, signer of the Declaration of Independence, member Const. Convention, and member APS.

23. JD, Feb. 9, 1786.

24. AM to D'Angiviller, New York, May 3, 1786, AN doc. (authors' trans.).

25. Ibid.

26. Ibid.

27. AM to Cuvillier, New York, May 12, 1786, AN doc. (authors' trans.).

28. AM to D'Angiviller, Philadelphia, June 11, 1786, AN doc. (authors' trans.).

29. Kalm, *Travels,* pp. 117–25 passim.

30. AM to Cuvillier, New York, July 15, 1786. AN doc. (authors' trans.).

31. Struthers Burt, *Philadelphia, Holy Experiment,* p. 229.

32. AM to D'Angiviller, New York, July 15, 1786, AN doc.

33. The Bartram garden on the Schuylkill, near Philadelphia, the first botanical garden in America, was founded by John Bartram (1699–1777), farmer and self-taught botanist, friend of Franklin and with him a founder of APS, widely known throughout the colonies over much of which he traveled on his botanical expeditions.

After his death the garden was carried on by his sons, William (1739–1823), naturalist and botanical explorer of the southeastern states and author of *Travels through North and South Carolina, Georgia, East and West Florida,* (Philadelphia, 1791) and John Bartram, Jr. (1743–1812), who succeeded his father as manager of the farm and botanical business.

34. *Franklinia alatamaha,* discovered by John and William Bartram on the Altamaha River in Georgia, the only place this rare and beautiful tree has ever been found growing wild.

35. The duc de Lauzon, who came to America soon after Lafayette, commanded a cavalry unit in the American Revolution. He returned to France after the war and was guillotined during the Terror 1793.

36. Donald Jackson and Dorothy Twohig, eds., *Diaries of George Washington,* IV:350, 354, V:1.

37. AM to D'Angiviller, New York, July 15, 1786, AN doc. (authors' trans.).

38. JD, July-Sept. 1786.

39. AM to D'Angiviller, New York, Aug. 18, 1786, AN doc. (authors' trans.).

40. Ibid.

41. JD, Sept. 2, 1786.

42. William Hamilton (1745–1813) introduced and cultivated rare and beautiful plants in his elegantly landscaped garden on the right bank of the Schuylkill, and is among those credited with the introduction of the Lombardy poplar (Darlington, ed., *Memorials,* p. 577). The Woodlands is now a part of Woodlawn cemetery.

43. It is a reasonable assumption that AM had purchased the horses with the intention of going south by land, stopping by Philadelphia en route, but his decision to go by sea instead necessitated this quick journey to that city before sailing.

Chapter 6 ?❧ *Carolina, 1786–1787*

1. The British had occupied Charleston from May 19, 1780, to Dec. 14, 1782.

2. Mrs. St. Julien Ravenel, *Charleston,* pp. 337–38.

3. Petry, serving in the absence of Chateaufort.

4. Gen. William Moultrie (1730–1805), Revolutionary hero and gov. of S.C., 1785–87. In the first important engagement in the South, Moultrie, then colonel, was in command of the unfinished fort on Sullivans Island at the entrance to Charleston harbor. His small band of defenders turned back the 50-vessel British fleet. The fort was named in honor of its commander. Later he was captured by the British and imprisoned until exchanged for Gen. Burgoyne.

5. AM to D'Angiviller, Charleston, Sept. 30, 1786, AN doc. (authors' trans.).

6. AM to D'Angiviller, Charleston, Nov. 12, 1786, AN doc. (authors' trans.).

7. The count was not unprepared for this proposal. Otto, after his first meeting with AM, suggested to the count: "Independently of the garden that M. Michaux proposes to establish here for the productions of the North of America, you will perhaps judge it apropos, Monsieur le Comte, to have orders given to M. Chateaufort, consul at Charleston, to make a similar establishment in Carolina for the trees and plants which grow only in the warm regions. I have occasion to believe that most of the productions of the two Carolinas and of Georgia could thrive in the south of France" (Otto to D'Angiviller, New York, Nov. 25, 1785, AN doc., authors' trans.).

8. AM to D'Angiviller, Charleston, Nov. 12, 1786. AN doc. (authors' trans.).

9. Ibid.

10. Ibid.

11. Francis Harper, ed., *The Travels of William Bartram,* p. 102.

12. Michaux wrote that the *Ilex cassine* is "called here the Yaupon or tea by the Indians," but it seems likely he had confused it with the closely related *Ilex vomitoria,* now sometimes called yaupon.

13. AM to D'Angiviller, Charleston, Nov. 12, 1786, AN doc. (authors' trans.).

14. JD, Dec. 1786.

15. AM to D'Angiviller, Charleston, Dec. 2, 1786, AN doc. (authors' trans.).

16. This transaction required four long documents, two leases, and two releases, all in the excessively convoluted and repetitious legal verbiage of scriveners of that day, expressing considerations of 5 shillings, 10 shillings, 10 shillings and 120 pounds, 14 shillings 3 pence and one peppercorn, for which John Rosemond and his wife Rachel and Lewis Beselieu conveyed "part of a plantation in the Paris of St. James, Goosecreek," upon which was located a family burying ground, "to the vendee-purchaser, Andrew Michaux." These documents are recorded in the office of the Register of Mesne Conveyances in Charleston in Book Y-5, pp. 129–32. The two leases bear the date Nov. 2, 1786, the releases Nov. 3, 1786. They were all recorded on July 12, 1787.

17. JD, Dec. 1786, AN doc.

18. AM to D'Angiviller, Charleston, Dec. 26, 1786, AN doc. (authors' trans.).

19. Ibid.

20. There is a poignance in reading the many hopes AM confidently expressed for the future of his plants in their French home at Rambouillet when one is aware of how few would survive the hazards of the times in France.

21. "Catalogue of plants shipped" sent by AM to D'Angiviller, Charleston, Dec. 26, 1786, AN doc. (authors' trans.).

22. JD, Jan.-Mar. 1787, AN doc.

23. "Always at least four workers employed. One pays them very dearly here, more dearly than in the French colonies" (AM to D'Angiviller, Charleston, Apr. 2, 1787, AN doc, authors' trans.).

24. Ibid.

25. AM to D'Angiviller, Charleston, Feb. 2, 1787, AN doc. (authors' trans.).

26. AM to D'Angiviller, Charleston, Mar. 10, 1787, AN doc. (authors' trans.). This letter lists 21 chests shipped; however, a letter written the same day on shipboard, by AM to Cuvillier, lists 22, and this is the figure referred to in later references.

27. AM to D'Angiviller, Charleston, Mar. 10, 1787, AN doc. (authors' trans.).

28. AM to Cuvillier, Charleston, Apr. 8, 1787, AN doc. (authors' trans.).

29. Ruellan (or Roland) and Company shipping agents at Le Havre, to Cuvillier, Le Havre, May 25, 1787, AN doc. (authors' trans.).

Chapter 7 ᘒᔰ *Botanizing in Carolina, 1787–1788*

1. See chap. 14.

2. The manuscript of Michaux's American journal in the surviving notebooks was edited with an introduction and explanatory notes by C. S. Sargent and published in the original French by APS as "Portions of the Journal of André Michaux." All references to or quotations from this journal, which AM entitled "Journal de Mon Voyage" (and which are cited here as *JAM*) are to this Sargent edition and are our translations unless otherwise indicated.

C. S. Sargent (1841–1927), botanist and arborculturist, a native of Boston and graduate of Harvard, became in 1872 director of the Harvard Botanic Garden and prof. of horticulture. He published (1891–1902) *The Silva of North America* in 14 folio volumes, and in 1905 his *Manual of the Trees of North America*, supplanting the *North American Sylva* of FAM and Thomas Nuttall.

3. John Fraser, Scottish plant hunter, made five expeditions to America between 1784 and 1795 and was associated with Thomas Walter, S.C. botanist. Fraser published an account of his 1787 visit to the Cherokee nation, *A Short History of the Agnostic Cornucopiae* (London, 1789) in which he recalls AM as "a French gentleman who had been sent to America . . . by his most Christian Majesty," and confesses his determination to excel the French botanist in discoveries, or at least to obtain for Great Britain equal honors in the field with France. To this end he attached himself to Michaux on the Cherokee expedition.

4. This account unless otherwise noted follows *JAM*.

5. This was the *Magnolia fraseri,* named for Fraser by Thomas Walter, eighteenth-century S.C. botanist.

6. Either the rare venomous coral snake, *Micrurus fulvius,* or its harmless mimic the scarlet kingsnake, *Lampropeltis doliata.*

7. Le Roy Hammond, owner of a mill and home on the road from Augusta to Cherokee Ponds. Hammond had served in the Am. Rev. as a partisan under Gen. Andrew Pickens (Margaret M. Seaborn, ed., *André Michaux's Journeys in Oconee County,* p. 59).

8. Andrew Pickens (1739–1817) Partisan leader in the Am. Revolution, eventually Brig. Gen., U.S. agent for Indian Affairs, whose frontier plantation, Hopewell, was near Seneca on the Keowee River. Presumably, after leaving Augusta, AM had made another and unrecorded visit to Hammond's place to receive this letter.

9. Probably a great horned owl, *Bubo virginianus,* wide ranging over most of the continent.

10. The Keowee (the Kiwi in *JAM*) has its source in N.C. and flows southwardly across S.C. to fall into the Savannah.

11. Andrew C. Kimmens, ed., *Tales of the Ginseng.*

12. For a follow-up of these purchases see, chap. 17, notes 17, 18, and 19.

13. *Pyrularia pubera* (Mich.), buffalo nut, fruit very poisonous, the only American species of a genus with but three species, the others being in Asia. This species, a discovery of AM, is thought to be parasitic on the roots of deciduous trees.

14. *JAM,* p. 18.

15. Deleuze, "Memoirs," p. 333.

16. Harper, ed., *Travels,* pp. 225–26.

17. *JAM,* p. 20.

18. Ibid., p. 21.

19. AM had traveled in all on this expedition approximately 900 miles across S.C. and Ga.

20. AM to D'Angiviller, New York, Aug. 2, 1787, AN doc. (authors' trans.).

21. Named for John Fothergill (1712–1780) English physician, naturalist, and philanthropist, a patron of Wm. Bartram.

22. AM to D'Angiviller, New York, Aug. 2, 1787, AN doc. (authors' trans.).

23. The two sums were to cover the expenses of the N.J. establishment and of the Keowee journey and to supply funds for future travels.

24. AM to D'Angiviller, Charleston, Aug. 29, 1787, AN doc. (authors' trans.).

25. AM to D'Angiviller, Charleston, Sept. 25, 1787, AN doc.; Florient Du Bertrand to D'Angiviller, Bordeaux, Nov. 16, 1787, AN doc. (authors' trans.). Four of the ducks reached France safely.

26. AM to D'Angiviller, Charleston, Sept. 25, 1787, AN doc. (authors' trans.).

27. AM to D'Angiviller, Charleston, Dec. 27, 1787, AN doc. (authors' trans.).

28. Ibid.

Chapter 8 ᘎᕉ *Florida, 1788*

1. Although Florida is entirely in the temperate zone, its climate is dominated by subtropical waters.

2. *JAM*, p. 27.

3. *Rhizophoraceae* (Federal Works Agency, WPA, *Florida: A Guide to the Southernmost State*, p. 23).

4. *JAM*, p. 28.

5. Bella Vista, plantation home of John Moultrie, Lt. Gov. of Fla. during the British occupation (1763–1783) who moved to the Bahamas with many other British when Spain resumed possession of the province.

6. Part of the network of shallow backwaters separating the mainland from the almost unbroken chain of barrier islands that guard the southeast U.S. coast from Md. to the tip of Fla., most of it utilized today by the Intracoastal Waterway.

7. After Britain ceded Fla. to Spain in 1783, more than 15,000 English settlers moved to the West Indies, abandoning their homes and plantations to Indians, plunderers, and the quick-growing jungle.

8. *JAM*, pp. 29–30. Michaux notes that this site is called "Musketo Shore" (côte des mosquitoes) on a map published in London some years before as "Nouvelle Carte de la Florida."

9. *JAM*, p. 32.

10. Ibid., and a letter of AM to D'Angiviller, St. Augustine, Apr. 24, 1788, AN doc. (authors' trans.).

11. *JAM*, p. 34.

12. Ibid.

13. *Gray's Manual of Botany*, 8th ed., p. 903.

14. *JAM*, p. 35.

15. It seems probable that this was Job Wiggins, William Bartram's friend and travel companion (Harper, ed., *Travels*, pp. 306, 363n).

16. Probably Salt Springs Run, Bartram's "Little River," flowing from Six Mile Springs (ibid., pp. 160–68).

17. *JAM*, p. 36. C. S. Sargent's footnote states that this rare and beautiful shrub, the yellow flowering star anise (*Illicium parviflorum*) has not been found growing wild in North America since AM's discovery of it in several places in this region of Fla. It is an aromatic shrub of a genus of the magnolia family of which there are but seven species, two in southeast U.S. and five in Asia. First described and named by AM.

18. *JAM*, p. 37.

19. Ibid.

20. Ibid., p. 38.

21. Ibid., p. 39. This Spalding may have been James, noted Scottish trader and scholar. Gen. MacIntosh was Lachlan MacIntosh (1725–1806), a native Scott, Ga. patriot in the Am. Revolution.

22. AM to D'Angiviller, Charleston, June 10, 1788, AN doc. (authors' trans.).

23. AM to D'Angiviller, Charleston, July 1, 1788, AN doc. (authors' trans.).

24. AM to D'Angiviller, Charleston, Aug. 2, 1788, AN doc. (authors' trans.).

25. AM to D'Angiviller, Charleston, Oct. 1, 1788, AN doc. (authors' trans.).

26. *JAM*, p. 41.

27. Ibid.

Chapter 9 ঈ Temperate Mountains and Tropical Isles, 1788–1791

1. *JAM*, p. 44.

2. Ibid., pp. 44–48.

3. Ibid., pp. 48–49. On this journey AM began a practice he thereafter followed of noting for future travels the desirable places to stop to insure avoidance of such experiences as this.

4. Ibid., p. 49.

5. AM to D'Angiviller, Charleston, Dec. 29, 1788, AN doc. (authors' trans.).

6. It remains disputed among botanists as to whether AM's *Magnolia cordata* was, in fact, a new species or a variety of *Magnolia acuminata*, the cucumber tree, or mountain magnolia. See J. K. Small, *Manual of Southeastern Flora* p. 534; W. C. Coker and H. R. Totten, *Trees of the Southeastern United States*, p. 167; A. E. Radford, H. E. Ahles, and C. R. Bell, *Manual of the Vascular Flora of the Carolinas*, p. 475.

7. Charles W. Short (1794–1863), physician and botanist, professor of botany at Transylvania Univ., collected and described the plants west of the Allegheny Mountains. His herbarium numbered 15,000 specimens.

8. The contents of AM's notebooks, "Journal de Mon Voyage" edited by Sargent, did not appear in print until 1889.

9. Ashton Chapman, "The Search for the Lost Shortia," pp. 112–15.

10. This account follows Chapman's article and that of C. S. Sargent, "Some remarks upon the journey of André Michaux to the high mountains of Carolina," pp. 466–73.

11. AM to D'Angiviller, Charleston, Jan. 5, 1789, AN doc. (authors' trans.).

12. Limosin, shipping agent at Le Havre, to D'Angiviller, Feb. 26, 1789, AN doc. (authors' trans.).

13. *JAM*, p. 50, has a list of AM's correspondents for one week, typical of many.

14. AM to D'Angiviller, Charleston, Apr. 28, 1789, AN doc. (authors' trans.). Most of these plants were shipped by AM for planting in the orangeries, or greenhouses, in France.

15. AM noted that a portion of his journal for 1789 had been lost so that "a great number of interesting observations will be abridged," an indication of the fidelity with which he usually kept his daily journal (*JAM*, p. 53n).

16. They observed the *Magnolia cordata* again at the foot of some moderately high mountains about 298 miles from Charleston (*JAM*, pp. 54–55).

17. Deleuze, "Memoirs," p. 337.

AM's last stop before entering the forest wilderness to the west was at the home of Col. Waightsill Avery (1741–1821), Rev. patriot and first attorney gen. of N.C. In the summer of 1788, he had been challenged to a duel by the fiery young Andrew Jackson. When the two met at the appointed time and place, both fired into the air (Marquis James, *Andrew Jackson, the Border Captain*, pp. 47–48).

18. *JAM*, p. 54. Mt. Mitchell, while not the highest mountain in North America, was the highest in the U.S. of that day.

19. *JAM*, p. 55.

20. "The Natural Bridge, the most sublime of Nature's works . . . so beautiful an arch, so elevated, so light, so springing, as it were, up to Heaven" (Jefferson, *Notes on the State of Virginia*, pp. 24–25).

21. *JAM*, p. 57.

22. François Barbe de Marbois (1745–1837). In 1780, as secretary of the French legation in Philadelphia, he had circulated a questionnaire seeking information on each of the states. Jefferson's responses touching on the state of Virginia became his famous *Notes on the State of Virginia*, first privately printed in Paris in May 1785. AM, who returned from Persia to Paris the following month, may well have seen a copy, since Jefferson was a friend of his colleague AT.

23. La Forest, Antoine René Charles Mathurin, comte de (1756–1846), French consul general, stationed first in New York, then in Philadelphia. Usually referred to by AM as De la Forest or Delaforest.

24. These gardens were, from 1802 to 1805, in the care of the German botanist Frederick Pursh (1774–1820), who later published a flora of North America, *Flora Americae Septentrionalis*, 1814.

25. *JAM*, p. 60.

26. The period covering this journey is treated very briefly in AM's journal, only some loose pages of notes.

27. These extraordinary springs and their beautiful environs are now submerged beneath the waters of the Santee impounded in Lake Marion.

28. James, *Andrew Jackson*, pp. 21–22.

29. *JAM*, p. 61.

30. *Magnolia glauca* is the name AM gave to the sweet bay, now *Magnolia Virginiana.*

31. *JAM*, p. 62.

32. What these difficulties were we can only conjecture, since neither AM's letter to Abbé Nolin nor the initial exchange of letters between the father and son after the latter's return to France has ever come to light. It seems probable that financial difficulties were the prime factor.

33. Abbé Nolin to D'Angiviller, Paris, Apr. 30, 1790, AN doc. (authors' trans.). The count had a residence at Rambouillet as well as others at Versailles and Paris.

34. AM to D'Angiviller, Charleston, Feb. 5, 1790, AN doc. (authors' trans.).

35. AM to D'Angiviller, Charleston, Feb. 23, 1790, AN doc. (authors' trans.).

36. AM to D'Angiviller, Charleston, Feb. 5, 1790, AN doc. (authors' trans.).

37. Ibid.

38. Deleuze, "Memoirs," p. 338.

39. AM to D'Angiviller, Charleston, Oct. 4, 1790, AN doc. (authors' trans.).

40. The year 1790 is almost a blank in AM's journal. The only entry for this year is for December 31.

41. *JAM,* p. 64.

42. *JAM,* pp. 63–65. Although AM may have had to reduce the number of his hired workers in order to save money, he still retained several hired, or rented, black workers, at least two of them slaves. He complained that no work could be done at the garden for five days, Jan. 18–23, because his laborers were needed by the parish to work the public highway, and again, on Feb. 6, they were absent all day to help a neighbor whose house had caught fire.

43. Ibid.

44. AM to John Bartram, Jr., Charleston, May 12, 1791, quoted by Joseph Ewan, ed., in his introduction to AM's *Flora Boreali-Americana,* p. xxxi.

45. *JAM,* p. 64.

46. FAM to D'Angiviller, Paris, Feb. 1791, AN doc. (authors' trans.). Young Michaux was then residing at 133 rue de la Harpe while pursuing his medical training.

47. AM to D'Angiviller, Charleston, Apr. 15, 1791, AN doc. (authors' trans.).

48. Ibid.

49. AM's regular journal entries cease in March 1791, and only a few entries on loose slips of paper cover this journey, the last dated May 22, 1791, when they returned to Charleston. Regular entries in the journal are resumed on March 27, 1792.

50. FAM, *The North American Sylva,* 1:260–61.

51. Charles Cotesworth Pinckney (1746–1825), soldier and statesman, born Charleston, S.C., son of colonial chief justice Charles Pinckney and Eliza Lucas, and educated abroad. He was sent to France with John Marshall and Elbridge Gerry when relations with the Director had deteriorated to the brink of war in 1796.

Chapter 10 ?❧ *The North Woods to Hudson Bay, 1792*

1. AM, mem. ab. (authors' trans.).

2. *JAM,* p. 67. John James Himely, Charleston merchant, probably Swiss born, with offices on Broad Street, a valued friend of both AM and FAM. To him AM entrusted the care of the Charleston garden in 1796 pending his return to the U.S. For some time he was part of the household of William Mills, father of famed architect Robert Mills, at the corner of Church and Tradd streets. There is evidence that he was the husband of a daughter of Mills's family.

3. Mem. ab. (authors' trans.). The transactions referred to are not on record in the Charleston courthouse. AM dates the act of acquistion made by Himely in April 1792, no day specified (*JAM*, p. 67).

4. Mem. ab. (authors' trans.).

5. There was mourning throughout America, England, and France for the beloved patriarch. In France a three-month period of mourning was proclaimed. Young FAM doubtless witnessed the elaborate memorial ceremonies in Paris.

6. Philadelphia remained the seat of government until 1800, when Washington became the capital.

7. The exact date of publication has not been determined, probably late in 1791, the year on its title page.

8. Benjamin Smith Barton (1766–1815), physician and naturalist. Educated in Philadelphia, Edinburgh, London, and Göttingen, mem. of APS, author of the first elementary botany by an American, *Elements of Botany* (1803).

9. Ralph Izard (1741–1804), one of the wealthiest and most distinguished of Carolina planters, was U.S. senator 1789–95.

10. Thomas Pinckney (1750–1828), younger brother of Charles Cotesworth Pinckney. Thomas likewise had distinguished careers in military, governmental, and diplomatic services.

11. Baron Palisot de Beauvois (1752–1820). After the slave uprising in Haiti, he was deported to the U.S., where he traveled in 1793–98 from N.Y. to Ga. and westward to the Ohio, amassing botanical collections which were lost by shipwreck en route to France in 1798 (F. D. Merrill, "Palisot de Beauvois as an Overlooked American Botanist," pp. 899–909).

12. Benjamin Rush (1745–1813). Physician, humanitarian, and social reformer. After college in U.S. he studied medicine at Edinburgh and London. Among the social reforms of which he was an early advocate were prison reform and the education of women. He also led in the advocacy of the panacea of bleeding. Member of APS, Cont. Congr., and signer of Dec. of Ind.

13. *JAM*, p. 68, dates this visit Apr. 26, not May 1.

14. Sir John Chardin (1643–1713), French traveler and author.

15. Benjamin Rush, *The Autobiography of Benjamin Rush*, p. 226.

16. Peter Pond (1740–1807). AM spells his name *Pound* (*JAM*, p. 69).

17. For no period of AM's American years is his journal more replete with botanical detail than during the six months of his Canadian expedition. His numerous botanical descriptions can be found in *JAM*, pp. 69–88.

18. Deleuze, "Memoirs," p. 339. This passage on the Indian canoe is but one of many in Deleuze providing descriptions and narrations given him by AM and found nowhere else.

19. Generally about four miles wides (*JAM*, p. 74).

20. In *JAM* it is spelled *Chicoutoumé*.

21. *JAM*, pp. 74–75.

22. Ibid., p. 75.

23. Ibid., p. 76.

24. Ibid., pp. 76–77.

25. Deleuze, "Memoirs," p. 340; *JAM*, p. 77. Such mishaps were common on this journey, in some instances soaking plant specimens, baggage, and provisions.

26. *JAM,* p. 82; blueberries: *Vaccinium corymbosum.*

27. Ibid., p. 80.

28. Ibid.

29. Ibid., p. 81.

30. Ibid., p. 82.

31. Deleuze, "Memoirs," p. 342.

32. Limitation of space prevents us following in more detail AM's venture into the Canadian wilderness and his return journey. More details may be found in Jacques Rousseau, *Le Voyage d'André Michaux au Lac Mistassini en 1792;* Abbé Ernest Le Page and P. Arthème Dutilly, "Retracing the Route of Michaux's Hudson Bay Journey of 1792."

33. Owen Connelly, *French Revolution/Napoleonic Era,* pp. 126–27.

34. *JAM,* p. 85.

35. Mem. ab. (authors' trans.).

Chapter 11 ૐ࿙ All Eyes on the West, 1793

1. *JAM,* p. 85.

2. The APS had been founded by a group of scientific-minded colonists at the instigation of Franklin and the elder Bartram as a learned society for the promotion of useful knowledge. At the time of AM's request its membership comprised the most distinguished intellectual leaders in the U.S.

3. Rush, *Autobiography,* p. 303. AM's comments on the medicinal and nutritional properties of plants suggest the broad range of his observations. His conclusion here that fresh fruits in one's diet prevent scurvy precedes by two years the British navy's pioneer 1795 action to eliminate scurvy among its sailors by prescribing lime or lemon juice as part of their daily diet.

4. David Rittenhouse (1732–1796), instrument maker, astronomer, and mathematician, a leading scientist of eighteenth-century America, president of APS from 1791 until his death.

5. Barton to Jefferson, Philadelphia, Jan. 4, 1793, Massachusetts Historical Society, Jefferson Letters, Thomas Jefferson Coolidge bequest. The margin of the manuscript is torn, partially defacing the word given in brackets, which seems to be "expedient."

6. John Ledyard (1751–1789), American explorer, son of a Groton, Conn., sea captain. He sailed with Capt. James Cook on his last voyage to the Pacific. Encouraged by Sir Joseph Banks, he undertook an expedition to explore the sources of the Niger, but died en route at Cairo, Egypt.

7. Subscription List for Michaux Expedition, APS Archives, 1793, 1980, 1654 MS.

8. "Copy of the Conditions AM submitted to Mr. Jefferson, Secretary of State, Jan. 20, 1793," APS Arc. 1980, 1654 MS. (authors' trans.).

9. AM has no comment in his journal on the execution of Louis XVI on Jan. 21, 1793; news of that event probably reached Philadelphia within six or seven weeks, putting a final closing seal on AM's royal connection.

10. Louis Augustin Guillaume Bosc (1759–1828), French naturalist

whose prodigious activities in wide areas of natural history represent a distinguished contribution to the natural sciences. As a member of the Acad. of Sci. he participated in many scientific missions including one to the U.S., probably 1796–98, during which AM's Carolina garden became his residence. Bosc became AT's successor as "professor of culture" at Jardin des Plantes.

11. A. A. Lipscomb and A. E. Bergh, eds., *The Writings of Thomas Jefferson,* 17:335–39, date this document in Jan. 1793, but Bernard de Voto in *The Course of Empire,* p. 600n, convincingly sets the date as Apr. 30, 1793. AM himself refers to it in Mem. ab. as being "toward the end of March."

12. Obviously, by this time AM had received the confirmation of his status as botanist to the French Republic.

13. AM, "Exposition of the Basis upon which I have resolved to undertake the journey to the West of the Mississippi," Mich. Papers (authors' trans.).

14. Ibid.

15. Edmond Charles Genet (1763–1834), first minister to the U.S. from the French Republic. The immense complexities involved in the Genet affair are beyond the scope of this work except insofar as AM was involved. Interested readers will find an excellent account of it in Harry Ammon, *The Genet Mission.* Our description is based on the above and on Frederick Jackson Turner, "The Origin of Genet's Projected Attack on Louisiana and the Floridas," pp. 650–71; Turner, ed., *Correspondence of the French Ministers to the United States, 1791–1797;* pertinent articles in the AHA *Reports* and the relevant pages in *JAM,* pp. 90–103.

16. "Memoir to serve as instructions to Citizen Genet," Turner, *Correspondence of the French Ministers,* 1:201–11 (authors' trans.).

17. Michel Ange Mangouret (1752–1829), named consul at Charleston, Mar. 2, 1792; dismissed with other French agents following the indiscretions of Genet.

18. Ammon, *Genet,* p. 56.

19. The attorney general ruled that the *Grange,* which had been illegally captured in American waters, must be released, and Genet acceded to this (Ammon, *Genet,* p. 54).

20. Thomas Jefferson to Jack Eppes, May 12, 1793, quoted in Dumas Malone, *Jefferson and the Ordeal of Liberty,* p. 81.

21. Genet to Min. of Foreign Affairs, Philadelphia, May 18, 1793, Turner, ed., *Correspondence of the French Ministers,* 1:214 (authors' trans.).

22. Ammon, *Genet,* p. 55.

23. *JAM,* p. 90. The day of the month is omitted in the journal.

24. Ibid.

25. Mem. ab.

26. Neither the memoir of observations on the French colonists nor this financial statement has been available to us.

27. *JAM,* p. 91.

28. Genet to Min. of Foreign Affairs, Philadelphia, July 25, 1793, Turner, ed., *Correspondence of the French Ministers,* 1:222 (authors' trans.).

29. George Rogers Clark (1752–1818), frontier leader in the Revolution. Born in Va., the elder brother of William Clark of the Lewis and Clark Expedition, he gained recognition as the Conqueror of the Old Northwest, only to

become embittered when neither Virginia nor the U.S. Government properly recognized his services or reimbursed him for his expenses in his campaigns.

30. Turner, "Origin of Genet's Projected Attack," p. 665.

31. John Brown (1757–1837), U.S. Senator from Ky., (1792–1805) brother of James Brown of Lexington. He had received his legal training under Jefferson.

32. Ammon, *Genet*, p. 42.

33. This seems to have been the same day that news of Genet's arrival in Charleston reached Philadelphia, perhaps sparking the public announcement of U.S. neutrality.

34. For a lucid account of the complex affair of the *Little Democrat*, see Malone, *Jefferson*, pp. 115–20.

35. Ammon, *Genet*, p. 72.

36. Turner, *Correspondence of the French Ministers*, 2:217 (authors' trans.).

37. Ammon, *Genet*, p. 88.

38. "Jefferson's Minute of Conversation with Genet," Dept. of State, *Jefferson Papers*, 4th ser., vol. 3, no. 84, reprinted in AHA, *Report for 1896*, pp. 984–85.

39. Isaac Shelby (1750–1826), military hero in the Am. Rev. and first governor of the state of Kentucky.

40. Turner, "Origin of Genet's Projected Attack," p. 66.

41. "Michaux's Instructions" and "Authorization to Michaux" (from Genet), Correspondence of Clark and Genet, Archives des Affaires Etrangères, reprinted in AHA, *Report for 1896*, pp. 990–96 (authors' trans.).

42. Genet was unaware of the change in Gen. Clark's situation and character since the days of his historic role in the Revolution. The general was now deep in debt, often befuddled with drink, and quite unable to organize and lead the expedition that he had proposed to the French government (Ammon, *Genet*, p. 83).

43. "Michaux's Instructions"; "Authorization to Michaux," pp. 990–96.

44. Ammon, *Genet*, p. 86.

Chapter 12 ➣ Two Missions West, 1793–1794

1. *JAM*, p. 91. From this point through p. 101 in *JAM* we have followed the translation of Reuben Gold Thwaites, ed., *Early Western Travels*, vol. 3. Citations will be both to the Sargent edition of the French text and to the Thwaites translation.

2. *JAM*, p. 91, Thwaites, p. 27. Nothing is known of Humeau; Thwaites says, "Le Blanc was a citizen of New Orleans, well-affected to the French cause." Ammon suggests that these two were, in fact, engaged by Genet as secret agents familiar with Louisiana (Ammon, *Genet*, p. 85).

3. Hugh H. Brackenridge (1748–1816), lawyer and writer, a native of Pa., classmate of James Madison and Philip Freneau at Princeton, author of *Modern Chivalry*, the first "literary" work of the American West and founder of the first paper of Pittsburgh and its first bookstore; later became a justice of the Pa. Supreme Court.

4. *JAM*, p. 94, *Thwaites*, p. 34. For the history of this unfortunate French settlement, see FAM's *Travels*, Thwaites, p. 182.

5. Mayesville, site of the first blockhouse in Ky., 1783.

6. Alexander D. Orr (1765–1835) emigrated from his native Va.; at the time of AM's visit was member of U.S. Congress from Ky.

7. *JAM*, p. 95, *Thwaites*, p. 36.

8. *JAM*, p. 96, *Thwaites*, p. 38.

9. Benjamin Logan (c. 1743–1802), Ky. pioneer and Indian fighter. A native of Va., he came to Ky. in 1775, where he served in several governmental capacities.

10. *JAM*, p. 96, Thwaites, pp. 39–40. AM went to see Logan at his place in Lincoln County. Next to Clark, Logan was the best-known figure in Ky.

11. AHA, *Report for 1896*, p. 934.

12. AM visited Clark at his father's home, Mulberry Hill, outside of Louisville, where Clark then resided (Thwaites, p. 42n).

13. *JAM*, p. 97, Thwaites, p. 42.

14. *JAM*, p. 97, Thwaites, p. 43.

15. Clark to Genet, Louisville, Oct. 3, 1793, AHA, *Report for 1896,* pp. 1007–9.

16. Clark to AM, Louisville, Oct. 3, 1793, ibid., p. 1009.

17. AM to Clark, Danville, Oct. 10, 1793, ibid., p. 1012 (in AM's English).

18. Clark to AM, Louisville, Oct. 15, 1793, ibid., p. 1013.

19. Clark to Genet, Louisville, Oct. 25, 1793, ibid., p. 1016.

20. *JAM*, p. 98, Thwaites, p. 45. C. S. Sargent lists this fern as *Lygodium palmatum.*

21. *JAM,* pp. 100–101. Here, with the entry for Dec. 15, the Thwaites translation ends and our trans. is resumed.

22. Clark to Genet, Louisville, Oct. 3, 1793, AHA, *Report for 1896,* pp. 1007–9.

23. The queen was executed on Oct. 16, 1793.

24. AM to Clark, Philadelphia, Dec. 27, 1793 ("The second year of the French Republic"), AHA, *Report for 1896,* pp. 1024–26.

25. *JAM,* pp. 101–2.

26. The reference is to Catesby's *Natural History of Carolina.*

27. *JAM*, p. 102. Linnaeus' great work, *Systema Naturae,* was then revolutionizing botanical classification systems.

28. *JAM*, p. 103. "La Société des amis de la liberté et de l'égalité" was an organization of Frenchmen living in Philadelphia whose meetings were devoted largely to discussions of current and political events (Ammon, *Genet,* p. 79).

29. *JAM*, p. 102.

30. Genet lived for the remaining 40 years of his life in the U.S., becoming a citizen. His marriage to Cornelia, daughter of the prosperous Governor George Clinton of N.Y. brought security and a large family. After her death he married Martha Osgood, daughter of Pres. Washington's postmaster general.

31. *JAM*, p. 106.

32. Ibid., p. 103.

33. Ibid., p. 107.
34. Ibid., p. 108.
35. Ibid., pp. 108–14.
36. Ibid., p. 111.
37. Ibid., p. 112.
38. Ibid., p. 114.
39. The unpublished diaries of Dr. Charles Drayton, Drayton Family Papers. Our references are to diary entries for the dates noted in the text.

Chapter 13 ౿❧ West to the Mississippi and American Finale, 1795–1796

1. *JAM,* p. 114. The Thwaites translation of AM's journal is resumed here and continues through page 140 of the French version. Thwaites, pp. 53–104.
2. *JAM,* p. 116, Thwaites, pp. 56–57.
3. *JAM,* p. 117–18, Thwaites, p. 59.
4. *JAM,* p. 118, Thwaites, p. 63.
5. *JAM,* p. 121, Thwaites, p. 67.
6. *JAM,* p. 121, Thwaites, pp. 67–68.
7. *JAM,* p. 122, Thwaites, pp. 67–70.
8. *JAM,* p. 122, Thwaites, p. 71.
9. *JAM,* p. 123, Thwaites, p. 73.
10. *JAM,* p. 129, Thwaites, pp. 82–83.
11. Ibid.
12. *JAM,* p. 131, Thwaites, pp. 86–87.
13. *JAM,* p. 131, Thwaites, pp. 87–89.
14. *JAM,* p. 132, Thwaites, pp. 89–91 and 167n.
15. Col. Robert Hays, brother-in-law of Andrew Jackson, and first U.S. marshall of Tenn.
16. *JAM,* p. 134, Thwaites, p. 93.
17. *JAM,* p. 185, Thwaites, p. 94.
18. *JAM,* p. 135, Thwaites, p. 95. This handsome tree is the only species of *Cladrastis* found in North America. Its other three species are found in China.
19. *JAM,* p. 140, Thwaites, p. 101.
20. Min. of Int. to AM, Paris, July 12, 1796, Mich. Papers (authors' trans.).
21. *JAM,* p. 140. The Thwaites translation ended with AM's arrival back in Charleston.

Chapter 14 ౿❧ Return to France, 1796–1800

1. The account of AM's shipwreck ordeal and rescue are from *JAM* unless otherwise noted. *JAM,* pp. 141–43.

2. AM to AT, Amsterdam, Oct. 14, 1796, AN doc. This letter appears also in *Bot. FA*, pp. 247–48 (authors' trans.).

3. AM to L'Héritier, Egmont, Nov. 7, 1796, *Bot. FA*, pp. 248 and facsimile copy as an illustration (authors' trans.). Charles L'Héritier de Brutelle was then Dir. of the Plant Conservatory in Paris and a member of the French Institute.

4. Min. of For. Affairs to Min. of Int., Paris, Nov. 10, 1796, AN doc. (authors' trans.).

5. *JAM*, p. 143. AM calls these finches *Pinson d'Ardennes.*

6. Brothers named Gever had established a notable ornithological museum in Rotterdam (*JAM*, p. 143).

7. Deleuze, "Memoirs," p. 346.

8. Jacques Philippe Martin Cels (1740–1806), Mem. of Council of Ag. in whose celebrated garden and nursery at Montrouge rare and little-known plants from around the world, including many collected by AM, could be seen. He is credited with great influence in saving the royal parks and châteaux during the Revolution and in the establishment of national forests.

Louis Daubenton (1716–1800), French naturalist and collaborator with Buffon in his *Histoire Naturelle* and the development of the Merino sheep.

Louis-Claude-Marie Richard (1754–1821), French botanist, member of the National Institute and professor of botany at the Faculty of Medicine in Paris. Later he was a collaborator of AM and FAM in preparing AM's *Flora Boreali-Americana.*

René Lourche (1750–1833), French botanist from Brittany.

9. AM to AT, Amsterdam, Oct. 14, 1796, AN doc. (authors' trans.).

10. Elias M. Durand (1794–1873) French emigré to the U.S., where he became an eminent pharmacist in Philadelphia and an able amateur botanist. He eventually acquired the herbaria of both Thomas Nuttall and Samuel Rafinesque.

11. Elias Durand, "Biographical Memoir of the late François André Michaux," p. 164.

12. Jean Nicholas Corvisart (1755–1821), professor of practical medicine at the College de France and personal physician for Napoleon (Durand, "Biographical Memoir, p. 164).

13. *Tr. FAM*, pp. 244, 299. See also ch. 8, n. 8.

14. Durant, and Durant, *Age of Napoleon*, pp. 33–90; Gordon Wright, *France in Modern Times*, pp. 49–66.

15. FAM to Comité d'Instruction de la Convention Nationale, Apr. 15, 1795, AN doc., published in *Bot. FA*, p. 249 (authors' trans.).

16. Gen. Pinckney was in Paris from Dec. 1796 to Feb. 1797, awaiting recognition from the Directory to serve as Min. to France, succeeding James Monroe. When objectionable preconditions were required, Pinckney "in a proper rage, left Paris for Amsterdam."

17. Robert Fulton was in Paris at this time seeking financial backing for his work on the torpedo.

18. Almost certainly "Monsieur du Pont" was Pierre Samuel du Pont de Nemours, head of the powerful du Pont Family. See chap. 17, n. 7.

19. *JAM*, p. 145.

20. AM to the Pres. of the Executive Directory, Paris, Oct. 28, 1797, Mich. Papers (authors' trans.).

21. This Prospectus is undated, but from its content we conclude this proposal could have been made by AM only in the period between his return from the U.S. and his departure on the Baudin expedition in 1800.

22. "Prospectus of the Establishment of a Nursery of Foreign Trees and Plants in Southern Provinces," "Project concerning the Establishment of a Nursery of Trees and Foreign Plants in the Environs of Bayonne," Mus. of Nat. Hist. docs. (authors' trans.).

23. Napoleon seized power from the Directory in the famous coup d'état of Nov. 9, 1799, which resulted in his election as first consul with plenary powers of a virtual dictator.

24. Nicolas Thomas Baudin (1756–1803).

25. Jean-Paul Faivre, "Baudin in His Time," Foreword to *Journal de mer: The Journal of Post Captain Nicolas Baudin*, pp. 9–13.

26. AM to Min. of Int., Paris, June 13, 1800, AN doc. (authors' trans.).

27. Min. of Int. to AM, Paris, Aug. 15, 1800, AN doc. (authors' trans.).

28. Min. of Int. to Citizen Michaux, Paris, Aug. 17, 1800; AM to Min. of Int., Paris, Aug. 28, 1800, AN docs. (authors' trans.).

29. AM to Min. of Int., Paris, Sept. 17, 1800, AN doc. (authors' trans.).

30. Report to Min. of Int., Paris, Sept. 18, 1800, AN doc. Italics are the authors' (authors' trans.).

Chapter 15 ❦ Expedition to the South Seas, 1800–1802

1. Jacques Gérard Milbert, *Picturesque Itinerary of the Hudson River and the Peripheral Parts of North America*, pp. xi–xii.
Jacques Gérard Milbert (1767–1840), professor of design at L'Ecole des Mines, Paris. Sent on royal missions to the Pyrenees, the Alps, the Rhone. Geographer on Baudin Expedition. Spent seven years in America, 1815–22, sent back natural history shipments to France, vegetable, mineral, and animal, including live opossum, moose, and bison for the king's menagerie.

2. "Plan of Itinerary for Citizen Baudin," Baudin, *Journal*, p. 1.

3. James Felix Emmanual Hamelin.

4. Baudin, *Journal*, p. 11.

5. Duval, *King's Garden*, p. 136.

6. Baudin, *Journal*, p. 20.

7. Ibid., p. 35.

8. Deleuze, "Memoirs," p. 348.

9. Baudin, *Journal*, pp. 37–38.

10. Ibid., pp. 45–120 passim.

11. Ibid., p. 96.

12. Duval, *King's Garden*, pp. 78–79.

13. Deleuze, "Memoirs," p. 348.

14. Ibid., p. 349. Probably the "M. Martin" who traveled with the Rousseau party in the East as the consul's personal physician.

15. Ibid., pp. 349–50.

16. Baudin, *Journal,* p. 138.

17. Duval, *King's Garden,* p. 140. For a defense of Baudin, see Jean-Paul Faivre, Foreword, Baudin, *Journal,* pp. ix-xii.

18. Pierre Joseph Redouté (1759–1840), French artist, most notable for his botanical paintings, particularly those of roses, illustrator of many natural history works, court artist of Marie Antoinette and the Empress Josephine.

19. AM to FAM, Île de France, Oct. 12, 1801, Mich. Papers (authors' trans.). This letter was addressed to "Citizen Michaux, son, Recommended to the Kindness of Citizen Ventenat at Paris." Etienne-Pierre Ventenat was then librarian of the Panthéon and a member of the Institute.

20. Jean-Baptiste-George-Marie Bory de Saint Vincent (1780–1846), French naturalist who later headed expeditions to Morea and Algeria; he left an account of his visit to Île de France.

21. Deleuze, "Memoirs," p. 350.

22. Various dates have been suggested as the time of AM's death. Ewan, in the chronology of AM prefacing the facsimile edition of AM's *Flora* gives Nov. 13, 1802.

Sargent in his introduction to *JAM* says AM died "late in November 1802" (*JAM,* p. 6).

Deleuze offers no date for AM's death but says his final illness began at the beginning of Frimaire, year 11 (Nov. 22, 1802): "As he was preparing to depart for the interior of the island, according to his original plan, he caught the fever of the country, of which he expired on the second attack" (Deleuze, "Memoirs," p. 351).

23. Ibid.

24. Peattie, *Green Laurels,* p. 201.

25. Deleuze, "Memoirs," p. 355.

26. Ibid.

Chapter 16 ❰ *The Legacies of André Michaux*

1. Deleuze, "Memoirs," p. 351.

2. Before FAM sailed for the U.S. on Aug. 25, 1801.

3. *Histoire des chênes de l'Amérique, ou Déscriptions et figures de toutes les espèces et variétés de Chênes de l'Amérique Septentrionale.* Par André Michaux, Membre associé de l'Institut national de France, de la Société d'Agriculture de Charleston, Caroline meridionale, etc. A Paris, chez Levrault frères, Quai Malaquais. An IX-1801. Large folio. With 36 fine copperplates.

4. AM, *Histoire des chênes,* preface (authors' trans.). The summary of his travels referred to by AM in his preface did not appear in the *Flora*; it was perhaps lost in transit back to France.

5. AM, *Histoire des chênes,* introduction, p. 4; trans. in *The New York Medical Repository,* 6 (1803): 64–70.

6. AM, *Histoire des chênes,* p. 4.

7. Ibid., p. 5.

8. Ibid.

9. *JAM*, p. 7.

10. "Michaux's cultivation and literary ability, judged by his journal, were not great" (ibid., p. 6).

11. "Mémoire sur les Dattiers, avec des observations sur quelque moyens utile auz progrès d'agriculture dans les colonies Occidentales."

The article has a footnote by AM's brother-in-law: "This scholar has just set out, in the capacity of naturalist, with Captain Baudin."

12. The memoir was read to the Colonial Society on May 5, 1799, nine days after being presented to the Institute.

13. "Memoire sur les Dattiers," p. 329 (authors' trans.).

14. Ibid., pp. 329–30.

15. Ibid., p. 331.

16. Ibid., p. 333.

17. Ibid., p. 334.

18. *Flora Boreali-Americana*, 2 vols. (Paris and Strasbourg, 1803); facsimile reprint, edited by Joseph Ewan.

19. Ibid., Introduction, pp. xiii–xiv.

20. Ibid., pp. xxiv–xxv.

21. *New York Medical Repository* 8 (1805): 394–95.

22. *JAM* p. 7.

23. Report of the Bur. of Ag. to the Min. of Int., Paris, Jan. 17, 1801, AN doc. (authors' trans.).

24. Report of the Consultant Bur. of Ag. to the Min. of the Int., July 2, 1801, AN doc. (authors' trans.).

25. FAM's commission, dated Thermidor, year 9, AN doc. (authors' trans.).

26. Baron de Augustin-François Silvestre (1762–1851), French naturalist, agriculturist, and official in the Bur. of Ag.

27. Undated memo from Min. of the Int. to Deshayer and memo from Chief, 2d Div. of Bur. of Ag., July 7, 1801, AN docs. (authors' trans.).

28. The Charleston Library Society has a presentation copy of the work delivered to it by FAM. When he reached Philadelphia the following summer, he delivered a copy to APS. A receipt for $10 paid for it is dated July 29, 1802, Mich. Papers.

Chapter 17 ❧ Mission to America, Carolina, 1801–1802

1. Not until the Treaty of Amiens in 1802, which provided a brief, uneasy peace, was there any cessation of war between France and England throughout the entire post-Revolutionary period.

2. FAM to Secy. of Bur. of Ag., 2d Div., Nov. 4, 1801, AN doc.; *Tr. FAM*, p. 117.

3. *Tr. FAM*, pp. 117–22. FAM goes on to discuss the disease, uncritically reporting the prevailing popular beliefs of the frightened populace. His interest in the malady persisted. A half century later, in 1852, he published in Paris a paper, *Mémoire sur les causes de la fièvre jaune*. We have not found a copy and only know its title and his continuing interest in the malady.

4. The title continues: *dans les états de l'Ohio, du Kentucky et du Tennessée, et retour a Charleston par les hautes-Carolines; Contenant des détails sur l'état actuel de l'agriculture et les productions naturelles de ces contrées, ainsi des renseignemens sur les rapports commerciaux qui existent entre ces Etats et ceux situés à l'est des montagnes et la Basse-Louisiane; Entrepris pendent l'an X-1802, sous les auspices de Son Excellence M. Chaptal, Ministre de l'Intérior. Avec une Carte trèsoignée de états du centre, de l'ouest et du sud des Etats-unis.*

5. FAM to Min. of Int., Charleston, Nov. 4, 1801, AN doc.

6. *Tr. FAM*, pp. 121–23. Converted to U.S. currency of 1801, the price of a cord of firewood comes to about $8 in marked contrast to the quoted price of beef of 7¢ a pound.

7. Pierre Samuel du Pont de Nemours (1739–1817), a notable French economist and agriculturist, longtime friend of Lafayette and Jefferson, he had held prominent positions in both the old regime and the revolutionary government, as had his son, Victor Marie du Pont (1767–1827).

7. Report from Bur. of Ag. to Min. of Int., Feb. 28, 1802, AN doc.

8. W. C. Coker, "The Garden of André Michaux," pp. 65–72; *Tr. FAM*, p. 124; Ann Leighton, *American Gardens in the Eighteenth Century*, p. 389.

9. "Catalogue of rare seeds sent during the year 10," AN doc. This list was reproduced in *Am. Midland Naturalist*, vol. 23. The Revolutionary calendar's year 10 (Sep. 23, 1801–Sep. 22, 1802) covered FAM's first seed season at the French Garden. Receipt of this list was acknowledged by Bur. of Ag., Apr. 26, 1802, AN doc.

10. FAM to Min. of Int., Charleston, Jan. 1, 1802, AN doc. (authors' trans.). The words "almost total neglect" exaggerate the garden's lack of care since his father's departure. The facts that there was due Himely for its care the sum of 4,200 fr. and that botanist Bosc had resided there in 1796–98 indicate that it did receive some care.

11. The Institut Nationale, founded by the Convention in 1794, later called the Institute of France, was reorganized by Napoleon and given the name Académie Française.

12. Du Pont to Min. of Int., New York, Feb. 9, 1802; Préfet d'Alliers to Min. of Int., Alliers, Mar. 1802; du Pont to Nat. Inst., New York, Mar. 8, 1802, all AN docs.

13. Min. of Int. to Nekelman, Paris, Apr. 3, 1802; Min. of Int. to FAM, Paris, Apr. 1, 1802, AN docs.

14. Report of Bur. of Ag., Silvestre, Chief, Apr. 18, 1802; Report of a Committee of Nat. Inst., undated by rec'd. Apr. 30, 1802; Memoir on the French gardens in U.S. by Citizen du Pont de Nemours, undated, Bur. of Ag. Doc. no. 448, all AN docs.

15. Report of Min. of Int. to Bur. of Ag., Apr. 2, 1802; Report to Min. of Int. from Chief of Bur. of Ag., Apr. 27, 1802, AN docs.

16. *Tr. FAM*, p. 124.

17. Deed of Andrew Michau (*sic*) to John James Himely, dated Mar. 15,

1802, in Book G-7, p. 102, of the Register of Mesne Conveyances for Charleston Co., signed by both Francis Andrew Michau and John J. Himely.

18. Deed of John James Himely to the Agricultural Society of S.C., Feb. 28, 1803, office of the Register of Mesne Conveyances for Charleston Co. The Society retained the property until 1820, when it was conveyed to John Carvile, Book F-9, p. 337.

19. These three grant conveyances, all dated Jan. 7, 1788, from Thomas Pinckney, governor, to Andrew Michaux of lands in the Ninety-Six District of S.C., are recorded in the Office of the Register of Mesne Conveyances of Charleston Co., in Book 22, pp. 281 and 273, and Book 23, p. 175; the plat of 888 acres, dated June 15, 1787, in Book 21, p. 279; of 1,000 acres, dated June 16, 1787, in Book 21, p. 280; and of the other 1,000 acres, also dated June 16, 1787, in Book 21, p. 281.

20. FAM to Gen. Andrew Pickens, Charleston, May 1, 1802, APS doc., Letters of Scientists. This letter to Pickens is the earliest attempt of FAM to write to a correspondent in English that we have seen.

21. Private correspondence with Margaret M. Seaborn, Feb. 1982. She cites details of the sale of a large tract in Oconee County embracing the three tracts in the grants to AM, now in the Town of Walhalla, and the *German Colony Protocol*, Oconee County Library, 1960, original pages 11–16.

Chapter 18 ᙖ New York and Philadelphia, 1802

1. *Tr. FAM*, p. 123.

2. Dr. David Hosack (1769–1835), physician, botanist, professor, and later editor of a leading scientific journal, son of a Scottish officer in the British army, and graduate of Princeton College.

3. *Tr. FAM*, pp. 126–29.

4. Ibid., pp. 127–29.

5. Min. of Int. to Min. of Finance, May 6, 1802, shows that a copy went to FAM; Min. of Int. to FAM, Apr. 28, 1802; Min. of Int. to du Pont de Nemours, Apr. 29, 1802; Report of Bur. of Ag. to Min. of Int., April 18, 1803, all AN docs.

6. AN doc. (authors' trans.). Both FAM and du Pont continued to call the N.J. gardener "Saulnier."

7. *Tr. FAM*, pp. 129–30.

8. Ibid., p. 130–31. The introduction of the Lombardy poplar, referred to by FAM as Italian poplar, has by some been credited to FAM, through Saunier's garden, probably because early descriptions of the garden report avenues bordered by them. It is probable that there were several introductions independent of each other.

9. Charles Willson Peale (1741–1827), portrait painter, naturalist, and collector; a native of Md., he moved to Philadelphia as a young man. Two of his numerous children, Raphael and Rembrandt, became artists. C. W. Peale painted the best-known portrait of William Bartram, Rembrandt one of FAM and one of ornithologist Alexander Wilson. For more on Peale's Museum see Charles Coleman Sellers, *Mr. Peale's Museum*.

10. John Vaughan (1756–1841), librarian, merchant and long-term sec-

retary of APS, "the voice and heart of Franklin's Philosophical Society." For 35 years JV and FAM were steady correspondents. At the same time he served as merchant representative of Irenée du Pont's nearby Wilmington powder factory.

11. Mich. Papers. The receipt is dated July 29, 1802.

12. *Tr. FAM*, p. 132.

13. FAM to Min. of Int., June 22, 1802; Report of Bur. of Ag. to Min. of Int., Oct. 6, 1802; Kin to Min. of Int., Nov. 16, 1802, all AN docs.

14. FAM to Com. for Com. Af. in Georgetown, June 12, 1802; FAM to Min. of Int., Philadelphia, June 22, 1802; Com. (Pichon?) to FAM, Georgetown, undated; Com. Com. Af. to Min. of Int., Georgetown, July 8, 1802, all AN docs.

15. Report of Bur. of Ag. to Min. of Int., Paris, Oct. 6, 1802; Report of Min. of Int., Paris, May 17, 1802, AN docs.

16. *Tr. FAM*, p. 290.

Chapter 19 ᘌ West to the Alleghenies and down the Ohio, 1802

1. Henry Muhlenburg (1753–1815), clergyman and botanist, whose intensive study of the local botany culminated in his *Flora Lancastriensis.*

2. *Tr. FAM*, pp. 136–37.

3. Ibid., pp. 138–39. It is interesting that FAM thought it necessary to define for his readers the American "whiskey": "They give the name of whiskey in the United States, to a sort of brandy made with rye."

4. Ibid., p. 139.

5. Ibid., pp. 141–43.

6. Ibid., pp. 143–44.

7. A hospital in Paris, Charité had been established by St. Vincent de Paul in 1634. Presumably it still continued to be used as a teaching place for medical students in FAM's training years.

8. *Tr. FAM*, pp. 145–46.

9. Ibid., pp. 145–59. Thwaites says the shrub FAM sought is thought to have been a species of sumac (*Rhus*).

10. Ibid., pp. 157–58. Ginseng, *Panax ginseng* in the Orient, *Panax quinquefolium* in the U.S., the specially prepared roots of which were regarded as a panacea for all ills of man, was at the time of FAM's visit a highly profitable item in Philadelphia's trade with China. See Kimmens, *Tales of the Ginseng*, pp. 160–64, for an account of "shangen" in the U.S.

11. *Tr. FAM*, pp. 159–62.

12. Thomas D. Clark, *The Kentucky*, pp. 54–69, gives an excellent account of the river navigation and commerce of the early nineteenth century. See also Richard Bissell, *The Monongahela*, pp. 49–58. It contains also, pp. 66–67, drawings of the types of riverboats.

13. *Tr. FAM*, p. 166.

14. Ibid., pp. 168–71.

15. Ibid., pp. 172–77. They camped in what was then Northwest Territory; in 1803, however, this eastern part of the territory became the state of Ohio. For 200 miles below Wheeling the river then separated Va. from N.W. Territory.

16. Ibid., pp. 175–76. The sycamore they measured was more than a third larger than the largest known in the U.S. today. See "National Register of Big Trees," p. 45. Had FAM called it the largest hardwood in N.A., his claim would remain true today.

17. *Tr. FAM*, pp. 177–78. FAM was of course in error in identifying those earthen structures as "Indian fortifications." They have now been identified as religiously inspired temple sites and animal effigies, some containing tremendous volumes of earth. They are attributed to the Hopewell People who flourished between 400 B.C. and A.D. 1100 (*American Heritage Book of Indians*, p. 153).

18. *Tr. FAM*, p. 180.

19. Ibid., pp. 181–82.

20. Ibid., pp. 182–87. For an account of the tragic Gallipolis settlement, see Howard Mumford Jones, *America and French Culture, 1750–1848*, pp. 147–51; Francis S. Philbrick, *The Rise of the West, 1754–1830*, pp. 124–25.

21. *Tr. FAM*, p. 186.

22. Ibid., p. 187.

23. Ibid., pp. 187–95.

Chapter 20 ৪৯ *Kentucky, 1802*

1. *Tr. FAM*, pp. 195–99.

2. Samuel Brown (1769–1830), Kentucky physician and professor of medicine, one of three sons of a Va. Presbyterian minister, all of whom emigrated to Ky. and became prominent leaders; John and James both serving as its U.S. senators, while Samuel became a leading doctor and a member of APS.

3. *Tr. FAM*, pp. 199–202.

4. Ibid., p. 202; Henry Savage, Jr., *Discovering America, 1700–1875*, p. 81.

5. *Tr. FAM*, pp. 202–5.

6. Ibid., pp. 248–49.

7. Ibid., pp. 245–46.

8. Ibid., pp. 243–45. This reference to FAM having seen draft horses in England is the first of two indicating he had been in England. However, we have seen no other reference to his having been there. Since in the original Paris edition the reference is to draft horses he had seen in Picardy, the later substitution of "England" may indicate that he visited England to arrange for the publication of the English edition in 1805.

Thwaites, in a footnote, provides a pertinent historical note on the origin of horse breeding in Ky.: "The first legislative assembly for Transylvania, meeting in Boonesborough in 1775, passed an act for preserving the breed of horses."

9. *Tr. FAM*, p. 245.

10. Ibid., pp. 246–47.

11. Ibid., pp. 206–9; John James Defour (c. 1763–1827). Dufour's book, *The American Vine Dresser's Guide*, was published in Cincinnati by S. J. Browne in 1826. Dufour is recognized as having contributed an important chapter in American grape growing. For a more complete account of the Dufour story, which eventually involved Thomas Jefferson and Henry Clay, see Clark, *The Kentucky*, pp. 149–56.

12. *Tr. FAM*, p. 213.

13. Ibid., p. 214. The peach, a native of Persia, after being introduced into America by early Spanish settlers, soon went wild and became widely distributed by the Indians—a history similar to that of the mustang of the prairies and the marsh "tacky" of the southeast coast.

14. Ibid., pp. 214–22. It is generally accepted that such prairie areas owe their origin to wildfires destructive enough to kill the forest cover and frequent enough to prevent its return to the area.

15. Ibid., pp. 218–19.

16. Ibid., pp. 244–47.

17. Ibid., pp. 240–42.

18. Ibid., pp. 228–29.

19. Ibid., pp. 231–33. Also see Kimmens, *Tales of the Ginseng*, pp. 160–61.

Chapter 21 ᛜ *Tennessee and Return to Carolina, 1802–1803*

1. According to Thwaites, three years later those efforts culminated in the establishment of Cumberland College, the first building of which later housed Vanderbilt U. (*Tr. FAM*, p. 251n).

2. *Tr. FAM*, p. 275. The resemblance that AM had recognized is another example of the resemblance between the floras of the southeast U.S. and Southeast Asia. The genus *Cladastris* has but four species, one in southeast U.S., two in China, and one in Japan.

Samuel L. Mitchill (1764–1831), N.Y. physician and naturalist of note. Doubtless, FAM had made his acquaintance during his stay in N.Y.

3. Daniel Smith (1748–1818), Va.-born, William-and-Mary-educated surveyor, planter, and military leader, mem. of U.S. Constitutional Convention and the major draftsman of the Tennessee constitution.

4. *Tr. FAM*, p. 273.

5. James Winchester (1752–1826), soldier, statesman, and long-term leader of the Tenn. Senate, who later served in the War of 1812 and for the third time became a prisoner of war.

6. *Tr. FAM*, p. 258.

7. Ibid., pp. 258–60.

8. Ibid., p. 260; Radford et al., *Flora of the Carolinas*, pp. 472–75; Coker and Totten, *Trees*, pp. 165–78.

9. *Tr. FAM,* p. 262. Probably FAM was seeing one of the more devastating outbreaks of the endemic pine beetle.

10. Ibid., pp. 265–68.

11. Ibid., pp. 265–76.

12. Ibid., pp. 283–85. FAM apparently, even at the time of preparing his manuscript, had not received a full account of his father's last days.

13. Ibid., pp. 301–2.

14. Ibid., pp. 304–5.

15. See chap. 17.

16. Draft copy of letter from Min. of Int. to Min. of Marine and Colonies, Oct. 12, 1802, AN doc.

17. The contents of a barrel put aboard a vessel destined for Ostend are set forth in a letter from FAM to Min. of Int., Charleston, Feb. 9, 1803; the contents of two large shipments are summarized in FAM's report to Min. of Int. dated May 13, 1803, AN docs. See also *Tr. FAM,* p. 306.

18. This list in FAM's hand bears Bur. of Ag. no. 494, AN doc.

19. FAM's reference to the Orangerie is almost certainly to the greenhouses located on the grounds behind the right wing of the château at Versailles.

20. Undated list addressed to Larus, Chief, 2d Div. of Bur. of Ag., AN doc.; *Tr. FAM,* pp. 218, 260, 275.

21. See David Duncan Wallace, *History of South Carolina,* 3 vols. For the Library Soc., 3:56–57; Ag. Soc., 2:376; Med. Soc., 3:47–48.

David Ramsay (1749–1815), physician and historian, b. Lancaster, Pa., educated at College of N.J. (Princeton) and Univ. of Pa., moved to Charleston in 1773, where he became widely known in medical circles, and as the author of historical works.

22. Durant and Durant, *The Age of Napoleon,* pp. 182–96.

23. MacPhail, pp. 4–5.

Chapter 22 ᘒᕇ Paris, 1803–1804

1. Report of FAM to Min. of Int. Chaptal, May 17, 1803, AN doc.

2. Report of FAM to Bur. of Ag., Paris, July 7, 1803, AN doc. (authors' trans.).

3. Report of FAM to Min. of Int., Paris, May 17, 1803, p. 5 (authors' trans.).

4. Report of FAM relating to the nursery near N.Y., Bur. of Ag., no. 802, AN doc.

5. Saunier to Min. of Int., Apr. 23, 1802; du Pont to Min. of Int., Sept. 17, 1803; Report of Min. of Int., Oct. 12, 1803; Saunier to Min. of Int., Oct. 7, 1803; copy of letter of Min. of Int. to du Pont, Oct. 20, 1803; Min. of Int. to du Pont, Oct. 23, 1803; Min. of Int. to Saunier, Oct. 23, 1803, draft of Report from Bur. of Ag. to Min. of Int., Nov. 15, 1803; Min. of Int. to du Pont, Dec. 1803; Report of Min. of Int. to Bur. of Ag., Nov. 1, 1803, all AN docs.

6. Internal doc., Bur. of Ag., no. 811, July 16, 1803, AN doc.

7. MacPhail, p. 4.

8. Ibid., p. 5.

9. Report from Bur. of Ag. to Min. of Int., June 7, 1803, AN doc.

10. Chief, 2d Div. of Prefecture of Lys to Min. of Int., May 20, 1803, AN doc. (authors' trans.).

11. Préfect of Rouen to Min. of Int., July 31, 1805, reported that "these seeds have rested almost two years in the boxes, nobody having furnished funds for payment" (AN doc., authors' trans.).

12. AT to Min. of Int., Paris, June 9, 1803 (authors' trans.); copy of reply to Professors of Mus. of Nat. Hist., June 28, 1803; Min. of Int. to Goulard, June 15, 1803, authorizing a share for Vilmorin. There were other deserving supplicants for shares; Descamet, nurseryman at St. Denis nursery, was among them (Descamet to Min. of Int., June 10, 1803). All AN docs.

13. Title p. of first ed. of *Voyage a l'ouest des monts Alleghanys*, Paris, An. XII—1804; also title p. of 3d English ed., London, 1805, reproduced in Thwaites, p. 109.

14. Durant and Durant, *Age of Napoleon*, pp. 119–20, 234.

15. Charles-François Mirbel (1776–1854), Fr. botanist and prof. at the Mus. of Nat. Hist. at 23. Later gained wide recognition for his brilliant studies of the biology of plants.

16. Jean-Antoine-Claude Chaptal (1756–1832), Fr. physician, botanist, chemist, and statesman, b. rural central Fr. and educated at Montpellier, where he became prof. of chemistry, and later at Ecole Polytechnique in Paris. Min. of Int. 1801–4 when he resigned to accept appointment to the Senate.

17. Coker & Totten, *Trees*, pp. 175–77.

18. Draft of letters from Min. of Int. to Mme Bonaparte, Apr. 10 and 13, AN doc.

19. Draft of letters of Min. of Int. to FAM and to Mme Bonaparte, dated May 1804, AN docs.

20. Report of Bur. of Ag. to Min. of Int., Apr. 3, 1804; Min. of Int. to Saunier, Apr. 28, 1804; Mirbel to Min. of Int., May 30, 1804; Min. of Int. to Mme Bonaparte, June 1, 1804; du Pont to Laucel, Aug. 1804; Bur. of Ag. to du Pont de Nemours & Co., Sept. 30, 1804, all AN docs.

Chapter 23 ᘒ➤ Dr. F. A. Michaux, Author and Scientist, 1804–1806

1. The title page bears the date "An XII—1804," which describes it as being published sometime between Jan. 22 and Sept. 23, 1804. It was probably much nearer the latter since Levrault did not receive authorization to proceed until well into May (MacPhail, p. 5).

2. Durant and Durant, *The Age of Napoleon*, pp. 188–99.

3. Ibid., pp. 197–99.

4. Since the period of his close association with AM, AT's work had won recognition by membership in 72 learned societies. His great work on the

subject, published after his death: *Cours de Culture et de naturalisation des végétaux,* 3 vols. (Paris, 1827).

5. Extract from the *Mémoires de la Société du department de la Seine,* vol. 7; later published separately: *Mémoire sur la naturalisation des arbres forestiers* (Paris, 1805). (authors' trans.).

6. Henri Louis Duhamel-Dumonseau (1700–1782), French naturalist in many fields and renowned in several, but his greatest contributions were in agriculture and botany, particularly the naturalization of exotic plants in France.

7. This and the ensuing paragraph are based on FAM's *Mémoire,* pp. 5–9.

8. The authors suspect that FAM's failure to grow the live oak and longleaf pine in the Paris area was owing to the absence there of suitable sandy and acid soil, rather than to climate.

9. Fénille, *Mémoires sur l'Administration forestière,* 2:252.

Charles-Marie Varenne de Fénille (ca. 1750–1794), French agronomist and experimental forester, devoted his life to experimental farming and the introduction and culture of forest trees and the maintenance of equality between growth and use. In 1794 he was executed without trial.

10. This and the following five paragraphs are derived from FAM's *Mémoire,* pp. 13–21.

11. Ibid., p. 21.

12. Ibid. This and the following four paragraphs are based on pp. 22–29.

13. Ibid., pp. 29–31.

14. Léon Perthais de Laillevault (1757–1818), French agronomist and military engineer, gained fame for military design and construction but in retirement beginning in 1791 engaged in agriculture and forest culture on his estate near Auxerre.

15. José Francisco Correa de Serra (1750–1823), Portuguese Abbé and savant. Political refugee first in France, then England, where he became a friend of Sir Joseph Banks and a member of the Royal Society. Later took refuge in the U.S.

16. FAM, *Mémoire,* pp. 32–36 (authors' trans.). The Min. of Fin., then the duc de Gaete, did in fact approve FAM's new mission, to be performed under the auspices of the Administration of Waters and Forests (FAM, "Historical Anecdote of Robert Fulton," *Jour. of the Franklin Institute,* 3d ser., 18 [July 1849]).

17. MacPhail, p. 9. The paragraphs quoted from their report on FAM's *Mémoire* are the authors' translation.

18. Jean-Baptiste de Nompere Champagney (1756–1834), military hero, ambassador to Vienna, Min. of Int. 1804–7, then succeeded Talleyrand as Min. of Exterior Relations.

19. MacPhail, pp. 5–8.

20. Durant and Durant, *The Age of Napoleon,* pp. 200–207.

21. FAM to Min. of Int., Paris, Aug. 26, 1805, AN doc. (authors' trans.).

22. Draft of letters, Min. of Int. to FAM; to Museum of Nat. Hist.; to Dir. of nurseries of Roule and Luxembourg, all Aug. 30, 1805, AN docs.

23. FAM to Min. of Int., Paris, Jan. 17, 1806, AN doc.; undated note, FAM to Denton (?); undated note of Cubieres (?) to FAM Paris. Mich. Papers.

24. Neckelman to Min. of Int., Bordeaux, Feb. 20, 1806, AN doc. Through extrapolation between FAM's Paris letter of Jan. 17, 1806, and Neck-

elman's of Feb. 21, 1806, to Min. of Int. saying FAM had sailed almost a month ago, we conclude that FAM sailed about Feb. 1. All AN docs.

25. Report of Bur. of Ag. to Min. of Int., Jan. 31, 1806; Min. of Int. to FAM, "Naturaliste," and to "Saunier, Jardinier Botaniste," both Feb. 14, 1806, AN docs.

Chapter 24 ?❧ *Second Mission to America,* 1806–1808

1. FAM to C. C. Pinckney, New York, Oct. 21, 1806, S.C. Hist. Soc. doc. (authors' trans.).

2. *Annales du Muséum d'Histoire Naturelle,* vol. 8 (1806); and reported to have been reprinted in pamphlet form in the same year (MacPhail, Foreword).

3. Bette, ed., *Jefferson's Garden Book,* p. 311.

4. Saunier to Champagny, Min. of Int., Bergen Woods near N.Y., Oct. 15, 1806, AN doc.

5. Durant and Durant, *Age of Napoleon,* pp. 207–10.

6. Counsellor of State, Dir. of Post Offices, to Min. of Int., Jan. 21, 1807; Min. of Int. to Duruflé fils, banker in Paris, Mar. 5, 1807; Duruflé to Min. of Int., Mar. 21, 1807; Report from Bur. of Ag. to Min. of Int., Mar. 27, 1807; Report by Bur. of Ag. to Duruflé, Apr. 3, 1807; Report of Bur. of Ag. to Min. of Int., May 1, 1807; Bur. of Ag. to Duruflé, Banker, May 8, 1807, all AN docs.

7. FAM to Min. of Int. Champagny, Jan. 10, 1807, AN doc.

8. Benjamin Vaughan (1751–1835), Anglo-American doctor, lawyer, diplomat, agriculturalist, and political economist who had played an important role in the peace negotiations of 1782. B. in Jamaica, the eldest of 11 children of a London merchant and wealthy Bostonian mother. Correspondent of Franklin and the first five presidents of the U.S.

Charles Vaughan (1759–1839), Anglo-American promoter and developer, brother of Benjamin and John, FAM's long-term correspondent. One of the founders of the Mass. Soc. for Promoting Ag. and promoter of Boston's first block of brick houses, the Franklin, or Tontine, Crescent.

9. FAM, *Sylva,* Introduction, p. 11.

10. Bosc to Min. of Int., Paris, July 11, 1807, AN doc.

11. FAM to BV, Boston, Aug. 1, 1807, BV Papers (authors' trans.).

12. John C. Warren (1778–1856), surgeon and naturalist, son of the distinguished Dr. John Warren (1753–1815). Innovative prof. at Harvard Med. School and Pres. of Boston Soc. of Nat. Hist.

13. John Gorham (1783–1829), Boston physician and chemist, son-in-law and student of the elder Dr. John Warren.

14. Robert H. Gardiner (1782–1864), agriculturalist, a relative of the Vaughans and prime mover in founding the Gardiner Lyceum.

15. Prob. Prof. Aaron Dexter of Harvard.

16. John Davis (1761–1847), Plymouth jurist, successively comptroller of U.S. Treas. under Pres. Washington and federal judge under Pres. Adams.

17. The governing body of Boston. Deer Island, the locale of the party, is off the north lip of Boston Harbor.

18. Thomas Pinckney of S.C., brother of C. C.

19. Charles Bulfinch (1763–1844), Boston architect and builder, designer of the State House in Boston and successor to Latrobe as architect of the national capital, Chm. of the Boston Selectmen.

20. FAM to BV, Philadelphia, Oct. 4, 1807, BV Papers (authors' trans.).

21. FAM, "Historical Anecdote of Robert Fulton," *Jour. of the Franklin Inst.*, 3d ser., 18 (July 1849):37–40.

22. Ibid.

23. Durand, "Biographical Memoir," of pp. 161–77.

24. Robert R. Livingston (1746–1813), chancellor of N.Y. and statesman who served in the Continental Cong. and was a member of the drafting com. of the Dec. of Ind., a leading backer of Fulton's *Clermont*, named for the family seat on the Hudson.

25. Durand, "Biographical Memoir," p. 175.

26. Fortin to Min. of Int., Nov. 5, 1807; Fortin to Chief, Bur. of Agr., Nov. 20, 1807, freight bill; Chief, Bur. of Ag., to Bosc, Insp. of Nurseries of Luxembourg and Roule, Nov. 27, 1807; Bosc. to Min. of Int., Dec. 15, 1807; Min. of Int. to Dir. of Roule, Mar. 18, 1808; FAM to Min. of Int., Dec. 26, 1808, all AN docs.

27. FAM to BV, Philadelphia, Sept. 2, 1808, BV Papers (authors' trans.). It appears FAM returned to Phila. before making this second trasmontane expedition. On Apr. 7, 1808, he received a receipt for $20 from Mathias Kin for a seed shipment sent the Min. of Int. six years earlier.

28. Napoleon's Bayonne Decree, Apr. 17, 1808, had subjected to seizure any Am. vessel entering a French port (Smelser, *The Democratic Republic, 1801–1815*, pp. 172–73).

29. Alexander Wilson (1766–1845) Scottish-Am. ornithologist. After apprentice as a weaver he came to U.S. where he became successively school teacher, Phila. editor, and finally a self-taught ornithologist. His 9-vol. *Am. Ornithology* brought recognition as the father of Am. ornithology.
Thomas Nuttall (1786–1859), British-born Am. naturalist.

30. A. Raffeneau-Delile (1778–1850), Fr. botanist and M.D., accompanied Napoleon on his invasion of Egypt in 1801, where he began his great work on the flora of Egypt, later Fr. Commissioner at Wilmington, N.C., studied medicine at Phila. and updated AM's *Flora* (*Bot. FA*, pp. 54–67).

31. Caspar Wistar (1761–1818), Philadelphia scientist and physician. After studying med. in Phila. went for more study in London and Edinburgh, became prof. of Med. at U. of Pa., and wrote the first Am. textbook on anatomy. Nuttall gave his name to *Wistaria*, more commonly spelled *Wisteria*.

32. Raffeneau-Delile to Wistar, Paris, Nov. 24, 1808, CWL no. 11.

33. Report of Min. of Int., Jan. 7, 1809, memo of approval, Jan. 21, 1809, AN docs. (authors' trans.).

34. Min. of Fin. to Min. of Int., Dec. 9, 1808; Claim of FAM to Min. of Int., Dec. 26, 1808; FAM to Min. of Int., Dec. 19, 1808; draft of letter from Min. of Int. to Min. of Fin., Jan. 7, 1809; draft of letter from Min. of Int. to Chief, 3d Div., Bur. of Ag., Jan. 21, 1809, all AN docs.

35. *Rapport sur les Voyages pour la naturalisation des Arbres Foresteriers des*

Etats-Unis; Fait à la Société d'Agriculture du departmant de la Seine, dans la séance du 1er février 1809. Par Mm. Alliare, Bosc du Petit-Thouars, et J. Correa de Serra, Rapporteur, Extract from the minutes of the Société d'Agriculture, vol. XI, Paris, 1809 (authors' trans.).

Chapter 25 ⊗ Paris, 1809–1814, Franco-American Scientific Intermediary

1. FAM to Wistar, Paris, May 27, 1809, CWL, no. 17 (authors' trans.).

2. FAM to Wistar, Paris, Nov. 29, 1809, CWL, no. 18 (authors' trans.).

3. Robert Patterson (1743–1824), born in Ireland of Scottish parents, came to Philadelphia as a young man. Prof. of mathematics at 21 of Univ. of Pa.; became president of APS in 1819 and author of respected works on physics and mathematics.

4. Patterson had brought with him FAM's diploma from APS.

5. FAM to JV, Paris, Nov. 29, 1809, Mich. Papers (authors' trans.).

6. Karl L. Willdenow (1765–1812), Dir. of Berlin Bot. Garden. His 5th ed. of Linnaeus' *Species plantarum* was a completely rewritten work that included many Am. plants for the first time (Earl L. Core, *Plant Taxonomy*, p. 40).

7. David B. Warden (1772–1845), Am. diplomat, author, and book collector of N. Irish birth to Scottish parents. Emigrating to U.S., he soon became an Am. citizen, secy. to the Am. ambassador to Fr. and consul of Paris, and member of APS.

8. Robert Cantwell, *Alexander Wilson*, p. 234.

9. Alexander von Humboldt (1769–1859), native of Berlin, eventually became an international figure as a naturalist, geographer, and explorer and author of many works, the most noted being his *Kosmos*, gaining him the reputation of being "the most famous man in Europe except for Napoleon."

10. FAM to Wm. Bartram, Paris, Mar. 12, 1810, Darlington, ed., *Memorials*, pp. 447–48.

11. For more on the complex European blockades, see Smelser, *The Democratic Republic*, pp. 192 ff., and Durant and Durant, *Age of Napoleon*, pp. 693 ff.

12. FAM to JV, Paris, Mar. 19, 1810, Mich. Papers (authors' trans.).

13. Chinard, "André and François André Michaux and Their Predecessors," pp. 349–50.

14. Durant and Durant, *Age of Napoleon*, pp. 222–30.

15. Ibid., pp. 230–36; FAM to Wistar, Paris, Nov. 29, 1809, CWL, no. 18 (authors' trans.).

16. FAM to Wm. Bartram, Paris, Mar. 12, 1810, Darlington, ed., *Memorials*, pp. 477–78.

17. FAM to JV, Paris, Mar. 19, 1810, Mich. Papers (authors' trans.).

18. *Tr. FAM*, p. 166.

19. Rembrandt Peale (1778–1860), portrait and historical painter, was twice sent to France by his father, Charles Willson Peale, to secure paintings of

notable French artists and scientists, first in 1808 and then in 1809, returning in 1810.

20. FAM to JV, Paris, Aug. 20, 1810 (authors' trans.), FAM to JV, Paris, Aug. 21, 1810, Mich. Papers.

21. Joel Barlow (1754–1812), Conn.-born poet and political leader in Am. Rev.; Min. to Fr. in 1811 until his death from exposure in Poland, where he had gone to meet Napoleon for a conference. His best known work is his *Columbiad*.

22. Thomas Bradford (1745–1838), Philadelphia printer, publisher, and newspaper man; one of the founders of APS. Among his notable publications was Wilson's *American Ornithology*.

23. FAM, "American Edition," Sept. 1, 1810, Mich. Papers.

24. Cantwell, *Alexander Wilson*, pp. 145–64; Savage, *Lost Heritage*, pp. 255–72.

25. Smelser, *The Democratic Republic*, pp. 192–226.

26. FAM to JV, Paris, Jan. 18, 1811, Mich. Papers (authors' trans.).

27. It is a striking comment on the state of the times that the great Humboldt was, even as FAM, reduced to barter his notable work. There is also an interesting sidelight on the *Atlas* that accompanied this work. Its important new map of Mexico had already been reproduced without permission or credit by Zebulon Pike in his published report of his 1805–7 western expedition, to the mortification of Pres. Jefferson with whom, on a visit to Washington, Humboldt had left a prepublication copy. It required a friendly letter of regrets from Jefferson to Humboldt to quiet the storm of protest provoked by the impropriety of the then deceased Pike (Savage, *Discovering America, 1700–1875*, p. 145n).

28. FAM to JV, Paris, Apr. 1 and 10 and June 27, 1811, Mich. Papers (authors' trans.).

29. The full title of the French edition is: *Histoire des arbres forestiers de l'Amérique septentrionale, considérés principalement sous les rapports de leur usage dans les arts et de leur introduction dans le commerce, ainsi que d'après les avantages qu'ils peuvent affrir aux gouvernemens en Europe et aux personnes que veulent former de grandes plantations.*

30. FAM to JV, Paris, Dec. 3, 1811, Mich. Papers (authors' trans.).

31. FAM to Wistar, Dec. 5, 1811, CWL no. 20; FAM to JV, Paris, Dec. 5, 1811, FAM to JV, Dec. 11, 1811, FAM to JV, Paris, Dec. 17, 1811, Mich. Papers.

32. Durant and Durant, *Age of Napoleon*, pp. 693–711.

33. Ibid., pp. 525–27.

34. We have no other information as to when and where FAM and James Biddle traveled together.

James Biddle (1783–1848) Naval officer and scion of the notable Phila. Biddle family. After attending U. of Pa. he began a naval career that took him to Tripoli, where he suffered capture and imprisonment. He was in Paris in 1811 to deliver government dispatches to the U.S. minister. Subsequently he served in the War of 1812 and in 1814 took possession of Oregon Territory.

35. FAM to Wistar, Paris, Jan. 28, 1812, CWL, no. 21 (authors' trans.).

36. Nicholas Biddle (1766–1844), Philadelphia financier and editor; his most notable work was (with Paul Allen) the *History of the Expedition of Captains Lewis and Clark*, which appeared in 1812. FAM's request for a copy could not have been filled for another two years.

37. If Wilson had sent the volumes of his *Ornithology* that had appeared before 1812, there would have been but six of the ultimate nine, the last posthumously prepared by George Ord (Cantwell, *Alexander Wilson,* pp. 242–62).

38. FAM to Wistar, paris, Jan. 28, 1812, CWL, no. 21; FAM to JV, Feb. 29, 1812, FAM to JV, Apr. 11, 1812, both from Paris, Mich. Papers.

39. FAM to JV, Paris, May 14, 1812, Mich. Papers.

40. FAM to JV, Paris, Nov. 23, 1812, Mich. Papers (authors' trans.).

41. Durant and Durant, *Age of Napoleon,* pp. 712–28.

42. Ferdinand R. Hassler (1770–1843), Swiss-born geologist and first Sup. of U.S. Coast Sur., came to U.S. in 1805. On a mission to England to secure surveying instruments in 1811 he became stranded in Europe until the end of the War of 1812.

43. FAM to JV, Paris, May 14, 1813, Mich. Papers (authors' trans.).

44. FAM to JV, Paris, Sept. 7, 1813, Mich. Papers (authors' trans.).

45. Rich to JV, Georgetown (D.C.), Mar. 12, 1814, Mich. Papers. Obadiah Rich (1783–1850), Boston bibliographer, occasional publisher and sponsor of scientific literature. In 1816, when consul in Spain, he was of great assistance to Washington Irving, William Prescott, and George Bancroft.

46. FAM to Wistar, Paris, June 26, 1814, CWL, no. 22 (authors' trans.).

47. FAM to JV, Paris, July 1, 1814, Mich. Papers (authors' trans.).

48. William H. Crawford (1772–1824), U.S. senator, cabinet member, and two-time presidential candidate. Born in Va. of Scottish parents but grew up in S.C. and Ga. Min. to Fr. in 1815 but resigned to become Secy. of War.

49. FAM to JV, Paris, July 20, 1814, Mich. Papers.

50. FAM to JV, Paris, July 1, 1814, Mich. Papers (authors' trans.).

51. Darlington, ed., *Memorials.*

52. FAM to JV, Paris, Dec. 18, 1814, Mich. Papers (authors' trans.).

Chapter 26 ȝ~ *Paris, 1814–1819, THE NORTH AMERICAN SYLVA*

1. FAM to JV, Paris, Feb. 24, Apr. 27, Apr. 28, and May 1, 1815, Mich. Papers.

2. Durant and Durant, *Age of Napoleon,* pp. 734–40.

3. FAM to JV, Paris, May 1, 1815, Mich. Papers (authors' trans.).

4. FAM to Bradford, Paris, May 5, 1815, Mich. Papers (authors' trans.).

5. Durant and Durant, *Age of Napoleon,* pp. 740–49.

6. FAM to JV, Paris, Aug. 23, 1815, Mich. Papers (authors' trans.).

7. Thomas Sully (1783–1872), English-born Am. artist, emigrated to Charleston as a boy. Moving to Philadelphia, he had a long and successful career. One of his best-known works is *Washington Crossing the Delaware.*

8. Baron Louis-Felix de Beaujour, Fr. diplomat to U.S. from 1804 to 1816, where he gathered the material for a book on the U.S. His brother followed him at his Philadelphia post.

9. FAM to JV, Paris, May 5, 1815, Mich. Papers.

10. FAM to McMahon, Aug. 23, 1815, Mich. Papers.
Bernard McMahon (?–1816), Irish-born Philadelphia horticulturist. His greenhouses and garden became a gathering place for botanical talk. His place was the repository of plants brought back by Lewis and Clark. His *American Gardener's Calendar*, the earliest Am. horticultural work, went into eleven editions.

11. FAM to JV, Paris, Sept. 12 and 19 and Nov. 5, 1815; FAM to Barton, Paris, Nov. 7, 1815, all Mich. Papers.

12. FAM to JV, Paris, Dec. 3, 1815, Mich. Papers (authors' trans.).

13. FAM to JV, Paris, Dec. 27, 1815, Mich. Papers (authors' trans.).

14. Daniel Drake (1785–1852), physician and author. Son of poor N.J. farm parents, who moved to Ky. After meager backwoods schooling, he began his medical studies under a leading Cincinnati physician. He was the author of important books on the Ohio region and member of APS.

15. FAM to JV, Paris, Jan. 7, 1816; bills of lading and receipts of Le Roy, Bayard, and McEver, Mar. 22, June 29, Sept. 17, 1816; FAM to JV, Apr. 26, and Sept. 17, 1816, all Mich. Papers.

16. Edward Everett (1794–1865), Boston Unitarian clergyman, teacher, and noted antislavery orator. He became editor of the *North American Review* (Brooks, *The Flowering of New England, 1815–1865*, pp. 77–88).

17. George Ticknor (1791–1871), Boston educator, entered Dartmouth at 14 and entered upon a legal career, but on a visit to Monticello was inspired by Jefferson's plans for U. of Va. to undertake the advocacy of a similar plan to change Harvard from a college to a university (ibid.).

18. Albert Gallatin (1761–1845), Swiss-born Am. diplomat and secy of Treas., had first settled in the Ohio region where his financial talents were soon recognized. He later served as Jefferson's secy. of Treas., Am. negotiator at Ghent, Min. to Fr. and to G.B.

19. FAM to JV, Paris, Jan. 7, 1816, Mich. Papers (authors' trans.).

20. FAM to JV, Paris, Apr. 26, 1816, Mich. Papers (authors' trans.).

21. FAM to JV, Paris, May 12, 1816, Mich. Papers (authors' trans.).

22. FAM to JV, Paris, June 14, 1816, Mich. Papers (authors' trans.).

23. Thomas H. Gallaudet (1787–1851), pioneer Am. educator of the deaf, born in Philadelphia of Fr. Huguenot parents, grad. of Yale, studied under Abbé Siscard in Paris under sponsorship of Henry Clay. Established in 1816 a school for the deaf in Hartford which was continued by his sons Thomas (1822–1902) and Edward (1837–1917). The FAM quotation is the authors' trans.

24. FAM to Wistar, Paris, Sept. 17, 1816, CWL, no. 23. (authors' trans.).

25. FAM to JV, Paris, July 5 and Sept. 18, 1816, Mich. Papers (authors' trans.).

26. FAM to JV, Paris, Dec. 10, 1816, Mich. Papers (authors' trans.).
Henri Grégoire (1750–1831), Fr. revolutionist, bishop, and educator. Born of peasant parents, he rose to power in both the church and government, where he managed to stem some of its excesses. His later years were devoted to experimental agriculture, the establishment of libraries, and advancing education.

27. Aimé-Jacques-Alexandre Bonpland (1733–1858), Fr. botanical ex-

plorer and experimental tropical horticulturalist, was Humboldt's companion on his Orinoco and Amazon expeditions. Later settled on the La Platte; Durant and Durant, *Age of Napoleon,* pp. 608–9; Duval, *King's Garden,* pp. 152–80.

28. FAM to Bigelow, Paris, Aug. 13, 1817, Mass. Hist. Soc. doc., Bigelow Collection.

Jacob Bigelow (1786–1879), Mass. Botanist and physician, grad. of Harvard and U. of Pa. Published in 1814 a bot. manual, *Florula Bostoniensis,* N.E. authority until Gray's *Manual* (1848).

29. Stephen Elliott (1771–1830), S.C. banker, planter, and botanist, grad. of Yale. In 1812 became pres. of the S.C. State Bank; prof. of botany at S.C. Med. Col., and author of a 2-vol. manual of the regional flora, *Sketch of the Botany of South Carolina and Georgia.*

30. FAM to JV, Paris, Feb. 27, May 29, June 22, and Aug. 23, 1817, Mich. Papers (authors' trans.).

31. FAM to JV, Feb. 27, 1817.
William H. Keating (1794–1840), mineralogical chemist. Born in Del., educated at U. of Pa. after which he went to Fr. for advanced study; became a prof. of chem. of national note.

32. FAM to JV, Paris, May 10, 1817, Mich. Papers.
John Sargeant (1779–1852) Philadelphia lawyer and gov. official. In 1816 he was sent to Europe by the Second Bank of U.S. on an important monetary mission. Later refused appointments to U.S. Sup. Court and as ambassador to G.B.

33. FAM to JV, Paris, Aug. 23, 1817, Mich. Papers (authors' trans.).
Lardner Vanusin (1792–1848), Philadelphia geologist, grad. of Ecole des Mines, became prof. of S.C. College. He inaugurated a unified system of geological nomenclature.

34. FAM to Bigelow, Paris, Aug. 13, 1817. Mass. Hist. Soc., Bigelow Col.

35. FAM to JV, Paris, Jan. 27, 1817, Mich. Papers (authors' trans.).

36. Ibid. As it turned out, three additional volumes were necessary to complete the *Sylva* and cover the breadth of its title. Those supplemental volumes were prepared by Thomas Nuttall and published in Phila.: vol. 1, in parts in 1842 and 1843; vol. 2 in 1846, and vol. 3 in 1849 (Graustein, *Thomas Nuttall,* chaps. 19 and 21 and p. 457 n. 60).

37. FAM to JV, Paris, May 24, 1817, Mich. Papers (authors' trans.).

38. FAM to Wistar, Paris, Dec. 18, 1817, CWL, no. 24 (authors' trans.).

39. FAM to JV, Paris, June 27, 1818, Mich. Papers; Durant and Durant, *Age of Napoleon,* p. 107.

40. FAM to JV, Dec. 16, 1817, Mich. Papers (authors' trans.).

41. FAM to JV, Paris, Feb. 3, 1818, Mich. Papers (authors' trans.).

42. FAM to JV, Paris, June 20 and 27, 1818, Mich. Papers (authors' trans.).

43. FAM to JV, Paris, July 19, 1819, Mich. Papers. See also FAM to JV, Apr. 15, 1816. In one of the new half volumes being distributed to replace the original, FAM wrote that "for the translation of the present half volume I am indebted to my friend Augustus L. Hillhouse of Connecticut." It is generally thought that he was also the translator of all the rest of the English-text edition (MacPhail, pp. 17–19).

44. FAM to JV, Paris, Oct. 17, 1819, Mich. Papers (authors' trans.).

45. Howe to JV. New Haven, Nov. 3, 1817; Belair to JV, Phila., Mar. 17, and New York, Aug. 5, 1818, Mich. Papers.

46. FAM to JV, Paris, Sept. 2, 1817, Mich. Papers (authors' trans.).

47. FAM to JV, June 27, 1818, Mich. Papers.

48. FAM to Carr, Paris, July 1, 1818, Mich. Papers.

49. FAM to JV, Paris, Aug. 19, 1818, Mich. Papers.

50. William Maclure (1763–1840), Scottish-born philanthropist, social and educational reformer, promoter of science, founder of Phila. Acad. of Nat. Sci. and the New Harmony colony, where the press he helped establish published the first Am. ed. of FAM's *Sylva* in 1841 (MacPhail, pp. 24–26; George B. Lockwood, *The New Harmony Movement,* pp. 74–75, 322 ff.).

51. FAM to JV, Paris, Nov. 1, 1818, Mich. Papers (authors' trans.).

52. Durand, "Biographical Memoir."

53. FAM to JV, Paris, Oct. 28, 1819, Mich. Papers (authors' trans.).

54. Wright, *France in Modern Times,* p. 113, quoting Bertier de Sauvigny, *La restauration,* p. 628.

55. Institut de France, Académie Royale des descriptions et belles lettres to FAM, No. 19, 1819; FAM to JV, Paris, Nov. 26, 1819, Mich. Papers.

Chapter 27 ᘗᔍ Vauréal, 1820–1834

1. FAM to JV, Paris, Jan. 9, Mar. 25, May 3 and 24, 1820, (authors' trans.). A copy of this map of La. and Mex. engraved by P. A. F. Tardieu, Paris, 1820, presumably the one sent with FAM's Mar. 25 letter to JV, is in the archives of APS, doc, no, 73/1820.

2. FAM to M. Thory, Rue St. Honoré, No. 392, Aug. 31, 1820, BM doc.; FAM to AT, Sept. 9, 1820, BM doc., pub. in *Bot. FA,* pp. 249–50.

3. FAM to AT, Le Havre, June 17, 1821, BM doc., in *Bot. FA,* pp. 250–51.

4. FAM to JV, Paris, Nov. 12, 1821, Mich. Papers (authors' trans.).

5. Chinard, "Michaux and Their Predecessors," pp. 354–55.

6. FAM to JV, Paris, Feb. 21, 1823, Mich. Papers (authors' trans.).

7. Wright, *France in Modern Times,* pp. 115–16.

8. FAM to JV, Paris, July 17 and Apr. 28, 1823, Mich. Papers (authors' trans.).

9. FAM, presentation doc. of AM's journals dated Jan. 15, 1824 (authors' trans.), with a copy of the acknowledgment of APS on its 3d page, Mich. Papers. See also *Proc. APS* 26, no. 129 (1889):7.

10. FAM to JV, Paris, Apr. 25, 1827, Mich. Papers.

11. Those comments are drawn from a dozen letters of FAM to JV between June 1, 1827, and Aug. 1, 1832, and one from Ord to JV dated Mar. 17, 1830, all Mich. Papers.

12. *Description de l'Egypte* (Paris, 1809–28); see Durant and Durant, *Age of Napoleon,* p. 110.

13. Philadelphia, 1824–28. Quotation from Harry B. Weiss and Grace M.

Ziegler, *Thomas Say,* p. 190. Invoice of Judah Dobson to JV, Aug. 13, 1834, for Say's *Entomology,* Mich. Papers.

14. FAM to JV, July 12, 1827, and July 10, 1828, Mich. Papers.

15. FAM to JV, Paris, Jan. 9, 1830, Mich. Papers (authors' trans.); Chinard, "Michaux and Their Predecessors," p. 354. But see MacPhail, pp. 24–26.

16. Ord to JV, Paris, Mar. 17, 1830, Mich. Papers.

17. Ord to JV, Paris, May 18, 1830, Mich. Papers.

18. FAM to JV Paris, Nov. 27, 1830, Mich. Papers (authors' trans.); see also Wright, *France in Modern Times,* pp. 114–30.

19. FAM to JV, Paris, July 27, 1832, Mich. Papers (authors' trans.).

20. JV to FAM, Philadelphia, Sept. 8, 1832, sent in packet to D. B. Warden. Copy in Mich. Papers.

Chapter 28 ᘓ Harcourt, 1834–1856

1. Pierre Aubert, "Les Fôrets de l'Eure," *Connaissance de l'Eure,* no. 28 (1978). Chinard says FAM was named director of Harcourt in 1829 ("Michaux and Their Predecessors," pp. 334–35). However, there are two extant letters of FAM, written years later, suggesting he did not commence his work at Harcourt until 1831 or 1832 (FAM to Pres. of APS, Vauréal, Oct. 24, 1852, Mich. Papers; and FAM to Brongniart, Harcourt, Nov. 19, 1845, Ms. no. 1988, piece 714, BM doc.). Additionally we have this: "Michaux fils . . . effected numerous [forest] plantations from 1833 to 1848" (quoted from a distribution to visitors to Harcourt by the Acad. d'Agriculture de France, prepared by A. Jardiller).

2. Chinard, "Michaux and Their Predecessors," pp. 334–35; also copies of FAM's will and probate docs. relating thereto in Mich. Papers.

3. FAM to Brongniart, n. 1 above. See also *Bot. FA,* p. 234, and FAM to Pres. APS, n. 1 above.

4. A. Jardillier, "Château Féodal d'Harcourt," Acad. de Ag. de France (Le Neubourg); Pierre Aubert, "Forêt et Arboretum d'Harcourt," *Connaissance de l'Eure,* no. 28 (1978). See also *Domaine d'Harcourt Catalogue,* introduction.

5. FAM to Brongniart, n. 1 above.
Adolphe-Théodore Brongniart (1801–1876) son of Alexandre, pioneer paleobotanist, in whose researches Adolphe joined. Later he joined the faculty at the Museum of Nat. Hist. as prof. of botany. Later he became administrator of the Harcourt domain and arboretum.

6. FAM to Brongniart, n. 1 above.

7. *Echalas paisseaux et lattes.*

8. *Mémoire sur les causes de la fièvre jaune.*

9. This founding date has been questioned. Jardillier gives it as 1852 in his historical account; Aubert says 1853; see also *Domaine d'Harcourt Catalogue,* introduction.

10. FAM to pres. of APS, Vauréal, near Pontoise, Oct. 24, 1852, Mich. Papers (authors' trans.).

11. We have no explanation of FAM's seeming ignorance of the publication of the 3-vol. supplement to his *Sylva,* by Thomas Nuttall, Philadelphia, 1842–1849.

12. Isaac Lea (1792–1886), Philadelphia publisher and naturalist, was born of Quaker parents but lost that birthright when he enlisted for service in the War of 1812. He was the son-in-law of FAM's acquaintance Mathew Carey, and a mem. of Acad. of Nat. Sci. and of APS.

13. Lea to Patterson, Paris, 1852, Mich. Papers.

14. We use the generally reported place of FAM's death; however, the friend's report of his death mentions that he had spent the whole day supervising workmen planting Am. trees, strongly implying an activity scarcely possible at his modest, fully developed Vauréal estate but quite in keeping with activities then in progress at the Harcourt nursery and arboretum, particularly at that optimum planting time.

15. Chinard, "Michaux and Their Predecessors," p. 355.

16. Asa Gray to C. B. Trego (Sec. of APS), Boston, Sept. 15, 1856, Mich. Papers.
Asa Gray (1810–1888), one of eight children of rural N.Y. farm family; early dedicated himself to botany, a dedication that eventually brought him recognition as the foremost Am. botanist of his time, and most eminent botanical author. He traveled widely, visiting France in 1838 and again in 1850–51 to purchase botanical works for U. of Mich. It was on one of those trips that he had his association with FAM.

17. The correct date of FAM's death is Oct. 23, 1855.

18. Perhaps this was the presentation copy sent by FAM to Jefferson that he somehow reacquired after T. J.'s death.

19. The Mich. Papers at APS contain some 70 docs. bearing on the bequest and the activities relating to securing delivery of it. Among the more important are: *The Official Translation* of FAM's 1855 will from which the authors' quotations are made; APS to Boris Branet, Dec. 17, 1856; A. Germain to APS, Jan. 6, 1857; APS to A. Germain, Apr. 22, 1857; Germain to APS, May 19, 1857; Mass. Soc. to C. B. Trego, Apr. 11, 1859; Asa Gray to Trego, Mar. 6, 1859; Sheriff of Pontoise to APS, Feb. 1862, Summons; Report of Com. on Mich. Leg., May 1867; APS to Min. of Justice of Fr., May 1867; Summary of actions in Min. of APS from Sept. 19, 1856, to May 3, 1867; J. B. Lesley to G. B. Wood, Mar. 23, 1868; Mme Bezier to E. M. Durant, July 14, 1868; A. Carlier to Durand, Apr. 23, 1869; Carlier to Wood, Aug. 25, 1869; Carlier to Durand, Aug. 19, 1869.

20. The only records the authors have been able to find in respect to the legacy to the Mass. Soc. other than those previously cited are: (1) a resolution of the Soc. in French adopted at a meeting of its directors on Apr. 11, 1857, expressing condolences to Mme Micahaux (*sic*) and gratitude for the legacy bequeathed to it, found in the collections of the Mass. Hist. Soc. in Dr. C, Folder IV, no. 6; and (2) the minutes of the annual meeting of the Mass. Soc. for Promting Ag., on June 11, 1874, in which is recorded the following resolution: "Whereas by a second and final will of the late M. Michaux his bequest to the Society was freed from any conditions—therefore, Voted; That the part of the Resolution of the Trustees passed April 11, 1857, which relates to the disposition of the Gift be recinded and the amount received ($7807.67) be added to the general fund" (Archives of the Mass. Hist. Soc., Col. of Mass. Soc. for Promoting Ag.

Conclusion: The Michauxs and Forestry in America

1. Rutherford Platt, *The Great American Forest,* introduction.

2. Henry Clepper, *Professional Forestry in the United States,* pp. 14–38.

3. Gilbert Chinard, "The American Philosophical Society and the Early History of Forestry in America," pp. 444–88; Andrew D. Rodgers III, *Bernhard Eduard Fernow: A Story of North American Forestry.*

4. Rodgers, *Fernow,* pp. 19–20.

5. Ibid.

6. Chinard, "Early Hist. of For. in Am.," p. 467.

7. Joseph Trimble Rothrock (1839–1922), physician, botanist, and forester, received his scientific ed. at Harvard, where he served as asst. to Asa Gray, and medicine at U. of Pa. He headed a com. to study Pa. forests and then became the state's first forest commissioner.

8. J. R. Schramm, "Influence—Past and Present—of François André Micahux on Forestry and Forest Research in America," pp. 336–43; Chinard, "Early Hist. of For. in Am."

9. Rodgers, *Fernow,* p. 26.

10. Henry Clepper, *Crusade for Conservation: The Centennial History of the American Forestry Association,* p. 17.

11. Schramm, "Influence," p. 341.

12. Ibid., pp. 341–43.

13. Pennsylvania Forestry Advisory Services, Forest Resource Plan: *The Report for the Michaux State Forest, 1970–85.*
Rothrock, too, has now been memorialized with an even larger state forest in central Pa., and additionally by a memorial tablet that recognizes him as "The Father of Forestry in Pennsylvania," and at its unveiling on Oct. 29, 1923, a dedication pamphlet, *A Tribute to Dr. Joseph Trimble Rothrock.*

14. J. R. Schramm, "The Memorial to François André Michaux at the Morris Arboretum," pp. 145–49; idem, "Influence," pp. 336–43. More specifically, see J. R. Schramm and Ernst. J. Schreiner, "The Michaux Quercetum," *Morris Arboretum Bul.,* vol. 5(4), June 1954; Hui-Lin Li, "A Progress Report on the Michaux Quercetum," *Morris Arboretum Bul.,* vol. 6(4), Dec. 1955; J. M. F., Jr., "Michaux Quercetum," *Mor. Arb. Bul.,* vol. 11(1), Mar. 1960; S. B. B., "The Michaux Quercetum, *Mor. Arb. Bul.,* vol. 24(2), June 1973; J. J. Willaman, J. Y. Hsio, and H. L. Li, "A Progress Report: Status of Michaux Quercetum, *Mor. Arb. Bul.,* vol. 24(2), June 1973.

15. The constructive work of the Michauxs will continue, thanks to the Michaux Fund and its wise management by APS. Built now into a substantial fund producing about $12,000 annually, grants for the advancement of forestry and silviculture continue to be made from it (Whitfield J. Bell, Jr., APS, in private correspondence with the authors, Sept. 1, 1983).

ᴁᴄ Bibliography

A Note on the Primary Unpublished Sources

The American Philosophical Society's unpublished material pertinent to the lives of André Michaux and François André Michaux has proved to be the richest source of surviving letters and other unpublished documents. There collectively classified as Michaux Papers are many hundreds of items available nowhere else. There are many additional Michaux items at APS in collections designated APS Archives, Benjamin Vaughan Papers, Caspar Wistar Letters, and others, including the original eight notebooks containing André Michaux's journal of his American years.

Also the Society has obtained microfilms of many other hundreds of Michaux letters and official documents from collections in France, originally preserved in the Archives nationales, and others later deposited at Bibliothèque nationale, and still others at the Muséum national d'histoire naturelle.

The Bibliothèque de Versailles has in its archives a manuscript by André Michaux entitled "Journal de mon Voyage en Perse," providing his own account of the earliest of his major expeditions.

The Library of Congress has a copy of André Michaux's "Mémoire abrégé concernant mes Voyages dans l'Amérique Septentrionale," addressed to Citizen Genet; and other Michaux items.

Finally, there are to be found in institutions elsewhere still other Michaux documents. Among those repositories are the South Carolina Historical Society at Charleston, the Massachusetts Historical Society at Boston, and the Arnold Arboretum at Jamaica Plain and Cambridge, Mass. Full bibliographical data are given below.

Botanical Reference Works

The most frequently utilized botanical reference works include the following: Bailey, *Cyclopedia of Horticulture*; Coker and Totten, *Trees of the Southeastern States*; Core, *Plant Taxonomy*; Gray, *Manual of Botany*; Radford et al., *Manual of the Vascular Flora of the Carolinas*; Sargent, *Manual of the Trees of North America*; Small, *Manual of Southeastern Flora*. Full bibliographical data are given below.

Selected Bibliography

The Adams-Jefferson Letters: The Complete Correspondence between Thomas Jefferson and Abigail and John Adams. Edited by Lester J. Cappon. Chapel Hill: Univ. of North Carolina Press, 1959.

American Historical Association, *Report for 1896.* Vol. 1, 1896.

Ammon, Harry. *The Genet Mission.* New York: Norton, 1973.

Aubert, Pierre. "Forêt et Arboretum d'Harcourt." *Connaissance de l'Eure* (Eureux), no. 28 (1978).

Bailey, Liberty Hyde, ed. *Cyclopedia of Horticulture.* 3 vols. New York: Macmillan, 1928.

Bamford, Paul Walden. *Forests and French Sea Power, 1660–1789.* Toronto: Univ. of Toronto Press, 1956.

Bartram, William. *Travels through North and South Carolina, Georgia and East and West Florida.* Philadelphia, 1791.

Baudin, Nicolas. *Journal de Mer: The Journal of Post Captain Nicolas Baudin.* Edited and translated by Christine Cornell. Adelaide: Libraries Board of South Australia, 1974.

Bemis, Samuel Flagg. *Pinckney's Treaty.* Baltimore: Johns Hopkins Press, 1926.

Berkeley, Edmund, and Dorothy Smith. *Dr. Alexander Garden of Charles Town.* Chapel Hill: Univ. of North Carolina Press, 1969.

Bissell, Richard. *The Monongahela.* New York: Rinehart, 1949.

Betts, Edwin Morris, ed. *Thomas Jefferson's Garden Book.* Philadelphia: American Philosophical Society, 1944.

Blumenthal, Henry. *American and French Culture, 1800–1900.* Baton Rouge: Louisiana State Univ. Press, 1975.

Brooks, Van Wyck. *The Flowering of New England, 1815–1865.* New York: Dutton, 1940.

Brunet, Abbé Ovide. *Voyage d'André Michaux en Canada de puis le lac Champlain jusqu'a la Baie d'Hudson.* Quebec: Bureau de l'Abeille, 1861.

———. *Notice sur les plantes de Michaux et sur son voyage au Canada et a la baie d'Hudson d'apres son journal manuscrit et autres documents inedits.* Quebec: Bureau de l'Abeille, 1863.

———. "Michaux and his journey in Canada." *Canadian Naturalist* 1 (1864):331–43.

Burt, Struthers. *Philadelphia, Holy Experiment.* Garden City, N.Y.: Doubleday, 1945.

Cantwell, Robert. *Alexander Wilson, Naturalist and Pioneer.* Philadelphia: Lippincott, 1961.

Carmer, Carl. *The Hudson.* New York: Rinehart, 1959.

Carver, Capt. Jonathan. *Travels through the Interior Parts of North America in the Years 1766, 1767, 1768.* London, 1778. Reprint. Minneapolis, 1956.

Catesby, Mark. *The Natural History of Carolina, Florida and the Bahama Islands.* 2 vols. London, 1754, 1771.

Centre National de la Recherche Scientifique. *Les Botanistes Français en Amérique de Nord Avant 1850.* Paris, 1957.

Chapman, Ashton. "The Search for the Lost Shortia." *Audubon Magazine* 58 (May 1956):112–15.

Chardin, Sir John. *Journal du Voyage de Chardin en Perse et aux Indes Orientales.* London, 1671. Translated by E. Lloyd as *Sir John Chardin's Travels in Persia.* London: Argonaut Press, 1927.

Chateaubriand, François, Réné de. *Travels in America.* Translated by Richard Switzer. Lexington: Univ. of Kentucky Press, 1969.

Chinard, Gilbert. "The American Philosophical Society and the World of Science, 1768–1800." *Proceedings of the American Philosophical Society* 87, no. 1 (July 1943):1–12.

———. "Jefferson and the American Philosophical Society." *Proceedings of the American Philosophical Society* 87, no. 3 (July 1943):263–77.

———. "The American Philosophical Society and the Early History of Forestry in America." *Proceedings of the American Philosophical Society* 89, no. 2 (July 1945):444–88.

———. "André and François André Michaux and Their Predecessors." *Proceedings of the American Philosophical Society* 101, no. 4 (Aug. 1957):344–61.

Clark, Thomas D. *The Kentucky.* New York: Farrar and Rinehart, 1942.

Clepper, Henry. *Professional Forestry in the United States.* Baltimore: Johns Hopkins Univ. Press, 1971.

———. *Crusade for Conservation: The Centennial History of the American Forestry Association.* Washington, D.C.: American Forestry Association, 1975.

Coker, W. C. "The Garden of André Michaux." *Journal of the Elisha Mitchell Scientific Society.* July 1911, pp. 65–72.

———, and H. R. Totten. *Trees of the Southeastern United States.* Chapel Hill: Univ. of North Carolina Press, 1934.

Connelly, Owen. *French Revolution/Napoleonic Era.* New York: Holt, Rinehart and Winston, 1979.

Core, Earl L. *Plant Taxonomy.* Englewood Cliffs, N.J.: Prentice-Hall, 1955.

Coues, Elliott, ed., *History of the Expedition under the Command of Lewis and Clark.* 4 vols. New York: Francis P. Harper, 1893. Reprint. 3 vols. New York: Dover, 1965.

Crèvecoeur, J. Hector St. John. *Letters from an America Farmer.* Reprinted from the original edition, with a prefatory note by W. P. Trent and an introduction by Ludwig Lewisohn. New York, 1904.

Darlington, William, ed. *Memorials of John Bartram and Humphrey Marshall.* Facs. of 1849 ed. New York: Hafner, 1967.

Deleuze, J. P. F. "Notice Historique sur André Michaux." *Annales du Muséum National d'Histoire Naturelle* (Paris), 3 (1804): 191–227. Trans. Charles Konig and John Sims. "Memoirs of the Life and Botanical Travels of André Michaux." *Annals of Botany* (London), 1 (1805):321–55.

de Voto, Bernard. *The Course of Empire.* Boston: Houghton Mifflin, 1952.

Domaine d'Harcourt Catalogue. Académie d'Agriculture, Nancy, 1977.

Duke, Marc. *The DuPonts.* New York: Dutton, 1976.

Durand, Elias. "Biographical Memoir of the late François André Michaux." *Transactions of the American Philosophical Society* 2 (1856). Reprinted in *American Journal of Science and Arts,* 2d ser., 24 (Sept. 1857):161–77.

Durant, Will and Ariel. *The Age of Voltaire.* New York: Simon and Schuster, 1967.

———. *Rousseau and Revolution.* New York: Simon and Schuster, 1975.

———. *The Age of Napoleon.* New York: Simon and Schuster, 1975.

Duval, Marguerite. *The King's Garden.* Translated by Annette Tomarken and Claudine Cowen. Charlottesville: Univ. Press of Virginia, 1982.

Elliott, Stephen. *Sketch of the Botany of South Carolina.* 2 vols. Charleston, 1821, 1824.

Faÿ, Bernard. *Louis XVI.* Translated by Patrick O'Brien. Chicago: Henry Regnery, 1966.

———. *Franklin, the Apostle of Modern Times.* Boston: Little, Brown, 1929.

Federal Works Agency, W.P.A. *Florida: A Guide to the Southernmost State.* New York: Oxford Univ. Press, 1939.

Fitzpatrick, John C., ed. *Writings of George Washington.* 39 vols. Washington, D.C.: U.S. Govt. Printing Office, 1931–44.

Ford, Paul Leicester, ed. *Writings of Thomas Jefferson.* 10 vols. New York: Putnam, 1892–99.

Fraser, John. *A Short History of the Agnostic Cornucopiae: or the New American Grass.* London: Printed for the Author, Paradise-Row, Chelsia, 1789.

Graustein, Jeannette E. *Thomas Nuttall, Naturalist: Explorations in America, 1808–1841.* Cambridge: Harvard Univ. Press, 1967.

Gray, Asa. "Notes of a Botanical Excursion to the Mountains of North Carolina." *American Journal of Science* 42 (Dec. 1841).

———. *Gray's Manual of Botany.* 8th ed. of Gray's *Manual of the Botany of the Northern United States* (1848). Largely rewritten by Merritt Lyndon Fernald. Centennial Ed. New York: American Book Co., 1950.

Hamy, Ernest-Theodore. "Voyage d'André Michaux en Syrie et en Perse (1783–1785) d'apres son journal et sa correspondance." *9e* Congres international de geographia; Geneva, 1908. Compte-rendu des travaux du Congres, 3 (1911):351–88.

Harper, Francis, ed. *The Travels of William Bartram.* Naturalist's Ed. New Haven: Yale Univ. Press, 1958.

Hedrick, U. P. *A History of Horticulture in America to 1860.* New York: Oxford Univ. Press, 1950.

Hindle, Brooke. *The Pursuit of Science in Revolutionary American, 1735–1789.* Chapel Hill: Univ. of North Carolina Press, 1956.

Hodgins, M. D. "The Pride of India Tree." *American Forests* 85 (May 1979):22–25.

Hunt, K. W. "The Charleston Woody Flora." *American Midland Naturalist* 37, no. 3 (May 1947):671–72.

Illick, Joseph S. "Fifty Years Ago." *Forest Leaves* 21, no. 1 (1927).

Jackson, Donald, and Dorothy Twohig, eds. *The Diaries of George Washington.* 6 vols. Charlottesville: Univ. Press of Virginia, 1976–79.

James, James Alton. *The Life of George Rogers Clark.* Chicago: Univ. of Chicago Press, 1928.

James, Marquis. *Andrew Jackson, the Border Captain.* Indianapolis: Bobbs-Merrill, 1933.

Jardillier, A. "Château Féodal d'Harcourt." *Académie d'Agriculture* (Le Neubourg).

Jefferson, Thomas. *Notes on the State of Virginia.* Edited by William Peden. New York: Norton, 1972.

Jones, Howard Mumford. *America and French Culture, 1750–1848.* Chapel Hill: Univ. of North Carolina Press, 1927.

Kalm, Peter. *Travels in North America.* 2 vols. Edited by Adolph B. Benson. New York: Dover, 1966.

Kastner, Joseph. *A Species of Eternity.* New York: Knopf, 1977.

Kimmens, Andrew C., ed. *Tales of the Ginseng.* New York: William Morrow, 1975.

Lacroix, M. Alfred. *Notice Historique sur les Cinq de Jussieu Membres de l'Académie des Sciences (1712–1853).* Institut de France, Académie des Sciences. Paris, 1936.

Lamaute, Marie-Florence, "André Michaux et Son Exploration en Amérique du Nord (1785–1796), D'Apres Les Sources Manuscrites." Thesis, Univ. of Montreal, September 1981.

Leighton, Ann. *American Gardens in the Eighteenth Century.* Boston: Houghton Mifflin, 1976.

Le Page, Abbé Ernest, and P. Arthème Dutilly. "Retracing the Route of Michaux's Hudson's Bay Journey of 1792." *Revue de l'Université d'Ottawa,* Jan.-Mar., 1945.

Lipscomb, A. A., and A. E. Bergh, eds. *The Writings of Thomas Jefferson.* 20 vols. Washington, D.C.: Thomas Jefferson Mem. Assn., 1904–5.

Lockwood, George B. *The New Harmony Movement.* New York: Appleton, 1905. Reprint. Dover, 1971.

Locy, William A. *The Story of Biology.* Garden City, N.Y.: Garden City Publishing Co., 1925.

Lowenthal, David. *George Perkins Marsh.* New York: Columbia Univ. Press, 1958.

MacLeod, Dawn. *The Gardeners London.* London: Duckworth, 1972.

MacPhail, Ian. *André & François André Michaux.* The Sterling Morton Library Bibliographies in Botany and Horticulture. Lisle, Il: The Morton Arboretum, 1981.

Malone, Dumas. *Jefferson and the Ordeal of Liberty.* Boston: Little, Brown, 1962.

Marsh, George Perkins. *Man and Nature.* Edited by David Lowenthal. Cambridge: Harvard Univ. Press, 1965.

Martin, Edwin T. *Thomas Jefferson: Scientist*. New York: H. Schuman, 1952.

Merrill, F. D. "Palisot de Beauvois as an Overlooked American Botanist." *Proceedings of the American Philosophical Society* 76 (Apr. 1936):899–909.

Michaux, André. *Flora Boreali-Americana*. 2 vols. Sistens caracteres Plantarum quas in America septentrionali collegit et detexit Andreas Michaux. Paris and Strasbourg, 1803.

———. *Flora Boreali-Americana*. 2 vols. Facsimile reprint edited and with an introduction by Joseph Ewan. New York: Hafner, 1974.

———. *Histoire des Chênes de l'Amérique, ou Déscriptions et Figures de Toutes Espèces et Variétés de Chênes de l'Amérique Septentrionale*. Paris, Chez Levrault Frères, 1801.

———. "Journal de Mon Voyage." AM's manuscript journal of his eleven years in America which he recorded in small notebooks, or *cahiers*. The first notebook, covering the period from his arrival in New York in November 1785 until his setting out from Charleston in April 1787 on his first extensive botanical expedition in this country, was lost during his return voyage to France in 1796, when his vessel was shipwrecked off the coast of Holland. The remaining eight notebooks of the journal are in the custody of the APS.

———. "Journal de Mon Voyage." Edited and with an introduction and explanatory notes by C. S. Sargent, and published in the original French as "Portions of the Journal of André Michaux Botanist, written during his Travels in the United States and Canada, 1785–1796," *Proceedings of the American Philosophical Society*, 26, no. 129 (Jan.-July, 1889):1–146.

———. *Journal of André Michaux, 1793–1796*. Edited by Rueben Gold Thwaites. In *Early Western Travels*, vol. 3, pp. 27–104. Cleveland, 1907. Portions of the French version translated by the editor. Reprint. New York: AMS, 1966.

———. "Journal de Mon Voyage en Perse Année 1782." Manuscript, Bibliothèques de Versailles.

———. "Mémoire abrégé concernant mes Voyages dans l'Amérique Septentrionale." Manuscript, addressed to Citizen Genet, Philadelphia, May 21, 1793. Copy in Library of Congress.

———. "Mémoire sur les dattiers, avec des observations sur quelque moyens utile aux progrès de l'agriculture dans les colonies Occidentals." *Journal de Physique de Chemie, et d'Histoire Naturelle et des Arts* (Paris) 52, nivose a 1X [Apr. 1801]: 325–35.

———. *Quercus, or Oaks*. Dublin, 1809. Translated and with notes by Walter Wade. Dublin: Graisberry and Campbell, 1809.

———. "Prospectus de l'Etablissement d'une Pepinière d'Arbres et de Plantes Etrangères dans les Provinces Meridionales." Manuscript, Muséum national d'histoire naturelle.

Michaux, François André. *Voyage à l'ouest des monts Alleghanys*. Paris: Chez Levrault, Schoell et Compagne, An. XII—1804.

———. *Travels to the West of the Alleghany Mountains in the States of Ohio, Kentucky, and Tennesea, and Back to Charleston, by the Upper Carolines.* 3d English ed. London: B. Crosby and J. F. Hughes, 1805.

———. *Travels to the West of the Alleghany Mountains.* London, 1805 reprint. Edited by Rueben Gold Thwaites, with notes and introduction. In *Early Western Travels,* vol. 3. Cleveland, 1904. Facsimile reprint. New York: AMS, 1966.

———. *Mémoire sur la naturalisation des arbres forestiers.* Paris: Chez Levrault, Schoel et Compagnie, An XIII, 1805.

———. *Notice sur les îles Bermudes, et particulièrement sur l'île Saint Georges.* Reprinted from *Annales du Muséum d'Histoire Naturelle* (Paris) 8 (1806).

———. *Histoire des arbres Forestiers de l'Amérique septentrionale.* 3 vols. Paris: L. Haussmann et d'Hautel, 1810–13, 24 parts.

———. *The North American Sylva; or a description of the forest trees of the United States, Canada, and Nova Scotia.* 3 vols. Philadelphia. Printed by C. D. Hautel, Paris, 1817–18.

———. *Echalas paisseaux et lattes (Médoc) remplacés par des lignes de fer, mobiles.* Paris: Bouchard-Husard, 1845.

———. *Mémoire sur les causes de le fièvre jaune.* Paris: Bailliere, 1852.

———. *The North American Sylva.* 3 vols. With 3 vols. by Thomas Nuttall. Philadelphia. Printed by William Amphlett, New Harmony, Ind., 1841.

Milbert, Jacques Gérard. *Voyage pittoresque a l'Île de France au Cap de Bonne Espérance, et a l'île de Teneriffe.* 2 vols. and Atlas. Paris, 1812.

———. *Picturesque Itinerary of the Hudson River and the Peripheral Parts of North America.* Translated and annotated by Constance D. Sherman, Ridgewood, N.J.: Gregg Press, 1968.

Mitchill, Samuel Lathan. Unsigned review of A. Michaux's *Histoire des Chênes de l'Amérique.* In the *New York Medical Repository* 6 (1803).

———. Unsigned review of A. Michaux's *Flora Boreali-Americana.* In the *New York Medical Repository* 8 (1805).

Mitford, Nancy. *The Sun King: Louis XIV at Versailles.* New York: Harper and Row, 1866.

Morton, C. V. "Fern Herbarium of André Michaux." *American Fern Journal* 57 (1967):166–82.

"National Register of Big Trees." *American Forests* 88 (Apr. 1982):19–47.

New Jersey Laws. *An Act to enable Andre Michaux to purchase lands in the State of New Jersey under certain restrictions.* 1796 Acts of the General Assembly.

Nuttall, Thomas. *The North American Sylva; or A description of the forest trees of the United States, Canada and Nova Scotia, not described in the work of F. Andrew Michaux.* 3 vols. Vols. 4, 5, and 6 of Michaux's *North American Sylva.* Philadelphia. Printed by William Amphlett, New Harmony, Ind., 1842–49.

Peattie, Donald Culross. *An Almanac for Moderns.* New York: Putnam, 1935.

———. *Green Laurels.* New York: Garden City Publishing Co., 1938.

Pennsylvania Forestry Advisory Services. Forest Resource Plan. *The Report for the Michaux State Forest, 1970–1985.* Harrisburg, 1971.

Philbrick, Francis S. *The Rise of the West, 1754–1830.* New York: Harper and Row, 1965.

Pinchot, Gifford. *The Fight for Conservation.* New York: Doubleday Page, 1910. New ed. Seattle: Univ. of Washington Press, 1967.

———. *Breaking New Ground.* New York: Harcourt, Brace, 1947.

Platt, Rutherford. *The Great American Forest.* Englewood Cliffs, N.J.: Prentice-Hall, 1965.

Radford, A. E., H. E. Ahles, and C. R. Bell. *Manual of the Vascular Flora of the Carolinas.* Chapel Hill: Univ. of North Carolina Press, 1964.

Ravenel, Mrs. St. Julien. *Charleston: The Place and the People.* New York: Macmillan, 1925.

Rehder, Alfred. "Michaux's Earliest Note on American Plants." *Journal of the Arnold Arboretum* 4, no. 1 (Jan. 1923):1–8.

Rembert, David H., Jr. "The Carolina Plants of André Michaux." *Journal of the Southern Appalachian Botanical Club* 44, no. 2 (June 1979):65–80.

Rice, Howard C., Jr. *Thomas Jefferson's Paris.* Princeton, N.J.: Princeton Univ. Press, 1976.

Robbins, William J. "French Botanists and the Flora of the Northeastern United States: J. G. Milbert and Elias Durand." *Proceedings of the American Philosophical Society* 101, no. 4 (Aug. 1957):362–68.

———, and Mary Christine Howson. "André Michaux's New Jersey Garden and Pierre Paul Saunier, Journeyman Gardener." *Proceedings of the American Philosophical Society* 102, no. 4 (Aug. 1958):351–70.

Rodgers, Andrew D., III. *Bernhard Eduard Fernow: A Story of North American Forestry.* Princeton, N.J.: Princeton Univ. Press, 1951.

Rogers, George C., Jr. *Charleston in the Age of the Pinckneys.* Norman: Univ. of Oklahoma Press, 1969.

Rothrock, [Joseph Trimble]. *Memorial Tablet Dedication Proceedings.* Harrisburg, Pa., Oct. 29, 1923.

Rousseau, Jacques. *Le Voyage d'André Michaux au Lac Mistassini en 1792. Memoirs of the Montreal Botanic Garden,* no. 3 (1948).

Rusby, H. H. "Michaux's New Jersey Garden." *Torrey Botanical Club Bulletin* 11 (1984): 88–90.

Rush, Benjamin. *The Autobiography of Benjamin Rush.* Edited by George W. Corner. Princeton, N.J.: Princeton Univ. Press, 1948.

Sargent, C. S. "Some remarks upon the journey of André Michaux to the high Mountains of Carolina in December, 1788, in a letter addressed to Professor Asa Gray." *American Journal of Science,* 3d ser., 32 (1886):466–73.

———. *Manual of the Trees of North America.* 2d corrected ed. 2 vols. New York: Dover, 1965.

Savage, Henry, Jr. *River of the Carolinas: The Santee.* New York: Rinehart, 1956. Reprint. Chapel Hill: Univ. of North Carolina Press, 1968.

————. *Lost Heritage.* New York: William Morrow, 1970.

————. *Discovering America, 1700–1875.* New York: Harper and Row, 1979.

Schramm, J. R. "The Memorial to Francois André Michaux at the Morris Arboretum, University of Pennsylvania." *Proceedings of the American Philosophical Society* 100, no. 2 (June 1956):145–49.

————. "Influence—Past and Present—of Francois André Michaux on Forestry and Forest Research in America." *Proceedings of the American Philosophical Society* 101, no. 4 (Aug. 1957):336–43.

Seaborn, Margaret Mills, ed. *André Michaux's Journeys in Oconee County, South Carolina, in 1787 and 1788.* Walhalla, S.C.: Oconee County Library, 1976.

Sellers, Charles Coleman. *Mr. Peale's Museum.* New York: Norton, 1980.

Sherrill, Charles H. *French Memories of Eighteenth Century America.* New York: B. Bloom, 1971.

Small, J. K. *Manual of Southeastern Flora.* New York: Published by the Author, 1933.

Smelser, Marshall. *The Democratic Republic, 1801–1815.* New York: Harper and Row, 1968.

Smith, H. A. M. "The Ashley River: Its Seats and Settlements." *South Carolina Historical and Geneological Magazine,* vol. 20, p. 120, and vol. 29, pp. 8–11.

Société d'Agriculture du department de la Seine. M. M. Allaire, Bosc, Du Petit Thouars et J. Correa de Serra, Rapporteur. *Rapport sur les Voyages de M. Michaux, Pour la Naturalisation des Arbres Forestiers des Etats-Unis.* Vol. 11. Paris: Imprimerié de Madama Huzard, 1809.

Sparhawk, W. N. "The History of Forestry in America." In *Trees: The Yearbook of Agriculture, 1949.* Washington, D.C.: U.S. Govt. Printing Office, 1949.

Stark, Freya. *The Valley of the Assassins and Other Persian Travels.* London: John Murray, 1934.

Thesinger, Wilfred. *The Marsh Arabs.* London: Longmans, Green, 1964. Reprint. Penguin ed., Middlesex, Eng., 1967.

Torrey, H. H. "Michaux's New Jersey Botanical Garden." *Torrey Botanical Club Bulletin* 7 (1884).

True, Rodney H. "Francois André Michaux, the Botanist and Explorer." *Proceedings of the American Philosophical Society* 78, no. 2 (Dec. 1937): 313–37.

Turner, Frederick Jackson, ed. *Correspondence of the French Ministers to the United States, 1791–1797. Report of the American Historical Association for the year 1903,* Washington, D.C., vol. 2 (1904). Reprint 2 vols. New York: Da Capo Press, 1972.

————. *The Frontier in American History.* New York: Holt, Rinehart and Winston, 1920.

————. "The Origin of Genet's Projected Attack on Louisiana and the Floridas." *American Historical Review* (1897–98): 650–73.

U.S. Department of Agriculture. *Trees: The Yearbook of Agriculture, 1949.* Washington, D.C.: U.S. Govt. Printing Office, 1949.

U.S. Department of State. "Jefferson's Minute of Conversation with Genet."

Jefferson Papers, 4th ser., vol. 3, no. 84. Reprinted in the *Report of the American Historical Association, 1896*, pp. 984–85.

U.S. National Park Service. *Celebrated Conservationists and Naturalists in Our National Parks*. Washington, D.C.: press release, 1938.

Wallace, David Duncan. *The History of South Carolina*. 3 vols. New York: American Historical Society, 1934.

Weiss, Harry B., and Grace M. Ziegler. *Thomas Say, Early American Naturalist*. Springfield, Ill: Charles C. Thomas, 1931.

West, George H. "The Michaux Lectures." *Forest Leaves* 26, no. 4.

Wilson, Alexander. *American Ornithology*. 9 vols. Philadelphia: Bradford and Inskeep, 1809–14.

Wister, John C., ed. *Garden Book*. New York: Doubleday, 1947.

Woodress, James. *A Yankee's Odyssey: The Life of Joel Barlow*. Philadelphia: Lippincott, 1958.

Wright, Gordon. *France in Modern Times*. Chicago: Rand McNally, 1974.

Wright, Louis B., *The Cultural Life of the American Colonies: 1607–1763*. New York: Harper and Row, 1957.

Zweig, Stefan. *Marie Antoinette*. New York: Viking, 1933.

ᴥⱹ *Index*

NOTE: Page numbers in *italics* indicate pictures. Quotation marks indicate species names used mistakenly by the Michauxs or superseded.

Abies balsamea, 118, 120, 122
Acer pennsylvanicum, 120
Acer rubrum, 63
Adams, John, 128
Administration of Waters and Forests, 281, 292
Aesculus, 93
  A. glabra, 291
  A. octandra, 63, 102, 243, 251
Agricultural plants, introduced into America from France, 36
Agricultural Society (France), report on FAM's 1805–8 mission, 292–94
  of South Carolina, transfer of title of French garden to, 207, 212
Aix sponsa (summer duck), 54, 60, 63, 80, 162
Akebia quinata, 5–6
Albany, 116, 287
Albizzia julibrissin, 4, 57, 202, 258
Aleppo, 18–20, 32
Alexandretta (İskenderun), Turkey, 16–17
Alleghenies, FAM's journey to, 1802, 216–26
Alligators, 70, 89–90
Alnus cordata, 343
Altamaha River, 69
Amaryllis, 32
America, botanical exchanges with France, 36
American character, AM's description of, 44, 47–48, 52
American Entomology (T. Say), 336
American Gazeteer (J. Morse), 320
American Philosophical Society, 121–27, *125,* 129–30, 146. *See also* Vaughan, John, correspondence with FAM
  AM's journal presented to by FAM, 334–35
  AM's western journey and, 127–30
  FAM's bequest to, 345, 348, 350–55
  mishandling of, 353–55
  FAM's election to, 297–98
  FAM's final letter to, 346–49

shipment of journals to from FAM, 297–301, 303–4, 307, 309–10.
  See also Vaughan, John
American Vine Dresser's Guide (Dufour), 238
American yellow lotus (*Nelumbo lutea*), 62, 81, 326
Amygdalus juncea, 22
Anatomy of the Elephant, 320
"*Andromeda arborea*" (*Oxydendrum arboreum*), 78, 106, 203, 251
Andromeda formossissima, 84
Andromeda glaucophylla, 120, 122
"*Andromeda rosmarinfolia*" (*A. glaucophylla*), 122
Animals, in AM's instructions as king's botanist, 38
Anisostichus capreolata, 92
Annals of the Museum of Natural History, 295, 297
"*Annona*" (*Asimina*), 87, 90, 93, 203
Annona grandiflora, 90
Antioch, 17–18
Apothecaries' Garden, 10
Appalachians, southern, AM's journeys through, 64–77, 94–97, 101–3, 105–6, 149–50
  fertility of, 253
Arabs, hostile, 18–21, 25–26, 28
Aralia spinosa, 90
"Arbuste," 98–100
Arbutus, trailing (*Epigaea repens*), 72
Archibald, Patrick, 223
Aristolochia macrophylla, 76
Arrow root, Florida (*Zamia*), 83
Arundinaria, 243–44
  A. gigantea, 244, 246
  A. macrosperma (*A. gigantea*), 244, 246
Ashley River, 150
Asimina, 87, 90, 93
  A. triloba, 203, 243
Astragalus, 106
Auduin, 336
Augusta, Georgia, 71, 93–94
Aureolaria, 240
Australia, 174